VIEWS OF ROME

Oklahoma Series in Classical Culture

Oklahoma Series in Classical Culture

VIEWS OF ROME

A GREEK READER

Adam Serfass

UNIVERSITY OF OKLAHOMA PRESS : NORMAN

Library of Congress Cataloging-in-Publication Data

Name: Serfass, Adam, editor.
Title: Views of Rome: a Greek reader / edited by Adam Serfass.
Other titles: Oklahoma series in classical culture; v. 55.
Description: Norman: University of Oklahoma Press, 2018. | Series: Oklahoma series in classical culture; volume 55
Identifiers: LCCN 2017023323 | ISBN 978-0-8061-5793-1 (pbk. : alk. paper)
Subjects: LCSH: Greek language—Readers. | Rome—History—Sources.
Classification: LCC PA3416.A5 Z3 2018 DG207 | DDC 488.6/421—dc23
LC record available at https://lccn.loc.gov/2017023323

Views of Rome: A Greek Reader is Volume 55 in the Oklahoma Series in Classical Culture.

The paper in this book meets the guidelines for permanence and durability of the Committee on Production Guidelines for Book Longevity of the Council on Library Resources, Inc. ∞

CONTENTS

ILLUSTRATIONS

Figures

Maps

ACKNOWLEDGMENTS

In the final selection found in this reader, excerpted from the historian Procopius writing in the sixth century C.E., the Byzantine general Belisarius considers the centuries-long history of Rome and concludes that the city "was not made through the ability of one man" but grew little by little through the cumulative contributions of many over a long period of time. What Belisarius says about Rome is no less true of this book. Many, many people—students, colleagues, friends, and family—helped this reader see the light of day, a process that took, if not centuries, several years.

This volume originated in a Greek course designed to complement the curriculum of the Intercollegiate Center for Classical Studies in Rome (ICCS), where I taught as a visiting professor in 2010–11. I am deeply obliged to the adventurous students there who braved nascent versions of this book. Since my return to Kenyon College, I have been able to try out passages from this reader in Greek courses three times. The comments and corrections offered by the students of ICCS and Kenyon shaped the notes on and introductions to the selections found within. Their candor and insight much improved this book. Three student assistants, Natalie Ayers, Eva Buchanan-Cates, and Anna Coppelman, contributed to the research for and revision of this volume, and two Kenyon alumnae edited parts of the manuscript, the eagle-eyed Sarah Eisenlohr and Kate Markey.

My fellow faculty at ICCS and here at Kenyon have provided much aid and advice: R. Scott Smith, Christopher Gregg, and Rhodora Vennarucci in Rome; Evelyn Adkins, Michael Barich, Carolin Hahnemann, N. Bryant Kirkland, Zoë S. Kontes, and Micah Myers at Kenyon. Colleagues generously read and offered useful critiques of the proposal for the book: Josh Levithan, Michael Maas, William McCulloh, Josiah Osgood, and R. Scott Smith. David Eastman and Steve Mason gave crucial assistance with particular authors included in the reader. Elizabeth Williams-Clymer shared digital images made from the splendid edition of Piranesi's *Vedute di Roma* housed in Kenyon's Greenslade Special Collections and Archives; these images illustrate this volume. Two anonymous readers for the University of Oklahoma Press provided extensive and thoroughgoing commentary on the manuscript. At the press, Brian Bowles, Stephanie Evans, and Alessandra Tamulevich have ably shepherded the project through the publication process.

But I owe the greatest thanks to my family, who have supported my academic pursuits in myriad ways. I dedicate this book to them: my brothers, Matthew and Joshua; my parents, Jane and Jerry; and my wife, Abby, without whose unflagging encouragement this book would never have been completed.

ABBREVIATIONS AND ACRONYMS

In the notes to the selections, the following reference works are frequently cited:

BDAG	Frederick W. Danker, ed. *A Greek-English Lexicon of the New Testament and Other Early Christian Literature*. 3rd ed. Chicago, 2000.
LSJ	H. G. Liddell and R. Scott, eds. *A Greek-English Lexicon*. 9th ed. with revised supplement. Oxford, 1996. Also available, without the supplement, at multiple sites online.
Lampe	G. W. H. Lampe, ed. *A Patristic Greek Lexicon*. Oxford, 1961.
Mason, *Greek Terms*	H. J. Mason. *Greek Terms for Roman Institutions: A Lexicon and Analysis*. American Studies in Papyrology 13. Toronto, 1974.
Smyth	H. W. Smyth. *Greek Grammar*. Cambridge, Mass., 1956. Also available online.

The following abbreviations are used throughout. Commonly encountered abbreviations (such as e.g., i.e., C.E., B.C.E.) are not listed below.

acc.	accusative
act.	active

ad loc. *ad locum* = "at the place." Indicates that further information may be found about the passage under study in the commentary cited.
adj. adjective
adv. adverb
aor. aorist
dat. dative
dep. deponent
esp. especially
fem. feminine
fl. *floruit* = "s/he flourished." Used when an individual's dates of birth and death are especially unsure.
fut. future
gen. genitive
impf. imperfect
impv. imperative
ind. indicative
inf. infinitive
lit. literally
mas. masculine
mid. For verbs and participles that could be either middle or passive, the most likely possibility is usually listed.
neu. neuter
nom. nominative
NRSV New Revised Standard Version, an English translation of the Bible.
NT New Testament
opt. optative
OT Old Testament
part. participle
pass. passive. For verbs and participles that could be either middle or passive, the most likely possibility is usually listed.
pf. perfect
pl. plural
plupf. pluperfect

pres. present

reg. *regnavit, regnaverunt* = "s/he ruled," "they ruled." Indicates the dates on which a monarch or monarchs assumed and vacated the throne.

s.v. *sub voce* = "under the entry." Here typically refers to an entry in a dictionary. When such an entry is long, reference is often made to subdivisions thereof.

sc. *scilicet* = supply what follows the abbreviation.

sg. singular

subj. subjunctive

vel sim. "or something similar"

VIEWS OF ROME

INTRODUCTION

Who were the ancient Romans? This book presents thirty-five annotated selections from authors writing in Greek that address this question, one that is germane to broader issues within the discipline of Classics and beyond, such as identity and imperialism. The answers of these authors are legion: they characterize the Romans as barbarians, fellow Hellenes, civilizers, rubes, sybarites, money-grubbers, divine agents, Satan's spawn, peacemakers, warmongers, persecutors, traditionalists, innovators, copycats, bureaucrats, technocrats, syncretists, multiculturalists. In short, the authors' viewpoints are far from monolithic; they are diverse. This book seeks to make these authors, who bridge the worlds of Greece and Rome, accessible to advanced undergraduate and graduate-level students of ancient Greek. Since these authors write in a variety of styles, dialects, genres, and periods, it should also help students appreciate more fully the range of expression possible in the language.

The book assembles passages that are of paramount importance for understanding Roman civilization and yet are mostly unavailable in student-friendly editions: for example, Dionysius of Halicarnassus on the founding of Rome (A3.2–A6); Polybius on the city's tripartite government (Senate, magistrates, people) and the state funerals of its great leaders (B1–B2); Cassius Dio on the accession of the first emperor, Augustus (C2); Eusebius on the emperor Constantine's endorsement of Christianity (E1–E3); Procopius on

Rome's deliverance from destruction on the cusp of the Middle Ages (E7). Authors who may be less familiar but nonetheless offer valuable perspectives are also included, such as Phlegon of Tralles (B5), Philo of Alexandria (C4), and the emperor Julian (E4). With more than a dozen selections related to polytheism, Judaism, and Christianity, including multiple passages from Josephus (D3–D6) and the New Testament (D1–D2), students of ancient religion should also discover much of interest.

This reader has been designed so that artifacts and monuments from classical antiquity may be studied together with many of the texts. For instance, when reading Strabo on the sack and looting of Corinth (B7), one could examine the temples of republican Rome, many of which were built from the spoils won by Roman generals campaigning in the eastern Mediterranean. When reading the Greek version of Augustus's *Res Gestae* (C3), preserved in inscriptions from Asia Minor, one could study the Roman monuments described in the text as well as the architectural settings in which the inscriptions were displayed. When reading about the Whore of Babylon portrayed in the New Testament book of Revelation (D2), one could study the representation of the goddess Roma, found on a coin circulating in Asia Minor, that may have inspired the image. The passages here may be fruitfully read on their own or in conjunction with an examination of material culture from the ancient Mediterranean.

How This Reader Is Organized

The thirty-five selections in this volume are grouped into five parts (A through E) with seven assignments in each (A1–A7, B1–B7, etc.). The five parts are part A, Early Rome; part B, Expansion in the Republic; part C, From Republic to Empire; part D, Jews and Christians; and part E, Late Antiquity. Selections are assigned to sections according to the dates of the events described rather than when an author was writing. Within each part, the selections are typically arranged chronologically. Some exceptions have been made, however, so that contrasting texts appear sequentially: for example, Plutarch's philhellene Flamininus and antihellene Cato the Elder sit side by side (B3–B4), and Boudicca's fiery denunciation of Rome is followed by Aelius Aristides's panegyrical praise of the empire (C5–C6). It is likely that thirty-five assignments are too many to be covered in a single semester: this surfeit allows the instructor to select passages in order to shape the course as she wishes—to emphasize certain themes, for example, or to concentrate on certain time periods.

Each selection typically includes one Greek passage; occasionally, shorter, related excerpts are presented together, as when two snippets from the gospel of Luke are juxtaposed with one from Paul's letter to the Christians in Rome (D1.1–2). Important writers such as Polybius (A7.2, B1–B2) and Plutarch (B3–B4, C7) appear in multiple selections: this allows instructors to delve more deeply into these authors and acclimates students to their prose. The varying lengths of the passages reflect the varying difficulty of the authors. Each selection is appropriate for an hour-long class; for a longer session, an instructor could supplement the Greek with a discussion based on one or more of the additional readings recommended in the introduction to every selection.

The introductory paragraphs that precede each of the individual selections provide key information about the author and elucidate the immediate context within the work from which the excerpt is drawn. When possible, I briefly discuss the author's views of Rome as evinced in other parts of his oeuvre. Yet an effort is made not to reveal too much about the content of the selection, for in my experience those who have elected to study ancient Greek like to discover things for themselves. Spoilers are kept to a minimum. As noted, suggestions for further reading in English are provided at the end of the introduction to each selection: these may be longer portions of the text under study, book chapters, or journal articles. In making selections from the vast bibliography on the authors here represented, I kept the needs of the classroom in mind. I favored readings that were not only clear and informative but also relatively brief and likely to foster lively discussion. These suggestions offer guidance to students looking to dig deeper as well as to instructors looking for readings to complement the Greek assigned for class.

Then follows the Greek text itself, accompanied by lemmatic notes keyed to the section numbers of the Greek. These notes offer assistance with morphology (forms), syntax, and vocabulary. (Definitions are printed in *italics*;

other information is in Roman type.) They regularly refer to portions of Smyth's Greek grammar and entries in Liddell, Scott, and Jones's unabridged Greek lexicon and other major dictionaries so that students may refresh their grammatical knowledge and deepen their vocabulary. These notes also comment from time to time on literary and historical matters. If the notes on a passage owe a special debt to a particular commentary, whether it is written in English or another language, I reference that work at the beginning of the notes.

Recurring Themes

This reader is polyphonic. It brings together the voices of Greek authors who lived across the Mediterranean—Greece, Asia Minor, the Levant, Egypt, Sicily, Italy—over a vast expanse of time. Most of the authors flourished between 200 B.C.E. and 400 C.E., though the inclusion of Herodotus (A3.1) and Procopius (E7) means that this reader encompasses nearly a millennium of Greek literature. Despite this geographical and chronological sweep, the authors in this volume share a common interest in Rome as the state that ruled or was soon to rule them. (Or, in two exceptional cases, as the state that they ruled, for two emperors are numbered among the authors.) Certain subjects thread through the selections. It may be helpful to consider these recurring themes here, before they are encountered severally in the individual passages. They are grouped below under one-word titles. Although this scheme is convenient, it is also artificial, in that many of the themes are interrelated and thus resist easy categorization, and reductionist, in that authors often treat them in subtle and complex ways. The goal here is to stimulate thought rather than provide definitive answers, so questions rather than statements predominate in the paragraphs below.

Empire

Polybius famously reckons that Rome came to dominate the inhabited world in a shade under fifty-three years (1.1.5). Rome's empire spanned three continents and lasted for centuries—until as late as 1453, by the reckoning of the great eighteenth-century historian Edward Gibbon, the year in which the fall of Constantinople marked the end of the eastern Roman or

Byzantine Empire. How did the Romans, once just one among many peoples in Italy, come to control the Mediterranean? What explains the rapidity of Rome's rise and the durability of its rule? Should it be chalked up to τύχη, a word that could be translated as "luck," "fortune," or "providence"? Does geography—where Rome is sited, where Italy is located in the Mediterranean—play a role? Is the secret to Rome's success its military might, or its diplomatic savvy? Are the reasons for its rise to be sought in its social institutions or cultural characteristics, for example, its "absorbency," its capacity to adopt what's best from other peoples and to incorporate those it conquers into the state? Or is Rome's success really a matter of morals—of the virtue of its citizens, an enduring "national character" that is transmitted from generation to generation?

Politics

Or should Rome's success be attributed primarily to the nature of its government? Selections in this volume offer snapshots of Roman politics at key moments in the state's development: for example, Polybius as Rome faces dire circumstances during the Second Punic War (B1), Cassius Dio on the transition from republic to principate (C2), Eusebius on the emperor Constantine's decision to ally himself with the Christian god (E1–E3). How do authors make sense of Roman government through the analytical framework provided by Greek political thought and the vocabulary of Greek politics? For instance, is Rome, in fact, a πόλις, or something else? When Rome comes to be ruled by emperors, how should they be viewed? As philosopher-kings, bloodthirsty persecutors, distant figureheads? How does the character of individual emperors affect the empire? Is rule by one the best form of government? And in the administration of this vast monarchic state, what role should an ambitious Greek politician play?

Religion

In Rome, religion was intertwined with politics and indeed all aspects of life. Many of the authors excerpted in this book, including Polybius, Plutarch, Eusebius, and Libanius (A7, E1–E3, E5–E6), recognize that Rome's religion supported the state. According to these writers, how, exactly, does Rome's religious system foster social stability? Is Rome's rise the result of divine favor, which its religious system is designed to curry? How does Roman polytheism—at once conservative and innovative, inclusive and restrictive—make room for monotheistic Jews and Christians? Can the latter serve both God and the state? Can they pledge allegiance to emperors who are nearly gods on earth? When Christianity begins to supplant traditional religious practices, is the state weakened or strengthened?

Identity

Religion may serve as one among many constituents of a person's identity. Identity is a slippery and protean concept. For what is it that defines who we are? Do we have one identity, or several identities that we put on and lay aside according to circumstances? Many of the selections in this book evince a concern with questions of identity. Sometimes authors tackle such questions explicitly; at other times, the questions seem to bubble up while the writers are ostensibly focused on other matters. As the introductions to the individual passages make clear, the identities of the authors included in this reader are often complex. Through their varied backgrounds and experiences, they cross geographical, religious, linguistic, and cultural boundaries that turn out to be more permeable than might be assumed. The same author may be an "insider" in one way and an "outsider" in another.

One bundle of questions about identity concerns the Romans, both as individuals and as a people. What are the core components of Roman identity? In other words, what makes the Romans Roman? Are the Romans similar to or different from those groups with which the author self-identifies? Consider the traditional Greek binarism by which peoples are categorized as either Hellenes or barbarians. To which group should the Romans be assigned? If this binarism is (rightly) understood to be, in reality, a continuum, does that make things any easier? And how might the identity of an individual Roman differ from the Roman people's as a whole? In short, "categorizing" the Romans and interpreting their identity, both when viewed corporately and case by case, is a difficult business.

There is another bundle of questions related to Greek identity. Before introducing them, it should first be made clear: whereas all the authors here excerpted write *in* Greek, not all of them would identify *as* Greek, though many do. For the latter, what constitutes Greekness? How does Roman rule affect what it means to be Greek? Here much depends on when an author is writing. The perspective of an author like Polybius (A7.2, B1–B2), who not only witnesses but participates in the process by which Greece comes under Roman control in the second century B.C.E., is different from that of an author like Plutarch (B3–B4, C7), deeply Hellenic in his cultural outlook but living in a Greece that had been under Roman control for more than two centuries. How is Hellenic identity tied to ethnicity? To what extent is it grounded in common customs, such as similar ways of worshipping the gods, or in a shared set of cultural values? If the Romans share those values, does that mean that they are Greeks? In trying to make sense of the Romans, Greeks confront questions about their own identity.

Style

An author's identity is also shaped by the language and style in which he writes. This claim, too, warrants further explanation. There are many reasons why an author may write in a certain way. He may do so to align his work with that of an earlier author whom he sees as a model: for example, Cassius Dio (C2, C5) and Procopius (E7) sometimes channel the style of Thucydides, and Julian echoes that of Plato (E4). A later author may thus share in an earlier author's authority, as the writers of the New Testament (D1–D2) do when they adopt the distinctive idiom of the Septuagint, the Greek translation of the Old Testament, which itself imports the vocabulary, syntax, and style of the Hebrew original. Style may also reflect the conventions of a particular genre; hence Eusebius (E1–E3), in his laudatory biography of Constantine, employs the elevated, pleonastic style of panegyric. A particular style (or literary form) may serve as a rhetorical stratagem, as when the author of the martyrdom of Agape and her companions (D7) renders the exchange between prisoners and persecutors as dialogue, which lends verisimilitude and drama to the proceedings. But for our purposes, it may be most important to note that style is also influenced by the evolution of the Greek language over time, by linguistic trends that some have seen as reactions to Roman rule.

After the death of Alexander the Great in 323 B.C.E., a shared or "common" (κοινή) version of the Greek language, evolving mainly from the dialects of Athens and Ionia, came to be employed in the vast territory that was conquered by the Macedonian monarch. The dialectical diversity of archaic and classical Greece was gradually supplanted by this more homogeneous κοινή, which became the favored idiom of Greek notables from Alexandria to Antioch to Athens. (Among the nonelite, κοινή tended to exhibit greater regional variation.) Polybius, who lived during the second century B.C.E., is an example of an author writing in elevated κοινή (A7.2, B1–B2). During the reign of Augustus (27 B.C.E.–14 C.E.), Dionysius of Halicarnassus advocated a return to "classicism" in Greek prose. For peace under Rome offered an opportunity for Greeks to unify around a common cultural heritage: the universal values of classical Athens as expressed in the language of that period. So the style in which Dionysius writes his history of early Rome (A3.2–A6) reflects this political-literary program.

Beginning in the later first century C.E., Greeks like Aelius Aristides (C6) took Dionysius's classicism a step further. They spoke and wrote in only the purest Attic, purging their language of elements not native to the dialect. They revived the moribund dialect of classical Athens as an artificial language; their mastery of it marked them as members of an elite. Before an adoring public, many of these linguistic purists delivered display speeches, known as "declamations," in the balanced, antithetical periods favored by sophists like Protagoras and Gorgias who had taught in classical Athens. Hence this movement is termed by moderns the "Second Sophistic," which reached its zenith in the second century C.E. Was the Second Sophistic a reaction to Rome? Were these latter-day sophists seeking refuge from the realities of Roman rule in the rarefied language of a bygone age? Should we see this reassertion of Hellenic identity as anti-Roman? Might the Romans have viewed the Greek pride manifested by the movement as beneficial to the state? Did the orators of the Second Sophistic serve to connect Greek cities with the empire's capital, since they declaimed there before Roman literati and the imperial court? There is no consensus about how these questions should be answered, but the case of the Second Sophistic reminds us to be aware of the broader implications of the styles reflected in the passages presented in this reader.

The authors in this volume also faced a particular stylistic challenge: how to convey in Greek the distinctive Latin vocabulary for Roman political officials, institutions, and concepts. In approaching this problem, some authors tended to stick to convention—they observed practices well attested in writers of their time—whereas others tended to go their own way. There were three possible ways forward. One was simply to transliterate a Latin word into the Greek alphabet, as the author of the martyrdom of Agape and her companions (D7) does when referring to specialized state officials: for example, the Latin *stationarius,* a sort of military policeman, is simply transliterated into Greek as στατιωνάριος. Luke (D1.1) likewise transliterates the name of the first emperor, Augustus (Αὔγουστος), in his account of Jesus's nativity. For an author writing toward the end of the first century C.E., Luke's decision is unusual. Until about the year 200 C.E., it was commoner to render Augustus as Σεβαστός (*revered, venerable*)—that is, with a "calque," a literal equivalent. (The connotations of Augustus vs. Σεβαστός are explored further in C2.) Another calque encountered in this reader is ῥάβδοι (*rods*) for *fasces,* the bundle of sticks bound with a leather thong that was carried before some Roman officials as a symbol of their power. Transliteration and calquing, then, were two possible solutions for authors seeking to adapt Roman political vocabulary for a Hellenophone readership. Finally, there was translation. For some Latin words, there were translations, such as ἐπαρχεία for *provincia* (*province*), that became normative, in that they were more or less consistently adopted by authors regardless of when and where they were writing. Sometimes translation might be a less straightforward process. A couple of closing examples may exemplify some of the knottier problems of translation faced by our authors. First, how should a Latin word be rendered for which there was no ready equivalent in Greek? A good example is the Latin adjective *divus* (*deified*), an appellation added postmortem to many emperors' names. Until the later Roman Empire, the usual solution was to employ the noun θεός, as Strabo (A1) does when he renders Divus Julius (*Deified Julius*) as ὁ θεὸς Καῖσαρ (*The God Caesar*). Something, of course, is lost in translation. Second, what should be done with an especially multivalent word? A good example is the word *imperium,* which was a crucial concept in Roman notions of political power. The Greek version of the *Res Gestae Divi*

Augusti (C3) translates *imperium,* which appears eight times in the Latin original, in five different ways. Eschewing consistency, the translator chooses to highlight different facets of the word by employing different renderings. These two examples remind us of something that every reader of this book knows: translation is not always easy.

PIRANESI'S *VIEWS OF ROME*

To close this introduction, a word about this book's title, *Views of Rome.* It is a translation of *Vedute di Roma,* the engravings of the city made by the architect, draftsman, author, entrepreneur, and antiquarian Giovanni Battista Piranesi (1720–78). Like many of the authors in this volume, Piranesi was both an insider and an outsider, a man of multiple identities, who spent much of his life seeking to make sense of Rome's past and present, though he was not a native of the city. He was born and lived for his first twenty years in and around Venice, where he was educated in classical literature and history and studied drawing, architecture, engineering, and stonemasonry. In his published works, he recognized his roots by adding after his name the epithet "Venetian Architect." Like many of the Greek authors in this book, he gravitated toward the Eternal City, which he left infrequently in the remaining thirty-eight years of his life, finding there fame and fortune and discovering in Rome an inexhaustible font of fascination and inspiration. His masterly copperplate engravings meticulously portrayed the monuments of Rome, including many that have since been lost. They represented the grand sites as living spaces, populated by strolling dandies and gesticulating shepherds, hoop-skirted ladies and less lofty women hanging laundry on clotheslines attached to ancient walls. Like Piranesi, the Greek authors collected in *Views of Rome* present, often in meticulous, masterly prose, personal perspectives on a lost civilization. Like Piranesi, each offers a unique view of Rome.

FURTHER READING

Those wishing to follow up on the subjects presented in this introduction or in search of general works on Greek-language writers' views of Rome should find among the sources below good places to start. There are many relevant studies in other languages, but the selections below are limited to works in English. Additional bibliography on particular authors and passages may be found in the introductions to the individual selections.

Alexander, L., ed. *Images of Empire*. Sheffield, 1991.

Ando, C. "Was Rome a *Polis*?" *Classical Antiquity* 18 (1999): 5–34.

Bakker, E. J., ed. *A Companion to the Ancient Greek Language*. Malden, 2010.

Balsdon, J. P. V. D. *Romans and Aliens*. Chapel Hill, 1979.

Bammel, E., and C. F. D. Moule, eds. *Jesus and the Politics of His Day*. Cambridge, 1984.

Beard, M., J. North, and S. Price. *Religions of Rome*. 2 vols. Cambridge, 1998.

Bowersock, G. W. *Augustus and the Greek World*. Oxford, 1965.

Bowersock, G. W. *Greek Sophists in the Roman Empire*. Oxford, 1969.

Bowersock, G. W. *Hellenism in Late Antiquity*. Ann Arbor, 1990.

Clark, G. *Christianity and Roman Society*. Cambridge, 2004.

Cooley, A. E. "The Publication of Roman Official Documents in the Greek East." In *Literacy and the State in the Ancient Mediterranean*, edited by K. Lomas, R. D. Whitehouse, and J. B. Wilkins, 203–18. London, 2007.

Dench, E. *Romulus' Asylum: Roman Identities from the Age of Alexander to the Age of Hadrian*. Oxford, 2005.

Feldherr, A., and G. Hardy, eds. *The Oxford History of Historical Writing*. Vol. 1, *Beginnings to A.D. 600*. Oxford, 2011.

Forte, B. *Rome and the Romans as the Greeks Saw Them*. Papers and Monographs of the American Academy in Rome 24. Rome, 1972.

Gabba, E. "The Historians and Augustus." In *Caesar Augustus: Seven Aspects*, edited by F. Millar and E. Segal, 61–88. Oxford, 1984.

Gabba, E. "Political and Cultural Aspects of the Classicistic Revival in the Augustan Age." *Classical Antiquity* 1 (1982): 43–65.

Garnsey, P. D. A., and C. R. Whittaker, eds. *Imperialism in the Ancient World: The Cambridge University Research Seminar in Ancient History*. Cambridge, 1978.

Goldhill, S., ed. *Being Greek under Rome: Cultural Identity, the Second Sophistic and the Development of Empire*. Cambridge, 2001.

Gruen, E. S. *Culture and National Identity in Republican Rome.* Ithaca, 1992.

Gruen, E. S. *The Hellenistic World and the Coming of Rome.* 2 vols. Berkeley, 1984.

Hadas-Lebel, M. *Jerusalem against Rome.* Translated by R. Fréchet. Leuven, 2006.

Hall, J. M. *Hellenicity: Between Ethnicity and Culture.* Chicago, 2002.

Hyde Minor, H. *Piranesi's Lost Words.* University Park, 2015.

Kaldellis, A. *Hellenism in Byzantium: The Transformations of Greek Identity and the Reception of the Classical Tradition.* Cambridge, 2007.

Kokkinia, C. "The Governor's Boot and the City's Politicians. Greek Communities and Rome's Representatives under the Empire." In *Herrschaftsstrukturen und Herrschaftspraxis: Konzepte, Prinzipien und Strategien der Administration im römischen Kaiserreich,* edited by A. Kolb, 181–89. Berlin, 2006.

Madsen, J. M., and R. Rees, eds. *Roman Rule in Greek and Latin Writing: Double Vision.* Leiden, 2014.

Marincola, J., ed. *A Companion to Greek and Roman Historiography.* 2 vols. Malden, 2007.

Markus, R. A. "The Roman Empire in Early Christian Historiography." *The Downside Review* 81 (1963): 340–53. Reprinted as chapter 4 in R. A. Markus. *From Augustine to Gregory the Great: History and Christianity in Late Antiquity.* London, 1983.

Mason, H. J. *Greek Terms for Roman Institutions: A Lexicon and Analysis.* American Studies in Papyrology 13. Toronto, 1974.

Mason, H. J. "The Roman Government in Greek Sources: The Effect of Literary Theory on the Translation of Official Titles." *Phoenix* 24 (1970): 150–59.

Momigliano, A. *Alien Wisdom: The Limits of Hellenization.* Cambridge, 1975.

Momigliano, A. "Pagan and Christian Historiography in the Fourth Century A.D." In *The Conflict between Paganism and Christianity in the Fourth Century,* edited by A. Momigliano, 79–99. Oxford, 1963.

Momigliano, A. "Some Preliminary Remarks on the 'Religious Opposition' to the Roman Empire." In *Opposition et résistances à l'Empire d'Auguste à Trajan,* 103–33. Fondation Hardt Entretiens 33. Geneva, 1987.

North, J. A. *Roman Religion.* Greece & Rome New Surveys in the Classics 30. Oxford, 2000.

Sandwell, I. *Religious Identity in Late Antiquity: Greeks, Jews and Christians in Antioch.* Cambridge, 2007.

Schmitz, T. A., and N. Wiater, eds. *The Struggle for Identity: Greeks and their Past in the First Century* B.C.E. Stuttgart, 2011.

Spawforth, A. J. S. *Greece and the Augustan Cultural Revolution.* Cambridge, 2012.

Swain, S. *Hellenism and Empire: Language, Classicism, and Power in the Greek World,* A.D. *50–250.* Oxford, 1996.

Wengst, K. Pax Romana *and the Peace of Jesus Christ.* Translated by J. Bowden. Philadelphia, 1987.

Whitmarsh, T. *The Second Sophistic.* Greece & Rome New Surveys in the Classics 35. Oxford, 2005.

Wilton-Ely, J. *The Mind and Art of Giovanni Battista Piranesi.* London, 1978.

Woolf, G. "Becoming Roman, Staying Greek: Culture, Identity and the Civilizing Process in the Roman East." *Proceedings of the Cambridge Philological Society* 40 (1994): 116–43.

Yarrow, L. M. *Historiography at the End of the Republic: Provincial Perspectives on Roman Rule.* Oxford, 2006.

Yourcenar, M. *The Dark Brain of Piranesi and Other Essays.* Translated by R. Howard. New York, 1984.

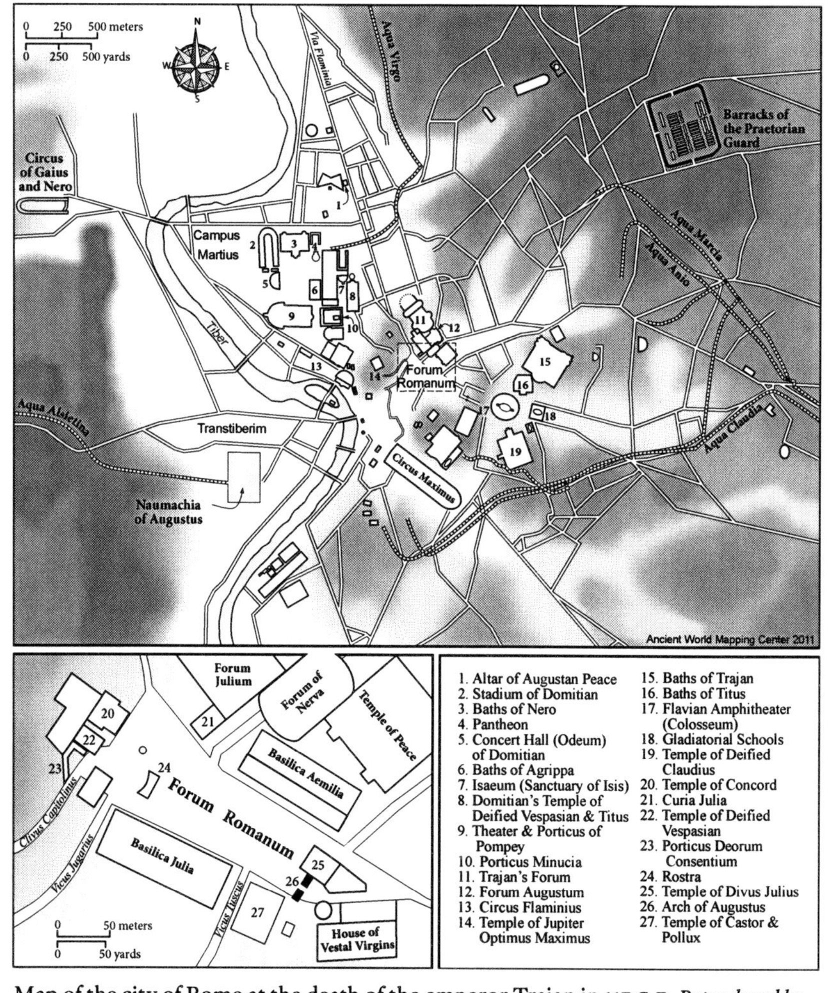

Map of the city of Rome at the death of the emperor Trajan in 117 C.E. *Reproduced by permission of the Ancient World Mapping Center, 2016. http://awmc.unc.edu/wordpress/.*

PART A

EARLY ROME

This reader's first selection comes from the geographer Strabo (A1). After considering why Rome was founded where it was, he presents an eyewitness account of its splendid cityscape in the early empire. The historian Diodorus Siculus next offers an ethnographic description of the Etruscans, the people living north of Rome who contributed to the development of the nascent Roman city-state (A2). The Etruscans, according to Herodotus (A3.1), migrated to Italy from Asia Minor, whereas Dionysius of Halicarnassus argues that they were natives (A3.2). Where the Etruscans came from is important because it is relevant to the question of whether foreign or Italic influences were more important in shaping Rome's culture. Then follow three more passages from Dionysius's *Roman Antiquities,* our most voluminous source for the history of early Rome. Dionysius tells of the birth of Romulus and Remus, Rome's founding fathers. He downplays fanciful elements in the story yet also finds a way for the twins to be educated in Greek (A4). The significance of this last detail is revealed in the next passage, where Dionysius drives home the thesis of his work: the Romans are in fact Greeks (A5). The Romans are also culturally "absorbent," as indicated by measures taken by Romulus, the city's first king, to incorporate other peoples into the state (A6). According to Plutarch, Romulus's successor Numa civilized the city's bellicose populace by founding many of its religious institutions (A7.1). The historian Polybius likewise argues that religion secures social stability in Rome (A7.2). In this excerpt, Polybius is not, strictly speaking, writing about the city's early history. But by placing this passage at the end of this section, Polybius may serve as a bridge to the next, which begins with two further selections from the author.

A1. SITE OF ROME

Strabo 5.3.7–8

Like many other authors in this volume, Strabo crossed cultural boundaries; he bridged the worlds of Greece and Rome. He was born to a distinguished family in the Hellenized city of Amasia in Pontus c. 65–60 B.C.E., when that region was coming under Roman control; in the preceding decades, it had been ruled by the wily, expansionist, Greco-Persian monarch Mithridates VI (reg. 120–63 B.C.E.; see further C1), arguably Rome's most resilient enemy since Hannibal. Strabo received an excellent education in Greek *paideia,* first in Asia Minor and then in Rome, which by the late republic had become a center of Greek learning: living in the capital for years, he mingled there with Greek intellectuals and Roman notables. He accompanied Aelius Gallus, prefect of Egypt, on expeditions up the Nile and into Arabia in the 20s B.C.E. Strabo's extensive travels there and elsewhere informed his systematic geography of the inhabited world, which he wrote in seventeen sprawling books. Fifty years in the making, Strabo's colossal work—he himself terms it a κολοσσουργία (1.1.23)—surveys the diverse lands united under Roman rule. It is meant as a useful guide for Romans who govern and for Greeks seeking to know more about the vast empire to which they now belong. Strabo praises Rome's treatment of Greece, which he thinks is more benevolent than its treatment of other regions it had conquered; he casts Augustus (reg. 27 B.C.E.–14 C.E.), Rome's first emperor, as a pious, pacifying monarch, a great builder and legislator influenced by

Greek intellectuals. At the same time, he believes in the Greeks' cultural superiority to the Romans.

The passage below is excerpted from the fifth book of Strabo's geography, on central and northern Italy; it describes the site of Rome for a Greek-speaking audience that may be unfamiliar with it. While other authors such as Cicero laud Romulus's foresight in choosing such a strategic location for the city, Strabo argues, to the contrary, that the city's topography makes it difficult to defend. He thus offers an alternative explanation for Rome's apparent impregnability in the opening of the excerpt. He goes on to marvel at Rome's state-of-the-art infrastructure and its splendid cityscape. As a Greek born in distant Asia Minor who had lived in Rome as an expatriate, a seasoned traveler who could compare the capital with countless other cities he had seen, Strabo offers an invaluable view of Rome during its remarkable transformation into the seat of world empire.

Further Reading

Strabo 6.4; Cicero *On the Republic* 2.10–11; G. W. Bowersock, *Augustus and the Greek World* (Oxford, 1965), 122–39; D. Dueck, *Strabo of Amasia: A Greek Man of Letters in Augustan Rome* (London, 2000), 85–129; D. Favro, "Making Rome a World City," in *The Cambridge Companion to the Age of Augustus*, ed. K. Galinsky, 234–63 (Cambridge, 2005); F. Coarelli, *Rome and Environs: An Archaeological Guide*, trans. J. J. Clauss and D. P. Harmon, new ed. (Berkeley, 2014), on the buildings mentioned below.

❧

(7) καί μοι δοκοῦσιν οἱ πρῶτοι τὸν αὐτὸν λαβεῖν διαλογισμὸν περί τε σφῶν αὐτῶν καὶ περὶ τῶν ὕστερον, διότι Ῥωμαίοις προσῆκεν οὐκ ἀπὸ τῶν ἐρυμάτων ἀλλὰ ἀπὸ τῶν ὅπλων καὶ τῆς οἰκείας ἀρετῆς ἔχειν τὴν ἀσφάλειαν καὶ τὴν ἄλλην εὐπορίαν, προβλήματα νομίζοντες οὐ τὰ τείχη τοῖς ἀνδράσιν ἀλλὰ τοὺς ἄνδρας τοῖς τείχεσι. κατ' ἀρχὰς μὲν οὖν ἀλλοτρίας τῆς κύκλῳ χώρας οὔσης ἀγαθῆς τε καὶ πολλῆς, τοῦ δὲ τῆς πόλεως ἐδάφους εὐεπιχειρήτου, τὸ μακαρισθησόμενον οὐδὲν ἦν τοπικὸν εὐκλήρημα· τῇ δ' ἀρετῇ καὶ τῷ πόνῳ τῆς χώρας οἰκείας γενομένης, ἐφάνη συνδρομή τις ἀγαθῶν ἅπασαν εὐφυΐαν

ὑπερβάλλουσα, δι' ἣν ἐπὶ τοσοῦτον αὐξηθεῖσα ἡ πόλις ἀντέχει τοῦτο μὲν τροφῇ τοῦτο δὲ ξύλοις καὶ λίθοις πρὸς τὰς οἰκοδομίας . . .

[In the remainder of 5.3.7, Strabo relates that the natural resources of Rome's environs, easily transported by river, are more than sufficient for the constant construction that goes on in the city. He adds that, to protect the city's fabric, Augustus has promulgated zoning regulations and created a squad of freedmen firefighters (*vigiles*).]

(8) ταῦτα μὲν οὖν ἡ φύσις τῆς χώρας παρέχεται τὰ εὐτυχήματα τῇ πόλει, προσέθεσαν δὲ Ῥωμαῖοι καὶ τὰ ἐκ τῆς προνοίας. τῶν γὰρ Ἑλλήνων περὶ τὰς κτίσεις εὐστοχῆσαι μάλιστα δοξάντων, ὅτι κάλλους ἐστοχάζοντο καὶ ἐρυμνότητος καὶ λιμένων καὶ χώρας εὐφυοῦς, οὗτοι προὐνόησαν μάλιστα ὧν ὠλιγώρησαν ἐκεῖνοι, στρώσεως ὁδῶν καὶ ὑδάτων εἰσαγωγῆς καὶ ὑπονόμων τῶν δυναμένων ἐκκλύζειν τὰ λύματα τῆς πόλεως εἰς τὸν Τίβεριν. ἔστρωσαν δὲ καὶ τὰς κατὰ τὴν χώραν ὁδούς, προσθέντες ἐκκοπάς τε λόφων καὶ ἐγχώσεις κοιλάδων, ὥστε τὰς ἁρμαμάξας δέχεσθαι πορθμείων φορτία· οἱ δ' ὑπόνομοι συννόμῳ λίθῳ κατακαμφθέντες ὁδοὺς ἁμάξαις χόρτου πορευτὰς ἐνίας ἀπολελοίπασι. τοσοῦτον δ' ἐστὶ τὸ εἰσαγώγιμον ὕδωρ διὰ τῶν ὑδραγωγίων, ὥστε ποταμοὺς διὰ τῆς πόλεως καὶ τῶν ὑπονόμων ῥεῖν, ἅπασαν δὲ οἰκίαν σχεδὸν δεξαμενὰς καὶ σίφωνας καὶ κρουνοὺς ἔχειν ἀφθόνους, ὧν πλείστην ἐπιμέλειαν ἐποιήσατο Μάρκος Ἀγρίππας, πολλοῖς καὶ ἄλλοις ἀναθήμασι κοσμήσας τὴν πόλιν. ὡς δ' εἰπεῖν, οἱ παλαιοὶ μὲν τοῦ κάλλους τῆς Ῥώμης ὠλιγώρουν, πρὸς ἄλλοις μείζοσι καὶ ἀναγκαιοτέροις ὄντες· οἱ δ' ὕστερον καὶ μάλιστα οἱ νῦν καὶ καθ' ἡμᾶς οὐδὲ τούτου καθυστέρησαν, ἀλλ' ἀναθημάτων πολλῶν καὶ καλῶν ἐπλήρωσαν τὴν πόλιν. καὶ γὰρ Πομπήιος καὶ ὁ θεὸς Καῖσαρ καὶ ὁ Σεβαστὸς καὶ οἱ τούτου παῖδες καὶ οἱ φίλοι καὶ γυνὴ καὶ ἀδελφὴ πᾶσαν ὑπερεβάλοντο σπουδὴν καὶ δαπάνην εἰς τὰς κατασκευάς· τούτων δὲ τὰ πλεῖστα ὁ Μάρτιος ἔχει κάμπος πρὸς τῇ φύσει προσλαβὼν καὶ τὸν ἐκ τῆς προνοίας κόσμον. καὶ γὰρ τὸ μέγεθος τοῦ πεδίου θαυμαστὸν ἅμα καὶ τὰς ἁρματοδρομίας καὶ τὴν ἄλλην ἱππασίαν ἀκώλυτον παρέχον τῷ τοσούτῳ πλήθει τῶν σφαίρᾳ καὶ κρίκῳ καὶ παλαίστρᾳ γυμναζομένων·

καὶ τὰ περικείμενα ἔργα καὶ τὸ ἔδαφος ποάζον δι' ἔτους καὶ τῶν λόφων στεφάναι τῶν ὑπὲρ τοῦ ποταμοῦ μέχρι τοῦ ῥείθρου σκηνογραφικὴν ὄψιν ἐπιδεικνύμεναι δυσαπάλλακτον παρέχουσι τὴν θέαν. πλησίον δ' ἐστὶ τοῦ πεδίου τούτου καὶ ἄλλο πεδίον καὶ στοαὶ κύκλῳ παμπληθεῖς καὶ ἄλση καὶ θέατρα τρία καὶ ἀμφιθέατρον καὶ ναοὶ πολυτελεῖς καὶ συνεχεῖς ἀλλήλοις, ὡς πάρεργον ἂν δόξαιεν ἀποφαίνειν τὴν ἄλλην πόλιν.

[Strabo's description of the Mausoleum of Augustus is omitted.]

πάλιν δ' εἴ τις εἰς τὴν ἀγορὰν παρελθὼν τὴν ἀρχαίαν ἄλλην ἐξ ἄλλης ἴδοι παραβεβλημένην ταύτῃ καὶ βασιλικὰς στοὰς καὶ ναούς, ἴδοι δὲ καὶ τὸ Καπιτώλιον καὶ τὰ ἐνταῦθα ἔργα καὶ τὰ ἐν τῷ Παλατίῳ καὶ τῷ τῆς Λιβίας περιπάτῳ, ῥᾳδίως ἐκλάθοιτ' ἂν τῶν ἔξωθεν. τοιαύτη μὲν ἡ Ῥώμη.

Notes to Strabo 5.3.7–8

These notes are indebted to the commentary of S. Radt, *Strabons Geographika* (Göttingen, 2002).

(7) οἱ πρῶτοι. *the first men*; i.e., Rome's founders.

διαλογισμός, -οῦ (mas.). *careful consideration, rational calculation.*

διότι. *that is, namely*; the clause that follows explains the founders' διαλογισμός.

προσῆκεν. 3rd sg. impf. act. ind. < προσήκω. Here, as often (LSJ, s.v. II.2), the verb is used impersonally: *it was fitting* + dat.

εὐπορία, -ας (fem.). *prosperity, abundance*: LSJ, s.v. 2.

προβλήματα. predicative with τὰ τείχη and τοὺς ἄνδρας; note too the neat chiasmus (Smyth 3020) that, following οὐ, caps the sentence.

κατ' ἀρχὰς. *at first*: LSJ, s.v. ἀρχή, b.

Giovanni Battista Piranesi, "Veduta di Campo Vaccino," c. 1748–1778. What was known in Piranesi's Rome as the Cow Field (Campo Vaccino) is the site of the ancient Forum Romanum. *Reproduced by permission of Greenslade Special Collections and Archives, Kenyon College, Gambier, Ohio.*

μὲν οὖν. *certainly, in fact*: Smyth 2901.

ἀλλοτρίας . . . εὐεπιχειρήτου. Translate the gen. absolutes as causal; gen. absolutes abound in the passage.

κύκλῳ. adverbial: *around.*

ἔδαφος, -εος (neu.). *foundation, lowland*; i.e., while Rome's hills served as a natural defense, the city's lower elevations were vulnerable.

εὐεπιχείρητος, -ον. *easily attacked.* sc. ὄντος.

μακαρισθησόμενον. neu. sg. nom., fut. pass. part.

τὸ . . . εὐκλήρημα. The syntax is not entirely clear; translate perhaps as *there was no good fortune regarding the location* (τοπικὸν) *that would have been praised.* In other words, the site of Rome had little to recommend it to those seeking to found a new settlement.

οἰκείας. predicative with τῆς χώρας in another gen. absolute.

ἐπὶ τοσοῦτον. *to such a degree.*

αὐξηθεῖσα. Translate as concessive.

ἀντέχω. *have enough* + dat.

τοῦτο μὲν . . . τοῦτο δὲ. *partly . . . partly*: Smyth 1256.

(8) ταῦτα. Strabo is referring to the natural resources—timber, stone, metal—provided by Rome's hinterlands, which were described in the portion of section 7 omitted here.

παρέχεται. mid., emphasizing that nature provides these resources freely.

τὰ εὐτυχήματα. predicative with ταῦτα.

καὶ τὰ. sc. εὐτυχήματα. This looks forward to what follows.

ἐρυμνότης, -ητος (fem.). *security, defensibility*; cf. the cognate ἐρυμάτων in (7).

οὗτοι = the Romans; ἐκεῖνοι = the Greeks.

προὐνόησαν < προνοέω. The prefix indicates foresight: *consider in advance* + gen.

ὀλιγωρέω. *value little* + gen.

ὑπονόμων. Dionysius of Halicarnassus also marvels at the Romans' sewers: *Roman Antiquities* 3.67.5.

ἔστρωσαν < στόρνυμι. *pave*; cf. στρώσεως above.

ἐκκοπή, -ῆς (fem.). *pass* carved out of a mountainous landscape.

ἔγχωσις, -εως (fem.). *building-up, heaping-up.* Cf. the prophet Isaiah (40.3–4) in the OT: "Make straight in the desert a highway for our God. Every valley shall be lifted up, and every mountain and hill be made low" (NRSV).

ἁρμάμαξα, -ης (fem.). *wagon.*

πορθμεῖον, -ου (neu.). *barge, cargo vessel.*

σύννομος, -ον. *closely joined, well fitted.*

κατακάμπτω. *vault*: LSJ, s.v. II; Radt, *Geographika*, ad loc.

πορευτός, -ή, -όν. *passable by* + dat.

ὑδραγωγίων. i.e., *aqueducts*.

δεξαμενή, -ῆς (fem.). *cistern*; cf. δέχομαι.

Μάρκος Ἀγρίππας. With Augustus's approval, Marcus Vipsanius Agrippa, the emperor's longtime friend and sometime son-in-law, worked to improve the infrastructure of Rome, especially its water supply and wastewater system; he famously inspected the Cloaca Maxima, the city's largest sewer, by boat.

ἀνάθημα, -ατος (neu.). lit., *that which is put up* (cf. ἀνατίθημι); here, *public building*: Radt, *Geographika,* ad loc.

ὡς . . . εἰπεῖν. *in sum*: LSJ, s.v. ὡς, B.II.3.

πρός + dat. *intent upon, occupied with*: Smyth 1695.2.

οἱ δ' ὕστερον . . . οἱ νῦν καὶ καθ' ἡμᾶς are contrasted with οἱ παλαιοὶ.

τούτου. i.e., in adorning Rome.

ἐπλήρωσαν. Verbs of filling take a gen. or both gen. and acc. (of what is being filled): Smyth 1369.

καὶ γὰρ indicates that the new sentence is moving from the general to the specific.

Πομπήιος. Gnaeus Pompeius, a.k.a. Pompey, the gifted general and rival of Julius Caesar, dedicated a massive theater-temple complex in the Campus Martius in 55 B.C.E.

ὁ θεὸς Καῖσαρ. i.e., Julius Caesar, whose postmortem deification was connoted by the addition of the Latin adjective *divus* (*deified*) to his name. It was typical to render this adjective in Greek, as Strabo does here, with the noun θεός: Mason, *Greek Terms,* 124–25.

ὁ Σεβαστὸς. i.e., Augustus. On the title, see note on section **(16.8)** of C2.

Μάρτιος . . . κάμπος. i.e., the Campus Martius or "Field of Mars," the low-lying region on the east bank of the Tiber nestled within the river's bend.

πρός + dat. *in addition to, besides*: Smyth 1695.2.

ἅμα + dat. *together with.*

ἀκώλυτος, -ον. *unhindered, open.*

παρέχον agrees with τὸ μέγεθος . . . θαυμαστὸν.

κρίκος, -ου (mas.). *hoop.* Rolling a hoop with a stick was a common pastime in ancient Greece and Rome (as well as in many other cultures).

ἔργον, -ου (neu.). *work of art, monument*: LSJ, s.v. III.

ῥεῖθρον, -ου (neu.). *channel* (of the Tiber): LSJ, s.v. II.

ἐπιδεικνύμεναι. This part. agrees with its nearest subject, στεφάναι, though it also modifies ἔργα and ἔδαφος: Smyth 1030.

δυσαπάλλακτος, -ον. *hard to take your eyes off.*

θέα, -ας (fem.). *sight, spectacle.* Note accent; cf. θεά, *goddess.*

ἄλλο πεδίον. The identity of this *other field* is disputed, but it would seem to be the Campus Flaminius, a subregion of the southern Campus Martius.

θέατρα τρία. i.e., the Theaters of Pompey, Balbus, and Marcellus.

ἀμφιθέατρον. probably the Amphitheater of Statilius Taurus or the Circus Flaminius.

πάρεργος,- ον. *subordinate, ancillary.*

τὴν ἀγορὰν . . . τὴν ἀρχαίαν. i.e., the Forum Romanum. By Strabo's day, this Forum was contiguous with the Forum Julium, started by Julius Caesar and finished by Augustus, which in turn abutted the Forum Augustum, built by Augustus.

ἄλλην ἐξ ἄλλης. *one after another*; for double ἄλλος, see Smyth 1274.

παραβάλλω. *place beside* + dat.

βασιλικὰς στοὰς = Latin *basilicae,* rectangular, colonnaded, multistory, multipurpose public buildings. In the Forum Romanum, there were mulitple *basilicae*; Augustus contributed to the renovation of two of them.

Καπιτώλιον. i.e., the Capitoline Hill.

Παλατίῳ. i.e., the Palatine Hill.

Λιβίας περιπάτῳ. i.e., the Porticus of Livia, Augustus's last wife. The Latin consonant "v," pronounced like the "w" in English "when," is rendered in Greek by ου or, as here, by β.

ἐκλάθοιτ(ο). 3rd sg. aor. mid. opt. < ἐκλανθάνω; the subject is still τις.

A2. A SKETCH OF THE ETRUSCANS

Diodorus Siculus 5.40

In antiquity, Etruria was the region to the north of Rome and to the west of the Apennine Mountains as far as the Arno River. A distinctive Etruscan culture, its growth fostered by contact with Phoenician and Greek traders, gradually emerged in the eighth and seventh centuries B.C.E. In Etruria developed the first Italic city-states, which were more or less politically autonomous but linked by a shared language that is only partly understood today. The Etruscans are thus best known through art and archaeology; especially famous are their necropolises dotted with tombs, many of them still decorated with lively, colorful frescoes that portend a sunny afterlife of eternal banqueting and general relaxation for the deceased. Ancient authors and modern scholars agree that the Etruscans shaped the development of Rome, but how and to what degree they did so has long been a matter of dispute. Most experts today now reject the idea of "Etruscan domination," according to which prosperous Etruscans came to control Rome politically; rather, their influence seems largely to have been cultural. Another matter that has been debated since antiquity is whether the Etruscans were native to Italy or migrants from elsewhere. This is the subject of the next selection (A3).

The passage below, which offers an ethnographic sketch of the Etruscans, is excerpted from Diodorus Siculus's *Library,* a universal history of the Mediterranean from the mythological past through 60 B.C.E. in forty books, of which fifteen are fully extant today. Born in Sicily in the early first century B.C.E., Diodorus, like Strabo (A1, B7), traveled to Egypt and lived for many years in Rome, a magnet for Greek intellectuals in the late republic and early empire. Unlike Strabo, he seems to have cultivated few connections with other Greek authors and Roman politicians in the capital. Again unlike Strabo, his assessment of Roman rule was, on the balance, negative. In composing a work as vast as the *Library,* Diodorus often drew on earlier authors' writings; the passage below is derived from Posidonius (c. 135–c. 51 B.C.E.), a Stoic philosopher well connected to Roman political luminaries, who wrote an influential sequel to Polybius's history (A7.2, B1–B2). Both Posidonius and Diodorus wrote when Etruria's distinctive culture was disappearing, as the region grew increasingly Romanized. This passage introduces themes that recur elsewhere in this volume: for example, it showcases the Romans as culturally absorbent, borrowing from and improving on what they find useful in other cultures (A6), and as sensitive to the symbolic, visual representation of political power (B2). It also introduces a trope, one that may derive more from Posidonius than Diodorus himself, that is echoed by other Greek and Roman authors, namely, that the latter-day influx of luxury (τρυφή) may etiolate a culture's martial spirit.

Further Reading

L. Bonfante, "Daily Life and Afterlife," in *Etruscan Life and Afterlife: A Handbook of Etruscan Studies,* ed. L. Bonfante, 232–78 (Detroit, 1986); K. S. Sacks, *Diodorus Siculus and the First Century* (Princeton, 1990), 23–54; T. J. Cornell, *The Beginnings of Rome: Italy and Rome from the Bronze Age to the Punic Wars (c. 1000–264 B.C.)* (London, 1995), 151–72.

(1) λείπεται δ' ἡμῖν εἰπεῖν περὶ τῶν Τυρρηνῶν. οὗτοι γὰρ τὸ μὲν παλαιὸν ἀνδρείᾳ διενεγκόντες χώραν πολλὴν κατεκτήσαντο καὶ πόλεις ἀξιολόγους καὶ πολλὰς ἔκτισαν. ὁμοίως δὲ καὶ ναυτικαῖς δυνάμεσιν ἰσχύσαντες καὶ πολλοὺς χρόνους θαλαττοκρατήσαντες τὸ μὲν παρὰ τὴν Ἰταλίαν πέλαγος ἀφ' ἑαυτῶν ἐποίησαν Τυρρηνικὸν προσαγορευθῆναι, τὰ δὲ κατὰ τὰς πεζὰς δυνάμεις ἐκπονήσαντες τήν τε σάλπιγγα λεγομένην ἐξεῦρον, εὐχρηστοτάτην μὲν εἰς τοὺς πολέμους,

ἀπ᾽ ἐκείνων δ᾽ ὀνομασθεῖσαν Τυρρηνήν, τό τε περὶ τοὺς ἡγουμένους στρατηγοὺς ἀξίωμα κατεσκεύασαν, περιθέντες τοῖς ἡγουμένοις ῥαβδούχους καὶ δίφρον ἐλεφάντινον καὶ περιπόρφυρον τήβενναν, ἔν τε ταῖς οἰκίαις τὰ περίστῳα πρὸς τὰς τῶν θεραπευόντων ὄχλων ταραχὰς ἐξεῦρον εὐχρηστίαν· ὧν τὰ πλεῖστα Ῥωμαῖοι μιμησάμενοι καὶ πρὸς τὸ κάλλιον αὐξήσαντες μετήνεγκαν ἐπὶ τὴν ἰδίαν πολιτείαν. (2) γράμματα δὲ καὶ φυσιολογίαν καὶ θεολογίαν ἐξεπόνησαν ἐπὶ πλέον, καὶ τὰ περὶ τὴν κεραυνοσκοπίαν μάλιστα πάντων ἀνθρώπων ἐξειργάσαντο· διὸ καὶ μέχρι τῶν νῦν χρόνων οἱ τῆς οἰκουμένης σχεδὸν ὅλης ἡγούμενοι θαυμάζουσί τε τοὺς ἄνδρας καὶ κατὰ τὰς ἐν τοῖς κεραυνοῖς διοσημείας τούτοις ἐξηγηταῖς χρῶνται. (3) χώραν δὲ νεμόμενοι πάμφορον, καὶ ταύτην ἐξεργαζόμενοι, καρπῶν ἀφθονίαν ἔχουσιν οὐ μόνον πρὸς τὴν ἀρκοῦσαν διατροφήν, ἀλλὰ καὶ πρὸς ἀπόλαυσιν δαψιλῆ καὶ τρυφὴν ἀνήκουσαν. παρατίθενται γὰρ δὶς τῆς ἡμέρας τραπέζας πολυτελεῖς καὶ τἄλλα τὰ πρὸς τὴν ὑπερβάλλουσαν τρυφὴν οἰκεῖα, στρωμνὰς μὲν ἀνθεινὰς κατασκευάζοντες, ἐκπωμάτων δ᾽ ἀργυρῶν παντοδαπῶν πλῆθος καὶ τῶν διακονούντων οἰκετῶν οὐκ ὀλίγον ἀριθμὸν ἡτοιμακότες· καὶ τούτων οἱ μὲν εὐπρεπείᾳ διαφέροντές εἰσιν, οἱ δ᾽ ἐσθῆσι πολυτελεστέραις ἢ κατὰ δουλικὴν ἀξίαν κεκόσμηνται. (4) οἰκήσεις τε παντοδαπὰς ἰδιαζούσας ἔχουσι παρ᾽ αὐτοῖς οὐ μόνον οἱ θεράποντες, ἀλλὰ καὶ τῶν ἐλευθέρων οἱ πλείους. καθόλου δὲ τὴν μὲν ἐκ παλαιῶν χρόνων παρ᾽ αὐτοῖς ζηλουμένην ἀλκὴν ἀποβεβλήκασιν, ἐν πότοις δὲ καὶ ῥᾳθυμίαις ἀνάνδροις βιοῦντες οὐκ ἀλόγως τὴν τῶν πατέρων δόξαν ἐν τοῖς πολέμοις ἀποβεβλήκασι. (5) συνεβάλετο δ᾽ αὐτοῖς πρὸς τὴν τρυφὴν οὐκ ἐλάχιστον καὶ ἡ τῆς χώρας ἀρετή· πάμφορον γὰρ καὶ παντελῶς εὔγειον νεμόμενοι παντὸς καρποῦ πλῆθος ἀποθησαυρίζουσιν. καθόλου γὰρ ἡ Τυρρηνία παντελῶς εὔγειος οὖσα πεδίοις ἀναπεπταμένοις ἐγκάθηται καὶ βουνοειδέσιν ἀναστήμασι τόπων διείληπται γεωργησίμοις· ὑγρὰ δὲ μετρίως ἐστὶν οὐ μόνον κατὰ τὴν χειμερινὴν ὥραν, ἀλλὰ καὶ κατὰ τὸν τοῦ θέρους καιρόν.

Notes to Diodorus Siculus 5.40

(1) Τυρρηνός, -οῦ (mas.). *Tyrrhenian*; i.e., Etruscan.

τὸ . . . παλαιὸν. adverbial. *formerly, in the distant past*: LSJ, s.v. παλαιός, II.2.

διενεγκόντες < διαφέρω. *excel in, be superior in* + dat.: LSJ, s.v. III.4.

ναυτικαῖς δυνάμεσιν. The Etruscans were often represented as gifted mariners, active in overseas trade and naval warfare.

ἐκπονέω. *practice (to perfection), perfect.*

σάλπιγξ, -ιγγος (fem.). The *salpinx* was a long trumpet—one extant example is more than five feet in length—used to summon and direct troops.

ἀξίωμα, -ατος (neu.). *ornamentation, trappings.*

περιτίθημι. lit., *place around*; here, *confer X* (+ acc.) *upon Y* (+ dat.).

ῥαβδοῦχος, -ου (mas.). *lictor,* a herald-cum-bodyguard who attended Roman magistrates possessing *imperium*; the Greek term derives from the bundle of rods (ῥάβδοι; Latin *fasces*) tied with a leather thong that lictors carried before magistrates as a symbol of those officials' power. This Greek word for lictor metonymically (Smyth 3033) identifies this official by what he bears.

δίφρον ἐλεφάντινον. Some Roman magistrates were permitted to sit in public on a *sella curulis,* a distinctive variety of ivory chair.

περιπόρφυρον τήβενναν. The *toga praetexta* worn by Roman magistrates sported a distinctive purple stripe along its hem.

ταῖς οἰκίαις τὰ περίστῳα. Found within a Roman house, a peristyle was an open-air courtyard surrounded by covered colonnades.

εὐχρηστία, -ας (fem.). *expedient, aid*; predicative with τὰ περίστῳα.

μεταφέρω. *adapt.* Many Greek and Roman writers commented on the Romans' ability not only to borrow from other cultures but also to improve on what they had adopted: see A6.

(2) φυσιολογία, -ας (fem.). *the natural sciences.*

ἐξεπόνησαν < ἐκπονέω. The Etruscans, not the Romans, are the subject.

ἐπὶ πλέον. *further*: LSJ, s.v. πλείων, II.1.

κεραυνοσκοπία, -ας (fem.). *divination through thunder and lightning.* Cicero's speech *On the Haruspices' Responses* offers an example of Etruscan ceraunoscopy in action.

μάλιστα here takes a partitive gen.: LSJ, s.v. μάλα, III.

διοσημεία, -ας (fem.). lit., *sign from Zeus*; i.e., a portent appearing in the sky.

(3) νεμόμενοι. The Etruscans are the subject.

ἀρκοῦσαν and ἀνήκουσαν are predicative with ἀφθονίαν.

δαψιλῆ. fem. sg. acc. < δαψιλής, -ές. *abundant.*

ἀνήκω + πρός + acc. *be enough for, approach the point of.* Those who have visited rural Tuscany may be unsurprised by Diodorus's claims.

τἄλλα = τὰ ἄλλα.

οἰκεῖος, -α, -ον or -ος, -ον + πρός. *appropriate to, suitable for*: LSJ, s.v. οἰκεῖος, IV.

στρωμνή, -ῆς (fem.). *dining-couch.*

ἀνθεινός, -ή, -όν. *flowered, brightly colored.* Such couches, often portrayed in polychromatic plaids, are commonplace in Etruscan wall paintings.

ἡτοιμακότες. mas. pl. nom., pf. act. part. < ἑτοιμάζω. *prepare.*

(4) ἰδιάζω. *be private.*

ἀποβεβλήκασι < ἀποβάλλω. *jettison, discard.*

ῥᾳθυμία, -ας (fem.). *pastime.*

οὐκ ἀλόγως. litotes (Smyth 3032). lit., *not contrary to reason*; i.e., *understandably.* In other words, since latter-day

Etruscans have become sybarites, it makes sense that their once-famed reputation for martial valor has faded.

(5) συμβάλλω. in mid., *contribute*: LSJ, s.v. 9.

οὐκ ἐλάχιστον. more litotes.

ἀναπεπταμένοις. neu. pl. dat., pf. pass. part. < ἀναπετάννυμι. In pf. pass., *be open.*

βουνοειδής, -ές. *hilly, lofty.*

ἀνάστημα, -ατος (neu.). *projection, ridge*; take with τόπων.

διείληπται. 3rd sg. pf. pass. ind. < διαλαμβάνω. *divide, criss-cross.* As often with the pf. pass., the agent is expressed in the dat.: Smyth 1488, 1490.

ὑγρά, -ᾶς (fem.). *moisture, precipitation.*

A3. ORIGINS OF THE ETRUSCANS

Herodotus 1.94 and Dionysius of Halicarnassus *Roman Antiquities* 1.30.1–3

Whence came the Etruscans, the people north of Rome who influenced the development of the nascent city (A2)? The answer to this particular question, which has been disputed since antiquity, is important, for the answer is germane to a broader question often raised by ancient authors of whether foreign, especially Greek, or native Italic influences were more influential in Rome's early evolution. The answer has also played a role in modern political discourse: for example, under Mussolini, the Etruscans were portrayed as native Italians, robust forerunners to the idealized Italians promoted by fascist ideology. The two passages below offer contrasting, legendary etiologies of the Etruscans.

In the first passage below, Herodotus (c. 484–c. 425 B.C.E.), that pioneering historian of classical Greece, obliquely offers an account of Etruscan origins that is found at the end of his account of the kingdom of Lydia. Herodotus writes in the dialect of his home region of Ionia. The second passage presents a different take on Etruscan origins, that of Dionysius of Halicarnassus (c. 60–c. 7 B.C.E.), who is introduced more fully in A4. In its opening lines, Dionysius raises but then rejects one theory of Etruscan origins, namely, that the Etruscans descended from the Pelasgians, a mysterious, bellicose people who (he argued earlier) had migrated from Greece to Italy but were later ejected by the Tyrrhenians (*Roman Antiquities* 1.17, 27–28). After rejecting this theory, he offers his own.

Further Reading

M. Pallottino, *The Etruscans,* ed. D. Ridgway, trans. J. Cremona, rev. ed. (Bloomington, 1975), 64–81; G. Forsythe, *A Critical History of Early Rome: From Prehistory to the First Punic War* (Berkeley, 2005), 28–58; P. Perkins, "DNA and Etruscan Identity," in *Etruscan by Definition: The Cultural, Regional and Personal Identity of the Etruscans. Papers in Honour of Sybille Haynes, MBE,* ed. J. Swaddling and P. Perkins, 95–111 (London, 2009).

A3.1. Herodotus 1.94

(1) Λυδοὶ δὲ νόμοισι μὲν παραπλησίοισι χρέωνται καὶ Ἕλληνές, χωρὶς ἢ ὅτι τὰ θήλεα τέκνα καταπορνεύουσι, πρῶτοι δὲ ἀνθρώπων τῶν ἡμεῖς ἴδμεν νόμισμα χρυσοῦ καὶ ἀργύρου κοψάμενοι ἐχρήσαντο, πρῶτοι δὲ καὶ κάπηλοι ἐγένοντο. (2) φασὶ δὲ αὐτοὶ Λυδοὶ καὶ τὰς παιγνίας τὰς νῦν σφίσι τε καὶ Ἕλλησι κατεστεώσας ἑωυτῶν ἐξεύρημα γενέσθαι· ἅμα δὲ ταύτας τε ἐξευρεθῆναι παρὰ σφίσι λέγουσι καὶ Τυρσηνίην ἀποικίσαι, ὧδε περὶ αὐτῶν λέγοντες. (3) ἐπὶ Ἄτυος τοῦ Μάνεω βασιλέος σιτοδείην ἰσχυρὴν ἀνὰ τὴν Λυδίην πᾶσαν γενέσθαι, καὶ τοὺς Λυδοὺς τέως μὲν διάγειν λιπαρέοντας, μετὰ δὲ ὡς οὐ παύεσθαι, ἄκεα δίζησθαι, ἄλλον δὲ ἄλλο ἐπιμηχανᾶσθαι αὐτῶν. ἐξευρεθῆναι δὴ ὦν τότε καὶ τῶν κύβων καὶ τῶν ἀστραγάλων καὶ τῆς σφαίρης καὶ τῶν ἀλλέων πασέων παιγνιέων τὰ εἴδεα, πλὴν πεσσῶν τούτων γὰρ ὦν τὴν ἐξεύρεσιν οὐκ οἰκηιοῦνται Λυδοί. (4) ποιέειν δὲ ὧδε πρὸς τὸν λιμὸν ἐξευρόντας, τὴν μὲν ἑτέρην τῶν ἡμερέων παίζειν πᾶσαν, ἵνα δὴ μὴ ζητέοιεν σιτία, τὴν δὲ ἑτέρην σιτέεσθαι παυομένους τῶν παιγνιέων. τοιούτῳ τρόπῳ διάγειν ἐπ' ἔτεα δυῶν δέοντα εἴκοσι. (5) ἐπείτε δὲ οὐκ ἀνιέναι τὸ κακὸν ἀλλ' ἔτι ἐπὶ μᾶλλον βιάζεσθαι οὕτω δὴ τὸν βασιλέα αὐτῶν δύο μοίρας διελόντα Λυδῶν πάντων κληρῶσαι τὴν μὲν ἐπὶ μονῇ τὴν δὲ ἐπὶ ἐξόδῳ ἐκ τῆς χώρης, καὶ ἐπὶ μὲν τῇ μένειν αὐτοῦ λαγχανούσῃ τῶν μοιρέων ἑωυτὸν τὸν βασιλέα προστάσσειν, ἐπὶ δὲ τῇ ἀπαλλασσομένῃ τὸν ἑωυτοῦ παῖδα, τῷ οὔνομα εἶναι Τυρσηνόν. (6) λαχόντας δὲ αὐτῶν τοὺς ἑτέρους ἐξιέναι ἐκ τῆς χώρης καταβῆναι ἐς Σμύρνην καὶ μηχανήσασθαι πλοῖα, ἐς τὰ ἐσθεμένους τὰ πάντα ὅσα σφι ἦν χρηστὰ ἐπίπλοα, ἀποπλέειν κατὰ βίου τε καὶ γῆς ζήτησιν, ἐς ὃ ἔθνεα πολλὰ παραμειψαμένους ἀπικέσθαι ἐς Ὀμβρικούς, ἔνθα σφέας ἐνιδρύσασθαι πόλιας καὶ οἰκέειν

τὸ μέχρι τοῦδε. (7) ἀντὶ δὲ Λυδῶν μετονομασθῆναι αὐτοὺς ἐπὶ τοῦ βασιλέος τοῦ παιδός, ὅς σφεας ἀνήγαγε, ἐπὶ τούτου τὴν ἐπωνυμίην ποιευμένους ὀνομασθῆναι Τυρσηνούς.

Notes to Herodotus 1.94

As noted in the introduction to this passage, Herodotus writes in Ionic dialect. For many of the more elusive Ionic forms, Attic equivalents are provided below; others are left unglossed. These notes are indebted to D. Asheri, A. Lloyd, and A. Corcella, *A Commentary on Herodotus Books I–IV* (Oxford, 2007).

(1) Λυδοὶ. Lydia was located in west-central Asia Minor.

χρέωνται = Attic χρῶνται.

χωρὶς ἢ ὅτι. *other than that.*

καταπορνεύουσι. The Lydians are the subject.

τῶν = Attic ὧν; on the forms of the relative pronouns in Herodotus, see Smyth 338.D.3. As the direct object of ἴδμεν, this pronoun should, strictly speaking, be acc. pl. But here, as often, the relative pronoun is attracted into the gen. case of its antecedent: Smyth 2522.

ἴδμεν = Attic ἴσμεν < οἶδα.

νόμισμα. Herodotus's claim that the Lydians pioneered the use of coinage is generally considered to be correct. Their earliest coins date to the seventh century B.C.E.

χρυσοῦ καὶ ἀργύρου. gen. of material: Smyth 1323.

κάπηλοι. i.e., "shopkeepers, hucksters, retail traders": Asheri, Lloyd, and Corcella, *Commentary on Herodotus,* ad loc.

(2) σφίσι = Attic αὐτοῖς. For a chart of the forms of the personal pronouns used by Herodotus, see Smyth 325.2.

κατεστεώσας < καθίστημι. in pf. part., *established, customary*: LSJ, s.v. B.6.

ἑωυτῶν = Attic ἑαυτῶν.

Τυρσηνίη, -ης (fem.) = Attic Τυρρηνία, -ας. *Tyrrhenia*; i.e., central Italy, as will become clear later in the passage.

ὧδε. *in the following way*: LSJ, s.v. I.3.

(3) ἐπὶ Ἄτυος . . . βασιλέος. ἐπί + gen. (usually with a personal name). *in the time of X*: Smyth 1689.1.b. Atys reigned c. 1200 B.C.E.; cf. Herodotus 1.7.

τοῦ Μάνεω. *son of Manes.*

διάγω + part. *continue to do X*: LSJ, s.v. II.2.d. In indirect discourse, the pres. inf. may stand in for an original impf. ind.: Smyth 1866.a.

ἄλλον δὲ ἄλλο ἐπιμηχανᾶσθαι αὐτῶν. *one of them tried one thing, another (one of them tried) another (thing)*: for double ἄλλος, see Smyth 1274.

ὦν = Attic οὖν.

ἀστράγαλοι, -ων (mas. pl.). *knuckle-bones*, used like dice.

παιγνιέων = Attic παιγνιῶν; in Ionic, the gen. pl. is uncontracted; cf. ἀλλέων πασέων.

εἴδεα. In Attic, the final vowels would contract to form εἴδη.

πεσσός, -οῦ (mas.). *stone* used for playing checkers, backgammon, vel sim.

οἰκηιοῦνται = Attic οἰκειοῦνται.

(4) δέοντα. neu. pl. acc., pres. act. part. < δέω. *lack* + gen. In other words, the Lydians stuck to this plan for eighteen years.

(5) τὸ κακὸν is the subject of ἀνιέναι.

διαιρέω. *divide X* (+ gen.) *into Y* (+ acc.): LSJ, s.v. II, citing this passage.

ἐπί + dat. here implies supervision: Smyth 1689.2.b.

μονή, -ῆς (fem.). *staying.*

αὐτοῦ. *there, in that place.*

λαγχάνω. *obtain by lot*; a paraphrase may be better here: *whose lot it was.*

τῶν μοιρέων. partitive gen.

ἑωυτὸν = Attic ἑαυτὸν.

τὸν βασιλέα is the subject of προστάσσειν.

οὔνομα = Attic ὄνομα.

(6) Σμύρνην. Smyrna, modern-day Izmir, is a city on the Aegean coast of Asia Minor.

ἐσθεμένους = Attic εἰσθεμένους < εἰστίθημι.

σφι = Attic αὐτοῖς: Smyth 325.D.2.

ἐπίπλοα = Attic ἔπιπλα < ἔπιπλα, ων (neu. pl.). *movable property.*

ἐς ὃ = Attic εἰς ὃ. *until.*

Ὀμβρικούς. i.e., the residents of the region of Umbria in central Italy.

ἐνιδρύω. *establish, found.*

πόλιας = Attic πόλεις.

(7) ἐπί + gen., with verbs of naming. *after*: LSJ, s.v. A.III.2.

A3.2. Dionysius of Halicarnassus *Roman Antiquities* 1.30.1–3

(1) τούτῳ μὲν δὴ τῷ τεκμηρίῳ χρώμενος ἑτέρους εἶναι πείθομαι τῶν Τυρρηνῶν τοὺς Πελασγούς. οὐ μὲν δὴ οὐδὲ Λυδῶν τοὺς Τυρρηνοὺς ἀποίκους οἶμαι γενέσθαι· οὐδὲ γὰρ ἐκείνοις ὁμόγλωσσοί εἰσιν, οὐδ᾽ ἔστιν εἰπεῖν ὡς φωνῇ μὲν οὐκέτι χρῶνται παραπλησίᾳ, ἄλλα δέ τινα διασώζουσι τῆς μητροπόλεως γῆς μηνύματα. οὔτε γὰρ θεοὺς Λυδοῖς τοὺς αὐτοὺς νομίζουσιν οὔτε νόμοις οὔτ᾽ ἐπιτηδεύμασι κέχρηνται παραπλησίοις, ἀλλὰ κατά γε ταῦτα πλέον Λυδῶν διαφέρουσιν ἢ Πελασγῶν. **(2)** κινδυνεύουσι γὰρ τοῖς ἀληθέσι μᾶλλον ἐοικότα λέγειν οἱ μηδαμόθεν ἀφιγμένον, ἀλλ᾽ ἐπιχώριον τὸ ἔθνος ἀποφαίνοντες, ἐπειδὴ ἀρχαῖόν τε πάνυ καὶ οὐδενὶ ἄλλῳ γένει οὔτε ὁμόγλωσσον οὔτε ὁμοδίαιτον ὂν εὑρίσκεται. ὠνομάσθαι δ᾽ ὑφ᾽ Ἑλλήνων αὐτὸ τῇ προσηγορίᾳ ταύτῃ οὐδὲν κωλύει, καὶ διὰ τὰς ἐν ταῖς τύρσεσιν οἰκήσεις καὶ ἀπ᾽ ἀνδρὸς δυνάστου. **(3)** Ῥωμαῖοι μέντοι ἄλλαις αὐτὸ προσαγορεύουσιν ὀνομασίαις· καὶ γὰρ ἐπὶ τῆς χώρας, ἐν ᾗ ποτε ᾤκησαν, Ἑτρουρίας προσαγορευομένης Ἑτρούσκους καλοῦσι τοὺς ἀνθρώπους· καὶ ἐπὶ τῆς ἐμπειρίας τῶν περὶ τὰ θεῖα σεβάσματα λειτουργιῶν, διαφέροντας εἰς αὐτὴν ἑτέρων, νῦν μὲν Τούσκους ἀσαφέστερον, πρότερον δ' ἀκριβοῦντες τοὔνομα ὥσπερ Ἕλληνες Θυοσκόους ἐκάλουν· αὐτοὶ μέντοι σφᾶς αὐτοὺς ἐπὶ τῶν ἡγεμόνων τινὸς Ῥασέννα τὸν αὐτὸν ἐκείνῳ τρόπον ὀνομάζουσι.

Notes to Dionysius of Halicarnassus Roman Antiquities *1.30.1–3*

These notes are indebted to V. Fromentin, *Denys d'Halicarnasse, Antiquités romaines, Tome 1: Introduction générale et Livre I* (Paris, 1998).

(1) τούτῳ . . . τῷ τεκμηρίῳ. Dionysius is referring to his argument in the preceding section: the Pelasgians and Tyrrhenians cannot be one and the same, as their languages are quite different.

οἶμαι = οἴομαι. *think, suppose*; commonly used to express courteous but firm disagreement: LSJ, s.v., III, IV.2.

ἐκείνοις. i.e., the Lydians; the subject is the Tyrrhenians. The Lydians, Tyrrhenians, and Pelasgians each speak a different language.

ἔστιν. *it is possible*; on the accent, see Smyth 187.b.

ἄλλα. Note accent.

μήνυμα, -ατος (neu.). *indication*: LSJ, s.v. II.

ἐπιτήδευμα, -ατος (neu.). *habit, custom*; in. pl., *way of life.*

(2) κινδυνεύω. *be likely* + inf.: LSJ, s.v. 4.b.

ἐοικώς, -υῖα, -ός. *seem like, resemble* + dat.

ἀποφαίνω. *demonstrate logically, prove* + part.: LSJ, s.v. II.2.

ὁμοδίαιτος, -ον. lit., *similar in dining customs*; by extension, *similar* generally.

εὑρίσκεται. pass., with supplementary part. The subject is τὸ ἔθνος; i.e., the Tyrrhenians.

προσηγορία, -ας (fem.). *name.* Dionysius considers the etymology of Τυρρηνοί, which in dialects other than Attic would be Τυρσηνοί. He argues that this people may have been named for the distinctive forts or "towers" (τύρσεις) in which they dwelt; see further 1.26.2. Dionysius often presents arguments from etymology; see, e.g., A4.

κωλύω. *hinder, prevent* + acc. and inf.: Smyth 1993; LSJ, s.v. 1.

(3) σέβασμα, -ατος (neu.). *worship.*

διαφέρω. *excel* + gen.: LSJ, s.v. II.8.

εἰς αὐτὴν. i.e., in religiosity.

Θυοσκόους. According to Dionysius, the Romans originally called the Etruscans Θυοσκόοι, reflecting the latter's expertise in religion: θύω means *sacrifice.* Over time this evolved into Τούσκοι (cf. English "Tuscans"), a shift that made the word's original derivation less clear (ἀσαφέστερον). In fact, Tuscus, Etruscus, and Tyrrhenus share the same root: Fromentin, *Denys,* ad loc.

τὸν αὐτὸν ἐκείνῳ τρόπον. *after him*; i.e., Rasenna. The word *rasna* appears in many Etruscan inscriptions, but its meaning is unclear: Fromentin, *Denys,* ad loc.

A4. RATIONALIZING ROME'S PAST

Dionysius of Halicarnassus *Roman Antiquities* 1.84.1–5

Born around 60 B.C.E. into a prominent family from the Greek city of Halicarnassus in southwest Asia Minor, Dionysius, like Strabo (A1, B7), Diodorus Siculus (A2), and other Greek intellectuals of his time, spent many years in Rome, where he lived from approximately 30 to 7 B.C.E. In classicizing Attic dialect, he wrote a variety of prose works, including rhetorical treatises and literary criticism. These writings laid out, among much else, the historiographical principles that informed Dionysius's history of Rome from its prehistory through the outbreak of the First Punic War in 264 B.C.E. The first eleven books of Dionysus's twenty-book history are extant. Early Rome was a hot topic during the reign of Augustus (reg. 27 B.C.E.–14 C.E.), when authors such as Vergil, Livy, and, most fully, Dionysius wrote about it. Dionysius rejects claims, mooted by other Greek writers (*Roman Antiquities* 1.4.2–3), that Rome had been settled by rustic, lowborn natives and that its rise to power could be chalked up to luck (τύχη). On the contrary, the city's founders, he argues, were Greeks who established the city and fostered its expansion in accordance with Greek civic values: this was the secret of Rome's success, from the city's earliest years through Dionysius's own day.

In researching his history, Dionysius read deeply in both Greek and Latin sources, including antiquarian writers like the Roman Varro (116–27 B.C.E.), who had gathered lore about the city's past. Drawing on this material,

Dionysius regularly records multiple versions of events but, as exhibited in the selection below, tends to favor rationalizing narratives that downplay the role of supernatural phenomena in human affairs. Just before the passage below, he relates the birth of Romulus and Remus as narrated by Fabius Pictor (fl. 200 B.C.E.), a Roman senator who was also Rome's first historian. (Interestingly, he wrote in Greek.) In Fabius's version, Amulius (in Greek, Ἀμόλιος) had unjustly seized the throne of Alba Longa, a town located about twelve miles southeast of Rome, from his elder brother Numitor (Νεμέτωρ). When Numitor's daughter Ilia gave birth, Amulius, fearing that her progeny would eventually challenge his rule, ordered his servants to expose the children, who were left on the banks of the Tiber. There they were suckled by a she-wolf and then raised by the shepherd Faustulus (Φαιστύλος). Here Dionysius presents an alternate version of the twins' exposure, discovery, and education.

Further Reading

Roman Antiquities 1.1–5, 75–83, 84.6–88; J. N. Bremmer and N. M. Horsfall, *Roman Myth and Mythography* (London, 1987), 25–48; E. Gabba, *Dionysius and* The History of Archaic Rome (Berkeley, 1991), 1–22; M. Fox, *Roman Historical Myths: The Regal Period in Augustan Literature* (Oxford, 1996), 49–95.

❧

(1) ἕτεροι δὲ οὐδὲν τῶν μυθωδεστέρων ἀξιοῦντες ἱστορικῇ γραφῇ προσήκειν τήν τε ἀπόθεσιν τὴν τῶν βρεφῶν οὐχ ὡς ἐκελεύσθη τοῖς ὑπηρέταις γενομένην ἀπίθανον εἶναί φασι, καὶ τῆς λυκαίνης τὸ τιθασόν, ᾗ τοὺς μαστοὺς ἐπεῖχε τοῖς παιδίοις, ὡς δραματικῆς μεστὸν ἀτοπίας διασύρουσιν· **(2)** ἀντιδιαλλαττόμενοι δὲ πρὸς ταῦτα λέγουσιν ὡς ὁ Νεμέτωρ, ἐπειδὴ τὴν Ἰλίαν ἔγνω κύουσαν, ἕτερα παρασκευασάμενος παιδία νεογνὰ διηλλάξατο τεκούσης αὐτῆς τὰ βρέφη καὶ τὰ μὲν ὀθνεῖα δέδωκε τοῖς φυλάττουσι τὰς ὠδῖνας ἀποφέρειν εἴτε χρημάτων τὸ πιστὸν τῆς χρείας αὐτῶν πριάμενος εἴτε διὰ γυναικῶν τὴν ὑπαλλαγὴν μηχανησάμενος, καὶ αὐτὰ λαβὼν Ἀμόλιος ὅτῳ δή τινι τρόπῳ ἀναιρεῖ· τὰ δ' ἐκ τῆς Ἰλίας γενόμενα περὶ παντὸς ποιούμενος ὁ μητροπάτωρ διασῴζεσθαι δίδωσι τῷ Φαιστύλῳ. (3) τὸν δὲ Φαιστύλον τοῦτον Ἀρκάδα μὲν εἶναί φασι τὸ γένος ἀπὸ τῶν σὺν Εὐάνδρῳ, κατοικεῖν δὲ περὶ τὸ Παλλάντιον ἐπιμέλειαν ἔχοντα τῶν Ἀμολίου κτημάτων. χαρίσασθαι δὲ Νεμέτορι τὴν ἐκτροφὴν τῶν παίδων τἀδελφῷ πειθόμενον ὄνομα Φαυστίνῳ τὰς περὶ τὸν Αὐεντῖνον τρεφομένας τοῦ Νεμέτορος ἀγέλας ἐπιτροπεύοντι· (4) τήν τε τιθηνησαμένην τὰ παιδία καὶ μαστοὺς ἐπισχοῦσαν οὐ λύκαιναν εἶναί φασιν, ἀλλ' ὥσπερ εἰκὸς γυναῖκα τῷ Φαιστύλῳ συνοικοῦσαν Λαυρεντίαν ὄνομα, ᾗ δημοσιευούσῃ ποτὲ τὴν τοῦ σώματος ὥραν οἱ περὶ τὸ Παλλάντιον διατρίβοντες ἐπίκλησιν ἔθεντο τὴν Λούπαν· ἔστι δὲ τοῦτο Ἑλληνικόν τε καὶ ἀρχαῖον ἐπὶ ταῖς μισθαρνούσαις τἀφροδίσια τιθέμενον, αἳ νῦν εὐπρεπεστέρᾳ κλήσει ἑταῖραι προσαγορεύονται. ἀγνοοῦντας δέ τινας αὐτὸ πλάσαι τὸν περὶ τῆς λυκαίνης μῦθον, ἐπειδὴ κατὰ τὴν γλῶτταν, ἣν τὸ Λατίνων ἔθνος φθέγγεται, λούπα καλεῖται τοῦτο τὸ θηρίον. (5) ἡνίκα δὲ τῆς ἐν τῷ γάλακτι τροφῆς ἀπηλλάγη τὰ παιδία, δοθῆναι πρὸς τῶν τρεφόντων εἰς Γαβίους πόλιν οὐ μακρὰν ἀπὸ τοῦ Παλλαντίου κειμένην, ὡς Ἑλλάδα παιδείαν ἐκμάθοιεν, κἀκεῖ παρ' ἀνδράσιν ἰδιοξένοις τοῦ Φαιστύλου τραφῆναι γράμματα καὶ μουσικὴν καὶ χρῆσιν ὅπλων Ἑλληνικῶν ἐκδιδασκομένους μέχρις ἥβης.

Notes to Dionysius of Halicarnassus **Roman Antiquities** *1.84.1–5*

These notes are indebted to V. Fromentin, *Denys d'Halicarnasse, Antiquités romaines, Tome 1: Introduction générale et Livre I* (Paris, 1998).

(1) ἕτεροι. i.e., other historians of early Rome.

μυθώδης, -ες. *legendary, mythical,* often in a pejorative sense; the word is common in philosophical discourse and discussions of historical method: LSJ, s.v.

προσήκω + dat. *befit, be suitable for.*

ἐκελεύσθη. Translate impersonally.

ἀπίθανον. As often in *Roman Antiquities,* Dionysius employs an argument from probability: since (the ancients assumed) slaves obey their masters, Amulius's slaves are unlikely to have disobeyed his order to throw the twins into the Tiber.

τιθασός, -όν. *tame, docile.*

μεστός, -ή, -όν + gen. *full of*: LSJ, s.v. II.

διασύρω. *shred, tear apart.*

(2) ἀντιδιαλλάττομαι + πρός + acc. *differ with respect to*: LSJ, s.v. ἀντιδιαλλάσσομαι, II. Where other dialects employ double sigma, Attic uses double tau.

κύω. *be pregnant.*

τὰ . . . ὀθνεῖα. i.e., the "substitute" children—not Romulus and Remus.

τοῖς φυλάττουσι τὰς ὠδῖνας. i.e., persons attending / watching over the birth.

ἀποφέρειν. The object is τὰ ὀθνεῖα.

τὸ πιστὸν τῆς χρείας αὐτῶν. *the trustworthiness of their services.*

πριάμενος. aor. part. < ὠνέομαι. *purchase X* (+ acc.) *with Y* (+ gen.)

ὅτῳ . . . τινι = ᾧτινι.

ἀναιρεῖ. As the narrative turns to the fate of Ilia's children, Dionysius switches to the historical present: Smyth 1883.

περὶ παντὸς ποιέω. *consider of great value*: Smyth 1373; LSJ, s.v. περί, A.IV.

διασώζεσθαι. inf. of purpose, common after verbs of giving: Smyth 2008–09.

(3) Φαιστύλος = Latin Faustulus; Φαυστίνος = Faustinus. Paired characters abound in this story (Numitor-Amulius, Romulus-Remus). The Latin names of these shepherds suggest both the Latin adjective *faustus* (*fortunate*) and Faunus, the Roman god of the forest, who is identified with the Greek Pan; Faunus/Pan is closely associated with Rome's foundation myths.

Ἀρκάς, -άδος (mas.). *(an) Arcadian.* Arcadia is a mountainous region of the Peloponnese. Evander is said to have established a settlement on Rome's Palatine Hill well before the city's foundation; see *Roman Antiquities* 1.31 and, famously, the eighth book of Vergil's *Aeneid*.

εἶναί. In indirect discourse, the pres. inf. may stand in for an original impf. ind.: Smyth 1866.a.

τὸ γένος. acc. of respect: Smyth 1600.

τὸ Παλλάντιον. i.e., the Palatine Hill, said by Dionysius to be named for the town of Pallantium (*Roman Antiquities* 1.31.4), whence the Arcadians had emigrated; on and near the hill were several sites associated with Rome's foundation, including the Lupercal, the cave wherein the twins were purportedly suckled by the she-wolf.

χαρίζομαι. *do X* (+ acc.) *as a favor to Y* (+ dat.).

πειθόμενον. Acceding to his brother Faustinus's request (τἀδελφῷ πειθόμενον), Faustulus raises Ilia's children; moreover, by securing his brother's assistance, Faustinus curries favor with Numitor, whose flocks he tends.

ὄνομα. again, acc. of respect: Smyth 1600.

τὸν Αὐεντῖνον: i.e., the Aventine Hill, located southwest of the Palatine.

(4) δημοσιεύω. *make public property*; i.e., *prostitute*: LSJ, s.v. 3, citing this passage.

ὥρα, -ας (fem.). *time, season*, especially *springtime*, in which sense the word is a euphemism for youth.

διατρίβω. *spend time*: LSJ, s.v. II. As in A3.1, Dionysius here presents an argument from etymology, a proper knowledge of which, he implies, is essential to an investigation of the distant past.

τἀφροδίσια = τὰ ἀφροδίσια.

ἀγνοοῦντας δέ τινας. Acc. + inf. indirect discourse resumes.

(5) ἀπηλλάγη. 3rd sg. aor. pass. ind. < ἀπαλλάττω. *release from*; i.e., *wean from* + gen.

πρὸς = ὑπὸ, with pass. verb: Smyth 1695.1.b.

Γαβίους. i.e., Gabii, an ancient city founded, according to Dionysius (*Roman Antiquities* 4.53), by the kings of Alba Longa, lay c. 12 miles east of Rome.

ἰδιόξενος, ου (mas.). *personal friend* who resides in a different place.

μουσικὴν. i.e., poetry.

A5. GREEK ROME

Dionysius of Halicarnassus
Roman Antiquities 1.89–90.1

When Dionysius published the first book of *Roman Antiquities* in 7 B.C.E., the idea that Greece had contributed to Rome's early development was nothing new. As early as the end of the fifth century, the Greek historian Hellanicus had claimed that Odysseus had played a role in the city's foundation (*Roman Antiquities* 1.72.2). Cato the Elder (234–149 B.C.E.; see B4), though he adopted in public life an antihellenic persona, conceded in his *Origins* that Rome was founded by Greeks (ibid. 1.11.1, 1.13.2). But no ancient author argued more fervently, learnedly, and voluminously for the Greekness of early Rome than Dionysius. As indicated by the passage below—Dionysius's concluding summary of his investigations in book 1 of his work—Rome's founding fathers descended from Greek migrants to Italy and established the city as a Greek colony (ἀποικία). Moreover, Dionysius, like others of his time, argues that Latin is a Greek dialect—one that, based on phonology, is closely related to the Aeolic dialect spoken in northwest Asia Minor and the islands there offshore. Later Romans still preserve the Greek virtues that guided the city's founding fathers. Dionysius is implicitly claiming that Greekness is grounded less in ethnicity or geography than in a shared set of cultural values.

These arguments had important implications for Dionysius's readers. With its classicizing, approachable prose, Dionysius's history of early Rome was meant for a wide audience of both Romans and Greeks. (Scholars debate which of these groups was the primary audience.) The work served to remind Roman aristocratic readers not only to avoid the στάσις—the fissiparous civic infighting—that occasionally threatened the nascent city-state (and that had recently rocked Rome after the death of Julius Caesar) but also to live up to the example of Rome's founders. For Greeks living under Rome, Dionysius made Roman rule more palatable. The seat of empire had been founded by noble fellow Hellenes; they were ruled not by barbarians but by Greeks.

Further Reading

E. J. Bickerman, "*Origines Gentium*," *Classical Philology* 47 (1952): 65–81; C. Schultze, "Dionysius of Halicarnassus and His Audience," in *Past Perspectives: Studies in Greek and Roman Historical Writing*, ed. I. S. Moxon, J. D. Smart, and A. J. Woodman, 121–41 (Cambridge, 1986); N. Wiater, "Writing Roman History—Shaping Greek Identity: The Ideology of Historiography in Dionysius of Halicarnassus," in *The Struggle for Identity: Greeks and Their Past in the First Century B.C.E.*, ed. T. A. Schmitz and N. Wiater, 61–91 (Stuttgart, 2011).

(89.1) ἃ μὲν οὖν ἐμοὶ δύναμις ἐγένετο σὺν πολλῇ φροντίδι ἀνευρεῖν Ἑλλήνων τε καὶ Ῥωμαίων συχνὰς ἀναλεξαμένῳ γραφὰς ὑπὲρ τοῦ τῶν Ῥωμαίων γένους, τοιάδ᾽ ἐστίν. ὥστε θαρρῶν ἤδη τις ἀποφαινέσθω πολλὰ χαίρειν φράσας τοῖς βαρβάρων καὶ δραπετῶν καὶ ἀνεστίων ἀνθρώπων καταφυγὴν τὴν Ῥώμην ποιοῦσιν Ἑλλάδα πόλιν αὐτήν, ἀποδεικνύμενος μὲν κοινοτάτην τε πόλεων καὶ φιλανθρωποτάτην, ἐνθυμούμενος ὅτι τὸ μὲν τῶν Ἀβοριγίνων φῦλον Οἰνωτρικὸν ἦν, τοῦτο δὲ Ἀρκαδικόν· **(2)** μεμνημένος δὲ τῶν συνοικησάντων αὐτοῖς Πελασγῶν, οἳ Θετταλίαν καταλιπόντες Ἀργεῖοι τὸ γένος ὄντες εἰς Ἰταλίαν ἀφίκοντο· Εὐάνδρου τε αὖ καὶ Ἀρκάδων ἀφίξεως, οἳ περὶ τὸ Παλλάντιον ᾤκησαν, Ἀβοριγίνων αὐτοῖς παρασχόντων τὸ χωρίον· ἔτι δὲ Πελοποννησίων τῶν σὺν Ἡρακλεῖ παραγενομένων, οἳ κατῴκησαν ἐπὶ τοῦ Σατορνίου· τελευταῖον δὲ τῶν ἀπαναστάντων ἐκ τῆς Τρωάδος καὶ συγκερασθέντων τοῖς προτέροις. τούτων γὰρ ἂν οὐδὲν εὕροι τῶν ἐθνῶν οὔτε ἀρχαιότερον οὔτε Ἑλληνικώτερον. **(3)** αἱ δὲ τῶν βαρβάρων ἐπιμιξίαι, δι᾽ ἃς ἡ πόλις πολλὰ τῶν ἀρχαίων ἐπιτηδευμάτων ἀπέμαθε, σὺν χρόνῳ ἐγένοντο. καὶ θαῦμα μὲν τοῦτο πολλοῖς ἂν εἶναι δόξειε τὰ εἰκότα λογισαμένοις, πῶς οὐχ ἅπασα ἐξεβαρβαρώθη Ὀπικούς τε ὑποδεξαμένη καὶ Μαρσοὺς καὶ Σαυνίτας καὶ Τυρρηνοὺς καὶ Βρεττίους Ὀμβρικῶν τε καὶ Λιγύων καὶ Ἰβήρων καὶ Κελτῶν συχνὰς μυριάδας ἄλλα τε πρὸς τοῖς εἰρημένοις ἔθνη τὰ μὲν ἐξ αὐτῆς Ἰταλίας, τὰ δ᾽ ἐξ ἑτέρων ἀφιγμένα τόπων μυρία ὅσα οὔτε ὁμόγλωττα οὔτε ὁμοδίαιτα, ὧν οὔτε φωνὰς οὔτε δίαιταν καὶ βίους σύγκλυδας ἀναταραχθέντας ἐκ τοσαύτης διαφωνίας πολλὰ τοῦ παλαιοῦ κόσμου τῆς πόλεως νεοχμῶσαι εἰκὸς ἦν· **(4)** ἐπεὶ ἄλλοι γε συχνοὶ ἐν βαρβάροις οἰκοῦντες ὀλίγου χρόνου διελθόντος ἅπαν τὸ Ἑλληνικὸν ἀπέμαθον, ὡς μήτε φωνὴν Ἑλλάδα φθέγγεσθαι μήτε ἐπιτηδεύμασιν Ἑλλήνων χρῆσθαι, μήτε θεοὺς τοὺς αὐτοὺς νομίζειν, μήτε νόμους τοὺς ἐπιεικεῖς, ᾧ μάλιστα διαλλάσσει φύσις Ἑλλὰς βαρβάρου, μήτε τῶν ἄλλων συμβολαίων μηδ᾽ ὁτιοῦν. ἀποχρῶσι δὲ τὸν λόγον τόνδε ὡς ἀληθῆ εἶναι Ἀχαιῶν οἱ περὶ τὸν Πόντον ᾠκημένοι τεκμηριῶσαι, Ἠλείων μὲν ἐκ τοῦ Ἑλληνικωτάτου γενόμενοι, βαρβάρων δὲ συμπάντων τῶν νῦν ὄντες ἀγριώτατοι.

(90.1) Ῥωμαῖοι δὲ φωνὴν μὲν οὔτ᾽ ἄκρως βάρβαρον οὔτ᾽ ἀπηρτισμένως Ἑλλάδα φθέγγονται, μικτὴν δέ τινα ἐξ ἀμφοῖν, ἧς ἐστιν ἡ πλείων Αἰολίς, τοῦτο μόνον ἀπολαύσαντες ἐκ τῶν πολλῶν ἐπιμιξιῶν, τὸ μὴ πᾶσι τοῖς φθόγγοις ὀρθοεπεῖν, τὰ δὲ ἄλλα, ὁπόσα γένους Ἑλληνικοῦ μηνύματ᾽ ἐστὶν ὡς οὐχ ἕτεροί τινες τῶν ἀποικησάντων διασώζοντες, οὐ νῦν πρῶτον ἀρξάμενοι πρὸς φιλίαν ζῆν, ἡνίκα τὴν τύχην πολλὴν καὶ ἀγαθὴν ῥέουσαν διδάσκαλον ἔχουσι τῶν καλῶν οὐδ᾽ ἀφ᾽ οὗ πρῶτον ὠρέχθησαν τῆς διαποντίου τὴν Καρχηδονίων καὶ Μακεδόνων ἀρχὴν καταλύσαντες, ἀλλ᾽ ἐκ παντὸς οὗ συνῳκίσθησαν χρόνου βίον Ἕλληνα ζῶντες καὶ οὐδὲν ἐκπρεπέστερον ἐπιτηδεύοντες πρὸς ἀρετὴν νῦν ἢ πρότερον.

Notes to Dionysius of Halicarnassus Roman Antiquities *1.89–90.1*

These notes are indebted to V. Fromentin, *Denys d'Halicarnasse, Antiquités romaines, Tome 1: Introduction générale et Livre I* (Paris, 1998).

(89.1) ἅ. neu. pl. acc., object of ἀνευρεῖν. An example of "incorporation," where the antecedent appears not before but within the relative clause; here, as often, the incorporated antecedent (τοιάδ') comes at the clause's end: Smyth 2536–37.

μὲν οὖν. *certainly, in fact*: Smyth 2901.

τοιάδ'. This word flags the transition from the thoroughgoing analysis found in the preceding pages to the conclusive summary with which book 1 ends.

θαρρέω. *take courage, be confident.*

τις ἀποφαινέσθω. *let someone* (i.e., the reader) *declare his opinion*: LSJ, s.v. ἀποφαίνω, B.II.2. This verb, as well as the participle ἀποδεικνύμενος below, are reminiscent of another Halicarnassian, Herodotus, whom Dionysius admired.

πολλὰ χαίρειν + dat. *utterly reject X*: LSJ, s.v. χαίρω, III.2.c; take the phrase closely with φράσας.

ποιοῦσιν. mas. pl. dat., pres. act. part.

αὐτήν. i.e., Rome. The word is predicative with Ἑλλάδα πόλιν; all three are acc. objects of ἀποφαινέσθω above.

Ἀβοριγίνων. Some historians thought the Aborigines—lit. those who were there "from the beginning" (Latin *ab origine*)—were natives of Italy; others, including Cato the Elder, thought they had originally migrated to Italy from Greece: *Roman Antiquities* 1.11.

Οἰνωτρικὸν. Dionysius argued earlier (1.12–13) that the Aborigines descended from the Oenotrians, an early Italic people who had originally emigrated from Arcadia in the Peloponnese. The Aborigines, therefore, were Greeks.

(2) Θετταλίαν καταλιπόντες Ἀργεῖοι. According to Dionysius, the Pelasgians, originally from Argos, were a people prone to frequent migration; before coming to Italy, they had lived in Thessaly: *Roman Antiquities* 1.17.

ἀφίξεως. Like Πελασγῶν, a complement of μεμνημένος; verbs of memory often take the gen.: Smyth 1356–58.

παρασχόντων. On Evander, see note on section (3) of A4, s.v. Ἀρκάς.

Ἡρακλεῖ. After conquering Spain, Hercules and his companions returned to Greece via Italy: *Roman Antiquities* 1.34–44.

ἐπὶ τοῦ Σατορνίου. The Saturnian was an old designation for the Capitoline Hill: *Roman Antiquities* 1.34.1.

ἀπαναστάντων < ἀπανίστημι. *emigrate.*

τῶν ἀπαναστάντων ἐκ τῆς Τρωάδος. i.e., Aeneas and his men. Dionysius identified no fewer than four waves of Greek immigration to Italy *before* Aeneas arrived.

συγκεράννυμι. in pass., *be mixed with, form a close friendship with*: LSJ, s.v. II.

εὕροι. sc. τις as the subject.

(3) σὺν χρόνῳ. *over time, later*: LSJ, s.v. χρόνος, 4.l.

θαῦμα . . . τοῦτο. Take the latter as the subject and the former as a predicate nom.; τοῦτο is a placeholder for the indirect question (πῶς . . . ὁμοδίαιτα) in apposition: Smyth 1248. Translate as *this may seem to be a source of wonder to the many people who have considered what was likely (to happen), (namely) how . . .*

εἰκότα. neu. pl. acc., pf. act. part. < ἔοικα.

Ὀπικούς . . . Κελτῶν. *Opicans, Marsians, Samnites, Tyrrhenians, Bruttians, Umbrians, Ligurians*—so far, all Italic peoples—*Iberians, Celts.*

ἄλλα. Note the accent.

εἰρημένοις. mas. pl. dat., pf. pass. part. < ἐρῶ. in pass., *be mentioned*: LSJ, s.v. III.

οὔτε φωνὰς οὔτε δίαιταν. Some editors think these words should be deleted from the text.

σύγκλυς, -υδος. *diverse, divergent.*

ἀναταράττω. *mix, blend,* with an implication of disorder.

πολλὰ . . . νεοχμόω. *cause many changes.*

τοῦ παλαιοῦ κόσμου. gen. of separation.

εἰκὸς ἦν + acc. and inf. may introduce an unfulfilled possibility in the pres.: Smyth 1774–79, 1905. Translate as *it might seem probable that their ways of life* (ὧν καὶ βίους) . . .

(4) ὡς = ὥστε.

ἐπιτήδευμα, -ατος (neu.). *habit, custom*; in pl., *way of life.*

διαλλάττω. *differ from X* (+ gen.) *in Y* (+ dat.): LSJ, s.v. διαλλάσσω, IV. The verb may imply not just difference but also superiority, as it seems to do here. Where other dialects employ double sigma, Attic uses double tau.

συμβόλαιον, -ου (neu.). *human activity, affair.*

ὁστισοῦν, ὁτιοῦν. *anybody at all, anything at all*: LSJ, s.v. ὅστις, IV.2.b.

ἀποχράω + inf. *be sufficient to X.*

ὡς ἀληθῆ εἶναι. Some editors also think these words should be deleted from the text.

Ἀχαιῶν οἱ περὶ τὸν Πόντον ᾠκημένοι. *those (of the) Achaeans dwelling around the Black Sea.*

'Ηλείων. gen. of source. Elis was a region in the Peloponnese just west of Achaea; however, the word is variously reported in the manuscripts and has been often emended. Even if the name is corrupt, the point is clear: the descendants of the Greekest of Greeks have so lost their Hellenic identity over time that they are now the most barbaric of barbarians; contrast with them the Romans.

(90.1) ἀπηρτισμένως. *entirely.*

ἀπολαύω + acc. *have the benefit of X.* Here, as often, the verb is ironic: LSJ, s.v. II.

τὸ μὴ πᾶσι τοῖς φθόγγοις ὀρθοεπεῖν is in apposition with τοῦτο μόνον. Dionysius, in his works on rhetoric, exhibits much interest in pronunciation.

μήνυμα, -ατος (neu.). *indication*: LSJ, s.v. II.

οὐ νῦν πρῶτον ἀρξάμενοι πρὸς φιλίαν ζῆν. This important sentiment, especially its last three words, is difficult to capture in English: *having not, just recently, begun to live in accordance with friendship.* Dionysius suggests that the Romans have lived in line with the Greek concept of φιλία (and all the virtues related thereto) from the beginning and have continued to do so through Dionysius's own day.

διδάσκαλον. predicative: *as a teacher.*

ἀφ' οὗ. *from the time when, since.*

ὠρέχθησαν < ὀρέγω + gen. in mid. and pass., *grasp at, take aim at, attack*: LSJ, s.v. II.2.

Καρχηδονίων καὶ Μακεδόνων. After fighting a series of wars against the Carthaginians and Macedonians, Rome annexed the territory of both these peoples in 146 B.C.E.

A6. INCLUSIVE ROME

Dionysius of Halicarnassus
Roman Antiquities 2.15.1, 2.15.3–17.1

In most accounts of Rome under the kings (traditionally, 753–510 B.C.E.), such as the historian Livy's, there is a tendency to associate the development of particular aspects of the state with particular monarchs. Rome's second king, Numa, for example, is said to have established many of the city's religious institutions (A7.1); Servius Tullius, its sixth monarch, is said to have revamped its social organization. Dionysius's approach differs. Since Rome is a Greek colony (ἀποικία), Dionysius models its foundation on Greek narratives of colonization (κτίσεις). Such narratives emphasize the preeminent role of the colony's founder in laying down the settlement's laws and customs; hence he is often called the lawgiver (νομοθέτης). So in Dionysius's account of Rome's regal period, Romulus is essentially responsible for establishing all the fundamental features of Roman society; the later kings cultivate the seeds that he planted.

In the passage below, part of a long account of Romulus's organization of the newborn city-state, Dionysius highlights two innovations that made the city inclusive and thereby helped Rome grow. Dionysius suggests that this inclusivity was integral to Rome's success. Above all, Dionysius emphasizes—and admires—Rome's clemency toward the cities it conquered and its willingness, in many cases, to convert them into colonies and even to share Roman citizenship with their residents. (Dionysius was not the only foreigner to argue that Rome's readiness to enroll new citizens strengthened the state; indeed, as early as the 210s B.C.E., Philip V, king of Macedon, had made such a claim. See W. Dittenberger, ed., *Sylloge Inscriptionum Graecarum,* 3rd ed. [Leipzig, 1917], no. 543.) Yet as Rome absorbed new peoples, it still preserved the Greek virtues under which it was founded. In other words, Roman expansion depended on a paradoxical combination of adherence to tradition and openness to inclusion.

Further Reading

Livy 1.8; E. Gabba, *Dionysius and* The History of Archaic Rome (Berkeley, 1991), 190–216; E. Dench, *Romulus' Asylum: Roman Identities from the Age of Alexander to the Age of Hadrian* (Oxford, 2005), 1–35; R. MacMullen, *The Earliest Romans: A Character Sketch* (Ann Arbor, 2011), vii–xi, 3–28.

(15.1) τεταγμένην μὲν οὖν καὶ κεκοσμημένην πρὸς εἰρήνην τε ἀποχρώντως καὶ πρὸς τὰ πολέμια ἐπιτηδείως ἐκ τούτων τῶν πολιτευμάτων τὴν πόλιν ὁ Ῥωμύλος ἀπειργάσατο, μεγάλην δὲ καὶ πολυάνθρωπον ἐκ τῶνδε.

[In section 2, Dionysius describes how Romulus restricted the exposure of newborns, thereby effecting population growth.]

(3) ἔπειτα καταμαθὼν πολλὰς τῶν κατὰ τὴν Ἰταλίαν πόλεων πονηρῶς ἐπιτροπευομένας ὑπὸ τυραννίδων τε καὶ ὀλιγαρχιῶν, τοὺς ἐκ τούτων ἐκπίπτοντας τῶν πόλεων συχνοὺς ὄντας, εἰ μόνον εἶεν ἐλεύθεροι, διακρίνων οὔτε συμφορὰς οὔτε τύχας αὐτῶν ὑποδέχεσθαι καὶ μετάγειν ὡς ἑαυτὸν ἐπεχείρει, τήν τε Ῥωμαίων δύναμιν αὐξῆσαι βουληθεὶς καὶ τὰς τῶν περιοίκων ἐλαττῶσαι· ἐποίει δὲ ταῦτα πρόφασιν ἐξευρὼν εὐπρεπῆ καὶ εἰς θεοῦ τιμὴν τὸ ἔργον ἀναφέρων. **(4)** τὸ γὰρ μεταξὺ χωρίον τοῦ τε Καπιτωλίου καὶ τῆς ἄκρας, ὃ καλεῖται νῦν κατὰ τὴν Ῥωμαίων διάλεκτον μεθόριον δυεῖν δρυμῶν καὶ ἦν τότε τοῦ συμβεβηκότος ἐπώνυμον, ὕλαις ἀμφιλαφέσι κατ' ἀμφοτέρας τὰς συναπτούσας τοῖς λόφοις λαγόνας ἐπίσκιον, ἱερὸν ἀνεὶς ἄσυλον ἱκέταις καὶ ναὸν ἐπὶ τοὺτῳ κατασκευασάμενος (ὅτῳ δὲ ἄρα θεῶν ἢ δαιμόνων οὐκ ἔχω τὸ σαφὲς εἰπεῖν) τοῖς καταφεύγουσιν εἰς τοῦτο τὸ ἱερὸν ἱκέταις τοῦ τε μηδὲν κακὸν ὑπ᾽ ἐχθρῶν παθεῖν ἐγγυητὴς ἐγίνετο τῆς εἰς τὸ θεῖον εὐσεβείας προφάσει καὶ εἰ βούλοιντο παρ᾽ αὐτῷ μένειν πολιτείας μετεδίδου καὶ γῆς μοῖραν, ἣν κτήσαιτο πολεμίους ἀφελόμενος. οἱ δὲ συνέρρεον ἐκ παντὸς τόπου τὰ οἰκεῖα φεύγοντες κακὰ καὶ οὐκέτι ἑτέρωσε ἀπανίσταντο ταῖς καθ᾽ ἡμέραν ὁμιλίαις καὶ χάρισιν ὑπ᾽ αὐτοῦ κατεχόμενοι.

(16.1) τρίτον ἦν ἔτι Ῥωμύλου πολίτευμα, ὃ πάντων μάλιστα τοὺς Ἕλληνας ἀσκεῖν ἔδει, κράτιστον ἁπάντων πολιτευμάτων ὑπάρχον, ὡς ἐμὴ δόξα φέρει, ὃ καὶ τῆς βεβαίου Ῥωμαίοις ἐλευθερίας ἦρχε καὶ τῶν ἐπὶ τὴν ἡγεμονίαν ἀγόντων οὐκ ἐλαχίστην μοῖραν παρέσχε, τὸ μήτε κατασφάττειν ἡβηδὸν τὰς ἁλούσας πολέμῳ πόλεις μήτε ἀνδραποδίζεσθαι μηδὲ γῆν αὐτῶν ἀνιέναι μηλόβοτον, ἀλλὰ κληρούχους εἰς αὐτὰς ἀποστέλλειν ἐπὶ μέρει τινὶ τῆς χώρας καὶ ποιεῖν ἀποικίας τῆς Ῥώμης τὰς κρατηθείσας, ἐνίαις δὲ καὶ πολιτείας μεταδιδόναι. **(2)** ταῦτά τε δὴ καὶ τἆλλα τούτοις ὅμοια καταστησάμενος πολιτεύματα μεγάλην ἐκ μικρᾶς ἐποίησε τὴν ἀποικίαν, ὡς αὐτὰ τὰ ἔργα ἐδήλωσεν. οἱ μὲν γὰρ συνοικίσαντες μετ᾽ αὐτοῦ τὴν Ῥώμην οὐ πλείους ἦσαν ἀνδρῶν τρισχιλίων πεζοὶ καὶ τριακοσίων ἐλάττους ἱππεῖς· οἱ δὲ καταλειφθέντες ὑπ᾽ ἐκείνου, ὅτ᾽ ἐξ ἀνθρώπων ἠφανίσθη, πεζοὶ μὲν ἑξακισχίλιοι πρὸς τέτταρσι μυριάσιν, ἱππεῖς δ᾽ οὐ πολὺ ἀπέχοντες χιλίων. **(3)** ἐκείνου δὲ ἄρξαντος τῶν πολιτευμάτων τούτων οἵ τε βασιλεῖς οἱ μετ᾽ αὐτὸν ἡγησάμενοι τῆς πόλεως τὴν αὐτὴν ἐφυλάξαντο προαίρεσιν καὶ οἱ μετ᾽ ἐκείνους τὰς ἐνιαυσίους λαμβάνοντες ἀρχὰς ἔστιν ἃ καὶ προστιθέντες, οὕτως ὥστε μηδενὸς ἔθνους τοῦ δοκοῦντος εἶναι πολυανθρωποτάτου τὸν Ῥωμαίων γενέσθαι δῆμον ἐλάττονα.

(17.1) τὰ δὲ Ἑλλήνων ἔθη παρὰ ταῦτα ἐξετάζων οὐκ ἔχω πῶς ἐπαινέσω τά τε Λακεδαιμονίων καὶ τὰ τῶν Θηβαίων καὶ τῶν μέγιστον ἐπὶ σοφίᾳ φρονούντων Ἀθηναίων, οἳ φυλάττοντες τὸ εὐγενὲς καὶ μηδενὶ μεταδιδόντες εἰ μὴ σπανίοις τῆς παρ᾽ ἑαυτοῖς πολιτείας (ἐῶ γὰρ λέγειν ὅτι καὶ ξενηλατοῦντες ἔνιοι) πρὸς τῷ μηδὲν ἀπολαῦσαι ταύτης τῆς μεγαληγορίας ἀγαθὸν καὶ τὰ μέγιστα δι᾽ αὐτὴν ἐβλάβησαν.

Notes to Dionysius of Halicarnassus Roman Antiquities *2.15.1, 2.15.3–17.1*

(15.1) ἀποχρώντως. *adequately, sufficiently.*

ἐκ τούτων τῶν πολιτευμάτων. i.e., the institutions and policies described by Dionysius in the sections preceding this excerpt.

ἀπεργάζομαι here takes two accusatives, *make X (to be) Y*: LSJ, s.v. III.

ἐκ τῶνδε. sc. πολιτευμάτων.

(3) ἔπειτα. *next, secondly.*

ἐκπίπτω. act. here has pass. meaning. *be driven out, banished*: LSJ, s.v. 3.

εἰ μόνον εἶεν ἐλεύθεροι. protasis of a past general condition. In Livy's account of these events, slaves were also admitted: 1.8.6.

διακρίνω. *pass judgment on.*

ὡς + acc. *to.* When ὡς is used as a proposition, its object, as here, is usually a person, not a place: LSJ, s.v. C.III.

ἐπιχειρέω + inf. *endeavor to X.*

πρόφασις, -εως (fem.). an ambiguous word that can mean *motive,* either presumed or actual, as well as *pretext, pretense*: LSJ, s.v.

ἀναφέρω. *offer,* in a religious sense: LSJ, s.v. I.4.

(4) μεταξὺ χωρίον τοῦ τε Καπιτωλίου καὶ τῆς ἄκρας. The steep Capitoline Hill had two peaks: one to the north commonly called the Citadel (Latin Arx) and another, the Capitolium, to the south.

μεθόριον δυεῖν δρυμῶν. Livy uses a similar locution for the location: "between two groves" (*inter duos lucos*): 1.8.5.

ἦν τότε τοῦ συμβεβηκότος ἐπώνυμον. *it was named for how it existed at that time.* In other words, the landscape of the hilltop has since changed.

ἀμφιλαφής, -ές. *dense, thick.* The adj. is dat. after ἐπίσκιον.

κατ'. *upon*; i.e., *covering.*

λαγών, -όνος (usually fem., sometimes mas.). *side, flank* (of a mountain): LSJ, s.v. II.

ἀνεὶς. mas. sg. nom., aor. act. part. < ἀνίημι.

ὅτῳ δὲ ἄρα θεῶν. Contemporary scholars are likewise unsure about the identity of the god or gods enshrined at the Asylum.

καταφεύγουσιν. mas. pl. dat., pres. act. part.

τοῦ . . . παθεῖν. articular inf.

ἐγγυητής, -οῦ (mas.). *guarantor, protector.*

ἐγίνετο. The subject is Romulus; ἐγγυητὴς is predicate nom.

προφάσει. See note on (3) above.

πολιτείας . . . μοῖραν. i.e., citizenship.

ἀφελόμενος < ἀφαιρέω.

ἑτέρωσε. *elsewhere*: LSJ, s.v. II.2. The émigrés did not leave Rome once they had arrived there.

ἀπανίσταντο. 3rd pl. impf. pass. ind. < ἀπανίστημι. in pass., *depart again, emigrate.*

(16.1) ἔδει + acc. and inf. Used impersonally, ἔδει introduces an unfulfilled obligation: Smyth 1774–76. In other words, the Greeks ought to have followed a policy similar to Romulus's but didn't.

ὑπάρχον. neu. sg. acc., pres. act. part. < ὑπάρχω. *be.*

ἄρχω + gen. *initiate, introduce.*

οὐκ ἐλαχίστην. litotes: Smyth 3032.

ἡβηδόν. *young and old alike.*

ἁλούσας. fem. pl. acc., aor. dep. part. < ἁλίσκομαι. *be captured.*

ἀνίημι. *leave untilled, allow to grow wild*: LSJ, s.v. II.6.

κληροῦχος. *cleruch*; i.e., someone to whom a plot of land in a settlement is assigned.

αὐτὰς. The antecedent is πόλεις.

μεταδίδωμι. *give a share of X* (+ gen.) *to Y* (+ dat.); i.e., some colonies received Roman citizenship.

(2) τὴν ἀποικίαν. i.e., Rome.

πλείους, ἐλάττους. mas. pl. nom.

ἠφανίσθη < ἀφανίζω. On the different accounts of Romulus's "disappearance," see *Roman Antiquities* 2.56.

πρός + dat. *in addition to*: LSJ, s.v. B.III.

τέτταρσι. dat. of τέτταρες. *four*. 6,000 + (4 x 10,000) = 46,000 infantrymen.

(3) προαίρεσις, -εως (fem.). *policy, course of action*: LSJ, s.v. 3.

ἐνιαυσίους. Most Roman republican magistrates had one-year terms of office.

ἀρχή, -ῆς (fem.). *office, magistracy*.

ἔστιν ἃ καὶ προστιθέντες. *also adding to things as they are*. Romulus's successors both preserved his policies and, as needed, supplemented them.

ἐλάττονα. i.e., less populous.

(17.1) παρά + acc. *vis-à-vis, in comparison to*: Smyth 1692.3.c.

οὐκ ἔχω πῶς + subj. *I don't see how*: LSJ, s.v. ἔχω (A), III.2; Smyth 2546–47.

εἰ μὴ. *except for*.

ἐάω. *refrain from* + inf. Dionysius employs the rhetorical device known as preterition: by denying that he is going to say a certain thing, he draws attention to it.

ξενηλατέω. *deport foreigners*.

πρός + dat. *in addition to*, here followed by the articular inf. τῷ μηδὲν ἀπολαῦσαι . . . ἀγαθὸν.

ἀπολαύω. *gain X* (+ acc.) *from Y* (+ gen.).

μεγαληγορία, -ας (fem.). *braggadocio, haughty talk*, in this case, about nobility of birth (τὸ εὐγενὲς).

A7. RELIGION

Plutarch *Numa* 8.1–3 and Polybius 6.56.6–12

In ancient Rome, politics and religion were deeply intertwined and mutually supportive; harmonious relations with the gods fostered stability in the state. Indeed, religion permeated every facet of Roman life; the gods were everywhere, their shrines and images ubiquitous. Through public rituals—prayers, libations, sacrifices—the Romans propitiated the gods, who in turn made their will known, if opaquely, through signs and portents: Roman religion was transactional. It was also deeply conservative yet cautiously open to innovation. The Romans thought highly of their religion—Cicero opined that of all peoples the Romans were the most pious (*On the Haruspices' Responses* 19)—and many Greek authors did as well, though what inspired this admiration varied. Dionysius of Halicarnassus (A3.2–A6), for example, praised Rome's rejection of manic, frenzied religious rites; of new and foreign deities; and of shameful myths populated by immoral gods (*Roman Antiquities* 2.18–23). According to Dionysius, Rome's religious system mostly originated in one man's genius: that of its authoritative founder and lawgiver, Romulus (A6).

Unlike Dionysius and like most other writers, the prolific polymath Plutarch (who is more fully introduced in B3) attributes the establishment of Rome's religious system less to Romulus than to Numa (Νομᾶς), by tradition the city's second king. Plutarch introduces Numa as a learned mystic, a hermitic outlier detached from politics and dedicated to the divine. When he does reluctantly accept the crown, he rules, though perhaps imperfectly, like Plato's philosopher-king. In the first passage below, Plutarch shows how the monarch tempers Rome's bellicosity with piety. In the second passage, Polybius, who is introduced more fully in the next selection (B1), claims, like Cicero, that Rome's religious system is superior to those of other states. For both Polybius and Marx, religion is the "opiate of the masses"—but for Polybius this quality is admirable rather than deplorable.

Further Reading

Plutarch *Numa* 1–7; J. A. North, *Roman Religion,* Greece & Rome New Surveys in the Classics 30 (Oxford, 2000), 4–20; A. Erskine, "Polybios and Barbarian Rome," *Mediterraneo Antico* 3 (2000): 165–82; B. Boulet, "Is Numa the Genuine Philosopher King?," in *The Statesman in Plutarch's Works,* ed. L. de Blois et al., 2 vols., 2:245–56 (Leiden, 2005); P. A. Stadter, "*Paidagôgia pros to theion:* Plutarch's *Numa,*" published online in *Ancient Journeys: A Festschrift in Honor of Eugene Numa Lane,* ed. C. Callaway (2002), http://www.stoa.org/lane/, and reprinted in the author's *Plutarch and His Roman Readers* (Oxford, 2015), 246–57.

A7.1. Plutarch *Numa* 8.1–3

(1) ταῦτα δὲ ὁ Νομᾶς ἐπ' εὐνοίᾳ καὶ χάριτι τοῦ δήμου πολιτευσάμενος εὐθὺς ἐπεχείρει τὴν πόλιν, ὥσπερ σίδηρον, ἐκ σκληρᾶς καὶ πολεμικῆς μαλακωτέραν ποιῆσαι καὶ δικαιοτέραν. ἀτεχνῶς γὰρ ἣν Πλάτων ἀποκαλεῖ φλεγμαίνουσαν πόλιν ἐκείνη τότ' ἦν, συστᾶσα μὲν εὐθὺς ἐξ ἀρχῆς τόλμῃ τινὶ καὶ παραβόλῳ θρασύτητι τῶν θρασυτάτων καὶ μαχιμωτάτων ἐκεῖ πανταχόθεν ὠσαμένων, **(2)** ταῖς δὲ πολλαῖς στρατείαις καὶ τοῖς συνεχέσι πολέμοις τροφῇ χρησαμένη καὶ αὐξήσει τῆς δυνάμεως, καὶ καθάπερ τὰ καταπηγνύμενα τῷ σείεσθαι μᾶλλον ἐδράζεται, ῥώννυσθαι δοκοῦσα διὰ τῶν κινδύνων, οὕτω δὴ μετέωρον καὶ τετραχυμένον δῆμον οὐ μικρᾶς οὐδὲ φαύλης οἰόμενος εἶναι πραγματείας μεταχειρίσασθαι καὶ μετακοσμῆσαι πρὸς εἰρήνην, ἐπηγάγετο τὴν ἀπὸ τῶν θεῶν βοήθειαν, **(3)** τὰ μὲν πολλὰ θυσίαις καὶ πομπαῖς καὶ χορείαις, ἃς αὐτὸς ὠργίασε καὶ κατέστησεν, ἅμα σεμνότητι διαγωγὴν ἐπίχαριν καὶ φιλάνθρωπον ἡδονὴν ἐχούσαις, δημαγωγῶν καὶ τιθασεύων τὸ θυμοειδὲς καὶ φιλοπόλεμον ἔστι δ᾽ ὅτε καὶ φόβους τινὰς ἀπαγγέλλων παρὰ τοῦ θεοῦ καὶ φάσματα δαιμόνων ἀλλόκοτα καὶ φωνὰς οὐκ εὐμενεῖς, ἐδούλου καὶ ταπεινὴν ἐποίει τὴν διάνοιαν αὐτῶν ὑπὸ δεισιδαιμονίας.

Notes to Plutarch Numa *8.1–3*

(1) ταῦτα refers to the measures Numa made immediately after his accession, described in the preceding section: he disbanded Romulus's security detail and established a new priesthood dedicated to superintending the cult of the deified Romulus.

Νομᾶς, -ᾶ (mas.). Numa's name is variously spelled in Greek.

ἐπ᾽ . . . δήμου. By currying the favor of the people, Numa also cements his authority.

ἐπιχειρέω + inf. *try, attempt to X.* The word also has martial undertones; it can mean *attempt to attack, attack.*

ἀτεχνῶς. *absolutely, really*: LSJ, s.v. ἀτέχνως, II.

ἧν. Another example of "incorporation"; see first note on A5.

Πλάτων ἀποκαλεῖ φλεγμαίνουσαν. Plato *Republic* 2.372e, *Laws* 3.691e.

ἐκείνη. sc. πόλις; i.e., Rome.

συστᾶσα. fem. sg. nom., aor. act. part. < συνίστημι. *come together, come into existence.*

ὠσαμένων. mas. pl. gen., aor. mid. part. < ὠθέω. *thrust, push, shove.*

(2) τροφῇ, αὐξήσει. predicative with ταῖς . . . πολέμοις.

μετέωρος, -ον. *unstable, haughty, mindless.* Plutarch's vocabulary in this passage is remarkably rich.

τετραχυμένον < ταράσσω. *trouble, agitate.*

μετέωρον . . . δῆμον is the object of μεταχειρίσασθαι καὶ μετακοσμῆσαι.

οἰόμενος + inf. and predicative gen: Smyth 1305. Translate as *reckoning it to be neither a small nor easy business . . .*

ἐπάγω. in mid., *procure for oneself*; this verb also has martial connotations: *bring on as an ally*: LSJ, s.v. II. The use of the mid. may again raise the question of Numa's motives.

(3) τὰ . . . πολλὰ. *primarily, mostly*: LSJ, s.v. πολύς, III.a.

διαγωγή, -ῆς (fem.). *amusement, pastime*: LSJ, s.v. II.2.

δημαγωγέω. *lead the people,* usually in a pejorative sense: LSJ, s.v.

ἔστι . . . ὅτε. *sometimes, now and then*: LSJ, s.v. ὅτε, A.IV.2. The phrase should be taken with what follows.

φόβους. i.e., things that cause fear.

δεισιδαιμονία, -ας (fem.) here is a difficult word to translate, as it may mean, depending on the author and text, *fear of the gods, scrupulosity in religion* (positive connotations) as well as *superstition, irrational beliefs about the gods, excessive piety* (negative connotations). Plutarch wrote a treatise on δεισιδαιμονία (164e–174f), in which he adheres to the latter definitions. Yet in this passage the word's meaning seems more ambiguous: Numa fosters δεισιδαιμονία to benefit the populace, or so it appears. Cf. section (7) in A7.2.

A7.2. POLYBIUS 6.56.6–12

(6) μεγίστην δέ μοι δοκεῖ διαφορὰν ἔχειν τὸ Ῥωμαίων πολίτευμα πρὸς βέλτιον ἐν τῇ περὶ θεῶν διαλήψει. **(7)** καί μοι δοκεῖ τὸ παρὰ τοῖς ἄλλοις ἀνθρώποις ὀνειδιζόμενον, τοῦτο συνέχειν τὰ Ῥωμαίων πράγματα, λέγω δὲ τὴν δεισιδαιμονίαν· **(8)** ἐπὶ τοσοῦτον γὰρ ἐκτετραγῴδηται καὶ παρεισῆκται τοῦτο τὸ μέρος παρ' αὐτοῖς εἴς τε τοὺς κατ' ἰδίαν βίους καὶ τὰ κοινὰ τῆς πόλεως ὥστε μὴ καταλιπεῖν ὑπερβολήν. ὃ καὶ δόξειεν ἂν πολλοῖς εἶναι θαυμάσιον. **(9)** ἐμοί γε μὴν δοκοῦσι τοῦ πλήθους χάριν τοῦτο πεποιηκέναι. **(10)** εἰ μὲν γὰρ ἦν σοφῶν ἀνδρῶν πολίτευμα συναγαγεῖν, ἴσως οὐδὲν ἦν ἀναγκαῖος ὁ τοιοῦτος τρόπος· **(11)** ἐπεὶ δὲ πᾶν πλῆθός ἐστιν ἐλαφρὸν καὶ πλῆρες ἐπιθυμιῶν παρανόμων, ὀργῆς ἀλόγου, θυμοῦ βιαίου, λείπεται τοῖς ἀδήλοις φόβοις καὶ τῇ τοιαύτῃ τραγῳδίᾳ τὰ πλήθη συνέχειν. **(12)** διόπερ οἱ παλαιοὶ δοκοῦσί μοι τὰς περὶ θεῶν ἐννοίας καὶ τὰς ὑπὲρ τῶν ἐν ᾅδου διαλήψεις οὐκ εἰκῇ καὶ ὡς ἔτυχεν εἰς τὰ πλήθη παρεισαγαγεῖν, πολὺ δὲ μᾶλλον οἱ νῦν εἰκῇ καὶ ἀλόγως ἐκβάλλειν αὐτά.

Notes to Polybius 6.56.6–12

These notes on Polybius are indebted to F. W. Walbank, *A Historical Commentary on Polybius,* 3 vols. (Oxford, 1957–).

(6) διάληψις, -εως (fem.). *opinion, belief,* often implying that the author looks favorably on the notion: LSJ, s.v. III.

(7) δεισιδαιμονίαν. See note on section (3) of A7.1.

(8) ἐπὶ τοσοῦτον. *to such a degree.*

ἐκτραγῳδέω. a rare and striking verb: *speak as if in a tragedy*; here, *dress up in tragic garb*: LSJ, s.v., citing this passage. By using a verb associated with the stage, the reader is invited to compare the social functions of religion and drama.

παρεισῆκται. 3rd sg. pf. pass. ind. < παρεισάγω. *introduce, bring forward,* often in reference to the introduction of a character into a narrative or of an individual into a political assembly: LSJ, s.v.

μέρος, -εος (neu.). *matter, business*: LSJ, s.v. IV.

μὴ καταλιπεῖν ὑπερβολήν. *it does not leave room for overstatement*; i.e., one cannot overstate how embedded religion is in both public and private life.

(9) χάριν + gen. postpositive (i.e., appears after the word it governs). *on account of.*

(10) εἰ . . . ἦν. protasis of pres. contrafactual: *if it were possible* (and it is not).

ἴσως. *perhaps.*

(11) τραγῳδία, ας (fem.). probably *pomp, spectacle* (LSJ, s.v. II.3) and not *exaggerated speech,* as LSJ, s.v. II.2, citing this passage, claims.

(12) ἐν ᾅδου. sc. τῇ γῇ: Smyth 1027.b.

εἰκῇ (adv.). *thoughtlessly, foolishly.*

ὡς ἔτυχεν. lit., *as it happened*; i.e., *randomly, thoughtlessly.*

Map of Greece, the Aegean Sea, and western Asia Minor. *Reproduced by permission of the Ancient World Mapping Center, 2016. http://awmc.unc.edu/wordpress/.*

PART B

EXPANSION IN THE REPUBLIC

These selections offer views of Roman expansion during the republic, when the state became more and more enmeshed in the affairs of other Mediterranean powers, especially those in the east, and more and more territory overseas came under its influence and control. This section opens with two selections from Polybius, a historian writing in the second century B.C.E. In the sixth book of his work, Polybius suspends his chronological narrative to consider how Rome managed to weather crushing defeats at the hands of Hannibal during the Second Punic War. He argues that checks-and-balances in Roman government enabled the state to respond effectively to external threats and that, militarily, Rome was superior to Carthage (B1). In part, this military superiority may be traced to Rome's spectacular public funerals, where future generations are inspired to emulate the virtues of the great men who had come before them (B2). Next, two passages from Plutarch's biographies exemplify contrasting attitudes among Roman notables toward Greek culture. In flamboyant fashion the philhellenic Flamininus "liberated" Greece from Macedonian hegemony at the Isthmian Games in 196 B.C.E. (B3), whereas the apparently antihellenic Cato the Elder ejected charismatic Greek philosophers from Rome in 155 B.C.E. (B4). Then comes another pair of contrasting passages, the first hostile to Rome and the second complimentary: supernatural beings prophesied Rome's ruin after it had defeated a Seleucid army in 191 B.C.E. (B5), whereas in 161 B.C.E. Jewish leaders rebelling from their Seleucid overlords sought an alliance with Rome, a power praised for its martial might, fidelity to its friends, and stable government (B6). The section concludes with Strabo's account of the sack of Corinth by the Roman general Lucius Mummius in 146 B.C.E. and the subsequent looting of that city's art, which came to beautify the city of Rome (B7).

B1. SECRETS OF ROMAN SUCCESS

Polybius 6.18, 52

Polybius was no armchair quarterback: he was deeply involved in the geopolitics of his day. He was born around 200 B.C.E. to an aristocratic family from Megalopolis, a leading city in the Peloponnese. Like his father, he was an important figure, serving as an envoy and the second-highest official (ἵππαρχος), in the Achaean League, a confederation of city-states that promoted Greek autonomy. In 168, after the Romans' defeat of Perseus, king of Macedon, at the Battle of Pydna, Greece came under Rome's sway, and Polybius was one of a thousand Greek hostages detained in Italy. In Rome, he met the then-teenage Scipio Aemilianus, learned scion of a prestigious family who became one of the most celebrated generals and literati of his time. Polybius traveled widely, often while on campaign with Scipio, in Italy, the western provinces, and even beyond, into the Atlantic; he witnessed first-hand Scipio's victory over Carthage in 146, which extinguished Rome's great foe forever. He returned to Greece that same year to help negotiate the terms by which that region would be absorbed into the empire. He died around 118, having fallen from a horse.

As a Greek former power player with close ties to members of the Roman elite, Polybius was well positioned to write his history of Rome's rapid rise to interregional hegemony in forty books, focusing on the years 264–146 B.C.E. Only books 1 through 5 are extant in full; also preserved are quotations and excerpts, some lengthy, of the rest, including long excerpts from the crucial sixth book. After a now-lost account of Rome's disastrous defeat at Cannae by Hannibal in 216, Polybius in book 6 pauses from his chronological narrative to discuss what enabled Rome not just to weather this crisis but also to become master of the Mediterranean, namely, its πολιτεία—its interrelated political, religious, social, and military institutions and traditions. The first passage below immediately follows his famous discussion of Rome's mixed constitution, with its three branches of government: the magistrates, Senate, and people, which respectively represent monarchic, aristocratic, and democratic power within the state. The second, from later in book 6, compares the military strengths and weaknesses of Rome and Carthage. At the end of the passage, Polybius shows how Rome perpetuates its martial might, as one generation of Romans imprints a thirst for honor on the next.

Further Reading

Polybius 1.1–5, 6.2–17; F. W. Walbank, *Polybius* (Berkeley, 1972), 130–56; C. B. Champion, *Cultural Politics in Polybius's* Histories (Berkeley, 2004), 1–29, 67–99; F. Millar, "Polybius between Greece and Rome," in *Greek Connections: Essays on Culture and Diplomacy,* ed. J. T. A. Koumoulides, 1–18 (Notre Dame, 1987), reprinted in F. Millar, *Rome, the Greek World, and the East,* ed. H. M. Cotton and G. M. Rogers, 3 vols., 3:91–105 (Chapel Hill, 2006).

❧

(18.1) τοιαύτης δ' οὔσης τῆς ἑκάστου τῶν μερῶν δυνάμεως εἰς τὸ καὶ βλάπτειν καὶ συνεργεῖν ἀλλήλοις, πρὸς πάσας συμβαίνει τὰς περιστάσεις δεόντως ἔχειν τὴν ἁρμογὴν αὐτῶν, ὥστε μὴ οἷόν τ' εἶναι ταύτης εὑρεῖν ἀμείνω πολιτείας σύστασιν. **(2)** ὅταν μὲν γάρ τις ἔξωθεν κοινὸς φόβος ἐπιστὰς ἀναγκάσῃ σφᾶς συμφρονεῖν καὶ συνεργεῖν ἀλλήλοις, τηλικαύτην καὶ τοιαύτην συμβαίνει γίνεσθαι τὴν δύναμιν τοῦ πολιτεύματος **(3)** ὥστε μήτε παραλείπεσθαι τῶν δεόντων μηδέν, ἅτε περὶ τὸ προσπεσὸν ἀεὶ πάντων ὁμοῦ ταῖς ἐπινοίαις ἁμιλλωμένων, μήτε τὸ κριθὲν ὑστερεῖν τοῦ καιροῦ, κοινῇ καὶ κατ' ἰδίαν ἑκάστου συνεργοῦντος πρὸς τὴν τοῦ προκειμένου συντέλειαν. **(4)** διόπερ ἀνυπόστατον συμβαίνει γίνεσθαι καὶ παντὸς ἐφικνεῖσθαι τοῦ κριθέντος τὴν ἰδιότητα τοῦ πολιτεύματος. **(5)** ὅταν γε μὴν πάλιν ἀπολυθέντες τῶν ἐκτὸς φόβων ἐνδιατρίβωσι ταῖς εὐτυχίαις καὶ περιουσίαις ταῖς ἐκ τῶν κατορθωμάτων, ἀπολαύοντες τῆς εὐδαιμονίας, καὶ ὑποκολακευόμενοι καὶ ῥᾳθυμοῦντες τρέπωνται πρὸς ὕβριν καὶ πρὸς ὑπερηφανίαν, **(6)** ὃ δὴ φιλεῖ γίνεσθαι, τότε καὶ μάλιστα συνιδεῖν ἔστιν αὐτὸ παρ' αὑτοῦ ποριζόμενον τὸ πολίτευμα τὴν βοήθειαν. **(7)** ἐπειδὰν γὰρ ἐξοιδοῦν τι τῶν μερῶν φιλονεικῇ καὶ πλέον τοῦ δέοντος ἐπικρατῇ, δῆλον ὡς οὐδενὸς αὐτοτελοῦς ὄντος κατὰ τὸν ἄρτι λόγον, ἀντισπᾶσθαι δὲ καὶ παραποδίζεσθαι δυναμένης τῆς ἑκάστου προθέσεως ὑπ' ἀλλήλων, οὐδὲν ἐξοιδεῖ τῶν μερῶν οὐδ' ὑπερφρονεῖ. **(8)** πάντα γὰρ ἐμμένει τοῖς ὑποκειμένοις τὰ μὲν κωλυόμενα τῆς ὁρμῆς, τὰ δ' ἐξ ἀρχῆς δεδιότα τὴν ἐκ τοῦ πέλας ἐπίστασιν.

(52.1) τά γε μὴν κατὰ μέρος, οἷον εὐθέως τὰ πρὸς τὰς πολεμικὰς χρείας, τὸ μὲν πρὸς τὰς κατὰ θάλατταν, ὅπερ εἰκός, ἄμεινον ἀσκοῦσι καὶ παρασκευάζονται Καρχηδόνιοι διὰ τὸ καὶ πάτριον αὐτοῖς ὑπάρχειν ἐκ παλαιοῦ τὴν ἐμπειρίαν ταύτην καὶ θαλαττουργεῖν μάλιστα πάντων ἀνθρώπων, **(2)** τὸ δὲ περὶ τὰς πεζικὰς χρείας πολὺ δή τι Ῥωμαῖοι πρὸς τὸ βέλτιον ἀσκοῦσι Καρχηδονίων. **(3)** οἱ μὲν γὰρ τὴν ὅλην περὶ τοῦτο ποιοῦνται σπουδήν, Καρχηδόνιοι δὲ τῶν μὲν πεζικῶν εἰς τέλος ὀλιγωροῦσι, τῶν δ' ἱππικῶν βραχεῖάν τινα ποιοῦνται πρόνοιαν. **(4)** αἴτιον δὲ τούτων ἐστὶν ὅτι ξενικαῖς καὶ μισθοφόροις χρῶνται δυνάμεσι, Ῥωμαῖοι δ' ἐγχωρίοις καὶ πολιτικαῖς. **(5)** ᾗ καὶ περὶ τοῦτο τὸ μέρος ταύτην τὴν πολιτείαν ἀποδεκτέον ἐκείνης μᾶλλον· ἡ μὲν γὰρ ἐν ταῖς τῶν μισθοφόρων εὐψυχίαις ἔχει τὰς ἐλπίδας ἀεὶ τῆς ἐλευθερίας, ἡ δὲ Ῥωμαίων ἐν ταῖς σφετέραις ἀρεταῖς καὶ ταῖς τῶν συμμάχων ἐπαρκείαις. **(6)** διὸ κἂν ποτε πταίσωσι κατὰ τὰς ἀρχάς, Ῥωμαῖοι μὲν ἀναμάχονται τοῖς ὅλοις, Καρχηδόνιοι δὲ τοὐναντίον. **(7)** ἐκεῖνοι γὰρ ὑπὲρ πατρίδος ἀγωνιζόμενοι καὶ τέκνων οὐδέποτε δύνανται λῆξαι τῆς ὀργῆς, ἀλλὰ μένουσι ψυχομαχοῦντες, ἕως ἂν περιγένωνται τῶν ἐχθρῶν. **(8)** διὸ καὶ περὶ τὰς ναυτικὰς δυνάμεις πολύ τι λειπόμενοι Ῥωμαῖοι κατὰ τὴν ἐμπειρίαν, ὡς προεῖπον ἐπάνω, τοῖς ὅλοις ἐπικρατοῦσι διὰ τὰς τῶν ἀνδρῶν ἀρετάς· **(9)** καίπερ γὰρ οὐ μικρὰ συμβαλλομένης εἰς τοὺς κατὰ θάλατταν κινδύνους τῆς ναυτικῆς χρείας, ὅμως ἡ τῶν ἐπιβατῶν εὐψυχία πλείστην παρέχεται ῥοπὴν εἰς τὸ νικᾶν. **(10)** διαφέρουσι μὲν οὖν καὶ φύσει πάντες Ἰταλιῶται Φοινίκων καὶ Λιβύων τῇ τε σωματικῇ ῥώμῃ καὶ ταῖς ψυχικαῖς τόλμαις· μεγάλην δὲ καὶ διὰ τῶν ἐθισμῶν πρὸς τοῦτο τὸ μέρος ποιοῦνται τῶν νέων παρόρμησιν. **(11)** ἓν δὲ ῥηθὲν ἱκανὸν ἔσται σημεῖον τῆς τοῦ πολιτεύματος σπουδῆς, ἣν ποιεῖται περὶ τὸ τοιούτους ἀποτελεῖν ἄνδρας ὥστε πᾶν ὑπομένειν χάριν τοῦ τυχεῖν ἐν τῇ πατρίδι τῆς ἐπ᾽ ἀρετῇ φήμης.

Notes to Polybius 6.18, 52

These notes on Polybius are indebted to F. W. Walbank, *A Historical Commentary on Polybius,* 3 vols. (Oxford, 1957–).

(18.1) οὔσης. Translate the gen. absolute as causal.

μερῶν. i.e., the three branches of Rome's government: the magistrates, Senate, and people.

πρός + acc. *against.*

συμβαίνει. *it happens, it turns out* + inf.: LSJ, s.v. συμβαίνω, III. Note the prevalence of words prefixed by συμ-/ν-, which underscores the passage's theme: cooperation and (healthy) competition among the branches of government strengthens the state.

δεόντως. *as it ought.*

οἷόν τ᾽ ἐστί. *it is possible*: LSJ, s.v. οἷος, III.2.

πολιτεία, -ας (fem.). This Greek word has a broader meaning than its English cognate *polity*; as noted in the introduction to this passage, πολιτεία refers holistically to a state's political, social, military, and religious institutions and traditions.

(2) ὅταν is an important word, for it implies that the pattern here described is recurrent and has been observed repeatedly by the author either firsthand or in his research.

ἔξωθεν. Polybius's theory about the galvanizing effect of an external threat on the functioning of government is not original; e.g., some prominent Romans also endorsed the idea: Walbank, *Historical Commentary,* ad loc.

τηλικ-οῦτος, -αύτη, -οῦτο. *so great*: LSJ, s.v. τηλικόσδε, II.

πολίτευμα, -ατος (neu.). *government,* narrower than πολιτεία: LSJ, s.v. II.

(3) δεόντων. part. < δεῖ.

ἅτε + part. *since.*

προσπεσὸν < προσπίπτω. *happen, befall.*

ἁμιλλάομαι. *contend, strive,* often without negative connotations of rivalry: LSJ, s.v.

τοῦ προκειμένου. *of (the matter) lying before them.*

συντέλεια, -ας (fem.). *end, solution*: LSJ, s.v. III.

(4) ἀνυπόστατος, -ον. *irresistible.*

ἐφικνέομαι + gen. *succeed in, attain.*

ἰδιότης, -ητος (fem.). *variety, type, kind.*

(5) ὅταν. The repetition of this word marks a transition to the next phase of the analysis.

ἐνδιατρίβω + dat. *linger in, wallow in*: LSJ, s.v. II.2.

περιουσία, -ας (fem.). *profit, abundance,* often with a connotation of surfeit.

κατόρθωμα, -ατος (neu.). *success.*

ὑποκολακεύω. *flatter a bit.*

ῥᾳθυμέω. *grow lazy.*

(6) φιλεῖ γίνεσθαι. *is accustomed to happen*; i.e., *is what usually happens*: LSJ, s.v. II.2.

ἔστιν. Note accent (Smyth 187.b): *it is possible.*

αὐτὸ παρ' αὑτοῦ . . . τὸ πολίτευμα. i.e., the system itself generates the solution to the problem.

(7) ἐξοιδοῦν. neu. sg. nom., pres. act. part. < ἐξοιδέω. *swell.* The part. modifies τι, which is the subject. Polybius employs a metaphor common in antiquity: body politic as human body.

οὐδενὸς αὐτοτελοῦς ὄντος. gen. absolute; translate as causal.

κατὰ τὸν ἄρτι λόγον. i.e., according to the analysis just presented.

ἀντισπᾶσθαι . . . παραποδίζεσθαι. complementary infinitives triggered by δυναμένης.

παραποδίζω. *trip, hinder the feet.*

δυναμένης . . . προθέσεως. another gen. absolute.

ὑπερφρονέω. *be overly proud.*

(8) τοῖς ὑποκειμένοις. *in their present state*: cf. LSJ, s.v. ὑπόκειμαι, II.8.b. The system of checks-and-balances promotes equilibrium and stability.

ἐκ τοῦ πέλας. i.e., from the other branch(es) of government.

(52.1) τά γε μὴν κατὰ μέρος. *(taking) these things one by one*: LSJ, s.v. μέρος, II.2. In the preceding section, Polybius offers a general comparison of Roman and Carthaginian government. He argues that Carthage, before the Hannibalic War, had had a strong, mixed government resembling Rome's; then the people came to possess too much political power among the Carthaginians and consequently Rome emerged as the superior state. Polybius now selectively compares the two states in matters of detail.

οἷον εὐθέως. *for example.*

τὰ πρὸς τὰς πολεμικὰς χρείας. *things related to military affairs.* For this use of χρεία: LSJ, s.v. II.b.

τὸ μὲν . . . τὸ δὲ. *on the one hand . . . on the other*: Smyth 1111.

Καρχηδόνιος, -ου (mas.). *Carthaginian.*

ὑπάρχω. *belong to, exist, be,* here + dat. of possession.

τὴν ἐμπειρίαν ταύτην is predicative with τὸ . . . ὑπάρχειν. Translate as *both because this craft has been their national practice* (πάτριον αὐτοῖς) *from of old and because they work the seas* (θαλαττουργεῖν) *more than all other men.*

(2) πολὺ . . . τι. *much more, by far.*

(3) εἰς τέλος. *in the end, ultimately*: LSJ, s.v. τέλος, II.2.b.

(5) ᾗ. lit., *because of which thing*; i.e., *because of this, therefore.*

μέρος, -εος (neu.). *matter, business*: LSJ, s.v. IV.

ταύτην. i.e., Rome's. When they appear together, οὗτος often refers to what was just mentioned and ἐκεῖνος to what was mentioned earlier: Smyth 1240. Hence it may sometimes be convenient to translate these demonstratives as *the latter* and *the former*, respectively.

ἀποδεκτέον. impersonal verbal adj. < ἀποδέχομαι. *it must be admitted* + acc. Verbal adjs. that end in -τέος, -τέα, -τέον connote necessity: Smyth 473.

ἀρεταῖς. In the passage, Polybius draws on the traditional vocabulary of Greek virtue to characterize the Roman soldiers and their allies.

συμμάχων. Rome's Italian allies (Latin *socii*) were nominally independent but had to supply Rome with troops, which fought in their own units (Latin *auxilia*).

ἐπάρκεια, -ας (fem.). *help, support.*

(6) κἄν = καὶ ἐάν.

κατὰ τὰς ἀρχάς. *at first*: LSJ, s.v. ἀρχή, b.

τοὐναντίον = τὸ ἐναντίον. Supply "do" vel sim. as a verb.

(7) λῆξαι < λήγω. *stop, check* + gen.: LSJ, s.v. II.2.

ψυχομαχέω. *fight zealously to the point of death.*

(8) λειπόμενοι. Translate as concessive.

(9) οὐ μικρὰ. litotes: Smyth 3032.

συμβάλλω. in mid., *contribute*: LSJ, s.v. 9.

ἐπιβάτης, -ου (mas.). *marine*; i.e., soldier carried on a ship. According to Polybius, since the Romans' infantry is superior, the presence of marines on their ships offers a distinct advantage in naval engagements with the Carthaginians.

ῥοπή, -ῆς (fem.). *weight*, esp. a weight used on a balance.

(10) μὲν οὖν. *certainly, in fact*: Smyth 2901.

φύσει. This is an interesting claim, for rarely does Polybius attribute cultural differences to nature; indeed, in the subsequent analysis he seems to undercut this, arguing that Rome's πολιτεία, rather than natural superiority, is the source of its soldiers' excellence. On this, see further the excerpt from Champion recommended in this text's introduction.

μεγάλην modifies παρόρμησιν; hyperbaton (Smyth 3028) draws attention to the adj.

ἐθισμός, -οῦ (mas.). *imprinting.*

τῶν νέων. subjective gen.: Smyth 1330.

παρόρμησις, -εως (fem.). *eagerness.*

(11) ῥηθὲν. neu. sg. nom., aor. pass. part. < ἐρῶ. Essentially the word here means *example.*

χάριν + gen. *on account of*: LSJ, s.v. χάρις, VI.b. This preposition is usually postpositive (Smyth 1665.a)—i.e., it follows the word it governs—but here, as not uncommonly, it precedes the word.

B2. PUBLIC FUNERALS

Polybius 6.53–54

In the chapter of his history that precedes this passage below (B1), Polybius states that Rome is remarkably good at cultivating bravery, ambition, and patriotism among its youth; its ability to transmit these virtues across time helps explain its rise to hegemony in the Mediterranean. To evince his claim, Polybius describes how such values are imprinted on Rome's youth at the public funerals of its great men.

After the death of a prominent Roman, the deceased's whole household went into mourning. Within the *atrium* of the family's townhouse, the body, dressed in finery, lay in state, surrounded by mourners. Polybius's account focuses on the next part of the obsequies: in solemn pomp the body was conveyed to the Forum Romanum for the climax of the funeral rites, the public eulogy (in Latin, *laudatio funebris*) delivered from the Rostra or speaker's platform; this ritual blurred the boundaries between public and private, past and present, word and deed (λόγος and ἔργον), and even life and death. Thereafter the family and close friends proceeded outside the city for a private burial or cremation. The rites concluded on the ninth day after the death, when the family gathered for a meal at the tomb.

Further Reading

J. M. C. Toynbee, *Death and Burial in the Roman World* (Ithaca, 1971), 43–61; H. I. Flower, *Ancestor Masks and Aristocratic Power in Roman Culture*

(Oxford, 1996), 91–158; A. Erskine, "How to Rule the World: Polybius Book 6 Reconsidered," in *Polybius and His World: Essays in Memory of F. W. Walbank,* ed. B. Gibson and T. Harrison, 231–45 (Oxford, 2013).

❧

(53.1) ὅταν γὰρ μεταλλάξῃ τις παρ' αὐτοῖς τῶν ἐπιφανῶν ἀνδρῶν, συντελουμένης τῆς ἐκφορᾶς κομίζεται μετὰ τοῦ λοιποῦ κόσμου πρὸς τοὺς καλουμένους ἐμβόλους εἰς τὴν ἀγορὰν ποτὲ μὲν ἑστὼς ἐναργής, σπανίως δὲ κατακεκλιμένος. **(2)** πέριξ δὲ παντὸς τοῦ δήμου στάντος, ἀναβὰς ἐπὶ τοὺς ἐμβόλους, ἂν μὲν υἱὸς ἐν ἡλικίᾳ καταλείπηται καὶ τύχῃ παρών, οὗτος, εἰ δὲ μή, τῶν ἄλλων εἴ τις ἀπὸ γένους ὑπάρχει, λέγει περὶ τοῦ τετελευτηκότος τὰς ἀρετὰς καὶ τὰς ἐπιτετευγμένας ἐν τῷ ζῆν πράξεις. **(3)** δι' ὧν συμβαίνει τοὺς πολλοὺς ἀναμιμνησκομένους καὶ λαμβάνοντας ὑπὸ τὴν ὄψιν τὰ γεγονότα, μὴ μόνον τοὺς κεκοινωνηκότας τῶν ἔργων, ἀλλὰ καὶ τοὺς ἐκτός, ἐπὶ τοσοῦτον γίνεσθαι συμπαθεῖς ὥστε μὴ τῶν κηδευόντων ἴδιον, ἀλλὰ κοινὸν τοῦ δήμου φαίνεσθαι τὸ σύμπτωμα. **(4)** μετὰ δὲ ταῦτα θάψαντες καὶ ποιήσαντες τὰ νομιζόμενα τιθέασι τὴν εἰκόνα τοῦ μεταλλάξαντος εἰς τὸν ἐπιφανέστατον τόπον τῆς οἰκίας, ξύλινα ναΐδια περιτιθέντες. **(5)** ἡ δ' εἰκών ἐστι πρόσωπον εἰς ὁμοιότητα διαφερόντως ἐξειργασμένον καὶ κατὰ τὴν πλάσιν καὶ κατὰ τὴν ὑπογραφήν. **(6)** ταύτας δὴ τὰς εἰκόνας ἔν τε ταῖς δημοτελέσι θυσίαις ἀνοίγοντες κοσμοῦσι φιλοτίμως, ἐπάν τε τῶν οἰκείων μεταλλάξῃ τις ἐπιφανής, ἄγουσιν εἰς τὴν ἐκφοράν, περιτιθέντες ὡς ὁμοιοτάτοις εἶναι δοκοῦσι κατά τε τὸ μέγεθος καὶ τὴν ἄλλην περικοπήν. **(7)** οὗτοι δὲ προσαναλαμβάνουσιν ἐσθῆτας, ἐὰν μὲν ὕπατος ἢ στρατηγὸς ᾖ γεγονώς, περιπορφύρους, ἐὰν δὲ τιμητής, πορφυρᾶς, ἐὰν δὲ καὶ τεθριαμβευκὼς ἤ τι τοιοῦτον κατειργασμένος, διαχρύσους. **(8)** αὐτοὶ μὲν οὖν ἐφ' ἁρμάτων οὗτοι πορεύονται, ῥάβδοι δὲ καὶ πελέκεις καὶ τἄλλα τὰ ταῖς ἀρχαῖς εἰωθότα συμπαρακεῖσθαι προηγεῖται κατὰ τὴν ἀξίαν ἑκάστῳ τῆς γεγενημένης κατὰ τὸν βίον ἐν τῇ πολιτείᾳ προαγωγῆς. ὅταν δ' ἐπὶ τοὺς ἐμβόλους ἔλθωσι, **(9)** καθέζονται πάντες ἑξῆς ἐπὶ δίφρων ἐλεφαντίνων. οὗ κάλλιον οὐκ εὐμαρὲς ἰδεῖν θέαμα νέῳ φιλοδόξῳ καὶ φιλαγάθῳ· **(10)** τὸ γὰρ τὰς τῶν ἐπ' ἀρετῇ δεδοξασμένων ἀνδρῶν εἰκόνας ἰδεῖν ὁμοῦ πάσας οἷον εἰ ζώσας καὶ πεπνυμένας τίν᾽ οὐκ ἂν παραστῆσαι; τί δ᾽ ἂν κάλλιον θέαμα τούτου φανείη;

(54.1) πλὴν ὅ γε λέγων ὑπὲρ τοῦ θάπτεσθαι μέλλοντος, ἐπὰν διέλθῃ τὸν περὶ τούτου λόγον, ἄρχεται τῶν ἄλλων ἀπὸ τοῦ προγενεστάτου τῶν παρόντων, καὶ λέγει τὰς ἐπιτυχίας ἑκάστου καὶ τὰς πράξεις. **(2)** ἐξ ὧν καινοποιουμένης ἀεὶ τῶν ἀγαθῶν ἀνδρῶν τῆς ἐπ᾽ ἀρετῇ φήμης ἀθανατίζεται μὲν ἡ τῶν καλόν τι διαπραξαμένων εὔκλεια, γνώριμος δὲ τοῖς πολλοῖς καὶ παραδόσιμος τοῖς ἐπιγινομένοις ἡ τῶν εὐεργετησάντων τὴν πατρίδα γίνεται δόξα. **(3)** τὸ δὲ μέγιστον, οἱ νέοι παρορμῶνται πρὸς τὸ πᾶν ὑπομένειν ὑπὲρ τῶν κοινῶν πραγμάτων χάριν τοῦ τυχεῖν τῆς συνακολουθούσης τοῖς ἀγαθοῖς τῶν ἀνδρῶν εὐκλείας. **(4)** πίστιν δ᾽ ἔχει τὸ λεγόμενον ἐκ τούτων. πολλοὶ μὲν γὰρ ἐμονομάχησαν ἑκουσίως Ῥωμαίων ὑπὲρ τῆς τῶν ὅλων κρίσεως, οὐκ ὀλίγοι δὲ προδήλους εἵλοντο θανάτους, τινὲς μὲν ἐν πολέμῳ τῆς τῶν ἄλλων ἕνεκεν σωτηρίας, τινὲς δ᾽ ἐν εἰρήνῃ χάριν τῆς τῶν κοινῶν πραγμάτων ἀσφαλείας. **(5)** καὶ μὴν ἀρχὰς ἔχοντες ἔνιοι τοὺς ἰδίους υἱοὺς παρὰ πᾶν ἔθος ἢ νόμον ἀπέκτειναν, περὶ πλείονος ποιούμενοι τὸ τῆς πατρίδος συμφέρον τῆς κατὰ φύσιν οἰκειότητος πρὸς τοὺς ἀναγκαιοτάτους. **(6)** πολλὰ μὲν οὖν τοιαῦτα καὶ περὶ πολλῶν ἱστορεῖται παρὰ Ῥωμαίοις ἓν δ᾽ ἀρκοῦν ἔσται πρὸς τὸ παρὸν ἐπ᾽ ὀνόματος ῥηθὲν ὑποδείγματος καὶ πίστεως ἕνεκεν.

Notes to Polybius 6.53–54

These notes on Polybius are indebted to F. W. Walbank, *A Historical Commentary on Polybius,* 3 vols. (Oxford, 1957–).

(53.1) μεταλλάσσω. lit., *change, undergo a change*; a euphemism for *die,* so it would be appropriate to use a euphemism in English: *pass away.*

αὐτοῖς. i.e., the Romans.

μετὰ τοῦ λοιποῦ κόσμου. "*with every kind of honour*": Walbank, *Historical Commentary,* ad loc.

ἔμβολος, -ου (mas.). *bronze beak, ram.* οἱ ἔμβολοι. *Rostra*: LSJ, s.v. ἔμβολος, 3. The Rostra was a speaker's dais in the northwest part of the Forum Romanum bedizened with the bronze rams of enemy ships captured in the Battle of Antium in 338 B.C.E. and statues of those who had died on behalf of their country. This is important: the decoration of the Rostra whence the eulogy was delivered evoked Rome's martial might and those who served the city even unto death. The topographical backdrop is richly symbolic.

ἀγορὰν. i.e., the Forum Romanum.

ἑστὼς. mas. sg. nom., 2nd pf. act. part. < ἵστημι. *be placed upright.*

ἐναργής, -ές. *conspicuous, prominent.* The deceased is propped up so that he may be easily seen: Walbank, *Historical Commentary,* ad loc.

(2) πέριξ. adv., *all around,* an emphatic form of περί.

ἂν = ἐὰν.

λέγει. This is the fullest description of the *laudatio funebris*; although such speeches were frequently published or inscribed in antiquity, only a few, incomplete examples are extant.

ἐπιτετευγμένας < ἐπιτυγχάνω. *accomplish, achieve.*

(3) συμβαίνει. *it turns out that, it happens that* + acc. and inf.

λαμβάνοντας ὑπὸ τὴν ὄψιν. *seeing in their mind's eye*; cf. LSJ, s.v. λαμβάνω, I.9.

γεγονότα. neu. pl. acc., pf. act. part. < γίγνομαι.

ἐπὶ τοσοῦτον. *to such a degree.*

κηδεύω. *bury,* commonly used when the deceased is related to those burying him.

ἴδιον . . . κοινὸν. predicative with τὸ σύμπτωμα. Polybius's chiastic (Smyth 3020) deployment of these adjectives draws attention to the antithesis between public and private that is dissolved in the ceremony.

(4) ναΐδιον, -ου (neu.). *small shrine, cupboard.* (ναΐδιον is a diminutive of νεώς, νεώ [mas.] *temple.*) Notable families placed images of their illustrious ancestors in shrines known in Latin as *armaria,* which bore labels listing the names and accomplishments of the deceased. On special occasions, the doors of the *armaria* were opened and the images within decorated. The shrines were located in the *atrium,* the grand reception room of the Roman townhouse, where they reminded visitors of the family's multigenerational success.

(5) πρόσωπον, ου (neu.). *mask*: LSJ, s.v. III.

διαφερόντως. *especially.*

κατὰ τὴν πλάσιν καὶ κατὰ τὴν ὑπογραφήν. "*both in its modelling and complexion*": Walbank, *Historical Commentary,* ad loc.

(6) ἀνοίγνυμι. lit., *open*; i.e., *display.* Polybius calques—mimics in Greek—the Latin idiom *imagines aprire,* which lit. means *to open the images*; i.e., to open the *armaria* in which the images are displayed.

ἄγουσιν. The object is ταύτας . . . τὰς εἰκόνας.

δοκοῦσι. mas. pl. dat., pres. act. part.

(7) προσαναλαμβάνω. *put on besides, also assume.*

ὕπατος, -ου (mas.). *consul.*

στρατηγός, -οῦ (mas.). *praetor*: Mason, *Greek Terms,* 159.

ᾖ γεγονώς = γεγόνῃ. 3rd sg. pf. act. subj.

περιπορφύρους. The *toga praetexta* worn by Roman magistrates sported a distinctive purple stripe along its hem.

τιμητής. Censors (τιμηταί), two of whom were elected for eighteen-month terms in Polybius's day, brokered leases on public property and contracts for tax-collection in the provinces, took the census and thereby assigned citizens to different property classes, and had general oversight of public morals. Whether the censor indeed wore a purple toga is debated.

θριαμβεύω. *hold a triumph.* A triumph was a spectacular parade through the city of Rome that celebrated a general's victory and made manifest the might of Rome (see D5–D6). During the procession, the general wore purple garments elaborately embroidered with golden thread (διαχρύσους).

(8) ῥάβδος, -ου (fem.). *rod*; here in pl. and translating the Latin *fasces*; i.e., rods bundled and tied together with a leather thong and carried before some magistrates as a symbol of their authority. The fasces also contained axes, which, typically, were on display only when the magistrate was outside the city on campaign. See also note on section **(1)** of A2, s.v. ῥαβδοῦχος.

ἀρχή, -ῆς (fem.). *office, magistracy.*

εἰωθότα. neu. pl. nom., pf. act. part. < ἔθω. *be accustomed* + inf. The pf. of this defective verb should be translated as pres.; the plupf., as impf.: LSJ, s.v.

συμπαράκειμαι. *accompany* + dat.

προηγεῖται. The verb is sg. because the last element of the compound subject is neu. pl.

ἑκάστῳ. dat. of possession with τῆς γεγενημένης.

(9) δίφρων ἐλεφαντίνων. Some Roman magistrates were permitted to sit in public on a *sella curulis,* a distinctive variety of ivory chair.

οὗ. gen. of comparison after κάλλιον. As often, Greek employs a relative pronoun (*than which*) where English prefers a personal or demonstrative (*than this*) pronoun: Smyth 2490.

οὐκ εὐμαρὲς ἰδεῖν. sc. ἐστί.

(10) οἷον εἰ. *as if.*

παραστήσαι. 3rd sg. aor. act. opt. < παρίστημι. *inspire.* The optative is potential; the subject is the long articular infinitive τὸ . . . ἰδεῖν; the object is τίν' = τίνα. *whom.*

φανείη. 3rd sg. aor. pass. opt.

(54.1) πλήν. *however,* marking a transition.

ἐπιτυχία, -ας (fem.). *success.*

(2) ἐξ ὧν. Polybius is not celebrated as a stylist, but surely this sentence is artfully constructed.

καινοποιουμένης. Translate as causal.

τῆς ἐπ' ἀρετῇ φήμης. Polybius uses this exact phrase in 6.52.11 (B1). The repetition indicates that he is circling back to the issue that prompted the description of the funeral rites—namely, how Roman institutions engrain in young men a readiness to fight valiantly for Rome.

παραδόσιμος, -ον. *handed-down, transmitted.*

ἐπιγινομένοις. i.e., future generations.

(3) παρορμῶνται. cf. παρόρμησιν in 6.52.10 (B1).

χάριν τοῦ τυχεῖν. Another phrase paralleled in 6.52.11 (B1).

συνακολουθέω + dat. *accompany, follow closely upon.*

(4) πίστις, εως (fem.). *credence, trustworthiness.*

ἐκ τούτων. *from the following.*

πολλοὶ μὲν. Note the splendid use of μέν . . . δέ in this sentence.

κρίσις, -εως (fem.). *outcome.* Roman soldiers have willingly engaged in single combat to determine a battle's outcome.

ἕνεκεν = ἕνεκα.

(5) ἀρχὰς. adv. *early on* (in Rome's history).

περὶ πλείονος ποιούμενοι. *valuing X* (+ acc.) *more than Y* (+ gen. of comparison). See also note on section **(2)** of A4, s.v. περὶ παντὸς ποιέω.

συμφέρον, οντος (neu.). *benefit, advantage*: LSJ, s.v. συμφέρω, A.II.3.b.

κατὰ φύσιν. See note on section **(52.10)** of B1, s.v. φύσει.

οἰκειότης, -ητος (fem.). *relationship.*

ἀναγκαῖος, -α, -ον or -ος, -ον. *related by blood*: LSJ, s.v. II.5.

(6) ἐπ' ὀνόματος ῥηθὲν. *famed example*: LSJ, s.v. ὄνομα, II. On the form of ῥηθὲν, see note on section **(11)** of B1; the part. agrees with ἓν . . . ἀρκοῦν. In the next section, Polybius tells the story of Horatius Cocles, the early Roman hero who, in Polybius's version of the tale, saved the city from invasion at the cost of his own life.

B3. PHILHELLENE FLAMININUS

Plutarch *Flamininus* 10–11.2, 11.4

Although he traveled to Egypt, Asia Minor, and Italy, where he lectured in Rome, Plutarch (c. 45–c. 125 C.E.) spent most of his life in Greece, preferably among his books in his hometown of Chaeronea in western Boeotia, where his wealthy and locally prominent family had deep roots. His was a Greece wholly pacified: proudly Hellenic in culture but fully integrated into the Roman Empire. Plutarch wrote prolifically—more than 280 works were known in antiquity—including (but by no means limited to) practical essays on philosophical and ethical matters, antiquarian compendia of the lore of Greece and Rome, and political treatises, one of which will be excerpted later in this volume (C7). But Plutarch's most famous works are his *Lives,* which typically pair one Greek figure with one Roman; sometimes Plutarch appends a direct comparison (σύγκρισις) of the two. These biographies are treasure-troves for ancient historians—though Plutarch says that he narrates historical events only insofar as they reveal the character of individuals (see, e.g., *Alexander* 1)—and they have influenced later writers, including Shakespeare, Montaigne, Goethe, and Emerson.

Plutarch wrote a life of Titus Quinctius Flamininus (c. 229–174 B.C.E.), to whom Plutarch often refers by his praenomen, Titus. Consul in 198, Flamininus was tasked as proconsul (197–194) with continuing the war against Philip V, king of Macedon (reg. 221–179 B.C.E.), who exerted hegemony over

Greece. In 197, Flamininus defeated Philip at the Battle of Cynoscephalae in Thessaly. In the following year, the Senate issued a decree outlining the terms of the peace with Macedon and sent ten of its number to Greece to join Flamininus in the postwar settlement of the region. In June or July 196, at the Isthmian games, the philhellenic Flamininus, in flamboyant fashion, informed Greece of its fate.

Further Reading

Plutarch *Flamininus* all; Polybius 18.44–46; E. Badian, *Titus Quinctius Flamininus: Philhellenism and* Realpolitik (Cincinnati, 1970); E. S. Gruen, *The Hellenistic World and the Coming of Rome,* 2 vols., 1:250–72 (Berkeley, 1984).

(10.1) ἐπεὶ δὲ οἱ δέκα πρέσβεις, οὓς ἡ σύγκλητος ἔπεμψε τῷ Τίτῳ, συνεβούλευον τοὺς μὲν ἄλλους Ἕλληνας ἐλευθεροῦν, Κόρινθον δὲ καὶ Χαλκίδα καὶ Δημητριάδα διατηρεῖν ἐμφρούρους ἕνεκα τῆς πρὸς Ἀντίοχον ἀσφαλείας, ἐνταῦθα δὴ ταῖς κατηγορίαις λαμπροὶ λαμπρῶς τὰς πόλεις ἀνερρήγνυσαν Αἰτωλοί, τὸν μὲν Τίτον κελεύοντες τὰς πέδας τῆς Ἑλλάδος λύειν (οὕτω γὰρ ὁ Φίλιππος εἰώθει τὰς προειρημένας πόλεις ὀνομάζειν), **(2)** τοὺς δὲ Ἕλληνας ἐρωτῶντες εἰ κλοιὸν ἔχοντες βαρύτερον μὲν, λειότερον δὲ τοῦ πάλαι τὸν νῦν, χαίρουσι, καὶ θαυμάζουσι τὸν Τίτον ὡς εὐεργέτην, ὅτι τοῦ ποδὸς λύσας τὴν Ἑλλάδα τοῦ τραχήλου δέδεκεν. ἐφ᾽ οἷς ἀχθόμενος ὁ Τίτος καὶ βαρέως φέρων, καὶ δεόμενος τοῦ συνεδρίου, τέλος ἐξέπεισε καὶ ταύτας τὰς πόλεις ἀνεῖναι τῆς φρουρᾶς, ὅπως ὁλόκληρος ἡ χάρις ὑπάρξῃ παρ᾽ αὐτοῦ τοῖς Ἕλλησιν.

(3) Ἰσθμίων οὖν ἀγομένων πλῆθος μὲν ἀνθρώπων ἐν τῷ σταδίῳ καθῆστο τὸν γυμνικὸν ἀγῶνα θεωμένων, οἷα δὴ διὰ χρόνων πεπαυμένης μὲν πολέμων τῆς Ἑλλάδος ἐπ᾽ ἐλπίσιν ἐλευθερίας, σαφεῖ δὲ εἰρήνῃ πανηγυριζούσης· τῇ σάλπιγγι δὲ σιωπῆς εἰς ἅπαντας διαδοθείσης, **(4)** προελθὼν εἰς μέσον ὁ κῆρυξ ἀνεῖπεν ὅτι Ῥωμαίων ἡ σύγκλητος καὶ Τίτος Κοΐντιος στρατηγὸς ὕπατος καταπολεμήσαντες βασιλέα Φίλιππον καὶ Μακεδόνας, ἀφιᾶσιν ἀφρουρήτους καὶ ἐλευθέρους καὶ ἀφορολογήτους, νόμοις χρωμένους τοῖς πατρίοις, Κορινθίους, Λοκρούς, Φωκεῖς, Εὐβοέας, Ἀχαιοὺς Φθιώτας, Μάγνητας, Θετταλούς, Περραιβούς. τὸ μὲν οὖν πρῶτον οὐ πάνυ πάντες οὐδὲ σαφῶς ἐπήκουσαν, ἀλλ᾽ ἀνώμαλος καὶ θορυβώδης κίνησις ἦν ἐν τῷ σταδίῳ θαυμαζόντων καὶ διαπυνθανομένων καὶ πάλιν ἀνειπεῖν κελευόντων· **(5)** ὡς δὲ αὖθις ἡσυχίας γενομένης ἀναγαγὼν ὁ κῆρυξ τὴν φωνὴν προθυμότερον εἰς ἅπαντας ἐγεγώνει καὶ διῆλθε τὸ κήρυγμα, κραυγὴ μὲν ἄπιστος τὸ μέγεθος διὰ χαρὰν ἐχώρει μέχρι θαλάττης, ὀρθὸν δὲ ἀνειστήκει τὸ θέατρον, οὐδεὶς δὲ λόγος ἦν τῶν ἀγωνιζομένων, ἔσπευδον δὲ πάντες ἀναπηδῆσαι καὶ δεξιώσασθαι καὶ προσειπεῖν τὸν σωτῆρα τῆς Ἑλλάδος καὶ πρόμαχον.

(6) τὸ δὲ πολλάκις λεγόμενον εἰς ὑπερβολὴν τῆς φωνῆς καὶ μέγεθος ὤφθη τότε. κόρακες γὰρ ὑπερπετόμενοι κατὰ τύχην ἔπεσον εἰς τὸ στάδιον. αἰτία δὲ ἡ τοῦ ἀέρος ῥῆξις· ὅταν γὰρ ἡ φωνὴ πολλὴ καὶ μεγάλη φέρηται, διασπώμενος ὑπ᾽ αὐτῆς οὐκ ἀντερείδει τοῖς πετομένοις, ἀλλ᾽ ὀλίσθημα ποιεῖ καθάπερ κενεμβατοῦσιν, εἰ μὴ νὴ Δία πληγῇ τινι μᾶλλον ὡς ὑπὸ βέλους διελαυνόμενα πίπτει καὶ ἀποθνῄσκει, δύναται δὲ καὶ περιδίνησις εἶναι τοῦ ἀέρος, οἷον ἑλιγμὸν ἐν πελάγει καὶ παλιρρύμην τοῦ σάλου διὰ μέγεθος λαμβάνοντος.

(11.1) ὁ δ᾽ οὖν Τίτος, εἰ μὴ τάχιστα τῆς θέας διαλυθείσης ὑπιδόμενος τὴν φορὰν τοῦ πλήθους καὶ τὸν δρόμον ἐξέκλινεν, οὐκ ἂν ἐδόκει περιγενέσθαι τοσούτων ὁμοῦ καὶ πάντοθεν αὐτῷ περιχεομένων. ὡς δ᾽ ἀπέκαμον περὶ τὴν σκηνὴν αὐτοῦ βοῶντες ἤδη νυκτὸς οὔσης, αὖθις οὕστινας ἴδοιεν ἢ φίλους ἢ πολίτας ἀσπαζόμενοι καὶ περιπλεκόμενοι, πρὸς δεῖπνα καὶ πότους ἐτρέποντο μετ᾽ ἀλλήλων. **(2)** ἐν ᾧ καὶ μᾶλλον, ὡς εἰκὸς, ἡδομένοις ἐπῄει λογίζεσθαι καὶ διαλέγεσθαι περὶ τῆς Ἑλλάδος, ὅσους πολεμήσασα πολέμους διὰ τὴν ἐλευθερίαν οὔπω τύχοι βεβαιότερον οὐδὲ ἥδιον αὐτῆς, ἑτέρων προαγωνισαμένων ὀλίγου δεῖν ἀναίμακτος αὐτὴ καὶ ἀπενθὴς φερομένη τὸ κάλλιστον καὶ περιμαχητότατον ἆθλον.

[In the remainder of 11.2 and all of 11.3, the Greeks recall that most of the wars they had fought resulted in their own servitude, thanks mainly to their contentious and morally suspect leaders.]

(4) ἀλλόφυλοι δὲ ἄνδρες, ἐναύσματα μικρὰ καὶ γλίσχρα κοινωνήματα παλαιοῦ γένους ἔχειν δοκοῦντες, ἀφ' ὧν καὶ λόγῳ τι καὶ γνώμῃ τῶν χρησίμων ὑπάρξαι τῇ Ἑλλάδι θαυμαστὸν ἦν, οὗτοι τοῖς μεγίστοις κινδύνοις καὶ πόνοις ἐξελόμενοι τὴν Ἑλλάδα δεσποτῶν χαλεπῶν καὶ τυράννων ἐλευθεροῦσι.

Notes to Plutarch Flamininus *10–11.2, 11.4*

(10.1) σύγκλητος, -ου (fem.). *(Roman) Senate*: LSJ, s.v. II.2.

Κόρινθον δὲ καὶ Χαλκίδα καὶ Δημητριάδα. Corinth, Chalcis, and Demetrias were strategically important cities that Philip had garrisoned, and through them he exerted control over Greece. The ten commissioners, fearing an invasion from Antiochus III (on whom see below), thought that the Romans should garrison them with their own troops. The key points are that the status of these cities was a flashpoint in the complex diplomacy of the period and that the Senate had not given explicit instructions about the matter.

διατηρέω. *keep, maintain*: LSJ, s.v. 2.

ἔμφρουρος, -ον. *garrisoned.*

Ἀντίοχον. The Hellenistic monarch Antiochus III ruled the Seleucid kingdom 222–187 B.C.E.; he was ultimately a graver threat to Rome than Philip. Centered in Syria, the Seleucid kingdom also encompassed Mesopotamia and regions east as far as the Indus River. Antiochus expanded it westward. Coming to control much of Asia Minor and even some of Thrace, Antiochus threatened to extend further his hegemony in those regions as well as over mainland Greece. On Antiochus, see also B5, B6, C1.

ἐνταῦθα δή. *then, at that very moment*: LSJ, s.v. ἐνταῦθα, II.

λαμπροὶ λαμπρῶς. polyptoton: repetition of words with the same root but different endings.

ἀναρρήγνυμι. *excite greatly, flow forth,* in which sense this vivid verb is used to describe floods, volcanic eruptions, and suppurating sores: LSJ, s.v. II.

Αἰτωλοί. The Aetolian League, a confederacy of Greek city-states, had resented Macedon's hegemony over Greece and dispatched troops to fight alongside Flamininus's army at Cynoscephalae. Soon thereafter the League soured on the Romans and allied against them with Antiochus.

εἰώθει. 3rd sg. plupf. act. ind. < ἔθω, *be customary, accustomed.* The plupf. of this defective verb should be translated as impf.; see also note on section **(53.8)** of B2.

(2) κλοιός, -οῦ (mas.). *dog-collar,* wooden *collar* worn by prisoners: LSJ, s.v.

εὐεργέτης, -ου (mas.). *benefactor.* In Greek cities, wealthy εὐεργέται erected public buildings and subsidized cultural life; in return, donors earned intangible but invaluable cultural capital: honor and fame. Contemporary scholars refer to this phenomenon as euergetism. Despite the Aetolians' claims, extant Greek inscriptions, coins, and statues celebrate Flamininus as benefactor.

τοῦ ποδὸς . . . δέδεκεν. *having released Greece's foot, he bound (Greece) by the neck.*

δέδεκεν < δέω. *bind.*

τοῦ συνεδρίου. i.e., the envoys.

τέλος (adv.). *at last*: LSJ, s.v. II.2.a.

ἀνεῖναι < ἀνίημι + gen. of separation: Smyth 1392.

χάρις. A key word in the vocabulary of euergetism.

(3) Ἰσθμίων οὖν ἀγομένων. The Isthmian games took their name from the isthmus of Corinth, where they were held biennially in even years. They were one of the great Panhellenic festivals at which athletes, musicians, and poets competed. During the games, Corinth suspended hostilities with other powers so that athletes could travel to the isthmus and compete there in safety.

καθῆστο. 3rd sg. impf. dep. ind. < κάθημαι. *sit, be seated.*

οἷα. *since, as.*

διὰ χρόνων. *after a (long) time*: LSJ, s.v. χρόνος, 4.c.

πανηγυρίζω. *celebrate a festival.*

(4) Κοΐντιος = Latin Quinctius.

στρατηγὸς ὕπατος. lit., *highest general*; this phrase is used to render both *consul* and *proconsul* in Flamininus's day; only later were the two officials distinguished in Greek: Mason, *Greek Terms,* 104–5. Plutarch here preserves the archaic usage; indeed he seems to transmit the language of the decree accurately: cf. Polybius 18.46.5, Livy 33.32.5.

ἀφρούρητος, -ον. *free from garrisons.*

ἀφορολόγητος, -ον. *free from taxes.*

Κορινθίους . . . Περραιβούς. By waiting until the end of the decree to list these peoples, Flamininus builds suspense. Chalcis was located in Euboea, and Demetrias in Magnesia; hence none of the three cities in which the ten legates wished to leave garrisons was compelled to house Roman troops after Flamininus's declaration. On the locations and significance of the cities listed in the decree, see F. W. Walbank, *A Historical Commentary on Polybius,* 3 vols. (Oxford, 1957–), 2:613.

θορυβώδης, -ες. *turbulent, uproarious.*

(5) ἀνάγω. *lift, raise*: LSJ, s.v. I.6, 7.

ἐγεγώνει. 3rd sg. plupf. act. ind. < γέγωνα, defective verb. *shout, proclaim, make oneself heard.* Translate the plupf. as impf.: see note on section (1) above, s.v. εἰώθει.

τὸ μέγεθος. acc. of respect.

ἀνειστήκει. 3rd sg. plupf. act. ind. < ἀνίστημι. The plupf. here indicates that the event happened suddenly: Smyth 1953.

ἀναπηδῆσαι. cf. πέδας in section **(1)** above.

σωτῆρα. Extant inscriptions commemorate Flamininus as σωτήρ, indicating that he received divine honors, which were conveyed by Greeks on monarchs and extraordinary men.

(6) ὑπερβολή, -ῆς (fem.). *(extreme) power.*

φωνῆς. synaesthesia, when one of the senses is described in terms of another: here sight reveals the power of sound.

διασπώμενος < διασπάω. *tear apart.* sc. ὁ ἀήρ.

ἀντερείδω. *support, prop up* + dat.

κενεμβατέω. *step into a void.* With this word, Plutarch concludes the first of three explanations for how birds in flight may be felled by the human voice, a subject that engages him elsewhere: *Pompey* 25.7.

παλιρρύμη, -ης (fem.). *backward rush.*

σάλος, -ου (mas.). *tossing motion* (of the sea).

λαμβάνοντος agrees with τοῦ ἀέρος; ἑλιγμὸν and παλιρρύμην are objects of the part.

(11.1) θέα, -ας (fem.). *spectacle.* Note the accent; not θεά, *goddess.*

φορά, -ᾶς (fem.). *rush*: LSJ, s.v. A.II.3.

ἐξέκλινεν. 3rd sg. aor. act. ind. < ἐκκλίνω. *avoid*: LSJ, s.v. II.2.

ἀποκάμνω. *grow very tired of* + part.

ἴδοιεν. opt. in an indirect question introduced by οὕστινας in secondary sequence after aor. ἀπέκαμον.

(2) ἐπῄει. 3rd sg. impf. act. ind. < ἔπειμι. *happen to come into X's mind, happen to occur to X* + dat.: LSJ, s.v. ἔπειμι (B), I.2.b. Translate impersonally.

πολεμήσασα. Translate as concessive.

βεβαιότερον οὐδὲ ἥδιον. sc. ἐλευθερίαν.

ὀλίγου δεῖν. *almost, all but.*

ἆθλον. An apropos word, considering the setting of the proclamation. Indeed the vocabulary of spectacle and (athletic) competition threads throughout the excerpt.

(4) ἀλλόφυλοι . . . ἄνδρες. i.e., the Romans.

γλίσχρος, -α, -ον. lit., *sticky*; here, *enduring, persistent.*

τι. acc. subject in indirect discourse introduced by θαυμαστὸν ἦν.

τῶν χρησίμων. partitive gen. dependent on τι.

ἐξελόμενοι < ἐξαιρέω. in mid., *deliver*: LSJ, s.v. IV.

B4. ANTIHELLENE CATO

Plutarch *Cato the Elder* 22–23.3

While Greek culture had influenced Rome from the city's beginnings, never was its influence stronger than in the second century B.C.E., when Greece came under Roman control. This was a century of cultural politics when individual Roman politicians embraced a spectrum of views about the Greeks. Some, like Flamininus (B3), were philhellenes—though the jury is still out on whether Flamininus had a genuine enthusiasm for Greek culture or merely posed as a philhellene to ingratiate himself to the Greeks. Others rejected, or apparently rejected, Greek culture. There was, ostensibly, no more fervent antihellene than Marcus Porcius Cato (234–149 B.C.E.), also known as Cato the Elder and Cato the Censor.

Despite his humble origins as a *novus homo*, a "new man" who counted no senator among his ancestors, Cato was elected consul in 195 and, famously, censor in 184. Although he held no office after his censorship, he continued to have much clout as a gadfly, orator, and champion of old-fashioned Roman virtues as he conceived of them. Also a pioneering author of Latin prose, he wrote *On Agriculture,* a salmagundi of advice more or less related to running a country estate, complete with recipes for pickling, for Cato loved thrift and turnips. He also composed *Origins,* the first history of Rome in Latin. In seven books that are extant in more than one hundred fragments, the work covers the city's prehistory through the author's own day. It may be surprising to learn that, in this work, Cato argues for the influence of

Greek culture on Rome's early history (A5). For in the vignette below from Plutarch's biography of Cato, the aged protagonist counters the pernicious effects of Greek philosophy on impressionable Roman youths. Events date to 155.

Further Reading

Plutarch *Marcus Cato* all; A. E. Astin, *Cato the Censor* (Oxford, 1978), 157–81; E. S. Gruen, *Studies in Greek Culture and Roman Policy* (Leiden, 1990), 158–92; E. S. Gruen, *Culture and National Identity in Republican Rome* (Ithaca, 1992), 52–83.

(22.1) ἤδη δὲ αὐτοῦ γέροντος γεγονότος πρέσβεις Ἀθήνηθεν ἦλθον εἰς Ῥώμην οἱ περὶ Καρνεάδην τὸν Ἀκαδημαϊκὸν καὶ Διογένη τὸν Στωικὸν φιλόσοφον, καταδίκην τινὰ παραιτησόμενοι τοῦ δήμου τῶν Ἀθηναίων, ἣν ἐρήμην ὦφλον Ὠρωπίων μὲν διωξάντων, Σικυωνίων δὲ καταψηφισαμένων, τίμημα ταλάντων πεντακοσίων ἔχουσαν. **(2)** εὐθὺς οὖν οἱ φιλολογώτατοι τῶν νεανίσκων ἐπὶ τοὺς ἄνδρας ἵεντο, καὶ συνῆσαν ἀκροώμενοι καὶ θαυμάζοντες αὐτούς, μάλιστα δ᾽ ἡ Καρνεάδου χάρις, ἧς δύναμίς τε πλείστη καὶ δόξα τῆς δυνάμεως οὐκ ἀποδέουσα, μεγάλων ἐπιλαβομένη καὶ φιλανθρώπων ἀκροατηρίων ὡς πνεῦμα τὴν πόλιν ἠχῆς ἐνέπλησε. **(3)** καὶ λόγος κατεῖχεν, ὡς ἀνὴρ Ἕλλην εἰς ἔκπληξιν ὑπερφυὴς πάντα κηλῶν καὶ χειρούμενος ἔρωτα δεινὸν ἐμβέβληκε τοῖς νέοις, ὑφ᾽ οὗ τῶν ἄλλων ἡδονῶν καὶ διατριβῶν ἐκπεσόντες ἐνθουσιῶσι περὶ φιλοσοφίαν. ταῦτα τοῖς μὲν ἄλλοις ἤρεσκε Ῥωμαίοις γινόμενα, καὶ τὰ μειράκια παιδείας Ἑλληνικῆς μεταλαμβάνοντα καὶ συνόντα θαυμαζομένοις ἀνδράσιν ἡδέως ἑώρων· **(4)** ὁ δὲ Κάτων ἐξ ἀρχῆς τε τοῦ ζήλου τῶν λόγων παραρρέοντος εἰς τὴν πόλιν ἤχθετο φοβούμενος, μὴ τὸ φιλότιμον ἐνταῦθα τρέψαντες οἱ νέοι τὴν ἐπὶ τῷ λέγειν δόξαν ἀγαπήσωσι μᾶλλον τῆς ἀπὸ τῶν ἔργων καὶ τῶν στρατειῶν, ἐπεὶ δὲ προὔβαινεν ἡ δόξα τῶν φιλοσόφων ἐν τῇ πόλει καὶ τοὺς πρώτους λόγους αὐτῶν πρὸς τὴν σύγκλητον ἀνὴρ ἐπιφανὴς σπουδάσας αὐτὸς καὶ δεηθεὶς ἡρμήνευσε, Γάϊος Ἀκίλιος, ἔγνω μετ᾽ εὐπρεπείας ἀποδιοπομπήσασθαι τοὺς φιλοσόφους ἅπαντας ἐκ τῆς πόλεως, (5) καὶ παρελθὼν εἰς τὴν σύγκλητον ἐμέμψατο τοῖς ἄρχουσιν, ὅτι πρεσβεία κάθηται πολὺν χρόνον ἄπρακτος ἀνδρῶν, οἳ περὶ παντὸς οὗ βούλοιντο ῥᾳδίως πείθειν δύνανται· δεῖν οὖν τὴν ταχίστην γνῶναί τι καὶ ψηφίσασθαι περὶ τῆς πρεσβείας, ὅπως οὗτοι μὲν ἐπὶ τὰς σχολὰς τραπόμενοι διαλέγωνται παισὶν Ἑλλήνων, οἱ δὲ Ῥωμαίων νέοι τῶν νόμων καὶ τῶν ἀρχόντων ὡς πρότερον ἀκούωσι.

(23.1) ταῦτα δ' οὐχ, ὡς ἔνιοι νομίζουσι, Καρνεάδῃ δυσχεράνας ἔπραξεν, ἀλλ' ὅλως φιλοσοφίᾳ προσκεκρουκὼς καὶ πᾶσαν Ἑλληνικὴν μοῦσαν καὶ παιδείαν ὑπὸ φιλοτιμίας προπηλακίζων, ὅς γε καὶ Σωκράτη φησὶ λάλον καὶ βίαιον γενόμενον ἐπιχειρεῖν τρόπῳ δυνατὸς ἦν, τυραννεῖν τῆς πατρίδος, καταλύοντα τὰ ἔθη καὶ πρὸς ἐναντίας τοῖς νόμοις δόξας ἕλκοντα καὶ μεθιστάντα τοὺς πολίτας. (2) τὴν δ' Ἰσοκράτους διατριβὴν ἐπισκώπτων γηρᾶν φησὶ παρ' αὐτῷ τοὺς μαθητάς ὡς ἐν Ἅιδου παρὰ Μίνῳ χρησομένους ταῖς τέχναις καὶ δίκας ἐροῦντας. τὸν δὲ παῖδα διαβάλλων πρὸς τὰ Ἑλληνικά φωνῇ κέχρηται θρασυτέρᾳ τοῦ γήρως, οἷον ἀποθεσπίζων καὶ προμαντεύων, ὡς ἀπολοῦσι Ῥωμαῖοι τὰ πράγματα γραμμάτων Ἑλληνικῶν ἀναπλησθέντες. (3) ἀλλὰ ταύτην μὲν αὐτοῦ τὴν δυσφημίαν ὁ χρόνος ἀποδείκνυσι κενήν, ἐν ᾧ τοῖς τε πράγμασιν ἡ πόλις ἤρθη μεγίστη καὶ πρὸς Ἑλληνικὰ μαθήματα καὶ παιδείαν ἅπασαν ἔσχεν οἰκείως.

Notes to Plutarch Cato the Elder *22–23.3*

(22.1) αὐτοῦ γέροντος. i.e., Cato, who was 78 or 79 years old at the time.

περί + acc. *connected to, associated with*: LSJ, s.v. C.I.2.

Καρνεάδην. Carneades (214/13–129/28 B.C.E.) was a prominent philosopher at the Academy in Athens when that school embraced Scepticism, whose proponents suspended judgment about all things and rejected the possibility of real knowledge. In dazzling public disputations, Carneades skewered popular and philosophical ideas.

Διογένη τὸν Στωικὸν. Diogenes (c. 240–152 B.C.E.) headed the Stoic school in Athens. He is especially known for his writings on ethics and the philosophy of language; carbonized papyri from Herculaneum are slowly revealing more about his ideas. Plutarch does not mention Critolaus, head of the Peripatetic school, who also numbered among the envoys.

καταδίκη, -ης. *unfavorable judgment against* + gen. The envoys petition the Senate to overturn the ruling of the Sicyonians against Athens; on the legal situation, see further below.

παραιτησόμενοι. fut. part. indicating purpose < παραιτέομαι. *appeal.*

ἐρήμην ὀφλισκάνω. *receive by default*; i.e., by failing to attend the proceeding.

διώκω. *bring a complaint, prosecute*: LSJ, s.v. IV.

καταψηφίζομαι. *rule against.* In 158 or 157, Athens sacked Oropus, a city on its frontier once subject to it. The Oropians sought redress from the Roman Senate, which instructed the Sicyonians to arbitrate. When the Athenians failed to show up at the arbitration, the Sicyonians levied a fine of 500 talents. The Senate, on appeal, reduced the fine to 100 talents, the payment of which the Athenians still managed to avoid.

ταλάντων πεντακοσίων = about 2850 pounds of silver, a large sum.

ἔχουσαν agrees with καταδίκην; its object is τίμημα.

(2) φιλόλογος, -ον. *garrulous, fond of learning, fond of dialectic*: LSJ, s.v.

ἀκροάομαι. Like many of the words in this passage, this one has ominous overtones: *listen to* or *obey*: LSJ, s.v.

ἐπιλαμβάνω. in mid. + gen., *take, seize, attack,* also used of diseases: LSJ, II, III. Vocabulary associated with contagion and invasion appears throughout the passage.

ἀκροατήριον, -ου (neu.). *audience*: LSJ, s.v. II, citing this passage.

ὡς πνεῦμα. Several sources comment on the power and volume of Carneades's voice.

ἐνέπλησε. Verbs of filling take a gen. or both gen. and acc. (of what is being filled): Smyth 1369.

(3) κατέχω. *prevail*: LSJ, s.v. B.3.

εἰς ἔκπληξιν ὑπερφυὴς. *prodigious in his passion.*

κηλέω. *bewitch, beguile.* Carneades casts a spell over the city's youths.

χειρόω. lit., *handle*; here, *conquer, subdue.*

ἐνθουσιάω. *be possessed (by a god), be in ecstasy.*

μεταλαμβάνω + gen. *partake in.*

ἑώρων. 3rd pl. impf. act. ind. < ὁράω.

(4) παραρρέω. *flow in, sneak in*: LSJ, s.v.

φοβούμενος here introduces a positive fear clause (μή + subj.).

ἐνταῦθα. *thither, in that direction*; i.e., toward the philosophers.

προὔβαινεν < προβαίνω. *advance.*

σύγκλητος, -ου (fem.). *(Roman) Senate*: LSJ, s.v. II.2.

δεηθεὶς < δέομαι. dep., *beg, ask*: LSJ, s.v. δέω (B), II.2.

Γάϊος Ἀκίλιος. Gaius Acilius also wrote a history of Rome in Greek, further evidence of his bilingualism.

ἀποδιοπομπέομαι. a splendid verb: *escort from, free from, conjure away,* with connotations of purification: LSJ, s.v., citing this passage.

(5) κάθηται. 3rd sg. pres. dep. ind. < κάθημαι. *sit, be seated.*

οὗ. The relative pronoun, as often, is attracted into the case of its gen. antecedent: Smyth 2522.

δεῖν. Plutarch switches from ὅτι + ind. to acc. + inf. indirect discourse, which is not uncommon: Smyth 2628.

τὴν ταχίστην (sc. ὁδόν). *in the quickest way, very quickly*: LSJ, s.v. ταχύς, C.II.3.

γιγνώσκω. *decide, decree*: LSJ, s.v. II.

διαλέγω + dat. in mid. and pass., *converse with, practice dialectic with*: LSJ, s.v. B.

(23.1) δυσχεραίνω + dat. *dislike, be annoyed by*: LSJ, s.v.

προσκρούω + dat. lit., *collide with*; here, *take offense with*: LSJ, s.v.

φιλοτιμία, -ας (fem.). *ambition, love of honor.* In Plutarch, this important quality may be negative or positive, depending on how it is directed. This ambiguity allows for multiple interpretations of Cato's motives. Does Cato's antihellenic attitude reflect his zeal for preserving Roman honor, for self-promotion through political posturing, or a combination of both?

προπηλακίζω. *bespatter with mud*: LSJ, s.v.

Σωκράτη. It is not clear why Cato is so critical of Socrates.

φησὶ. The verb suggests that Plutarch here (and again when it recurs in the next section) is drawing on Cato's own writings, though from which work(s) is unclear.

(2) Ἰσοκράτους. Isocrates (436–338 B.C.E.) was a pioneer in rhetorical education, for which he established a school in Athens c. 392. Some students attended his school for as long as three or four years: Isocrates *Antidosis* 87–88.

ἐν Ἅιδου. sc. τῇ γῇ, a common omission with Hades: Smyth 1302.

Μίνῳ. After ruling Crete, Minos, son of Zeus and Europa, became one of the three judges of souls in the underworld.

χρησομένους . . . ἐροῦντας. more fut. participles indicating purpose.

ἐροῦντας. mas. pl. acc., fut. act. part. < ἐρῶ. *pronounce.*

διαβάλλω. *prejudice X* (+ acc.) *against Y* (+ πρός + acc.): LSJ, s.v. III.

γῆρας, -αος (contracting to -ως) (neu.). *old age.*

ἀπολοῦσι. Note the tense.

ἀναπλησθέντες < ἀναπίμπλημι. *fill* + gen.: LSJ, s.v. II.

(3) ἤρθη μεγίστη. *was exalted to its highest point*: LSJ, s.v. ἀείρω, II.

ἔχω οἰκείως πρός + acc. *be intimate with, familiar with*: LSJ, s.v. οἰκεῖος, B.

B5. PROPHECIES OF ROMAN RUIN

Phlegon of Tralles
On Wondrous Things 3.3–8, 3.12

Phlegon, a freedman originally from the Greek city of Tralles in Asia Minor who served in the court of Hadrian (117–38 C.E.), once came upon, in an imperial storehouse, an enbalmed centaur that was gifted to the emperor by an Arabian king. This extraordinary encounter is described in the author's *On Wondrous Things* (35), which compiles tales of unusual phenomena—of a four-headed child (20), for example, or of a giant tooth (14.2). Other authors produced similar works in antiquity; moderns refer to these writers as "paradoxographers," that is, recorders of marvels. Phlegon's penchant for assembling facts is also displayed in his list of *Long-Lived Persons* and his *Olympiads,* an almanac-like guide to the games as well as a chronicle of historical events. Both of these works are extant in fragments; Phlegon is known to have written yet more works, but they are now lost.

On Wondrous Things opens with three stories of revenants—that is, embodied ghosts—that admix realistic historical detail with macabre supernatural elements. The third story, excerpted below, begins just after the Battle of Thermopylae in 191 B.C.E. There the Romans under the consul Manius Acilius Glabrio had defeated forces led by Antiochus III, the Hellenistic monarch of the Seleucid Empire centered in Syria who in the previous year had invaded Greece. (On Antiochus, see also B3, B6, C1.) After their victory, the Romans met with dire prophecies of future defeat. Appearing below are three of these prophecies, which Phlegon claims to derive from the writings of a certain Antisthenes the Peripatetic, the identity of whom is much debated. While the prophecies do vary somewhat in tone and content, all seem to derive from the second century B.C.E. (even if they may have been stitched together at a later time) and evince a strong strain of anti-Roman sentiment during Rome's rise to power in the eastern Mediterranean.

Further Reading

E. Gabba, "True History and False History in Classical Antiquity," *Journal of Roman Studies* 71 (1981): 50–62; E. S. Gruen, *The Hellenistic World and the Coming of Rome,* 2 vols. (Berkeley, 1984), 1:316–56; W. Hansen, *Phlegon of Tralles'* Book of Marvels (Exeter, 1996), 1–22.

(3) Ἐν δὲ τῇ παρατάξει τῇ γενομένῃ πρὸς Ἀντίοχον ἐν Θερμοπύλαις ἐπιφανέστατα σημεῖα ἐγένετο Ῥωμαίοις. ἀποσφαλέντος γὰρ Ἀντιόχου καὶ φυγόντος τῇ ἐπιούσῃ ἡμέρᾳ ἐγίνοντο οἱ Ῥωμαῖοι περὶ ἀναίρεσιν τῶν ἐκ τῆς σφετέρας δυνάμεως πεπτωκότων καὶ περὶ συλλογὴν λαφύρων τε καὶ σκύλων καὶ αἰχμαλώτων. (4) Βούπλαγος δέ τις, τῶν ἀπὸ Συρίας ἱππάρχης, τιμώμενος παρὰ τῷ βασιλεῖ Ἀντιόχῳ, ἔπεσε καὶ αὐτὸς γενναίως ἀγωνισάμενος. ἀναιρουμένων δὲ τῶν Ῥωμαίων πάντα τὰ σκῦλα καὶ μεσούσης τῆς ἡμέρας ἀνέστη ὁ Βούπλαγος ἐκ τῶν νεκρῶν, ἔχων τραύματα δέκα δύο, καὶ παραγενόμενος εἰς τὸ στρατόπεδον αὐτῶν ἀνεῖπε λεπτῇ τῇ φωνῇ τούσδε τοὺς στίχους·

παῦσαι σκυλεύων στρατὸν Ἄιδος εἰς χθόνα βάντα·
ἤδη γὰρ Κρονίδης νεμεσᾷ Ζεὺς μέρμερα λεύσσων,
μηνίει δὲ φόνῳ στρατιᾶς καὶ σοῖσιν ἐπ' ἔργοις,
καὶ πέμψει φῦλον θρασυκάρδιον εἰς χθόνα τὴν σήν,
οἵ σ' ἀρχῆς παύσουσιν, ἀμείψῃ δ' οἷά γ' ἔρεξας.

(5) Ταραχθέντες δὲ οἱ στρατηγοὶ ἐπὶ τοῖς ῥηθεῖσιν διὰ ταχέων συνήγαγον τὸ πλῆθος εἰς ἐκκλησίαν καὶ ἐβουλεύοντο περὶ τοῦ γεγονότος φάσματος. ἔδοξεν οὖν τὸν μὲν Βούπλαγον παραχρῆμα μετὰ τὰ λεχθέντα ἔπη ἀποπνεύσαντα κατακαύσαντας θάψαι, καθαρμὸν δὲ

ποιήσαντας τοῦ στρατοπέδου θῦσαι Διὶ Ἀποτροπαίῳ καὶ πέμψαι εἰς Δελφοὺς ἐρωτήσοντας τὸν θεόν τί χρὴ ποιεῖν. **(6)** παραγενομένων δὲ Πυθῶδε τῶν θεωρῶν καὶ πυνθανομένων τί ποιητέον, ἀνεῖπεν ἡ Πυθία τόνδε τὸν χρησμόν·

ἴσχεο νῦν, Ῥωμαῖε, δίκη δέ τοι ἔμμονος ἔστω,
μή σοι ἐφορμήσῃ Παλλὰς πολὺ φέρτερον Ἄρη
χηρώσῃ τ' ἀγοράς· σὺ δέ, νήπιε, πολλὰ μογήσας
ἵξεαι ἐς χώρην τὴν σὴν πολὺν ὄλβον ὀλέσσας.

(7) Ἀκούσαντες οὖν τοῦ λόγου τούτου, τὸ μὲν ἐπιστρατεῦσαι ἐπί τινα τῶν ἐν τῇ Εὐρώπῃ κατοικούντων ἀπέγνωσαν τὸ παράπαν, ἀναζεύξαντες δὲ ἀπὸ τοῦ προειρημένου τόπου παρεγένοντο ἐπὶ Ναύπακτον τῆς Αἰτωλίας, οὗ ἐστιν ἱερὸν κοινὸν τῶν Ἑλλήνων, εὐτρέπιζόν τε θυσίας δημοτελεῖς ἀπαρχάς τε ἐξ ἔθους.

(8) Τούτων δὲ ἐπιτελουμένων ὁ στρατηγὸς Πόπλιος ἐμμανὴς γενόμενος καὶ παράφρων ἀποφθέγγεται πολλά τινα ἐνθουσιωδῶς, τὰ μὲν ἐν μέτρῳ, ἐστὶν δ' ἃ καὶ καταλογάδην. διαγγελθέντος δὲ τῷ πλήθει τοῦ πράγματος συνέθεον πάντες πρὸς τὴν σκηνὴν τοῦ Ποπλίου, ἅμα μὲν ὑπαγωνιῶντες καὶ ἐκπεπληγμένοι ἐπὶ τῷ τὸν κράτιστον αὐτῶν καὶ δυνάμενον ἀφηγεῖσθαι μετ' ἐμπειρίας ἠτυχηκέναι, ἅμα δὲ ἀκούειν βουλόμενοι τὰ λεγόμενα, ὥστε τινὰς αὐτῶν πιεσθέντας βιαιότερον ἀποπνιγῆναι. τὰ μὲν οὖν ἐν μέτρῳ ῥηθέντα ὑπ' αὐτοῦ, ἔτι ὄντος ἐν τῇ σκηνῇ, ἐστὶν τάδε·

ὦ πατρίς, οἷόν σοι λυγρὸν φέρει Ἄρη Ἀθήνη,
ἡνίκα πορθήσασ' Ἀσίην πολύολβον ἵκηαι
Ἰταλίην ἐς γαῖαν ἐυστεφάνους τε πόληας
Θρινακίης νήσου πολυηράτου, ἣν κτίσατο Ζεύς.
ἥξει γὰρ στρατιὴ πολυφέρτατος, ὀβριμόθυμος,
τηλόθεν ἐξ Ἀσίης, ὅθεν ἡλίου ἀντολαί εἰσιν,
καὶ βασιλεὺς διαβὰς στεινὸν πόρον Ἑλλησπόντου
ὅρκια πιστὰ τεμεῖ πρὸς κοίρανον Ἠπειρώτην·
ἥξει δ' Αὐσονίην στρατιὴν ἀνάριθμον ἀγείρας

πάντοθεν ἔκ τ' Ἀσίης ἠδ' Εὐρώπης ἐρατεινῆς,
καί σε δαμᾷ, χήρους δ' οἴκους καὶ τείχεα θήσει,
δουλοσύνην δ' ἐπὶ πᾶσιν ἐλεύθερον ἦμαρ ἀπούρας
τεύξει μήνιδος οὕνεκ' Ἀθηναίης μεγαθύμου.

[In 3.9–11, Publius delivers further prophecies.]

(12) Ἀποφθεγξάμενος δὲ ταῦτα ἐσιώπησεν καὶ πορευθεὶς ἔξω τοῦ στρατοπέδου ἀνέβη ἐπί τινα δρῦν. ἐπακολουθήσαντος δὲ τοῦ ὄχλου προσεκαλέσατο αὐτοὺς καὶ εἶπε τάδε· "ἐμοὶ μέν, ὦ ἄνδρες Ῥωμαῖοι καὶ οἱ λοιποὶ στρατιῶται, καθήκει τελευτήσαντι ὑπὸ λύκου πυρροῦ εὐμεγέθους καταβρωθῆναι ἐν τῇ σήμερον ἡμέρᾳ, ὑμεῖς δὲ τὰ ῥηθέντα ὑπ' ἐμοῦ γινώσκετε συμβησόμενα ὑμῖν πάντα, τεκμηρίοις χρώμενοι τῇ νῦν ἐσομένῃ ἐπιφανείᾳ τοῦ θηρίου τε καὶ τῇ ἐμῇ ἀναιρέσει, ὅτι ἀληθῆ εἴρηκα ἔκ τινος θείας ὑποδείξεως."

[In 3.13–14, the prophecy above is fulfilled: Publius jumps on the wolf's back; the beast eats him—or at least most of him. For the wolf leaves behind his disembodied head, which delivers one last prophecy to the Romans. Alarmed, they build a temple to Apollo of Lycia—i.e., Λύκιος, an epithet probably homonymous with λύκειος, *of the wolf*, in the Greek pronunciation of the day.]

Notes to Phlegon of Tralles On Wondrous Things *3.3–8, 3.12*

These notes are indebted to the commentaries of A. Stramaglia, Res inauditae, incredulae: *Storie di fantasmi nel mondo greco-latino* (Bari, 1999) and W. Hansen, *Phlegon of Tralles'* Book of Marvels (Exeter, 1996).

(3) ἀποσφαλέντος. mas. sg. gen, aor. pass. part. < ἀποσφάλλω, *trip up*. This is one of many emendations suggested for the problematic ἐπιφανέντος transmitted in the manuscripts.

ἐπιούσῃ. *following*: LSJ, s.v. ἔπειμι (B), II.

γί(γ)νομαι περί + acc. *be engaged with*: LSJ, s.v. γίγνομαι, s.v. II.3.c.

πεπτωκότων. mas. pl. gen., pf. act. part. < πίπτω.

λάφυρα, -ων (neu. pl.). *booty.*

σκῦλα, -ων (neu. pl.). more specific than λάφυρα; specifically, *spoils* taken from dead soldiers.

(4) Βούπλαγος is not otherwise known; his name would seem to mean "cattle prod." His story is similar to that of another revenant soldier who fought for Octavian against Sextus Pompey in the Sicilian War: Pliny *Natural History* 7.178–79.

μεσούσης τῆς ἡμέρας. In supernatural stories from Greece and Rome, midday is a not uncommon time for otherworldly phenomena to appear: Stramaglia, Res inauditae, ad loc.

λεπτῇ τῇ φωνῇ. Another topos: ancient ghosts speak with faint or shrill voices: Stramaglia, Res inauditae, ad loc.

παῦσαι. Translate the inf. as an impv. (Smyth 2013); the verb here takes a supplementary part. Why the Romans' behavior was objectionable is unclear, for the despoiling of a vanquished army by the victors was a usual practice in antiquity.

Ἀΐδας, -ος (mas.). *Hades.*

Κρονίδης. As often, the suffix -ίδης (mas. sg. nom.) indicates a patronymic: Smyth 845. Cronus's son is Zeus.

μέρμερα. i.e., the ill-conceived or baneful deeds of the Romans.

σοῖσιν = Attic σοῖς.

παύσουσιν < παύω, here in a different sense from παῦσαι above: *depose X* (+ acc.) *from Y* (+ gen.): LSJ, s.v. 2. The Romans did fear that Antiochus might launch an expedition against Italy and took special measures to defend against it.

ἀμείψῃ. 2nd sg. fut. mid. ind. < ἀμείβω. in mid., *pay for*: LSJ, s.v. B.3.

(5) ῥηθεῖσιν. neu. pl. dat., aor. pass. part. < ἐρῶ. *say.*

διὰ ταχέων. *swiftly*: LSJ, s.v. ταχύς, B.2.

ἀποπνεύσαντα. mas. sg. acc., aor. act. part. modifying τὸν . . . Βούπλαγον; take as objects of κατακαύσαντας θάψαι. Buplagus is dead once more.

Διὶ Ἀποτροπαίῳ. Zeus Apotropaios—Zeus who wards off evil.

ἐρωτήσοντας. Note the tense: fut. part. indicating purpose.

(6) Πυθώδε. adv., *to Pytho,* the region wherein Delphi lay. Whether the following prophecy is genuine or forged is debated.

θεωρός, -οῦ (mas.). *envoy sent to an oracle.*

ποιητέον. verbal adjective implying necessity; see note on section **(52.5)** of B1, s.v. ἀποδεκτέον.

Πυθία, -ας (fem.). the prophetic priestess of Apollo at Delphi.

ἴσχεο. 2nd sg. pres. mid. impv., uncontracted as is common in verse < ἴσχω. *restrain, check,* a poetic verb.

τοι = Attic σοι.

ἔστω. 3rd sg. pres. act. impv. < εἰμί.

μή here introduces a negative purpose clause.

Ἄρη. mas. sg. acc. < Ἄρης, -εος (Epic) / -εως (Attic); Ares is here used, as often, as a metonym (Smyth 3033) for war.

ἵξεαι. 2nd sg. fut. dep. ind., uncontracted < ἱκνέομαι.

(7) ἀναζευγνύω / ἀναζεύγνυμι. *withdraw* (an army): LSJ, s.v.

οὗ. *where.*

ἀπαρχή, -ῆς (fem.). *first-fruit*; i.e., the first portion of some product (e.g., grain, produce) given to the gods.

ἐξ ἔθους. *according to custom.*

(8) ὁ στρατηγὸς Πόπλιος. Buplagus exits the story, replaced by the generically named General Publius. Some identify the latter with Publius Cornelius Scipio Africanus, who served as his brother Lucius's legate in the campaign against Antiochus after the Battle of Thermopylae and about whom many legends circulated.

ἐνθουσιώδης, -ες. *be in ecstasy*; i.e., *possessed* or *inspired by a god.*

ἐστὶν δ' ἅ. Take this with the previous clause as well: *some (which are) in verse, and some which are in prose.*

ὑπαγωνιάω. *be somewhat anxious*: LSJ, s.v. This seems to be the word's only appearance in all of Greek literature.

ἐκπεπληγμένοι < ἐκπλήσσω + ἐπί + dat. *be astonished at*: LSJ, s.v. II.

ἐπὶ τῷ . . . ἠτυχηκέναι. articular inf.

ἀφηγεῖσθαι is a complementary inf. triggered by δυνάμενον.

ἠτυχηκέναι. pf. act. inf. < ἀτυχέω + μετά. *meet with.*

βιαιότερον. *too violently.* When a comparative "stands alone" (i.e., when what something is being compared with is not expressed), the comparative may imply excess: Smyth 1062.c.

ἀποπνιγῆναι. aor. pass. inf. < ἀποπνίγω. *suffocate.* So crammed together were those seeking to hear Publius that some of them died.

πορθήσασ(α) < πορθέω. *destroy.* The part. agrees with πατρὶς.

Ἀσίην. Although his troops were soundly defeated at Thermopylae, Antiochus managed to escape to Asia Minor. In 190, an army under Lucius Cornelius Scipio joined with Asian allies to defeat Antiochus near Magnesia ad Sipylum in Lydia; according to the treaty of Apamea in 188, the king was then compelled, among other things, to give up claims to lands west and north of the Taurus Mountains, hand over hostages (and the aged Hannibal who had fled to Antiochus's court), and pay an enormous indemnity. This prophecy must have been composed *after* Scipio's campaign in Asia and not delivered, as implied by the text, in the immediate aftermath of Thermopylae. It is thus a revenge fantasy: since the "west" invaded the "east," the "east" will invade the "west."

ἵκηαι. 2nd sg. aor. dep. subj., uncontracted < ἱκνέομαι. subj. in indefinite temporal clause referring to a future event; the ἄν is omitted, as often in verse: Smyth 2402.

πόληας = Attic πόλεις.

Θρινακίη, -ης (fem.). *Sicily.*

Ἑλλησπόντου. The narrow strait known as the Hellespont separates Europe and Asia.

ὅρκια . . . τέμνω. *swear oaths*; i.e., make a formal alliance: LSJ, s.v. τέμνω, II.2.

τεμεῖ. 3rd sg. fut. act. ind. < τέμνω.

πρός. here *with*, not *against*.

'Ηπειρώτην. It is not clear whether a particular king from Epirus in western Greece is meant.

Αὐσονίη, -ης (fem.). *Ausonia*; i.e., Italy.

δαμᾷ. 3rd sg. fut. act. ind., a poetic form < δαμάζω. *conquer*.

χῆρος, -α, -ον. lit., *widowed*; therefore, *bereft, desolated*. The adj. also modifies τείχεα; when an adj. modifies two nouns, it may agree with the one closest to it: Smyth 1030, 1053.

τείχεα. i.e., (walled) cities, by synecdoche (Smyth 3047).

ἀπούρας. mas. sg. nom., aor. act. part. < ἀπαυράω, a defective verb meaning *take away, wrest from*: LSJ, s.v. Its object is ἐλεύθερον ἦμαρ; the object of τεύξει is δουλοσύνην.

(12) ἀναβαίνω ἐπί + acc. *mount X*, usually for the purposes of public speaking: LSJ, s.v. ἀναβαίνω, II.6.

καθήκει + dat. impersonal, *it is fitting for X, suitable for X*. The use of this verb suggests that the manner of Publius's death is both appropriate and significant.

τελευτήσαντι agrees with ἐμοὶ; hyperbaton (Smyth 3028).

λύκου πυρροῦ. This strangely colored beast may be symbolic in at least three ways. First, its tawny-red coat evokes blood. Second, Rome is associated with a wolf; it is ironic that a general serving the Roman state is eaten by the animal that represents it. And third, the soldiers who witness Publius's demise believe that the wolf was sent by (or was perhaps even a manifestation of) Apollo; see the English summary of what occurs after the passage.

καταβρωθῆναι. aor. pass. inf. < καταβιβρώσκω. *devour*.

γινώσκετε. impv., not ind.

τεκμηρίοις. predicative with the datives that follow χρώμενοι.

B6. ROME AS ALLY

1 Maccabees 8.1–16

In 169 B.C.E., the Seleucid monarch Antiochus IV Epiphanes (reg. 175–164), son of Antiochus III (reg. 222–187; see B3, B5, C1) looted the Jewish Temple in Jerusalem. This Hellenistic king later garrisoned the city and promulgated measures that essentially outlawed the practice of Judaism in Judaea. This sparked a rebellion, led by the priest Mattathias and his sons, the most famous of whom was Judas Maccabaeus, the latter word apparently meaning "hammer-man." (Judas is perhaps best known for restoring the Temple, an event commemorated at Hanukkah, and for the oratorio composed about him by Handel.) This story of resistance is vividly told in 1 Maccabees, which is counted among the Apocrypha, works considered scriptural by Catholics and Orthodox, but not by Jews and most Protestants. Written in a Greek that may seem unusual to those used to Attic, 1 Maccabees includes many stylistic and syntactic features native to Hebrew. (Whether 1 Maccabees is a translation of a Hebrew text or is an original composition in Greek is debated.) Nothing is known about the author except through inference from his text: he was versed in the Hebrew scriptures and had some exposure to Greek literature, especially historiography, which is reflected in the work's structure; he therefore was likely to be a member of the Judaean elite. It was written sometime between 133 and 63 B.C.E., probably closer to the former than latter date; it was meant to laud the Hasmoneans, the descendants of the Maccabees, who ruled Judaea during those years.

On March 8, 161 B.C.E., a Seleucid army suffered a severe loss at the hands of the Judaeans, who cut off and publicly displayed the right arm and head of the enemy's commander. Perhaps fearing reprisal, Judas then sought an alliance with a powerful third party, Rome, which resulted in a treaty that is quoted in the work (8.17–32). To contextualize this alliance, the author first must introduce the Romans to his audience (8.1–16). In short, he gilds them, contrasting them with the Seleucids and underscoring the similarities between them and the Jews; this serves to make the alliance more palatable for a people warned in their scriptures to be wary of such diplomatic arrangements. To suggest that Rome would be a nonpareil ally, he emphasizes that state's military prowess and the stability of its republican government. Some of the author's views of Rome are paralleled in other authors, like Polybius. Yet the author also presents erroneous information about Rome's political institutions, which has puzzled commentators. This passage provides testimony about Rome during its great period of expansion from an author not subject to it.

Further Reading

1 Maccabees 1–7; M. Smith, "Rome and Maccabean Conversions: Notes on 1 Macc. 8," in Donum Gentilicium: *New Testament Studies in Honour of David Daube,* ed. E. Bammel, C. K. Barrett, and W. D. Davies, 1–7 (Oxford, 1978); E. S. Gruen, *Heritage and Hellenism: The Reinvention of Jewish Tradition* (Berkeley, 1998), xiii-xx, 1–40; L. M. Yarrow, *Historiography at the End of the Republic: Provincial Perspectives on Roman Rule* (Oxford, 2006), 133–38.

(1) Καὶ ἤκουσεν Ἰούδας τὸ ὄνομα τῶν Ῥωμαίων, ὅτι εἰσὶν δυνατοὶ ἰσχύι καὶ αὐτοὶ εὐδοκοῦσιν ἐν πᾶσιν τοῖς προστιθεμένοις αὐτοῖς, καὶ ὅσοι ἂν προσέλθωσιν αὐτοῖς, ἱστῶσιν αὐτοῖς φιλίαν, καὶ ὅτι εἰσὶ δυνατοὶ ἰσχύι. **(2)** καὶ διηγήσαντο αὐτῷ τοὺς πολέμους αὐτῶν καὶ τὰς ἀνδραγαθίας, ἃς ποιοῦσιν ἐν τοῖς Γαλάταις, καὶ ὅτι κατεκράτησαν αὐτῶν καὶ ἤγαγον αὐτοὺς ὑπὸ φόρον, **(3)** καὶ ὅσα ἐποίησαν ἐν χώρᾳ Σπανίας τοῦ κατακρατῆσαι τῶν μετάλλων τοῦ ἀργυρίου καὶ τοῦ χρυσίου τοῦ ἐκεῖ· **(4)** καὶ κατεκράτησαν τοῦ τόπου παντὸς τῇ βουλῇ αὐτῶν καὶ τῇ μακροθυμίᾳ, καὶ ὁ τόπος ἦν ἀπέχων μακρὰν ἀπ' αὐτῶν σφόδρα, καὶ τῶν βασιλέων τῶν ἐπελθόντων ἐπ' αὐτοὺς ἀπ' ἄκρου τῆς γῆς, ἕως συνέτριψαν αὐτοὺς καὶ ἐπάταξαν ἐν αὐτοῖς πληγὴν μεγάλην, καὶ οἱ ἐπίλοιποι διδόασιν αὐτοῖς φόρον κατ' ἐνιαυτόν· **(5)** καὶ τὸν Φίλιππον καὶ τὸν Περσέα Κιτιέων βασιλέα καὶ τοὺς ἐπηρμένους ἐπ' αὐτοὺς συνέτριψαν αὐτοὺς ἐν πολέμῳ καὶ κατεκράτησαν αὐτῶν· **(6)** καὶ Ἀντίοχον τὸν μέγαν βασιλέα τῆς Ἀσίας τὸν πορευθέντα ἐπ' αὐτοὺς εἰς πόλεμον ἔχοντα ἑκατὸν εἴκοσι ἐλέφαντας καὶ ἵππον καὶ ἅρματα καὶ δύναμιν πολλὴν σφόδρα, καὶ συνετρίβη ὑπ' αὐτῶν, **(7)** καὶ ἔλαβον αὐτὸν ζῶντα καὶ ἔστησαν αὐτοῖς διδόναι αὐτόν τε καὶ τοὺς βασιλεύοντας μετ' αὐτὸν φόρον μέγαν καὶ διδόναι ὅμηρα καὶ διαστολὴν **(8)** καὶ χώραν τὴν Ἰνδικὴν καὶ Μηδίαν καὶ Λυδίαν ἀπὸ τῶν καλλίστων χωρῶν αὐτῶν, καὶ λαβόντες αὐτὰς παρ' αὐτοῦ ἔδωκαν αὐτὰς Εὐμένει τῷ βασιλεῖ· **(9)** καὶ ὅτι οἱ ἐκ τῆς Ἑλλάδος ἐβουλεύσαντο ἐλθεῖν καὶ ἐξᾶραι αὐτούς, **(10)** καὶ ἐγνώσθη ὁ λόγος αὐτοῖς, καὶ ἀπέστειλαν ἐπ' αὐτοὺς στρατηγὸν ἕνα καὶ ἐπολέμησαν πρὸς αὐτούς, καὶ ἔπεσον ἐξ αὐτῶν τραυματίαι πολλοί, καὶ ᾐχμαλώτισαν τὰς γυναῖκας αὐτῶν καὶ τὰ τέκνα αὐτῶν καὶ ἐπρονόμευσαν αὐτοὺς καὶ κατεκράτησαν τῆς γῆς καὶ καθεῖλον τὰ ὀχυρώματα αὐτῶν καὶ κατεδουλώσαντο αὐτοὺς ἕως τῆς ἡμέρας ταύτης· **(11)** καὶ τὰς ἐπιλοίπους βασιλείας καὶ τὰς νήσους, ὅσοι ποτὲ ἀντέστησαν αὐτοῖς, κατέφθειραν καὶ ἐδούλωσαν αὐτούς, μετὰ δὲ τῶν φίλων αὐτῶν καὶ τῶν ἐπαναπαυομένων αὐτοῖς συνετήρησαν φιλίαν· **(12)** καὶ κατεκράτησαν τῶν βασιλέων τῶν ἐγγὺς καὶ τῶν μακράν, καὶ ὅσοι ἤκουον τὸ ὄνομα αὐτῶν, ἐφοβοῦντο ἀπ' αὐτῶν. **(13)** οἷς δ' ἂν βούλωνται βοηθεῖν καὶ βασιλεύειν, βασιλεύουσιν· οὓς δ' ἂν βούλωνται, μεθιστῶσιν· καὶ ὑψώθησαν σφόδρα. **(14)** καὶ ἐν πᾶσιν τούτοις οὐκ ἐπέθεντο αὐτῶν οὐδὲ εἷς διάδημα, οὐδὲ περιεβάλοντο πορφύραν ὥστε ἁδρυνθῆναι ἐν αὐτῇ· **(15)** καὶ βουλευτήριον ἐποίησαν ἑαυτοῖς, καὶ καθ' ἡμέραν ἐβουλεύοντο τριακόσιοι καὶ εἴκοσι βουλευόμενοι διὰ παντὸς περὶ τοῦ πλήθους τοῦ εὐκοσμεῖν αὐτούς· **(16)** καὶ πιστεύουσιν ἑνὶ ἀνθρώπῳ ἄρχειν αὐτῶν κατ' ἐνιαυτὸν καὶ κυριεύειν πάσης τῆς γῆς αὐτῶν, καὶ πάντες ἀκούουσιν τοῦ ἑνός, καὶ οὐκ ἔστιν φθόνος οὐδὲ ζῆλος ἐν αὐτοῖς.

Notes to 1 Maccabees 8.1–16

These notes are indebted to J. A. Goldstein, *I Maccabees: A New Translation with Introduction and Commentary,* The Anchor Bible (Garden City, 1976).

(1) Καὶ. The recurrent use of this conjunction at the beginning of clauses and sentences in this passage is a "Hebraism," a linguistic element of the Greek text that reflects the style, syntax, or vocabulary of Hebrew.

ἰσχύι. fem. sg. dat. < ἰσχύς, -ύος (fem.). *might, force.*

προστίθημι + dat. *side with, associate with.* This verb is drawn from the vocabulary of conversion; the Jewish author implies that, like his own coreligionists, the Romans are willing to accept "converts": Goldstein, *I Maccabees,* ad loc.

προσέλθωσιν also suggests conversion; indeed the Greek word for proselyte (προσήλυτος) is related to this verb. Political allegiance is cast in the language of religious affiliation.

(2) διηγήσαντο < διηγέομαι. *describe.* sc. a generic "they" as the subject.

αὐτῷ. i.e., Judas.

Γαλάται, -ων (mas. pl.), *Celts,* may refer to the Gauls who dwelled in southern France and northern Italy or the Galatians of Asia Minor; here the former are probably meant: Goldstein, *I Maccabees,* ad loc.

(3) τοῦ . . . τοῦ ἐκεῖ. partitive gen. dependent on ὅσος: LSJ, s.v. ὅσος, II.

(4) ἀπέχω. *be far from*: LSJ, s.v. III.

μακράν is an adv. The far-reaching ambit of Roman power would be an important desideratum for potential allies located in distant Judaea.

βασιλέων. That Rome had defeated Hellenistic monarchs was of special interest to Judas and his supporters, as their primary enemy, Antiochus IV, was one too. The author interestingly echoes the Romans' own claim that they acquired territory through "defensive imperialism"; i.e., not through aggression, but as a byproduct of protecting their interests and fending off attacks (τῶν βασιλέων τῶν ἐπελθόντων ἐπ' αὐτοὺς).

πατάσσω. *strike*, with an internal acc.: LSJ, s.v. II.

(5) Κιτιέων. In Hebrew, Macedonians were called "Kittim." Philip V was defeated in 197 at the Battle of Cynoscephalae (see B4); Perseus, in 168 at Pydna.

ἐπηρμένους. mas. pl. acc., pf. pass. part. < ἐπαίρω. *stir up, rouse.*

(6) Ἀντίοχον. sc. "they defeated" vel sim. as the verb. Antiochus III was defeated in 190 at the Battle of Magnesia ad Sipylum in Lydia.

συνετρίβη. anacoluthon (Smyth 3004–08): Antiochus is now the subject.

(7) ἔλαβον αὐτὸν ζῶντα. The Romans did not in fact capture Antiochus III, but they did take twenty hostages, among them Antiochus IV. See further note on section **(8)** of B5, s.v. Ἀσίην.

διαστολή, -ῆς (fem.). *separation (?).* The implication is that Antiochus III had to give up territory, but the text is difficult; emendations have been suggested, but none of them has emerged as a consensus candidate.

(8) Ἰνδικὴν καὶ Μηδίαν. Antiochus III did not in fact have to give up India and Media, but he did yield control of Asia west and north of the Taurus Mountains; most of this territory was given to Eumenes II, king of Pergamum (reg. 197–159/58 B.C.E.). See notes on **(7)** above and on section **(8)** of B5, s.v. Ἀσίην.

(9) ἐξᾶραι. aor. act. inf. < ἐξαίρω. *root out, excise, remove.*

(10) ἀπέστειλαν. sc. "the Romans" as the subject.

στρατηγὸν ἕνα. Lucius Mummius defeated the Achaean League and sacked Corinth in 146 B.C.E., bringing an end to Greek independence (see B7). This reference and much of what is described in the following verses is anachronistic, for Judas's alliance with Rome dated to 161.

ὀχύρωμα, -ατος (neu.). *fortress, stronghold.*

(11) ἐπαναπαύω + dat. *rely on, rest one's hopes on*: LSJ, s.v.

(12) φοβέω. in mid. and pass. + ἀπό. *be afraid of,* probably a Hebraism: LSJ, s.v. φοβέω, B.II.2.

(13) μεθίστημι. euphemistic. *remove*: LSJ, s.v. II.

(14) ἐπέθεντο. 3rd pl. aor. mid. ind. < ἐπιτίθημι. *put on.*

διάδημα. This claim—that Rome never had a king—is of course untrue. Assuming that the author is aware of Rome's regal period, he may elide it to strengthen the contrast between the Hellenistic monarchies and Rome. There is another possible motive. There was a Jewish tradition about the succession of world powers—that the third world-kingdom, that of the Greeks (i.e., of Alexander and his successors), would be succeeded by an all-powerful fourth and final kingdom during the end-times. Some Jews believed that this last kingdom would be theirs; the author may emphasize that Rome, never a monarchy, could not be an alternative candidate. See Goldstein, *I Maccabees,* ad loc.

ἁδρύνω. *strengthen.*

(15) βουλευτήριον, -ου (neu.). *Senate*: LSJ, s.v. II; Mason, *Greek Terms,* 123.

καθ' ἡμέραν. If the author knew this to be untrue, he may have claimed that the Senate met every day because he wanted to emphasize parallels between Jewish and Roman political institutions—the Sanhedrin, the Jews' own council, met daily (see Goldstein, *I Maccabees,* ad loc.)—or because it made the Romans seem especially dedicated to governance and thus a more attractive ally.

τριακόσιοι καὶ εἴκοσι. The Senate in fact had about 300 members before Sulla expanded the institution in 81 B.C.E.

(16) ἑνὶ ἀνθρώπῳ. An odd claim, for each year Rome was of course governed by *two* consuls.

οὐκ ἔστιν φθόνος οὐδὲ ζῆλος. Polybius also praises the cooperative spirit of Roman politics (B1).

B7. RAPACIOUS ROMANS

Strabo 8.6.23

As many of the readings in this section illustrate, the Romans intervened in Greek affairs during the second century B.C.E. through a combination of diplomacy and force. It was the Battle of Pydna, in which the legions of Lucius Aemilius Paullus won a strategic victory over the phalanxes of Perseus, king of Macedon (reg. 179–168 B.C.E.), that marked the transition in the year 168 B.C.E. from "soft imperialism" to "hard imperialism." After Pydna, when Rome involved itself in Greece, it tended to do so more decisively and violently. A striking example of hard imperialism may be found in the description of Corinth—the only city in mainland Greece the author explicitly claims to have visited—provided by the geographer Strabo, who is more fully introduced in A1. Strabo tells the story of the city's destruction in 146 B.C.E. by Lucius Mummius, cast in some ancient sources as the quintessentially boorish, avaricious Roman general, a lover of loot with no aesthetic sensibility.

Yet in Mummius's day looting was nothing new. The earliest literature from the Greco-Roman world testifies to the practice: for example, Odysseus, disguised as a beggar, explains to Penelope that her husband has not yet returned to Ithaca because he is off profitably plundering (Homer *Odyssey* 19.282–84). This long history of looting does not prevent Greek writers, beginning with Polybius, from criticizing it. Strabo's account remains remarkably relevant to current debates about cultural patrimony and the antiquities trade, museums as repositories for the fruits of empire, and the repatriation of artworks acquired in wartime.

Further Reading

Polybius 9.10; E. S. Gruen, *Culture and National Identity in Republican Rome* (Ithaca, 1992), 84–130; S. Pothecary, "*Kolossourgia:* 'A Colossal Statue of a Work,'" in *Strabo's Cultural Geography: The Making of a* Kolossourgia, ed. D. Dueck, H. Lindsay, and S. Pothecary, 5–26 (Cambridge, 2005); M. M. Miles, *Art as Plunder: The Ancient Origins of Debate about Cultural Property* (Cambridge, 2008), 73–95.

❧

Κορίνθιοι δ' ὑπὸ Φιλίππῳ ὄντες ἐκείνῳ τε συνεφιλονείκησαν καὶ ἰδίᾳ πρὸς Ῥωμαίους ὑπεροπτικῶς εἶχον, ὥστε τινὲς καὶ τῶν πρέσβεων παριόντων τὴν οἰκίαν αὐτῶν ἐθάρρησαν καταντλῆσαι βόρβορον. ἀντὶ τούτων μὲν οὖν καὶ ἄλλων ὧν ἐξήμαρτον ἔτισαν δίκας αὐτίκα· πεμφθείσης γὰρ ἀξιολόγου στρατιᾶς, αὐτή τε κατέσκαπτο ὑπὸ Λευκίου Μομμίου καὶ τἆλλα μέχρι Μακεδονίας ὑπὸ Ῥωμαίοις ἐγένετο, ἐν ἄλλοις ἄλλων πεμπομένων στρατηγῶν· τὴν δὲ χώραν ἔσχον Σικυώνιοι τὴν πλείστην τῆς Κορινθίας. Πολύβιος δὲ τὰ συμβάντα περὶ τὴν ἅλωσιν ἐν οἴκτου μέρει λέγων προστίθησι καὶ τὴν στρατιωτικὴν ὀλιγωρίαν τὴν περὶ τὰ τῶν τεχνῶν ἔργα καὶ τὰ ἀναθήματα. φησὶ γὰρ ἰδεῖν παρὼν ἐρριμμένους πίνακας ἐπ' ἐδάφους, πεττεύοντας δὲ τοὺς στρατιώτας ἐπὶ τούτων. ὀνομάζει δ' αὐτῶν Ἀριστείδου γραφὴν τοῦ Διονύσου, ἐφ' οὗ τινες εἰρῆσθαί φασι τὸ "οὐδὲν πρὸς τὸν Διόνυσον," καὶ τὸν Ἡρακλέα τὸν καταπονούμενον τῷ τῆς Δηιανείρας χιτῶνι. τοῦτον μὲν οὖν οὐχ ἑωράκαμεν ἡμεῖς, τὸν δὲ Διόνυσον ἀνακείμενον ἐν τῷ Δημητρείῳ τῷ ἐν Ῥώμῃ κάλλιστον ἔργον ἑωρῶμεν· ἐμπρησθέντος δὲ τοῦ νεὼ συνηφανίσθη καὶ ἡ γραφὴ νεωστί. σχεδὸν δέ τι καὶ τῶν ἄλλων ἀναθημάτων τῶν ἐν Ῥώμῃ τὰ πλεῖστα καὶ ἄριστα ἐντεῦθεν ἀφῖχθαι· τινὰ δὲ καὶ αἱ κύκλῳ τῆς Ῥώμης πόλεις ἔσχον. μεγαλόφρων γὰρ ὢν μᾶλλον ἢ φιλότεχνος ὁ Μόμμιος, ὥς φασι, μετεδίδου ῥᾳδίως τοῖς δεηθεῖσι. Λεύκολλος δὲ κατασκευάσας τὸ τῆς Εὐτυχίας ἱερὸν καὶ στοάν τινα χρῆσιν ᾐτήσατο ὧν εἶχεν ἀνδριάντων ὁ Μόμμιος, ὡς κοσμήσων τὸ ἱερὸν μέχρι ἀναδείξεως, εἶτ' ἀποδώσων· οὐκ ἀπέδωκε δέ, ἀλλ' ἀνέθηκε κελεύσας αἴρειν εἰ βούλεται· πράως δ' ἤνεγκεν ἐκεῖνος οὐ φροντίσας οὐδέν, ὥστ' ηὐδοκίμει τοῦ ἀναθέντος μᾶλλον. πολὺν δὲ χρόνον ἐρήμη μείνασα ἡ Κόρινθος ἀνελήφθη πάλιν ὑπὸ Καίσαρος τοῦ θεοῦ διὰ τὴν εὐφυΐαν, ἐποίκους πέμψαντος τοῦ ἀπελευθερικοῦ γένους πλείστους· οἳ τὰ ἐρείπια κινοῦντες καὶ τοὺς τάφους συνανασκάπτοντες εὕρισκον ὀστρακίνων τορευμάτων πλήθη, πολλὰ δὲ καὶ χαλκώματα· θαυμάζοντες δὲ τὴν κατασκευὴν οὐδένα τάφον ἀσκευώρητον εἴασαν, ὥστε εὐπορήσαντες τῶν τοιούτων καὶ διατιθέμενοι πολλοῦ νεκροκορινθίων ἐπλήρωσαν τὴν Ῥώμην· οὕτω γὰρ ἐκάλουν τὰ ἐκ τῶν τάφων ληφθέντα, καὶ μάλιστα τὰ ὀστράκινα. κατ' ἀρχὰς μὲν οὖν ἐτιμήθη σφόδρα ὁμοίως τοῖς χαλκώμασι τοῖς κορινθιουργέσιν, εἶτ' ἐπαύσαντο τῆς σπουδῆς, ἐκλιπόντων τῶν ὀστράκων καὶ οὐδὲ κατωρθωμένων τῶν πλείστων. ἡ μὲν δὴ πόλις ἡ τῶν Κορινθίων μεγάλη τε καὶ πλουσία διὰ παντὸς ὑπῆρξεν, ἀνδρῶν τε ηὐπόρησεν ἀγαθῶν εἴς τε τὰ πολιτικὰ καὶ εἰς τὰς τέχνας τὰς δημιουργικάς· μάλιστα γὰρ καὶ ἐνταῦθα καὶ ἐν Σικυῶνι ηὐξήθη γραφική τε καὶ πλαστικὴ καὶ πᾶσα ἡ τοιαύτη δημιουργία. χώραν δ' ἔσχεν οὐκ εὔγεων σφόδρα, ἀλλὰ σκολιάν τε καὶ τραχεῖαν, ἀφ' οὗ πάντες ὀφρυόεντα Κόρινθον εἰρήκασι καὶ παροιμιάζονται "Κόρινθος ὀφρυᾷ τε καὶ κοιλαίνεται."

Notes to Strabo 8.6.23

These notes are indebted to the commentary of S. Radt, *Strabons Geographika* (Göttingen, 2002).

ὑπό + dat. *subject to*: Smyth 1698.3.c.

Φιλίππῳ. Philip V, king of Macedon (reg. 221–179 B.C.E.; see also B3).

συμφιλονεικέω. *side with* + dat. Strabo's account here is somewhat confusing, for although Corinth was allied with Philip in the First Macedonian War (215–205 B.C.E.), in 197 it was freed of its Macedonian garrison (B3) and rejoined the

Achaean League, a confederation of Greek city-states, of which it soon became the leading member.

ἰδίᾳ. adv., *privately, personally*: LSJ, s.v. ἴδιος, VI.2.

ἔχω + adv. *behave X*: LSJ, s.v. ἔχω (A), B.II.2.

πρέσβεων. The Senate sent envoys to Corinth in 147 to mediate between the Achaean League and Sparta, which had declared its independence from the confederacy but was compelled by force to rejoin it.

παριόντων < πάρειμι (εἶμι). *pass by.*

καταντλέω. *pour X* (+ acc.) *upon Y* (+ gen.): LSJ, s.v.

βόρβορος, ου (mas.). *filth, (human) waste.* Some authors relay that the envoys were insulted or threatened with violence; only Strabo suggests that scatological abuse may have been the ordure of the day.

μὲν οὖν. *certainly, in fact*: Smyth 2901.

ὧν. The verb ἐξαμαρτάνω may take an acc. when it means *commit a fault,* but here that acc. is attracted into the gen. case of its antecedent, as is common with the relative pronoun: Smyth 2522. See also note on section **(22.5)** of B4, s.v. οὗ.

αὐτίκα. This adv.'s placement at the end of the clause, an emphatic position, draws attention to the rapidity of the Romans' response.

αὐτή = ἡ Κόρινθος.

κατέσκαπτο. 3rd pl. plupf. pass. ind. < κατασκάπτω. *utterly destroy.* Archaeology indicates that the destruction was not as total as the verb suggests. The plupf. hints that by the time Strabo was writing, the site had been resettled; see below.

τἆλλα = τὰ ἄλλα. i.e., the other parts of Greece.

ἄλλοις ἄλλων. On double ἄλλος, see Smyth 1274 and notes on section **(8)** of A1, s.v. ἄλλην ἐξ ἄλλης and section **(3)** of A3.1, s.v. ἄλλον δὲ ἄλλο.

Σικυώνιοι. The city of Sicyon was located about 11 miles northwest of Corinth.

τῆς Κορινθίας. sc. γῆς: Smyth 1027.b.

Πολύβιος. This portion of Polybius (39.2) is not otherwise attested; see F. W. Walbank, *A Historical Commentary on Polybius,* 3 vols. (Oxford, 1957–), 3:728–30.

ἐν οἴκτου μέρει. *with a measure of pity.*

ἐρριμμένους. mas. pl. acc., pf. pass. part. < ῥίπτω. *throw, snatch.*

πεττεύοντας (Attic) = πεσσεύοντας < πεσσεύω. *play checkers.*

αὐτῶν. i.e., the works of art.

Ἀριστείδου. The painter Aristides of Thebes (fl. 376–336 B.C.E.) was a pioneer in both technique and style: see, e.g., Pliny *Natural History* 35.98–100, 122.

ἐφ' οὗ . . . Διόνυσον. *about which some say the (phrase) "nothing compares to the Dionysus" was proclaimed* (εἰρῆσθαί < ἐρῶ). The phrase οὐδὲν πρὸς τὸν Διόνυσον was originally linked to early Greek tragedy, which some said had *nothing (to do with) Dionysus.* But πρός + acc. may also mean *in comparison to* (Smyth 1695.3.c), so the phrase was repurposed to refer to Aristides's incomparable painting.

χιτῶνι. Deianira gave her husband Hercules a tunic wetted with what she thought was a love potion but that was actually poison.

ἀνάκειμαι. *be dedicated, be set up* (as a votive); the word functions as the passive corollary to ἀνατίθημι, *dedicate* (as a votive), whence the noun ἀνάθημα, -ατος (neu.).

Δημητρείῳ. i.e., the Temple of Ceres, Liber, and Libera, located near the Circus Maximus. Because the Roman god Liber was often identified with Dionysus, the temple may have seemed an appropriate home for Aristides's painting. (Many Roman temples, decorated with pillaged artworks, functioned as de facto museums.) The temple burned down in 31 B.C.E., an important datum in the reconstruction of Strabo's biography, for it is a firm indicator that he had been to Rome before that date.

ἐμπρησθέντος. mas. sg. gen., aor. pass. part. < ἐμπίμπρημι. *kindle, set on fire.*

νεώς, νεώ (mas.). *temple*; for this noun's irregular declension: Smyth 238.

σχεδὸν . . . τι. *I suppose, I'd bet*; here the phrase "soften[s] a positive assertion": LSJ, s.v. σχεδόν, IV.2.

ἐντεῦθεν. i.e., Corinth.

ἀφῖχθαι. pf. dep. inf. < ἀφικνέομαι.

κύκλῳ. adverbial: *around.*

μεγαλόφρων, -ονος. perhaps ambiguous: the adj. can mean *great-minded, generous* (the usual way it is taken here), but also *big-headed, arrogant.*

δεηθεῖσι. aor. dep. part. < δέομαι. *beg, ask*: LSJ, s.v. δέω (B), II.2.

Λεύκολλος. Lucius Licinius Lucullus, consul in 151 B.C.E., dedicated a Temple of Good Fortune funded from booty collected while he was campaigning in Spain.

στοά, -ᾶς (fem.). *stoa*; i.e., a covered colonnade.

ὧν. The relative pronoun is again attracted from the acc. into the gen. of its antecedent ἀνδριάντων, which is "incorporated"; i.e., it appears after the pronoun as part of the relative clause: Smyth 2522, 2538.

κοσμήσων, ἀποδώσων. fut. participles indicating purpose.

ἀναδείξεως. The day of a temple's dedication was a grand, public event.

ἀνέθηκε. On this verb, see note on ἀνάκειμαι above. Items dedicated to a god became the deity's legal property.

βούλεται. The subject is Mummius.

αἴρειν. Note breathing: < αἴρω, not αἱρέω.

μᾶλλον. Markings in certain manuscripts may indicate that some text has been lost between this word and πολὺν at the beginning of the next sentence: Radt, *Geographika*, ad loc.

ἐρήμη. In 146 B.C.E., Mummius pillaged the city and then, in accordance with a senatorial decree, razed it and forbade the Greeks to rebuild.

ἀνελήφθη < ἀναλαμβάνω.

Καίσαρος τοῦ θεοῦ. i.e., Julius Caesar, who in 44 B.C.E. established a colony in Corinth; on the designation τοῦ θεοῦ, see note on section **(8)** of A1, s.v. ὁ θεὸς Καῖσαρ.

ἀπελευθερικός, -ή, -όν. (of a) *freedman*; i.e., a manumitted slave.

κινέω. *move,* but often pejorative: *disturb, mess with*: LSJ, s.v. A.2, II.1.

συνανασκάπτω. *dig up besides*: LSJ, s.v.

ὀστρακίνων. i.e., ceramic.

τόρευμα, -ατος (neu.). *relief.*

κατασκευή, -ῆς (fem.). *workmanship, style.*

εἴασαν. 3rd pl. aor. act. ind. < ἐάω. *leave.*

εὐπορέω + gen. *have plenty of*: LSJ, s.v. b.

διατίθημι. in mid., *sell for* + gen. of price: LSJ, s.v. B.2, 3; Smyth 1372.

νεκροκορίνθια, -ων (neu. pl.). Perhaps the translation *Corinthian-deathware* is not inappropriate.

ἐπλήρωσαν. Verbs of filling take a gen. or both gen. and acc. (of what is being filled): Smyth 1369.

κατ' ἀρχὰς. *at first*: LSJ, s.v. ἀρχή, b.

διὰ παντὸς. sc. χρόνου.

ὑπῆρξεν < ὑπάρχω. *be.* Does the use of the aorist lend the sentence an elegiac tone?

ηὔξήθη. 3rd sg. aor. pass. ind. < αὐξάνω. *grow, flourish*; here the pass. is act. in meaning.

εὔγεων. mas. sg. acc. < εὔγεως, ων. *of good earth, fertile.* Compounds formed with γῆ end in -γειος or -γεως: Smyth 888.e.

ὀφρυόεις, -εσσα, -εν. *ridged, beetling.*

ὀφρυάω. *be perched on a ridge.*

PART C

FROM REPUBLIC TO EMPIRE

The second-century C.E. historian Appian is a major source for Rome's wars against Mithridates VI, the formidable Greco-Persian king of Pontus, who overran Asia Minor in 89 B.C.E. It took the Roman general Lucius Cornelius Sulla three years to wrest the region back from Mithridates. In the winter of 85/84, he informed Asia's leading men, some of whom had sided with the Pontic king, of the consequences of spurning Rome (C1). Sulla was one of the politicians who came to possess extraordinary power in the fractious period known as the late republic (133–27 B.C.E.), as was Octavian, who became Rome's first emperor. The historian Cassius Dio analyzes events in January 27 B.C.E., a key time in the transition from republic to principate, when the first emperor's powers and privileges were more clearly defined and he assumed the name Augustus (C2). Augustus (reg. 27 B.C.E.–14 C.E.) shaped his legacy by writing an autobiographical account of his achievements, the *Res Gestae,* preserved in inscriptions found in Asia Minor. The *Res Gestae* is extant in Greek and Latin; excerpts from both are presented below side-by-side, which makes it easier for those who know both languages to appreciate the differences between the two versions (C3). Philo of Alexandria paints a vivid picture of the early months of the emperor Gaius Caligula's reign (37–41 C.E.) and suggests that, in a political system where so much power devolved on one man, the health of the empire was closely tied to the health of the emperor. Then follow two contrasting views of the Roman Empire. The British warrior-queen Boudicca, fomenting rebellion in 60 or 61 C.E., blasts the greedy, corrupt Romans in a speech fashioned by Cassius Dio (C5). By contrast the second-century C.E. orator Aelius Aristides praises Rome, which has ushered in an age of safety, stability, and peace (C6). In such a world, what role was there to play for a Greek who longed for a political career? Plutarch lays out a careful response to this question in his *Political Precepts,* excerpted in the final selection of this section (C7).

C1. SULLA SPEAKS AT EPHESUS

Appian *Mithridatic Wars* 61.250–63.261

In the first century B.C.E., Rome's most formidable rival was Mithridates VI Eupator (reg. 120–63 B.C.E.), the Greco-Persian king of Pontus whose military prowess, diplomatic acumen, and masterly agitprop made him a threat to Roman interests in the eastern Mediterranean for more than thirty years. In 89, while Rome was trying to squelch the rebellion of many of its Italian allies in the Social War (91–87 B.C.E.), Mithridates (whose name is variously spelled in English) overran most of Asia Minor and, in the following year, arranged, with the collusion of Greek cities that had sided with him, for all Romans and Italians resident in the region to be killed in a single day, a brutal act known as the "Asian Vespers"; as many as 150,000 may have died. Casting himself, like Flamininus (B3), as the liberator of Hellas, Mithridates next invaded Greece. A seasoned commander, Lucius Cornelius Sulla, was elected consul for 88 and tasked with taking on the Pontic king. Sulla eventually recovered Greece and Asia, and he brokered a peace with Mithridates that was surprisingly generous to the king. But what would Sulla do about the Greek cities of Asia that had sided with the enemy? In the passage below, Sulla informs them of their fate during the winter of 85/84 in a speech delivered in the theater of Ephesus, a splendid edifice still standing today. It is worth considering the motives, stated and unstated, behind Sulla's speech, not least his desire to return swiftly to Italy, leading soldiers whose loyalty had been secured through the provision of booty and with a war chest sufficient to fund the campaigns he would need to wage there against his rivals, especially Lucius Cornelius Cinna, who dominated Roman politics at the time and had Sulla declared an enemy of the state while he was campaigning against Mithridates.

Sulla's speech is excerpted from the *Roman History* of Appian, a native of Alexandria in Egypt, a cosmopolitan center of Hellenic culture; more than most cities, however, Alexandria was prone to outbursts of urban unrest (see C4), and some of its residents harbored resentment, even centuries after its conquest, toward Rome. Although Appian was proud of his Alexandrian roots, he emigrated to Rome during the reign of Hadrian (reg. 117–38 C.E.) and, receiving Roman citizenship, there worked as an advocate, probably on the legal staff of the imperial treasury; he was named a procurator by the emperor Antoninus Pius (reg. 138–61 C.E.). Written in direct, approachable Greek for an audience assumed to have little familiarity with Roman institutions, his work documents the expansion of Roman power region by region: Sulla's speech appears in his account of the Mithridatic Wars, for which Appian is a major source. Appian is an avowed monarchist and an admirer of Roman rule, which is providential and beneficial to its subjects. Yet he does not sugarcoat the shortcomings of Rome's leaders, especially when their infighting foments unrest, and the sometimes morally reprehensible ways in which they obtain and wield power.

Further Reading

B. C. McGing, *The Foreign Policy of Mithridates VI Eupator, King of Pontus* (Leiden, 1986), 89–131; A. M. Gowing, *The Triumviral Narratives of Appian and Cassius Dio* (Ann Arbor, 1992), 9–18, 273–87; S. Swain, *Hellenism and Empire: Language, Classicism, and Power in the Greek World, A.D. 50–250* (Oxford, 1996), 248–53; A. Mayor, *The Poison King: The Life and Legend of Mithradates, Rome's Deadliest Enemy* (Princeton, 2010), 1–26; J. Osgood, "*Breviarium Totius Imperii:* The Background of Appian's *Roman History,*" in *Appian's* Roman History: *Empire and Civil War,* ed. K. Welch, 23–44 (Swansea, 2015).

❧

(61.250) αὐτὴν δὲ τὴν Ἀσίαν καθιστάμενος, Ἰλιέας μὲν καὶ Χίους καὶ Λυκίους καὶ Ῥοδίους καὶ Μαγνησίαν καί τινας ἄλλους, ἢ συμμαχίας ἀμειβόμενος, ἢ ὧν διὰ προθυμίαν ἐπεπόνθεσαν οὗ ἕνεκα, ἐλευθέρους ἠφίει καὶ Ῥωμαίων ἀνέγραφε φίλους, ἐς δὲ τὰ λοιπὰ πάντα στρατιὰν περιέπεμπεν. **(251)** καὶ τοὺς θεράποντας, οἷς ἐλευθερίαν ἐδεδώκει Μιθριδάτης, ἐκήρυττεν αὐτίκα ἐς τοὺς δεσπότας ἐπανιέναι. πολλῶν δὲ ἀπειθούντων, καὶ πόλεων τινῶν ἀφισταμένων, ἐγίγνοντο σφαγαὶ κατὰ πλῆθος ἐλευθέρων τε καὶ θεραπόντων ἐπὶ ποικίλαις προφάσεσι, τείχη τε πολλῶν καθῃρεῖτο, καὶ συχνὰ τῆς Ἀσίας ἠνδραποδίζετο καὶ διηρπάζετο. **(252)** οἵ τε καππαδοκίσαντες ἄνδρες ἢ πόλεις ἐκολάζοντο πικρῶς, καὶ μάλιστα αὐτῶν Ἐφέσιοι, σὺν αἰσχρᾷ κολακείᾳ ἐς τὰ Ῥωμαίων ἀναθήματα ὑβρίσαντες. ἐπὶ δὲ τοῖσδε καὶ κήρυγμα περιῄει, τοὺς ἐν ἀξιώσει κατὰ πόλιν ἐς ἡμέραν ῥητὴν πρὸς τὸν Σύλλαν ἀπαντᾶν ἐς Ἔφεσον. καὶ συνελθοῦσιν αὐτοῖς ἐπὶ βήματος ἐδημηγόρησεν οὕτως.

(62.253) "ἡμεῖς στρατῷ πρῶτον ἐς Ἀσίαν παρήλθομεν Ἀντιόχου τοῦ Σύρων βασιλέως πορθοῦντος ὑμᾶς. ἐξελάσαντες δ᾽ αὐτόν, καὶ τὸν Ἅλυν καὶ Ταῦρον αὐτῷ θέμενοι τῆς ἀρχῆς ὅρον, οὐ κατέσχομεν ὑμῶν ἡμετέρων ἐξ ἐκείνου γενομένων, ἀλλὰ μεθήκαμεν αὐτονόμους, πλὴν εἴ τινας Εὐμένει καὶ Ῥοδίοις συμμαχήσασιν ἡμῖν ἔδομεν, οὐχ ὑποτελεῖς ἀλλ᾽ ἐπὶ προστάταις εἶναι. **(254)** τεκμήριον δ᾽ ὅτι Λυκίους αἰτιωμένους τι Ῥοδίων ἀπεστήσαμεν. ἡμεῖς μὲν δὴ τοιοίδε περὶ ὑμᾶς γεγόναμεν· ὑμεῖς δέ, Ἀττάλου τοῦ φιλομήτορος τὴν ἀρχὴν ἡμῖν ἐν διαθήκαις καταλιπόντος, Ἀριστονίκῳ καθ᾽ ἡμῶν τέτταρσιν ἔτεσι συνεμαχεῖτε, μέχρι καὶ Ἀριστόνικος ἑάλω καὶ ὑμῶν οἱ πλείους ἐς ἀνάγκην καὶ φόβον περιήλθετε. **(255)** καὶ ὧδε πράσσοντες ὅμως, ἔτεσιν εἴκοσι καὶ τέτταρσιν ἐς μέγα περιουσίας καὶ κάλλους κατασκευῆς ἰδιωτικῆς τε καὶ δημοσίας προελθόντες, ὑπὸ εἰρήνης καὶ τρυφῆς ἐξυβρίσατε αὖθις, καὶ τὴν ἀσχολίαν ἡμῶν τὴν ἀμφὶ τὴν Ἰταλίαν φυλάξαντες οἱ μὲν ἐπηγάγεσθε Μιθριδάτην, οἱ δ᾽ ἐλθόντι συνέθεσθε. **(256)** ὃ δ᾽ ἐστὶ πάντων μιαρώτατον, ὑπέστητε αὐτῷ μιᾶς ἡμέρας τοὺς Ἰταλιώτας ἅπαντας αὐτοῖς παισὶ καὶ μητράσιν ἀναιρήσειν, καὶ οὐδὲ τῶν ἐς τὰ ἱερὰ συμφυγόντων διὰ τοὺς ὑμετέρους θεοὺς ἐφείσασθε. **(257)** ἐφ' οἷς ἔδοτε μέν τινα καὶ αὐτῷ Μιθριδάτῃ δίκην, ἀπίστῳ τε ἐς ὑμᾶς γενομένῳ, καὶ φόνου καὶ δημεύσεων ἐμπλήσαντι ὑμᾶς, καὶ γῆς ἀναδασμοὺς ἐργασαμένῳ καὶ χρεῶν ἀποκοπὰς καὶ δούλων ἐλευθερώσεις, καὶ τυράννους ἐπ' ἐνίοις, καὶ ληστήρια πολλὰ ἀνά τε γῆν καὶ θάλασσαν, ὡς εὐθὺς ὑμᾶς ἔχειν ἐν πείρᾳ καὶ παραβολῇ οἵους ἀνθ' οἵων προστάτας ἐπελέγεσθε. **(258)** ἔδοσαν δέ τινα καὶ ἡμῖν δίκην οἱ τῶνδε ἄρξαντες. ἀλλὰ δεῖ καὶ κοινὴν ὑμῖν ἐπιτεθῆναι τοιάδε ἐργασαμένοις· ἣν εἰκὸς μὲν ἦν ὁμοίαν οἷς ἐδράσατε γενέσθαι, μή ποτε δὲ Ῥωμαῖοι σφαγὰς ἀσεβεῖς ἢ δημεύσεις ἀβούλους ἢ δούλων ἐπαναστάσεις, ἢ ὅσα ἄλλα βαρβαρικά, μηδ' ἐπὶ νοῦν λάβοιεν. **(259)** φειδοῖ δὲ γένους ἔτι καὶ ὀνόματος Ἑλληνικοῦ καὶ δόξης τῆς ἐπὶ τῇ Ἀσίᾳ, καὶ τῆς φιλτάτης Ῥωμαίοις εὐφημίας οὕνεκα, μόνους ὑμῖν ἐπιγράφω πέντε ἐτῶν φόρους ἐσενεγκεῖν αὐτίκα, καὶ τὴν τοῦ πολέμου δαπάνην, ὅση τε γέγονέ μοι καὶ ἔσται καθισταμένῳ τὰ ὑπόλοιπα. **(260)** διαιρήσω δὲ ταῦθ' ἑκάστοις ἐγὼ κατὰ πόλεις, καὶ τάξω προθεσμίαν ταῖς ἐσφοραῖς, καὶ τοῖς οὐ φυλάξασιν ἐπιθήσω δίκην ὡς πολεμίοις."

(63.261) τοσάδε εἰπὼν ἐπιδιῄρει τοῖς πρέσβεσι τὴν ζημίαν, καὶ ἐπὶ τὰ χρήματα ἔπεμπεν. αἱ δὲ πόλεις ἀποροῦσαί τε καὶ δανειζόμεναι μεγάλων τόκων, αἱ μὲν τὰ θέατρα τοῖς δανείζουσιν, αἱ δὲ τὰ γυμνάσια ἢ τεῖχος ἢ λιμένας ἢ εἴ τι δημόσιον ἄλλο, σὺν ὕβρει στρατιωτῶν ἐπειγόντων, ὑπετίθεντο. τὰ μὲν δὴ χρήματα ὧδε τῷ Σύλλᾳ συνεκομίζετο, καὶ κακῶν ἅδην εἶχεν ἡ Ἀσία.

Notes to Appian Mithridatic Wars *61.250–63.261*

These notes are indebted to P. Goukowsky, *Appien, Histoire romaine, Tome VII, Livre XII: La guerre de Mithridate* (Paris, 2001).

(61.250) καθίστημι. *set in order, settle*: LSJ, s.v. A.II. The subject is Sulla.

Μαγνησίαν. i.e., Magnesia on the Maeander River in Ionia.

ἀμείβω. in mid., *repay X* (+ acc.) *for Y* (+ gen.): LSJ, s.v. B.3.

ὧν διὰ προθυμίαν ἐπεπόνθεσαν οὗ ἕνεκα. *because of what they had suffered on account of their goodwill toward him*; i.e., Sulla.

ἐπεπόνθεσαν. 3rd pl. plupf. act. ind. < πάσχω.

ἠφίει. 3rd sg. impf. act. ind. < ἀφίημι.

(251) ἐλευθερίαν. In preparation for the Asian Vespers, Mithridates promised freedom to slaves who killed their Roman masters: Appian *Mithridatic Wars* 22.86. Later, when his power over Asia was wavering, he liberated slaves to secure their loyalty (48.190).

ἐκήρυττεν (Attic) = ἐκήρυσσεν.

ἐγίγνοντο. Appian does not explicitly say who carried out these acts of violence.

κατὰ πλῆθος. *in great numbers*: LSJ, s.v. πλῆθος, V.

ποικίλος, -η, -ον. *varied, manifold*, with a connotation of complexity: LSJ, s.v. III.

(252) καππαδοκίσαντες < καππαδοκίζω. *be allied with the Cappadocians*. Verbs in which the suffix -ίζω is attached to a proper name may indicate the adoption of a language or cultural practices (e.g., ἑλληνίζω, *speak Greek*) or, as here, political allegiance (e.g., μηδίζω, *side with the Medes*): Smyth 866.6.a. Mithridates had deposed Ariobarzanes I, the pro-Roman king of Cappadocia, a region in east-central Asia Minor, replacing him with an ally; Sulla restored Ariobarzanes to the throne.

κολακεία, -ας (fem.). *abject flattery*, in this case, toward Mithridates.

ἀναθήματα. Ephesus warmly welcomed Mithridates; its residents had torn down Roman statues in the city: Appian *Mithridatic Wars* 21.81.

περιῄει. 3rd sg. impf. act. ind. < περίειμι. *go round*.

τοὺς ἐν ἀξιώσει. i.e., the cities' notables; Appian here switches to acc. + inf. indirect discourse to report the content of Sulla's κήρυγμα.

κατὰ πόλιν. As often, κατά + acc. is distributive (Smyth 1690.2.c): *in every city*.

ἀπαντᾶν. pres. act. inf. < ἀπαντάω. *meet, gather*; the verb also has legal (*present oneself to a court, meet in court*) and military connotations (*meet in battle*): LSJ, s.v.

συνελθοῦσιν. mas. pl. dat., aor. act. part.

δημηγορέω. *speak to a political assembly*, but also *speak like a demagogue*: LSJ, s.v.

(62.253) Ἀντιόχου. Antiochus III ruled the Seleucid Empire, based in Syria, 222–187 B.C.E. He came to control much of Asia Minor and invaded mainland Greece, where he fought Rome as the self-proclaimed liberator of Hellas; the Romans defeated him at Thermopylae in 191 and at Magnesia ad Sipylum in Lydia in 190. According to the Treaty of Apamea in 188, Antiochus had to abandon all territorial claims over mainland Greece and Asia Minor to the west and north of the Taurus Mountains. See also B3, B5, B6.

τὸν Ἅλυν. The Halys River. It is not clear whether this river did in fact mark a boundary in the Treaty of Apamea.

ἡμετέρων ἐξ ἐκείνου γενομένων. Take the participle as concessive: *although you became ours from him* (i.e., Mithridates).

μεθήκαμεν. 1st pl. aor. act. ind. < μεθίημι + inf. *set free, permit to X.*

τινας. In fact, most of the territory was yielded to Rhodes and Eumenes II, the king of Pergamum (reg. 197–159/58 B.C.E.).

οὐχ ὑποτελεῖς . . . εἶναι. i.e., the Greek city-states do not pay taxes to Rhodes and Pergamum, but are under their patronage (ἐπὶ προστάταις)—just as Rome's allies are under *its* patronage.

(254) Λυκίους. In 178 or 177, Lycian envoys petitioned the Senate to check the abusive behavior of Rhodes toward Lycia; siding with the envoys, the Senate decreed that the Lycians were not to be treated as slaves but as clients and allies: Polybius 25.4–5; Livy 41.6.8–12.

Ἀττάλου τοῦ φιλομήτορος. In 133, Attalus III Philometor, king of Pergamum, died without issue; in his will, he bequeathed the bulk of his kingdom to Rome on the condition that the city of Pergamum itself would remain independent. Refusing to accept the terms of the will, Aristonicus, who may have been the illegitimate half-brother of Attalus, usurped the throne and led an uprising against Rome. In 129, the Romans put down the revolt, executed Aristonicus, and reorganized the kingdom of Pergamum as the province of Asia.

ἑάλω. 3rd sg. aor. dep. ind. < ἁλίσκομαι. *be captured.*

ἐς. *out of, because of.*

(255) πράσσοντες = Attic πράττοντες.

ἐς μέγα . . . προελθόντες. *having advanced to the height.*

κατασκευή, -ῆς (fem.). *construction* (of buildings).

ὑπὸ . . . αὖθις. This is a trope in ancient historiography—that prosperity in peacetime leads to a taste for luxury, which in turn corrodes public morality.

ἐξυβρίσατε αὖθις. Sulla draws attention to the cyclicity of the phenomenon.

ἐπάγω. in mid., *bring X* (+ acc.) *as an ally into one's country*: LSJ, s.v. II.2. Other sources credit Mithridates for taking the initiative: e.g., Justin 38.7.

συντίθημι. in mid., *support, make a covenant with* (+ dat.): LSJ, s.v. B.II.

(256) ὃ . . . μιαρώτατον. a rhetorically powerful use of an "incorporated" relative clause (i.e., one in which the antecedent follows the pronoun) at the beginning of a sentence: Smyth 2536.

μιαρός, -ά, -όν. *vile, foul, polluted by blood*; a potent word, esp. in the superlative.

ὑφίστημι + fut. inf. + dat. *promise to do X for Y*: LSJ, s.v. B.II.

αὐτοῖς παισὶ . . . μητράσιν. dat. of accompaniment.

(257) δίκην δίδωμι. *suffer punishment* + dat. of agent.

δήμευσις, -εως (fem.). *confiscation of property.*

ἐμπλήσαντι. Verbs of filling may take an acc. of what is being filled and a gen. of what does the filling: Smyth 1369.

ἀναδασμός, -οῦ (mas.). *redistribution of property.* When Mithridates's control over Asia faltered, he turned to increasingly radical social and economic measures to win supporters.

ἔχω. *understand,* here inf. in a result clause after ὡς.

οἵους . . . ἐπελέγεσθε. lit., *what sort of rulers you were choosing instead of what other sort.* In other words, the Asians came to appreciate the differences between Mithridates and the Romans.

(258) κοινὴν. sc. δίκην.

ἐπιτεθῆναι. aor. pass. inf. < ἐπιτίθημι. *inflict, impose*: LSJ, s.v. A.V.

ἥν. The antecedent is δίκην.

εἰκὸς ἦν + acc. and aor. inf. introduces an unfulfilled (and therefore contrafactual) possibility in the past: *it would have been fitting for*: Smyth 1774–79.

ὅμοιος, -α, -ον + dat. *in proportion to.* Sulla claims that the Greeks deserve to be punished according to the terms of the *lex talionis*—i.e., eye for an eye.

ἐπὶ νοῦν λαμβάνω. *countenance, envisage.*

λάβοιεν. opt. of wish.

(259) φειδοῖ. fem. sg. dat. < φειδώ, -όος (contracting to -οῦς). *sparing* + gen.

μόνους. Hyperbaton (Smyth 3028) draws attention to this adj.

ἐπιγράφω. *assign as penalty*: LSJ, s.v. III.

πέντε ἐτῶν φόρους. i.e., the taxes that Asia did not pay to Rome for the five years, 89–85, during which Mithridates had controlled it.

ὅση . . . τὰ ὑπόλοιπα. Sulla requires reimbursement for all expenses he has incurred in the war and will incur in settling the affairs of Asia.

(260) φυλάσσω. *observe, regard* what Sulla says.

(63.261) ἐπιδιαιρέω. *apportion, divide.*

ἀπορέω. *be poor, be at a loss.*

μεγάλων τόκων. i.e., the Greeks were forced to take out high-interest loans.

στρατιωτῶν ἐπειγόντων. Since the tax collectors of Asia had fled or had been killed in the war, Sulla's soldiers were tasked with collecting funds.

ὑποτίθημι. *mortgage*: LSJ, s.v. VII. To raise money, the Greeks took out mortgages on public buildings, which served as a collateral for their creditors (τοῖς δανείζουσιν).

C2. FIRST AUGUSTAN SETTLEMENT

Cassius Dio 53.16.4–17.3, 18.1–3

In both his political career and literary work, Cassius Dio blurs the boundaries between Greece and Rome. Born c. 164 C.E. into a prominent family with roots in Nicaea, a Greek city in Bithynia, Dio, following in his father's footsteps, pursued a life of public service. He occupied a succession of prominent positions, including praetor, consul (twice), and proconsul of Africa. Dio identified, above all, as a Roman senator, one who served mostly under the unstable and unpredictable Severan emperors (reg. 193–235 C.E.) or, as he puts it, during an age of "iron and rust" (72.36.4). Yet Dio believed that, for a vast and diverse empire like Rome's, μοναρχία (rule by one) was the best form of government, and that a good monarch fostered harmonious relations with the senatorial elite, the torchbearers of traditional Roman values.

Dio's history is indebted to the literary traditions of both Greece and Rome. On the one hand, its cynicism and interest in the disjunction between surface and reality recall Thucydides, and its speeches are composed in the style of the Second Sophistic, as is well illustrated by the other excerpt from Dio in this volume (C5). On the other hand, adhering to the traditions of Latin historiography, Dio's history is organized annalistically (i.e., it narrates events year by year), proceeding from the city's foundation through his own day. It covers those one thousand or so years in eighty books—many of which are preserved only in excerpts, some lengthy—and epitomes (i.e., abridgements). Books 36–55.9, spanning 69–6 B.C.E., are extant nearly in full and offer the only sustained, continuous account of the late republic and Augustus's early years. The passage below is from book 53, where Dio narrates events in 27 B.C.E., a crucial and formative year in Rome's transition from δημοκρατία (the usual Greek word for republican government) to μοναρχία. In particular, it treats, with analytical insight, the so-called First Settlement, a series of senatorial decrees and acts of political theater in January that sought to "settle" questions regarding the first emperor's title, honors, and powers. Of special interest is the care with which Dio renders key Latin political terms and titles in Greek.

Further Reading

Dio 53.1–16.3; Suetonius *Augustus* 7.2; F. Millar, *A Study of Cassius Dio* (Oxford, 1964), 73–118; J. W. Rich, "Dio on Augustus," in *History as Text: The Writing of Ancient History*, ed. A. Cameron, 86–110 (London, 1989); A. M. Gowing, *The Triumviral Narratives of Appian and Cassius Dio* (Ann Arbor, 1992), 19–32, 289–94; A. M. Kemezis, *Greek Narratives of the Roman Empire under the Severans: Cassius Dio, Philostratus and Herodian* (Cambridge, 2014), 90–149.

(16.4) ὁ δ' οὖν Καῖσαρ πολλὰ μὲν καὶ πρότερον, ὅτε τὰ περὶ τῆς ἐξωμοσίας τῆς μοναρχίας καὶ τὰ περὶ τῆς τῶν ἐθνῶν διανομῆς διελέχθη, ἔλαβε· καὶ γὰρ τό τε τὰς δάφνας πρὸ τῶν βασιλείων αὐτοῦ προτίθεσθαι, καὶ τὸ τὸν στέφανον τὸν δρύινον ὑπὲρ αὐτῶν ἀρτᾶσθαι, τότε οἱ ὡς καὶ ἀεὶ τούς τε πολεμίους νικῶντι καὶ τοὺς πολίτας σώζοντι ἐψηφίσθη. **(5)** καλεῖται δὲ τὰ βασίλεια παλάτιον, οὐχ ὅτι καὶ ἔδοξέ ποτε οὕτως αὐτὰ ὀνομάζεσθαι, ἀλλ' ὅτι ἔν τε τῷ Παλατίῳ ὁ Καῖσαρ ᾤκει καὶ ἐκεῖ τὸ στρατήγιον εἶχε, καί τινα καὶ πρὸς τὴν τοῦ Ῥωμύλου προενοίκησιν φήμην ἡ οἰκία αὐτοῦ ἀπὸ τοῦ παντὸς ὄρους ἔλαβε· **(6)** καὶ διὰ τοῦτο κἂν ἄλλοθί που ὁ αὐτοκράτωρ καταλύῃ, τὴν τοῦ παλατίου ἐπίκλησιν ἡ καταγωγὴ αὐτοῦ ἴσχει. ἐπεὶ δὲ καὶ τῷ ἔργῳ αὐτὰ ἐπετέλεσεν, οὕτω δὴ καὶ τὸ τοῦ Αὐγούστου ὄνομα καὶ παρὰ τῆς βουλῆς καὶ παρὰ τοῦ δήμου ἐπέθετο. **(7)** βουληθέντων γάρ σφων ἰδίως πως αὐτὸν προσειπεῖν, καὶ τῶν μὲν τὸ τῶν δὲ τὸ καὶ ἐσηγουμένων καὶ αἱρουμένων, ὁ Καῖσαρ ἐπεθύμει μὲν ἰσχυρῶς Ῥωμύλος ὀνομασθῆναι, αἰσθόμενος δὲ ὅτι ὑποπτεύεται ἐκ τούτου τῆς βασιλείας ἐπιθυμεῖν, **(8)** οὐκέτ' αὐτοῦ ἀντεποιήσατο, ἀλλὰ Αὔγουστος ὡς καὶ πλεῖόν τι ἢ κατὰ ἀνθρώπους ὢν ἐπεκλήθη· πάντα γὰρ τὰ ἐντιμότατα καὶ τὰ ἱερώτατα αὔγουστα προσαγορεύεται. ἐξ οὗπερ καὶ σεβαστὸν αὐτὸν καὶ ἑλληνίζοντές πως, ὥσπερ τινὰ σεπτόν, ἀπὸ τοῦ σεβάζεσθαι, προσεῖπον.

(17.1) οὕτω μὲν δὴ τό τε τοῦ δήμου καὶ τὸ τῆς γερουσίας κράτος πᾶν ἐς τὸν Αὔγουστον μετέστη, καὶ ἀπ' αὐτοῦ καὶ ἀκριβὴς μοναρχία κατέστη· μοναρχία γάρ, εἰ καὶ τὰ μάλιστα καὶ δύο καὶ τρεῖς ἅμα τὸ κῦρός ποτε ἔσχον, ἀληθέστατα ἂν νομίζοιτο. **(2)** τὸ μὲν γὰρ ὄνομα αὐτὸ τὸ μοναρχικὸν οὕτω δή τι οἱ Ῥωμαῖοι ἐμίσησαν ὥστε μήτε δικτάτορας μήτε βασιλέας μήτ' ἄλλο τι τοιουτότροπον τοὺς αὐτοκράτοράς σφων ὀνομάζειν· τοῦ δὲ δὴ τῆς πολιτείας τέλους ἐς αὐτοὺς ἀνακειμένου οὐκ ἔστιν ὅπως οὐ βασιλεύονται. **(3)** αἱ μὲν γὰρ ἀρχαὶ αἱ ἐκ τῶν νόμων ὡς πλήθει γενόμεναι καὶ νῦν πλὴν τῆς τῶν τιμητῶν καθίστανται, διάγεται δὲ καὶ διοικεῖται πάντα ἁπλῶς ὅπως ἂν ὁ ἀεὶ κρατῶν ἐθελήσῃ. καὶ ἵνα γε μὴ ἐκ δυναστείας ἀλλ' ἐκ τῶν νόμων τοῦτ' ἔχειν δοκῶσι, πάνθ' ὅσα ἐν τῇ δημοκρατίᾳ μέγα παρ' ἑκοῦσί σφισιν ἴσχυσεν, αὐτοῖς τοῖς ὀνόμασι χωρὶς τοῦ τῆς δικτατορίας προσεποιήσαντο.

[In 53.17.4–11, Dio describes the various magistracies and priesthoods whose powers were absorbed by the emperors.]

(18.1) ἤδη δὲ καὶ ἕτερόν τι, ὃ μηδενὶ τῶν πάλαι Ῥωμαίων ἐς πάντα ἄντικρυς ἐδόθη, προσεκτήσαντο, ὑφ' οὗπερ καὶ μόνου καὶ ἐκεῖνα ἂν καὶ τἆλλα αὐτοῖς πράττειν ἐξῆν. λέλυνται γὰρ δὴ τῶν νόμων, ὡς αὐτὰ τὰ Λατῖνα ῥήματα λέγει· τοῦτ' ἔστιν ἐλεύθεροι ἀπὸ πάσης ἀναγκαίας νομίσεώς εἰσι καὶ οὐδενὶ τῶν γεγραμμένων ἐνέχονται. **(2)** καὶ οὕτως ἐκ τούτων τῶν δημοκρατικῶν ὀνομάτων πᾶσαν τὴν τῆς πολιτείας ἰσχὺν περιβέβληνται ὥστε καὶ τὰ τῶν βασιλέων, πλὴν τοῦ φορτικοῦ τῆς προσηγορίας αὐτῶν, ἔχειν. ἡ γὰρ δὴ τοῦ Καίσαρος ἥ τε τοῦ Αὐγούστου πρόσρησις δύναμιν μὲν οὐδεμίαν αὐτοῖς οἰκείαν προστίθησι, δηλοῖ δ' ἄλλως τὸ μὲν τὴν τοῦ γένους σφῶν διαδοχήν, τὸ δὲ τὴν τοῦ ἀξιώματος λαμπρότητα. (3) καὶ ἥ γε τοῦ πατρὸς ἐπωνυμία τάχα μὲν καὶ ἐξουσίαν τινὰ αὐτοῖς, ἥν ποτε οἱ πατέρες ἐπὶ τοὺς παῖδας ἔσχον, κατὰ πάντων ἡμῶν δίδωσιν, οὐ μέντοι καὶ ἐπὶ τοῦτο ἀρχὴν ἐγένετο ἀλλ' ἔς τε τιμὴν καὶ ἐς παραίνεσιν, ἵν' αὐτοί τε τοὺς ἀρχομένους ὡς καὶ παῖδας ἀγαπῷεν καὶ ἐκεῖνοί σφας ὡς καὶ πατέρας αἰδῶνται.

Notes to Cassius Dio 53.16.4–17.3, 18.1–3

The notes below are indebted to J. W. Rich, *Cassius Dio: The Augustan Settlement (*Roman History *53–55.9)* (Warminster, 1990) and M.-L. Freyburger-Galland, *Aspects du vocabulaire politique et institutionnel de Dion Cassius* (Paris, 1997).

(16.4) Καῖσαρ. i.e., Octavian.

πολλὰ. sc. "honors."

ἐξωμοσία, -ας (fem.). *refusal, denial* (of an office): LSJ, s.v. II. In the sections preceding this passage, Dio explains how Octavian, by amassing political power, sets himself up as a de facto monarch, all the while carefully calibrating his public persona to suggest that he is doing no such thing.

τὰ περὶ τῆς τῶν ἐθνῶν διανομῆς. The administration of the provinces had just been discussed in 53.12–15.

τό . . . προτίθεσθαι, τὸ . . . ἀρτᾶσθαι. These articular infinitives serve as the subject of ἐψηφίσθη. The Senate voted these honors—namely, the right to decorate the doorway to his residence with laurels on either side and the civic crown above—to Augustus on January 13, 27 B.C.E. Their symbolism is complex and multivalent. Laurels were associated with Apollo, a god with whom Augustus aligned himself, and grew near religious buildings in Rome (e.g., the Temple of Vesta). Moreover, doorways were garlanded during festivals, and triumphators displayed spoils on the facades of their houses. The laurels, then, linked Augustus with victory and piety. The civic crown, made of oak leaves, was awarded to a soldier or political leader who had saved a citizen's life; that citizen was to consider his savior to be his father and had to obey him. The oak was also associated with Jupiter. Both the crown and laurels became integral elements of the first emperor's iconography and often appeared on the coinage and artworks of the era. See further Rich, *Cassius Dio,* ad loc. and notes on section **(34)** of C3.

οἱ = αὐτῷ. In this clause, Dio explains the significance of the honors.

(5) βασίλεια, -ων (neu. pl.). *royal residence,* a term that takes on further significance in the light of **(17)** below.

παλάτιον, -ου (neu.). *Palatium* (i.e., imperial residence), *Palatine Hill.*

πρός + acc. *as a consequence of*: LSJ, III.2.

προενοίκησις, -εως (fem.). *former home.*

(6) κἂν = καὶ ἐὰν.

αὐτοκράτωρ is the equivalent of Latin *imperator.* In the republic, *imperator* could refer to someone who had the legitimate right to command an army (*imperium*), but the term was also an honorific bestowed on a victorious general through the acclamation of his soldiers; the victor might adopt it as a title for some time thereafter. Although *imperator* still possessed these meanings under the principate, it also came to mean, more generically, *emperor.* From Vespasian on, it became part of the emperor's official titulature as a praenomen. See Rich, *Cassius Dio,* 149–50; Freyburger-Galland, *Aspects du vocabulaire,* 149–52, 202–205; and notes on section **(4)** of C3.

καταλύω. *lodge, take up residence*: LSJ, II.2.

Αὐγούστου. The Senate granted the title Augustus to Octavian on January 16, 27 B.C.E., at the suggestion of Lucius Munatius Plancus.

(7) βουληθέντων. The verb indicates that the debate occured in the Senate (βουλή).

σφων = αὐτῶν.

ἰδίως. *variously*: LSJ, s.v. ἴδιος, VI.

τῶν μὲν τὸ τῶν δὲ τὸ. *some . . . this (name), others . . . that (name).* In other words, various possible titles were introduced and discussed.

ἐπιθυμέω. *covet, want.* The verb may take a complementary inf. or a gen. of what is desired.

Ῥωμύλος. Only Dio claims that Augustus *wanted* to be called Romulus; cf. Suetonius, who says that the name was mooted by unidentified persons before Plancus proposed Augustus instead: *Augustus* 7.2.

ὑποπτεύω. *be suspected, held in suspicion.*

(8) ἀντιποιέω. in mid., *seek, lay claim to* + gen.: LSJ, s.v. II.

σεβαστός, -ή, -όν. *revered* < σεβάζομαι; cf. σέβας, *reverent dread, awe.* Before it is used as a title, this verbal adj. (Smyth 471) is rarely attested. σεβαστός conveys the associations with sanctity and divinity contained in the word *augustus*; it does not capture other connotations of the Latin word, which also suggests *authority, clout* (cf. Latin *auctoritas*); *growth, fertility* (cf. Latin *augere*); and *auspiciousness* (cf. Latin *augurium*). Before the third century, σεβαστός was the favored term for the emperor; under the Severans, it became common to transliterate Augustus instead, which is Dio's usual practice.

(17.1) γερουσίας. i.e., the Senate.

καθίστημι. in 2nd aor., *come into being, become*: LSJ, s.v. B.5. Elsewhere in book 53, Dio claims that the monarchy had come into existence in 31 or 29 B.C.E., and that Augustus, here in January 27, was not establishing but defining and strengthening the new monarchy: see Rich, *Cassius Dio,* ad loc.

εἰ καὶ τὰ μάλιστα. *even if, to introduce an extreme case*: LSJ, s.v. μάλα, III.2.

δύο καὶ τρεῖς. By Dio's day, there had been multiple coregent emperors.

(2) οὕτω δή τι. *to such a degree.*

τέλος, -εος (neu.). *supreme authority*: LSJ, s.v. 2.

οὐκ ἔστιν ὅπως. *it is not possible that*: Smyth 2551. Since all power lies with the emperors, Dio argues, they must in fact be monarchs.

(3) ἀρχή, -ῆς (fem.). *magistracy*: LSJ, s.v. II.3.

ὡς πλήθει. *mostly, for the most part.*

τιμητής, -οῦ (mas.). *censor.* The last censor was elected in 22 B.C.E. On the powers of the censor, see note on section **(53.7)** of B2, s.v.

διάγω. *manage.*

ὅπως ἄν + subj. *in whatever way*: LSJ, s.v. ὅπως, A.2.

δυναστεία, -ας (fem.). *absolute power*: Freyburger-Galland, *Aspects du vocabulaire,* 127–31.

παρ' ἑκοῦσί σφισιν ἴσχυσεν. lit., *possessed power from them* (σφισιν = αὐτοῖς = the Roman people), *being willing.* Authority was vested in the magistrates through the consent of the people who elected them.

αὐτοῖς τοῖς ὀνόμασι. *together with the names (of the magistracies) themselves.* In other words, the emperors assumed not just the powers of the magistrates but also their titles.

προσποιέω. *appropriate, lay claim to.*

(18.1) ἐς πάντα. *altogether, entirely*: LSJ, s.v. πᾶς, IV.

ἄντικρυς. adv., *openly, outright*: LSJ, s.v. 2.

προσεκτήσαντο. sc. "the emperors" as subject.

καὶ μόνου. i.e., the single principle that Dio is about to describe is sufficient to legitimate all of the emperors' actions.

τἆλλα = τὰ ἄλλα.

ἐξῆν. 3rd sg. impf. act. ind. < ἔξεστι + dat. impersonal, *it was possible for.*

λέλυνται γὰρ δὴ τῶν νόμων. By Dio's day, legal theorists had argued that the emperors were above the law. In language similar to the Greek found here, the jurist Ulpian, a contemporary of Dio, writes *princeps legibus solutus est,* "the emperor has been freed from the laws": Justinian *Digest* 1.3.31. Dio here applies this principle anachronistically to earlier emperors as well.

τοῦτ' ἔστιν. *that is*: LSJ, s.v. εἰμί, B.

(2) περιβάλλω. a suggestive verb, especially in the mid.: *surround, clothe, cloak oneself with* + acc.: LSJ, s.v.

οἰκεῖος, -α, -ον or -ος, -ον. *innate, of its own.*

τὸ μὲν . . . τὸ δὲ. *on the one hand . . . on the other*: Smyth 1111.

(3) τάχα. *perhaps.*

οἱ πατέρες ἐπὶ τοὺς παῖδας ἔσχον. i.e., *patria potestas,* the power, vast in theory, that the head of a Roman family (*paterfamilias*) had over its members.

οὐ μέντοι . . . ἐγένετο. *it did not come to existence at first for this reason*; i.e., the paternalistic power of the emperor did not yet have the significance just described. The Romans' political vocabulary often blurred the line between political and familial power: senators, for example, were called *patres,* fathers.

σφας = αὐτοὺς.

C3. AUGUSTUS ON AUGUSTUS

Res Gestae Divi Augusti 1–4, 13, 24, 34–35

According to the Roman polymath and biographer Suetonius, after the death of Augustus on August 19, 14 C.E., three sealed scrolls were brought forward by the Vestal Virgins, to whom the first emperor had entrusted them, and read aloud in the Senate (*Augustus* 101). One scroll contained an autobiographical account of the emperor's accomplishments, known as the *Res Gestae Divi Augusti (RG),* which, so the emperor ordered, was to be inscribed on bronze tablets and posted at the entrance to his mausoleum in the Campus Martius. These bronze originals have been lost, but three inscribed copies of this remarkable document have turned up in the province of Galatia in Asia Minor. One copy is in Latin, one in Greek, and one is bilingual, with copies in both languages.

The *Res Gestae* is of monumental importance for our understanding of the Augustan Age, for it offers direct evidence for how the emperor wished to present himself to his subjects and posterity. Related in form to *elogia,* epitaphs that read like résumés of the deceased, the document is nonetheless *sui generis.* Written in the first-person singular and peppered with first-person pronouns, the *Res Gestae* keeps the spotlight on Augustus and his family; indeed, other than consuls, no one outside the imperial family is named in the text. The Greek translation—the similiarity of the two Greek copies suggests that they were transcribed from a common original—differs from the original Latin in subtle but significant ways. On the one hand, the Greek softens the Latin's imperialistic tone, making the document more palatable for provincials; on the other, it more frankly recognizes the monarchic nature of Augustus's rule for a readership accustomed to the rule of Hellenistic kings. Key Roman political concepts like *imperium* are carefully and variously rendered for an audience unfamiliar with them. So that the reader may appreciate their differences, the Greek and Latin versions are printed side by side below. Finally, a few notes about the orthography of the inscription: (1) the Greek exhibits iota adscript, not subscript (e.g., τῆι not τῇ), (2) long iota is rendered by ει, (3) η replaces ει, and (4) before γ, κ, ξ, χ, gamma becomes nu (ἐνγύς, not ἐγγύς).

Further Reading

Augustus *Res Gestae* all; D. N. Wigtil, "The Ideology of the Greek 'Res Gestae,'" in *Aufstieg und Niedergang der römischen Welt,* ed. W. Haase, part 2, vol. 30.1, *Sprache und Literatur (Literatur der augusteischen Zeit),* 624–38 (Berlin, 1982); A. E. Cooley, "The Publication of Roman Official Documents in the Greek East," in *Literacy and the State in the Ancient Mediterranean,* ed. K. Lomas, R. D. Whitehouse, and J. B. Wilkins, 203–18 (London, 2007); A. E. Cooley, Res Gestae Divi Augusti: *Text, Translation, and Commentary* (Cambridge, 2009), 1–55.

(1) Ἐτῶν δεκαεννέα ὢν [44 B.C.E.] τὸ στράτευμα ἐμῆι γνώμηι καὶ ἐμοῖς ἀναλώμασιν ἡτοίμασα, δι' οὗ τὰ κοινὰ πράγματα ἐκ τῆς τῶν συνομοσαμένων δουλήας ἠλευθέρωσα. Ἐφ' οἷς ἡ σύνκλητος ἐπαινέσασά με ψηφίσμασι προκατέλεξε τῆι βουλῆι Γαΐωι Πάνσαι καὶ Αὔλωι Ἱρτίωι ὑπάτοις [43 B.C.E.] ἐν τῆι τάξει τῶν ὑπατευσάντων ἅμα τὸ συμβουλεύειν δοῦσα,	(1) Annos undeviginti natus exercitum privato consilio et privata impensa comparavi, per quem rem publicam a dominatione factionis oppressam in libertatem vindicavi. Eo nomine senatus decretis honorificis in ordinem suum me adlegit, C. Pansa et A. Hirtio consulibus, consularem locum sententiae dicendae simul dans, et imperium mihi dedit. Res publica ne quid detrimenti

ῥάβδους τ' ἐμοὶ ἔδωκεν. Περὶ τὰ δημόσια πράγματα μή τι βλαβῆι, ἐμοὶ μετὰ τῶν ὑπάτων προνοεῖν ἐπέτρεψεν ἀντιστρατήγωι ὄντι. Ὁδὲ δῆμος τῶι αὐτῶι ἐνιαυτῶι ἀμφοτέρων τῶν ὑπάτων ἐν πολέμωι πεπτωκότων ἐμὲ ὕπατον ἀπέδειξεν καὶ τὴν τῶν τριῶν ἀνδρῶν ἔχοντα ἀρχὴν ἐπὶ τῆι καταστάσει τῶν δημοσίων πραγμάτων εἵλατο.

caperet, me pro praetore simul cum consulibus providere iussit. Populus autem eodem anno me consulem, cum consul uterque bello cecidisset, et triumvirum rei publicae constituendae creavit.

(2) Τοὺς τὸν πατέρα μου φονεύσαντας ἐξώρισα κρίσεσιν ἐνδίκοις τειμωρησάμενος αὐτῶν τὸ ἀσέβημα καὶ μετὰ ταῦτα αὐτοὺς πόλεμον ἐπιφέροντας τῆι πατρίδι δὶς ἐνείκησα παρατάξει.

(2) Qui parentem meum interfecerunt, eos in exilium expuli iudiciis legitimis ultus eorum facinus, et postea bellum inferentis rei publicae vici bis acie.

(3) Πολέμους καὶ κατὰ γῆν καὶ κατὰ θάλασσαν ἐμφυλίους καὶ ὀθνείους ἐν ὅληι τῆι οἰκουμένηι πολλάκις ἐποίησα, νεικήσας τε πάντων ἐφεισάμην τῶν περιόντων πολειτῶν. Τὰ ἔθνη, οἷς ἀσφαλὲς ἦν συνγνώμην ἔχειν, ἔσωσα μᾶλλον ἢ ἐξέκοψα. Μυριάδες Ῥωμαίων στρατεύσασαι ὑπὸ τὸν ὅρκον τὸν ἐμον ἐγένοντο ἐνγὺς πεντήκοντα· ἐξ ὧν κατήγαγον εἰς τὰς ἀποικίας ἢ ἀπέπεμψα εἰς τὰς ἰδίας πόλεις ἐκπληρωθέντων τῶν ἐνιαυτῶν τῆς στρατείας μυριάδας ὀλίγωι

(3) Bella terra et mari civilia externaque toto in orbe terrarum saepe gessi, victorque omnibus veniam petentibus civibus peperci. Externas gentes, quibus tuto ignosci potuit, conservare quam excidere malui. Millia civium Romanorum sub sacramento meo fuerunt circiter quingenta. Ex quibus deduxi in colonias aut remisi in municipia sua stipendis emeritis millia aliquanto plura quam trecenta, et iis omnibus agros adsignavi aut pecuniam pro praemiis militiae dedi. Naves

πλείους ἢ τριάκοντα καὶ αὐτοῖς πᾶσιν ἀγροὺς ἐμέρισα ἢ χρήματα ἀντὶ δωρεῶν στρατείας ἔδωκα. Ναῦς εἷλον ἑξακοσίας ἐκτος τούτων, εἵτινες ἥσσονες ἢ τριήρεις ἐγένοντο.

cepi sescentas praeter eas, si quae minores quam triremes fuerunt.

(4) Δὶς ἐπὶ κέλητος ἐθριάμβευσα, τρὶς ἐφ' ἅρματος. Εἰκοσάκις καὶ ἅπαξ προσηγορεύθην αὐτοκράτωρ. Τῆς συνκλήτου ἐμοὶ πλείους θριάμβους ψηφισσαμένης, ὧν πάντων ἀπεσχόμην. Ἀπὸ τῶν ῥάβδων τὴν δάφνην κατεθέμην ἐν τῶι Καπιτωλίωι, τὰς εὐχάς, ἅς ἐν ἑκάστωι τῶι πολέμωι ἐποιησάμην, ἀποδούς. Διὰ τὰς ἐμὰς πράξεις ἢ τὰς τῶν πρεσβευτῶν μου, ἃς αἰσίοις οἰωνοῖς καὶ κατὰ γῆν καὶ κατὰ θάλατταν κατώρθωσα, πεντηκοντάκις καὶ πεντάκις ἐψηφίσατο ἡ σύνκλητος θεοῖς δεῖν θύεσθαι. Ἡμέραι οὖν αὐταὶ ἐκ συνκλήτου δόγματος ἐγένοντο ὀκτακόσιαι ἐνενήκοντα. Ἐν τοῖς ἐμοῖς θριάμβοις πρὸ τοῦ ἐμοῦ ἅρματος βασιλεῖς ἢ βασιλέων παῖδες προήχθησαν ἐννέα. Ὑπάτευον τρὶς καὶ δέκατον, ὅτε ταῦτα ἔγραφον, καὶ ἤμην τριακοστὸν καὶ ἕβδομον δημαρχικῆς ἐξουσίας.

(4) Bis ovans triumphavi et tris egi curulis triumphos et appellatus sum viciens et semel imperator. Decernente pluris triumphos mihi senatu, quibus omnibus supersedi. Laurum de fascibus deposui in Capitolio, votis quae quoque bello nuncupaveram solutis. Ob res a me aut per legatos meos auspicis meis terra marique prospere gestas quinquagiens et quinquiens decrevit senatus supplicandum esse dis immortalibus. Dies autem, per quos ex senatus consulto supplicatum est, fuere DCCCLXXXX. In triumphis meis ducti sunt ante currum meum reges aut regum liberi novem. Consul fueram terdeciens cum scribebam haec, et eram septimum et tricensimum tribuniciae potestatis.

(13) Πύλην Ἐνυάλιον, ἣν κεκλῖσθαι οἱ πατέρες ἡμῶν ἠθέλησαν εἰρηνευομένης τῆς ὑπὸ Ῥωμαίοις πάσης γῆς τε καὶ θαλάσσης, πρὸ μὲν ἐμοῦ, ἐξ οὗ ἡ πόλις ἐκτίσθη, τῶι παντὶ αἰῶνι δὶς μόνον κεκλεῖσθαι ὁμολογεῖται, ἐπὶ δὲ ἐμοῦ ἡγεμόνος τρὶς ἡ σύνκλητος ἐψηφίσατο κλεισθῆναι.

(13) Ianum Quirinum, quem claussum esse maiores nostri voluerunt, cum per totum imperium populi Romani terra marique esset parta victoriis pax, cum, priusquam nascerer, a condita urbe bis omnino clausum fuisse prodatur memoriae, ter me principe senatus claudendum esse censuit.

(24) Εἰς ναοὺς πασῶν πόλεων τῆς Ἀσίας νεικήσας τὰ ἀναθέματα ἀποκατέστησα, ἃ εἶχεν ἰδίαι ἱεροσυλήσας ὁ ὑπ᾽ ἐμοῦ διαγωνισθεὶς πολέμιος. Ἀνδριάντες πεζοὶ καὶ ἔφιπποί μου καὶ ἐφ᾽ ἅρμασιν ἀργυροῖ εἱστήκεισαν ἐν τῆι πόλει ἐνγὺς ὀγδοήκοντα, οὓς αὐτὸς ἦρα, ἐκ τούτου τε τοῦ χρήματος ἀναθέματα χρυσᾶ ἐν τῶι ναῶι τοῦ Ἀπόλλωνος τῶι τε ἐμῶι ὀνόματι καὶ ἐκείνων, οἵτινές με τούτοις τοῖς ἀνδριᾶσιν ἐτείμησαν, ἀνέθηκα.

(24) In templis omnium civitatium provinciae Asiae victor ornamenta reposui quae spoliatis templis is cum quo bellum gesseram privatim possederat. Statuae meae pedestres et equestres et in quadrigeis argenteae steterunt in urbe XXC circiter, quas ipse sustuli, exque ea pecunia dona aurea in aede Apollinis meo nomine et illorum qui mihi statuarum honorem habuerunt posui.

(34) Ἐν ὑπατείαι ἕκτηι καὶ ἑβδόμηι [28–27 B.C.E.] μετὰ τὸ τοὺς ἐνφυλίους ζβέσαι με πολέμους κατὰ εὐχὰς τῶν ἐμῶν πολειτῶν ἐνκρατὴς γενόμενος πάντων τῶν πραγμάτων, ἐκ τῆς ἐμῆς ἐξουσίας εἰς τὴν τῆς

(34) In consulatu sexto et septimo, postquam bella civilia exstinxeram, per consensum universorum potitus rerum omnium, rem publicam ex mea potestate in senatus populique Romani arbitrium transtuli. Quo

συνκλήτου καὶ τοῦ δήμου τῶν Ῥωμαίων μετήνεγκα κυριήαν. Ἐξ ἧς αἰτίας δόγματι συνκλήτου Σεβαστὸς προσηγορεύθην καὶ δάφναις δημοσίαι τὰ πρόπυλά μου ἐστέφθη, ὅ τε δρύινος στέφανος ὁ διδόμενος ἐπὶ σωτηρίαι τῶν πολειτῶν ὑπεράνω τοῦ πυλῶνος τῆς ἐμῆς οἰκίας ἀνετέθη, ὅπλον τε χρυσοῦν ἐν τῶι βουλευτηρίωι ἀνατεθὲν ὑπό τε τῆς συνκλήτου καὶ τοῦ δήμου τῶν Ῥωμαίων διὰ τῆς ἐπιγραφῆς ἀρετὴν καὶ ἐπείκειαν καὶ δικαιοσύνην καὶ εὐσέβειαν ἐμοὶ μαρτυρεῖ. Ἀξιώμὰτι πάντων διήνεγκα, ἐξουσίας δὲ οὐδέν τι πλεῖον ἔσχον τῶν συναρξάντων μοι.

pro merito meo senatus consulto Augustus appellatus sum et laureis postes aedium mearum vestiti publice coronaque civica super ianuam meam fixa est et clupeus aureus in curia Iulia positus, quem mihi senatum populumque Romanum dare virtutis clementiaeque iustitiae et pietatis caussa testatum est per eius clupei inscriptionem. Post id tempus auctoritate omnibus praestiti, potestatis autem nihilo amplius habui quam ceteri qui mihi quoque in magistratu conlegae fuerunt.

(35) Τρισκαιδεκάτην ὑπατείαν [2 B.C.E.] ἄγοντός μου ἥ τε σύνκλητος καὶ τὸ ἱππικὸν τάγμα ὅ τε σύνπας δῆμος τῶν Ῥωμαίων προσηγόρευσέ με πατέρα πατρίδος καὶ τοῦτο ἐπὶ τοῦ προπύλου τῆς οἰκίας μου καὶ ἐν τῶι βουλευτηρίωι καὶ ἐν τῆι ἀγορᾶι τῆι Σεβαστῆι ὑπὸ τῶι ἅρματι, ὅ μοι δόγματι συνκλήτου ἀνετέθη, ἐπιγραφῆναι ἐψηφίσατο. Ὅτε ἔγραφον ταῦτα, ἦγον ἔτος ἑβδομηκοστὸν ἕκτον.

(35) Tertium decimum consulatum cum gerebam, senatus et equester ordo populusque Romanus universus appellavit me patrem patriae, idque in vestibulo aedium mearum inscribendum et in curia Iulia et in foro Aug(usto) sub quadrigis, quae mihi ex s(enatus) c(onsulto) positae sunt censuit. Cum scripsi haec, annum agebam septuagensumum sextum.

For information about the Greek and Latin texts of the *Res Gestae* printed here, please see the sources and credits section at the end of this book.

Notes to Res Gestae Divi Augusti *1–4, 13, 24, 34–35*

These notes are indebted to P. A. Brunt and J. M. Moore, Res Gestae Divi Augusti: *The Achievements of the Divine Augustus* (Oxford, 1967); J. Scheid, Res Gestae Divi Augusti: *Hauts faits du Divin Auguste* (Paris, 2007); and A. E. Cooley, Res Gestae Divi Augusti: *Text, Translation, and Commentary* (Cambridge, 2009).

(1) δεκαεννέα ὢν. Augustus describes the immediate aftermath of Caesar's death on the Ides of March in 44 B.C.E.

ἐμῆι γνώμηι. i.e., Octavian acted on his own initiative. The Greek does not translate the Latin *privato,* which indicates that he acted not as a magistrate but as a private citizen.

συνομοσαμένων. mas. pl. gen., aor. mid. part. < συνομνύω / συνόμνυμι. *take an oath together*; i.e., *form a conspiracy.* In the Greek, Octavian liberated the state from those who conspired to assassinate Caesar; in the Latin, he did so from the domination of a faction.

δουλήας = Attic δουλείας.

σύνκλητος, -ου (fem.). *(Roman) Senate.*

προκαταλέγω. *add X* (+ acc.) *to Y* (+ dat.).

τὸ συμβουλεύειν. When the Senate's presider asked the assembled for their opinions, he did so in an order established by precedent. Octavian was now counted among the ex-consuls (ἐν τῆι τάξει τῶν ὑπατευσάντων), the first group consulted, though he had never held the consulship.

ῥάβδοι, -ων (fem. pl.). *fasces.* On the word, see also notes on sections **(1)** of A2 and **(53.8)** of B2. A bundle of rods tied with a leather thong carried before magistrates, the fasces manifested the licit right to command an army (*imperium*); hence ῥάβδοι here translates the Latin *imperium,* a word that is rendered variously in the Greek *RG*: see 8, 13, 26, 27, 30.

τι is the subject of βλαβῆι.

βλαβῆι. 3rd sg. aor. pass. subj. < βλάπτω. The verb is subj. in a negative purpose clause. The language indicates that the

Senate conveyed this authority through an emergency decree (*senatus consultum ultimum*).

ἀντιστράτηγος, -ου (mas.). *propraetor*: LSJ, s.v. II, 2; Mason, *Greek Terms,* 106–7.

πεπτωκότων. Hirtius and Pansa died in April 43; Octavian and Quintus Pedius were elected suffect (i.e., replacement) consuls on August 19 of that year.

τριῶν ἀνδρῶν. Octavian, Antony, and Lepidus were appointed triumvirs on November 27, 43 in a law proposed by the tribune Publius Titius.

εἵλατο = Attic εἵλετο. 3rd sg. aor. mid. ind. < αἱρέω. In later Greek, alpha often replaces the thematic vowels epsilon and omicron in the strong aorist endings.

(2) φονεύσαντας. This word is a conjecture, as the text here and for the corresponding Latin *interfecerunt* is unsure.

ἐξορίζω. *expel, banish.*

κρίσεσιν ἐνδίκοις. Caesar's killers were convicted *in absentia* by a special court established through a law proposed by Octavian's consular colleague, Pedius.

τειμωρησάμενος = τιμωρησάμενος. Long iotas are indicated in the inscription by the diphthong ει.

πατρίδι. The Greek renders *res publica* by the more emotionally charged πατρίς.

δὶς. This refers to the two battles fought on October 3 and 23 in the year 42, at Philippi in Macedonia between Octavian and Caesar's assassins, even though the first battle was a draw.

ἐνείκησα = ἐνίκησα; see gloss on τειμωρησάμενος above.

(3) Πολέμους. Instead of continuing chronologically, the text now proceeds topically.

ἐμφύλιος = ἔμφυλος, -ον. lit., *within the tribe*; here, *civil, internal.*

ἐν ὅληι τῆι οἰκουμένηι. This mention of worldwide conquest invites the reader to compare Augustus with Alexander the Great and his epigones, including, e.g., the Roman generalissimo and rival of Julius Caesar, Pompey the Great.

ἐφεισάμην. i.e., Octavian displays clemency, one of the four imperial virtues: see **(34)** below. The text may draw attention to this quality to counterbalance Octavian's reputation, evinced in other sources, for maltreating the vanquished.

περίειμι. *survive*: LSJ, s.v. περίειμι (εἰμί), III.

Μυριάδες . . . ἐνγὺς (= ἐγγὺς) πεντήκοντα. *nearly fifty ten-thousands*; i.e., five hundred thousand.

ἐκπληρωθέντων τῶν ἐνιαυτῶν. *when their years were fulfilled*; i.e., when the soldiers had finished their terms of military service.

ὀλίγωι. dat. degree of difference: Smyth 1513.

ἀντὶ. *as*.

δωρεῶν = δώρων. Roman generals were expected to provide veterans upon their discharge either donatives (cash payouts) or land.

εἴτινες = εἴ τινες.

(4) ἐπὶ κέλητος. In a triumph, a spectacular parade through the city of Rome that celebrated a general's victory, the commander rode in a chariot; in an ovation, a kind of junior-grade triumph, the general rode a horse or went on foot. Ovation is not easily translated into Greek; hence the Greek distinguishes that procession from a triumph by the general's mode of conveyance. See further note on section **(53.7)** of B2, s.v. θριαμβεύω; for a memorable account of a triumph, see D5–D6.

αὐτοκράτωρ. A victorious general might be hailed by his troops as αὐτοκράτωρ (= Latin *imperator*); see further note on section **(16.6)** of C2. Having been so declared, he would thereafter report his exploits to the Senate in dispatches decorated with laurel and adorn his fasces with the same plant, which was associated with victory. On laurel, see also note on section **(16.4)** of C2, s.v. τό . . . προτίθεσθαι, τὸ . . . ἀρτᾶσθαι.

ἀπέχω. in mid., *decline* + gen. In this text, Augustus is keen to document the honors and offices he licitly accepted as well as those he declined; his demurrals draw attention to his restraint and respect for traditional customs.

Καπιτωλίωι. At the end of the triumph, the general dedicated the laurels from his fasces to Jupiter Optimus Maximus in the god's temple on the Capitoline Hill; a general who did not receive a triumph but was acclaimed *imperator* might do the same.

ἀποδίδωμι. *pay for*; the verb illustrates well the transactional nature of Roman religion.

πρεσβευτής, -οῦ (mas.). *deputy, legate*: LSJ, s.v. II.2.

οἰωνός, -οῦ (mas.). *(ominous) bird*; i.e., a bird of divinatory significance: LSJ, s.v. II. Before he took significant action, a high Roman magistrate had to divine the gods' approval by taking the auspices; i.e., by ritually observing birds in flight. The Greek αἰσίοις οἰωνοῖς is an explanatory equivalent of the Latin "under my auspices" (*auspicis meis*), which indicates explicitly that Augustus's legates operate under his authority.

θεοῖς δεῖν θύεσθαι. After news of a victory, the Senate might order a *supplicatio,* a day or more of thanksgiving and sacrifice to the gods.

ὀκτακόσιαι ἐνενήκοντα. *890.*

προήχθησαν. 3rd pl. aor. pass. ind. < προάγω. Vanquished monarchs and their families were often paraded in the triumph.

ὅτε ταῦτα ἔγραφον. See final note on this selection.

ἤμην = ἦν.

τριακοστὸν καὶ ἕβδομον. *thirty-seventh (year).*

δημαρχικὴ ἐξουσία = Latin *tribunicia potestas,* the power of a tribune (without necessarily *being* a tribune). It gave the emperor the authority to summon the Senate and popular assembly, make motions in the former and propose legislation in the latter, veto other magistrates' actions, protect citizens from undue abuse from other magistrates, and compel citizens to do what he asked. It also made his person sacrosanct. Emperors dated their reigns by their receipt of tribunician power, which was renewed yearly. See further Brunt and Moore, Res Gestae, 10–12.

(13) Πύλην Ἐνυάλιον = Latin Janus Quirinus. The reader of the Latin text, presumably familiar with what is being described, knows that, by synecdoche (Smyth 3047), closing Janus Quirinus means shutting the gate (or gates) of that god's shrine, which stood in the northeast part of the Forum Romanum, near the Curia (Senate House) and the Forum of Julius Caesar. The Greek clarifies the situation for the reader, indicating that it was in fact a gate that was closed.

Ἐνυάλιος, -ου (mas.). Originally an epithet of Ares, the word is "divorced" from that god in order to stand in for the Roman divinity Quirinus, who does not have a Greek equivalent.

κεκλ(ε)ῖσθαι < κλείω. *shut.*

θαλάσσης. Conspicuously absent from the Greek is the Latin *parta victoriis pax,* "a peace born from victories," a key sentiment in Augustan ideology; also glossed over is the Latin phrase *per totum imperium,* "throughout the entire empire."

ἐξ οὗ. *since.*

δὶς μόνον. *only twice*; i.e., by Numa (A7.1), according to tradition, for forty-three years and again briefly in 235 B.C.E., after the First Punic War.

ὁμολογεῖται. Translate as an impersonal pass.

ἐπί + gen. *in the time of X*: LSJ, s.v. A.II.

ἡγεμών is a broader and more generic term than the Latin *princeps,* which is crucial to Augustus's self-presentation; for a nuanced discussion of the differences between the terms, see Cooley, Res Gestae, ad loc.

τρὶς. Although the Senate thrice authorized the closure, only twice were the gates closed.

(24) Ἀσίας. This is the first time that a location outside Italy is mentioned in the *RG*: Cooley, Res Gestae, ad loc. The Greek here omits the word "province" (*provincia*) found in the Latin; the word is translated elsewhere in the Greek *RG* (ἐπαρχείαι, 25), but only when it refers to western *provinciae.* Pillaging artworks from conquered regions was standard practice among Roman generals (B7).

ὁ ὑπ' ἐμοῦ διαγωνισθεὶς. Augustus does not mention his enemy, in this case Mark Antony, by name; see further the introduction to this passage. The Greek here is stronger than the Latin, which refers to Antony as "the one with whom I had waged war" (*is cum quo bellum gesseram*).

εἱστήκεισαν. 3rd pl. plupf. act. ind. < ἵστημι.

ἦρα. 1st sg. aor. act. ind. < αἴρω: Smyth 544.c.

ἐν τῶι ναῶι τοῦ Ἀπόλλωνος. A Temple of Apollo, a god with whom Augustus associated himself, was built by the emperor near his house on the Palatine Hill.

ἀνατίθημι. *dedicate* (as a votive), whence the noun ἀνάθημα, -ατος (neu.) above.

(34) ζβέσαι = σβέσαι. aor. act. inf. < σβέννυμι / σβεννύω. *quell, exstinguish.*

κατὰ . . . πολειτῶν. Cf. Latin *per consensum universorum*, "with the consent of all."

πολειτῶν. Again, the diphthong ει represents a long iota.

ἐνκρατής, -ές. *being in possession of, in control of* + gen.: LSJ, s.v. III.

κυριήαν = Attic κυριείαν < κυριεία, -ας (fem.). *proprietary rights.* The Greek is more explicit about Augustus's possession of quasi-monarchical power (as early as 28–27 B.C.E.) than the Latin: Cooley, Res Gestae, ad loc. The climax of the two-year "transfer of ownership" was the First Settlement of January 27 (C2).

Σεβαστὸς = Augustus, a title decreed by the Senate on January 16, 27. On its significance, see note on section **(16.8)** of C2.

δάφναις . . . ἀνετέθη. On the significance of the laurels and the oak crown, see note on section **(16.4)** of C2, s.v. τό . . . προτίθεσθαι, τὸ . . . ἀρτᾶσθαι.

δημοσίαι. adverbial, *publicly*: LSJ, s.v. δημόσιος, V.1.

πρόπυλα, -ων (neu. pl.). *entrance.*

ὅπλον is the subject of μαρτυρεῖ. While the shield from the Curia has been lost, a marble copy of it nearly a meter in diameter has been found in Arles; it is also frequently represented in art and coinage from the Augustan Age.

βουλευτηρίωι is a more generic reference to the Curia Iulia, as the Latin makes clear.

ἀνατεθὲν. neu. sg. nom., aor. pass. part.

ἀρετὴν . . . εὐσέβειαν = the four imperial virtues. The entire *RG* implicitly testifies to Augustus's possession thereof; here at the climax of the text, they are explicitly named. The Latin indicates that the shield was set up *because of* (*caussa*) Augustus's virtues, whereas the Greek indicates that the shield merely testifies to them.

διήνεγκα < διαφέρω. *excel X* (+ acc.) *in Y* (+ dat.).

(35) τὸ ἱππικὸν τάγμα. *the equestrian order.*

πατέρα πατρίδος = Latin *patrem patriae* = *father of the fatherland.* The title casts Augustus not just as a father figure but also as a savior and new founder of Rome: see Cooley, Res Gestae, ad loc. and notes on **(18.3)** of C2.

ἀγορᾶι τῆι Σεβαστῆι. i.e., the Forum of Augustus.

ἦγον ἔτος ἑβδομηκοστὸν ἕκτον. The text in its published form can thus be precisely dated: it was written on or after September 22, 13 C.E., Augustus's birthday, and before August 19, 14, the day of the emperor's death. Some have suggested that the document was drafted earlier and revised over time: Cooley, Res Gestae, 42–43.

C4. SOUND EMPEROR, SOUND EMPIRE

Philo *Embassy to Gaius* 2.8–3.21

Philo (c. 15 B.C.E.–c. 45 C.E.) belonged to a prominent Jewish family from Alexandria with ties to the Herods, Levantine client-kings who were supported by Rome (D1), and the imperial court: Philo's nephew, Tiberius Julius Alexander, was prefect of Egypt and the future emperor Titus's (reg. 79–81 C.E.) chief adviser in the Jewish War (D3–D6). Like other authors in this volume, Philo straddled worlds: he was a member of a large, semi-autonomous Jewish community in a cosmopolitan Greek city situated in Egypt and governed by a Roman prefect. Learned in both Hellenic *paideia* and the Hebrew scriptures, he wrote several studies of the Torah or Pentateuch, the first five books of the Old Testament, which demonstrate Philo's belief that Greek philosophy and Judaism are not only compatible but mutually illuminating.

What Philo thought about Rome is disputed, for he often discussed the topic obliquely. How did he square his belief that the Jews were God's elect with claims that Rome's universal rule was providential? Some scholars have read him as anti-Roman, a crypto-critic; others have seen him as more sanguine about his rulers. Also debated is how active Philo was in politics. We do know that after anti-Jewish riots broke out in Alexandria, a city prone to civic unrest, in August 38 C.E., Philo and a delegation of his coreligionists from that city sailed to Rome to seek redress from the emperor, Gaius Caligula (reg. 37–41 C.E.). Philo offers a vivid account of the riots and diplomatic mission in his *Embassy to Gaius,* written during the reign of that emperor's successor, Claudius (reg. 41–54), who seems to be the primary audience of this parenetic invective that warns against attacks on God's chosen people. In the passage below, which describes the early months of Gaius's reign, Philo adds a twist to the ancient commonplace that the body politic is like a human body. So influential is the *princeps* that the empire is only as healthy as the emperor himself. When he is well, a golden age is about to dawn; when he is unwell, the empire falls apart.

Further Reading

E. R. Goodenough, *An Introduction to Philo Judaeus,* 2nd ed. (Oxford, 1962), 52–74; D. R. Schwartz, "Philo, His Family, and His Times," in *The Cambridge Companion to Philo,* ed. A. Kamesar, 9–31 (Cambridge, 2009); K. Berthelot, "Philo's Perception of the Roman Empire," *Journal for the Study of Judaism* 42 (2011): 166–87; T. Seland, "Philo as Citizen: *Homo Politicus,*" in *Reading Philo: A Handbook to Philo of Alexandria,* ed. T. Seland, 47–74 (Grand Rapids, 2014).

(2.8) Τίς γὰρ ἰδὼν Γάιον μετὰ τὴν Τιβερίου Καίσαρος τελευτὴν παρειληφότα τὴν ἡγεμονίαν πάσης γῆς καὶ θαλάσσης ἀστασίαστον καὶ εὔνομον καὶ πᾶσι τοῖς μέρεσιν ἡρμοσμένην εἰς τὸ σύμφωνον, ἑῴοις, ἑσπερίοις, μεσημβρινοῖς, ἀρκτικοῖς—τοῦ μὲν βαρβαρικοῦ γένους τῷ Ἑλληνικῷ, τοῦ δ' Ἑλληνικοῦ τῷ βαρβαρικῷ, καὶ τοῦ μὲν στρατιωτικοῦ τῷ κατὰ πόλεις, τοῦ δὲ πολιτικοῦ τῷ στρατευομένῳ συμφρονήσαντος εἰς μετουσίαν καὶ ἀπόλαυσιν εἰρήνης—οὐκ ἐθαύμασε καὶ κατεπλάγη τῆς ὑπερφυοῦς καὶ παντὸς λόγου κρείττονος εὐπραγίας, **(9)** ἐξ ἑτοίμου τἀγαθὰ ἀθρόα σωρηδὸν κεκληρονομηκότα, παμπληθεῖς θησαυροὺς χρημάτων, ἄργυρον καὶ χρυσόν, τὸν μὲν ὡς ὕλην, τὸν δὲ ὡς νόμισμα, τὸν δὲ ὡς προκόσμημα δι' ἐκπωμάτων καί τινων ἑτέρων ἃ πρὸς ἐπίδειξιν τεχνιτεύεται, παμπληθεῖς δυνάμεις, πεζάς, ἱππικάς, ναυτικάς, προσόδους ὥσπερ ἐκ πηγῶν ἀενάῳ τινὶ φορᾷ χορηγουμένας, **(10)** ἀρχὴν ... [Philo details at some length the empire's vast geography] ... τὴν ἀφ' ἡλίου ἀνιόντος ἄχρι δυομένου τήν τε ἐντὸς ὠκεανοῦ καὶ ὑπερωκεάνιον; ἐφ' οἷς ὅ τε Ῥωμαίων δῆμος ἐγεγήθει καὶ πᾶσα Ἰταλία τά τε Ἀσιανὰ καὶ Εὐρωπαῖα ἔθνη. **(11)** ὡς γὰρ ἐπ' οὐδενὶ τῶν πώποτε γενομένων αὐτοκρατόρων ἅπαντες ἠγάσθησαν, κτῆσιν καὶ χρῆσιν ἰδίων τε καὶ κοινῶν ἀγαθῶν οὐκ ἐλπίζοντες ἕξειν, ἀλλ' ἔχειν ἤδη νομίζοντες πλήρωμά τινος εὐτυχίας, ἐφεδρευούσης εὐδαιμονίας. **(12)** οὐδὲν γοῦν ἦν ἰδεῖν ἕτερον κατὰ πόλεις ἢ βωμούς, ἱερεῖα, θυσίας, λευχειμονοῦντας, ἐστεφανωμένους, φαιδρούς, εὐμένειαν ἐξ ἱλαρᾶς τῆς ὄψεως προφαίνοντας, ἑορτάς, πανηγύρεις, μουσικοὺς ἀγῶνας, ἱπποδρομίας, κώμους, παννυχίδας μετ' αὐλῶν καὶ κιθάρας, τέρψεις, ἀνέσεις, ἐκεχειρίας, παντοίας ἡδονὰς διὰ πάσης αἰσθήσεως. **(13)** τότε οὐ πλούσιοι πενήτων προὔφερον, οὐκ ἔνδοξοι ἀδόξων, οὐ δανεισταὶ χρεωστῶν, οὐ δεσπόται δούλων περιῆσαν, ἰσονομίαν τοῦ καιροῦ διδόντος, ὡς τὸν παρὰ ποιηταῖς ἀναγραφέντα Κρονικὸν βίον μηκέτι νομίζεσθαι πλάσμα μύθου διά τε τὴν εὐθηνίαν καὶ εὐετηρίαν τό τε ἄλυπον καὶ ἄφοβον καὶ τὰς πανοικίας ὁμοῦ καὶ πανδήμους μεθ' ἡμέραν τε καὶ νύκτωρ εὐφροσύνας, αἳ μέχρι μηνῶν ἑπτὰ τῶν πρώτων ἄπαυστοι καὶ συνεχεῖς ἐγένοντο. **(14)** τῷ δὲ ὀγδόῳ κατασκήπτει βαρεῖα νόσος τῷ Γαΐῳ τὴν πρὸ μικροῦ δίαιταν, ὅτε ἔζη Τιβέριος, εὐκολωτέραν καὶ διὰ τοῦτο ὑγιεινοτέραν οὖσαν εἰς πολυτέλειαν μεθαρμοσαμένῳ. πολὺς γὰρ ἄκρατος καὶ ὀψοφαγίαι καὶ ἐπὶ πλήρεσι τοῖς ὄγκοις ἀπλήρωτοι ἐπιθυμίαι θερμολουσίαι τε ἄκαιροι καὶ ἔμετοι καὶ εὐθὺς πάλιν οἰνοφλυγίαι καὶ ἔφεδροι γαστριμαργίαι, λαγνεῖαι διὰ παίδων καὶ γυναικῶν, καὶ ὅσα ἄλλα καθαιρετικὰ ψυχῆς καὶ σώματος καὶ τῶν ἐν ἑκατέρῳ δεσμῶν συνεπέθετο. τὰ δὲ ἐπίχειρα ἐγκρατείας μὲν ὑγεία καὶ ἰσχύς, ἀκρασίας δὲ ἀσθένεια καὶ νόσος γειτνιῶσα θανάτῳ.

(3.15) Διαγγελείσης οὖν τῆς ὅτι νοσεῖ φήμης, ἔτι πλοΐμων ὄντων—ἀρχὴ γὰρ ἦν μετοπώρου, τελευταῖος πλοῦς τοῖς θαλαττεύουσιν, ἀπὸ τῶν πανταχόθεν ἐμπορίων εἰς τοὺς οἰκείους λιμένας καὶ ὑποδρόμους ἐπανιοῦσι, καὶ μάλιστα οἷς πρόνοια τοῦ μὴ διαχειμάζειν ἐπὶ ξένης ἐστί—μεθέμενοι τὸν ἁβροδίαιτον βίον ἐσκυθρώπαζον, συννοίας τε καὶ κατηφείας πᾶσα οἰκία καὶ πόλις γεγένητο μεστή, ἰσορρόπῳ λύπῃ τῆς πρὸ μικροῦ χαρᾶς ἀμφικλινοῦς γενομένης. **(16)** τὰ γὰρ μέρη πάντα τῆς οἰκουμένης αὐτῷ συνενόσησε, βαρυτέρᾳ νόσῳ χρησάμενα τῆς κατασχούσης Γάιον· ἐκείνη μὲν γὰρ σώματος ἦν αὐτὸ μόνον, ἡ δὲ τῶν πανταχοῦ πάντων, ψυχικῆς εὐσθενείας, εἰρήνης, ἐλπίδων, μετουσίας καὶ ἀπολαύσεως ἀγαθῶν. **(17)** ἀνεπόλουν γὰρ ὅσα καὶ ἡλίκα κακὰ ἐξ ἀναρχίας φύεται· λιμόν, πόλεμον, δενδροτομίας, δῃώσεις χωρίων, στερήσεις χρημάτων, ἀπαγωγάς, τοὺς περὶ δουλείας καὶ θανάτου φόβους ἀνηκέστους, ὧν ἰατρὸς ἦν οὐδείς, μίαν ἐχόντων θεραπείαν τὸ ῥωσθῆναι Γάιον. **(18)** ὅτε γοῦν ἤρξατο λωφᾶν ἡ νόσος, ἐν βραχεῖ καὶ οἱ μέχρι περάτων συνῄσθοντο—φήμης γὰρ οὐδὲν ὠκύτερον—, καὶ μετέωρος πᾶσα πόλις ἦν ἀκοῆς ἀεὶ διψῶσα βελτίονος, ἕως διὰ τῶν ἐπιφοιτώντων παντελὴς ῥῶσις εὐηγγελίσθη, δι᾽ ἣν πάλιν ἐξ ὑπαρχῆς ἐπὶ τὰς αὐτὰς ἐτρέποντο θυμηδίας, ἰδίαν ἑαυτῶν νομίζουσαι σωτηρίαν πᾶσαι μὲν ἤπειροι πᾶσαι δὲ νῆσοι. **(19)** μέμνηται γὰρ οὐδεὶς τοσαύτην μιᾶς χώρας ἢ ἑνὸς ἔθνους γενέσθαι χαρὰν ἐπὶ σωτηρίᾳ καὶ καταστάσει ἡγεμόνος, ὅσην ἐπὶ Γαΐῳ συμπάσης τῆς οἰκουμένης καὶ παραλαβόντι τὴν ἀρχὴν καὶ ῥωσθέντι ἐκ τῆς ἀσθενείας. **(20)** ὥσπερ γὰρ ἐκ νομάδος βίου καὶ θηριώδους νῦν πρῶτον ἀρχόμενοι μεταβάλλειν πρὸς τὸ σύννομον καὶ ὁμοδίαιτον καὶ ἐξ ἐρημίας καὶ σηκῶν καὶ ὑπωρειῶν εἰσοικίζεσθαι πόλεσι τειχήρεσι καὶ ἐξ ἀνεπιτροπεύτου ζωῆς ὑπὸ ἐπιτρόπῳ τάττεσθαι νομεῖ τινι καὶ ἀγελάρχῃ τῆς ἡμερωτέρας ἀγέλης ἐγεγήθεσαν ἀγνοίᾳ τῆς ἀληθείας· **(21)** τυφλώττει γὰρ ὁ ἀνθρώπινος νοῦς πρὸς τὴν τοῦ συμφέροντος ὄντως αἴσθησιν εἰκασίᾳ καὶ στοχασμῷ μᾶλλον ἢ ἐπιστήμῃ χρῆσθαι δυνάμενος.

Notes to Philo Embassy to Gaius *2.8–3.21*

These notes are indebted to E. M. Smallwood, *Philonis Alexandrini Legatio ad Gaium,* 2nd ed. (Leiden, 1970).

(2.8) παρειληφότα. mas. sg. acc., pf. act. part. < παραλαμβάνω. *inherit, succeed to.*

ἀστασίαστον, εὔνομον. These two-termination compound adjectives (Smyth 288–89) modify τὴν ἡγεμονίαν.

ἡρμοσμένην. fem. sg. acc., pf. pass. part. < ἁρμόζω. A suggestively multivalent verb: *join, fit together, regulate, tune.*

εἰς τὸ σύμφωνον. *harmoniously.* Philo gilds the empire's state at the time of Tiberius's death on March 16, 37 C.E., to make its decline under Gaius (read on) seem all the more steep.

τοῦ μὲν βαρβαρικοῦ γένους. gen. absolute, to be taken with συμφρονήσαντος below.

τῷ κατὰ πόλεις. i.e., the citizen, as opposed to the soldier. Philo employs chiasmus (Smyth 3020) to underscore the unity among the empire's residents.

ἐθαύμασε here takes a gen.; the subject is Τίς in the opening line.

κατεπλάγη. 3rd sg. aor. pass. ind. < καταπλήσσω. *astound, amaze* + gen. of what causes the astonishment.

παντὸς λόγου κρείττονος. *greater than all reckoning.*

εὐπραγία, -ας (fem.). *success, wellbeing.*

(9) ἐξ ἑτοίμου. *immediately.*

σωρηδόν. *en masse.*

κεκληρονομηκότα < κληρονομέω. *inherit.* The part. agrees with Γάιον. This section may not be as hyperbolic as it appears, for Tiberius, a sound financial manager, kept the imperial coffers full.

ὡς ὕλην. i.e., as bullion.

προκόσμημα, -ατος (neu.). *(gaudy) ornament.*

δι' = διὰ. *in the form of.*

ἐπίδειξις, -εως (fem.). *display.* There may be wordplay here, for ἐπίδειξις may also refer to a ceremonial or "display" speech of praise or blame, which is, arguably, what Philo's *Embassy* is. For another speech of such a kind, see C6.

δύναμις, -εως (fem.). *military force,* as the subsequent words suggest: LSJ, s.v. 3.

προσόδος, -ου (fem.). *revenue, income.*

χορηγέω. *supply (generously)*: LSJ, s.v. 3.

(10) ἀρχή, -ῆς (fem.). *empire*: LSJ, s.v. II.2.

ὑπερωκεάνιον; Note the punctuation; the question is finally coming to an end.

ἐγεγήθει < γηθέω. *rejoice.* This verb is defective; the pf. should be translated as pres. and the plupf. as impf.: Smyth 1947, 1952.a. Although the verb has multiple subjects, in number it agrees with the nearest one, δῆμος: Smyth 966.

(11) αὐτοκράτωρ, -ορος (mas.). *emperor*; see further notes on sections **(16.6)** of C2 and **(4)** of C3.

ἠγάσθησαν < ἄγαμαι. *be delighted with* + dat.: LSJ, s.v. I.5. Coins, statues, and inscriptions confirm that Gaius's accession was greeted favorably: Smallwood, *Philonis,* ad loc.

ἐφεδρεύω. *accompany, attend.* ἐφεδρευούσης εὐδαιμονίας is gen. absolute.

(12) οὐδὲν . . . ἕτερον is the object of ἰδεῖν, a complementary inf. triggered by ἦν, *it was possible.*

κατά + acc. here is distributive: *throughout, in each and every*: Smyth 1690.2.c.

θυσίας. Philo later says that Jews in Jerusalem thrice offered hecatombs in the Temple on Gaius's behalf: 45.356.

λευχειμονοῦντας. *people wearing white clothes*; white was associated with purity and the divine.

ἄνεσις, -εως (fem.). *relaxation, indulgence.* In this lavish list, asyndeton (Smyth 3016), pleonasm (Smyth 3042), and *accumulatio* (the "heaping up" of words) convey the superabundant goodwill felt by the empire's subjects toward Gaius.

ἐκεχειρία, -ας (fem.). *holiday*: LSJ, s.v. 2.

(13) προφέρω. *be superior to* + gen. Philo now deploys antithesis and parallel construction to great effect.

τοῦ καιροῦ διδόντος. Take the gen. absolute as causal.

ὡς here introduces a result clause.

Κρονικὸν βίον. As early as Hesiod (c. 700 B.C.E.), the reign of Cronus, Zeus's father, was reckoned a paradisaical golden age; at various points during the early empire, poets sang that a golden age was soon to return or had arrived (e.g., under Augustus and early in Nero's reign).

νομίζεσθαι functions here as a linking verb: LSJ, s.v. νομίζω, II.

πλάσμα is predicative with τὸν παρὰ ποιηταῖς ἀναγραφέντα Κρονικὸν βίον.

μεθ' = μετὰ. *during.*

μέχρι μηνῶν ἑπτὰ. i.e., from Gaius's accession on March 16 through mid-October, 37 C.E.

(14) κατασκήπτει. Here, at the turning point in the passage, Philo employs the historical present for vividness: Smyth 1883.

βαρεῖα νόσος. Scholars do not agree about what ailed Gaius.

τῷ Γαΐῳ agrees with μεθαρμοσαμένῳ at the sentence's end.

πρὸ μικροῦ. *until quite recently, just a bit before.*

ὅτε ἔζη Τιβέριος. Gaius lived with Tiberius on Capri from 31 C.E. until the latter's death; Suetonius contradicts Philo's account of Gaius's abstemiousness: *Gaius* 11.

εὔκολος, -ον. lit., *with a good colon*; i.e., *simple* or *moderate in diet.*

μεθαρμόζω. *change, alter*; the object is τὴν πρὸ μικροῦ δίαιταν.

ὀψοφαγία, -ας (fem.). *fancy food.*

ἐπὶ . . . ἐπιθυμίαι. i.e., even when his belly was full, Gaius's appetite was insatiable.

ἔφεδροι γαστριμαργίαι. *serial acts of gluttony.* Philo's over-the-top vocabulary suits Gaius's excessive behavior.

λαγνεία, -ας (fem.). *(salacious) sex.*

τῶν ἐν ἑκατέρῳ δεσμῶν. i.e., those things that link the soul and body.

συνεπέθετο < συνεπιτίθημι. *join in attacking X* + dat. (τῷ Γαΐῳ).

ἐπίχειρα, -ων (neu. pl.). *wages, rewards.*

ἐγκράτεια, -ας (fem.). *self-mastery, self-control.* Philo caps the description of Gaius's debauchery with a moralizing apothegm.

(3.15) Διαγγελείσης. fem. sg. gen., aor. pass. part., triggering indirect discourse.

ἔτι πλοΐμων ὄντων. *since (the season) was still favorable for sailing*: LSJ, s.v. πλώιμος, 2.

πλοῦς. contracted mas. sg. nom. < πλόος, -ος (mas.). *time of sailing.*

ὑπόδρομος, -ου (mas.). *haven, mooring.*

ἐπανιοῦσι. mas. pl. dat., pres. fut. part. < ἐπανέρχομαι. *return.*

οἷς. dat. of possession.

ἐπὶ ξένης. sc. γῆς: Smyth 1027.b.

ἁβροδίαιτος, -ον. *luxurious.* Philo is, apparently, not hyperbolizing; during Gaius's illness, anxiety pervaded the populace, among which socializing and even bathing were banned: Smallwood, *Philonis,* ad loc.

σκυθρωπάζω. *look sad* or *angry.*

σύννοια, -ας (fem.). *anxiety*: LSJ, s.v. 2.

γεγένητο. 3rd sg. plupf. dep. ind. The plupf. is not always augmented in later Greek.

ἰσόρροπος, -ον. *of equal weight*; ἰσορρόπῳ λύπῃ is dat. of cause.

ἀμφικλινής, -ές. *wavering, flagging.*

(16) ἐκείνη. i.e., Gaius's illness, contrasted with the illness afflicting the οἰκουμένη.

αὐτὸ μόνον. *only, merely.* In this phrase, which is common in Philo's Greek, the pronoun intensifies the adverb: Smallwood, *Philonis,* ad loc.

εὐσθένεια, -ας (fem.). *strength, toughness.*

μετουσίας καὶ ἀπολαύσεως. cf. εἰς μετουσίαν καὶ ἀπόλαυσιν in **(2.8)**.

(17) ἀναπολέω. here, inchoative impf. (Smyth 1900): *began to dig up*; i.e., *repeat, discuss again.* Gaius's accession portended a return of a golden age; his illness threatened a return to anarchy.

δενδροτομία, -ας (fem.). lit. *tree-cutting*; i.e., agricultural *devastation*. In an agrarian economy, the felling of trees is especially destructive, for it can take years for saplings to bear fruit.

δῄωσις, -εως (fem.). *destruction, ravaging.*

στέρησις, -εως (fem.). *confiscation.*

ἀνήκεστος, -ον. *incurable.*

ὧν . . . Γάιον. *for which (fears) there was no doctor, since they had as their only cure the recovery of Gaius.*

(18) λωφάω. *abate, wane*: LSJ, s.v. 4.

ἐν βραχεῖ. *in a short period of time, quickly.*

συνῄσθοντο. 3rd pl. aor. dep. ind. < συναισθάνομαι. *perceive simultaneously.*

μετέωρος, -ον. *in suspense*: LSJ, s.v. III.

διψάω. *thirst for* + gen.

ἐπιφοιτάω. *visit.*

ἐξ ὑπαρχῆς. *afresh, anew*: LSJ, s.v. ὑπαρχή, II.2.

θυμηδία, -ας (fem.). *gladness of heart, rejoicing*: LSJ, s.v.

(19) μέμνηται. 3rd sg. pf. mid. ind. < μιμνήσκω. Here the verb triggers acc. + inf. indirect discourse.

μιᾶς χώρας . . . ἑνὸς ἔθνους. subjective genitives: Smyth 1330.

(20) πρῶτον. *for the first time.* Philo likens the effects of Gaius's recovery to primordial humankind's emergence from a state of nature into civilized life.

ἀρχόμενοι here triggers complementary infinitives: *beginning to X.*

ὁμοδίαιτος, -ον. *shared, communal.*

σηκός, -οῦ (mas.). *pen, enclosure* (for animals). The manuscripts may here be corrupt, as the word seems odd in the context.

ὑπώρεια, -ας (fem.). *foothill* of a mountain range.

εἰσοικίζω. in mid., *settle (oneself) in* + dat.

ἀνεπιτρόπευτος, -ον. *without a guardian.*

νομεῖ τινι, ἀγελάρχῃ are in apposition with ἐπιτρόπῳ. The comparison of a ruler with a shepherd is as old as Homer: Smallwood, *Philonis,* ad loc.

ἐγεγήθεσαν. See note on section **(10)**, s.v. ἐγεγήθει.

(21) τυφλώττω. *be blind.* As in **(14)**, Philo marks a section's end with a maxim.

πρός + acc. *with respect to*: Smyth 1695.3.c.

τοῦ συμφέροντος ὄντως. *of what is truly beneficial.*

εἰκασία, -ας (fem.). *conjecture, misapprehension.*

στοχασμός, -οῦ (mas.). *guesswork.*

C5. BOUDICCA BASHES ROME

Cassius Dio 62.3–5

In 43 C.E., a Roman army invaded Britain, then populated by a patchwork of peoples, and over the next few years fought to bring the island under Roman control. Individual tribes continued to resist, including the powerful Iceni, who dwelled near modern-day Norfolk, northeast of London. The Iceni rebelled in 47; after quashing the revolt, the Romans installed Prasutagus on the Icenian throne as a client-king, hoping thereby to ensure the tribe's loyalty. In his will, Prasutagus, trying to keep the Romans at bay, named not only his two daughters but also the emperor Nero (reg. 54–68 C.E.) as his heirs. This testamentary arrangement backfired: the Romans confiscated the lands of the Icenian elite, raped Prasutagus's daughters, and beat his widow, Boudicca (a.k.a. Boudica, Boadicea). How did Boudicca respond? In 60 or 61, she led a rebellion that devastated three Roman settlements, including Londinium (London); in all, Tacitus claims, some seventy thousand Romans and allies were killed in these attacks (*Annals* 14.33.2). This figure may be hyperbolic, but it is hard to argue away the "Boudiccan destruction horizon," a stratum of debris that archaeologists have unearthed under the razed settlements. More than a meter thick in some locations, this is a layer of rubble, soot, and molten glass that burned in fires of more than 1800°F.

Tacitus attributes the uprising to a snowballing series of offensive acts perpetrated by the Romans. Our other major source for these events, Cassius

Dio (C2), argues that financial oppression fueled the revolt. Dio introduces Boudicca as a tall, terrifying, Amazonian queen with wild, waist-long, blond hair, a "noble savage" of manly courage and intelligence (φρόνημα). Brandishing a spear, she mounts an earthen platform and addresses her troops, 120,000 strong, urging them to join the fight against their Roman oppressors. When one is caught up in Boudicca's fiery speech, excerpted below, it is easy to forget that it is not a verbatim record of what she actually said; rather, like all speeches in Greek and Roman histories, it is an analytical and rhetorical showpiece written by the author. Boudicca's jeremiad was composed not by some anti-Roman firebrand but by a cultivated Roman senator from a Greek family who had served in many of the empire's highest offices. (On Dio, see further C2.) Moreover, Boudicca speaks in the polished, periodic style favored by rhetoricians of the Second Sophistic, a literary movement of Dio's day that was centered around declamation, the delivery of display speeches (C6). So a barbarian queen from the first century C.E. orates in the style favored by sophists in Athens of the fifth and fourth centuries B.C.E. and characterized by stylistic features such as antithesis, parallelism, isocolon (phrases of similar length and structure), and homoioteleuton (repetition of words with similar endings).

Further Reading

Cassius Dio 62.1–2, 6–12; Tacitus *Annals* 14.29–39; E. Adler, "Boudica's Speeches in Tacitus and Dio," *Classical World* 101 (2008): 173–95; M. Johnson, *Boudicca* (London, 2012), 21–38, 75–108.

❧

(3.1) "πέπεισθε μὲν τοῖς ἔργοις αὐτοῖς ὅσον ἐλευθερία τῆς δουλείας διαφέρει, ὥστ' εἰ καὶ πρότερόν τις ὑμῶν ὑπὸ τῆς τοῦ κρείττονος ἀπειρίας ἐπαγωγοῖς ἐπαγγέλμασι τῶν Ῥωμαίων ἠπάτητο, ἀλλὰ νῦν γε ἑκατέρου πεπειραμένοι μεμαθήκατε μὲν ὅσον ἡμαρτήκατε δεσποτείαν ἐπισπαστὸν πρὸ τῆς πατρίου διαίτης προτιμήσαντες, ἐγνώκατε δὲ ὅσῳ καὶ πενία ἀδέσποτος πλούτου δουλεύοντος προφέρει. **(2)** τί μὲν γὰρ οὐ τῶν αἰσχίστων, τί δ' οὐ τῶν ἀλγίστων, ἐξ οὗπερ ἐς τὴν Βρεττανίαν οὗτοι παρέκυψαν, πεπόνθαμεν; οὐ τῶν μὲν πλείστων καὶ μεγίστων κτημάτων ὅλων ἐστερήμεθα, τῶν δὲ λοιπῶν τέλη καταβάλλομεν; (3) οὐ πρὸς τῷ τἆλλα πάντα καὶ νέμειν καὶ γεωργεῖν ἐκείνοις, καὶ τῶν σωμάτων αὐτῶν δασμὸν ἐτήσιον φέρομεν; καὶ πόσῳ κρεῖττον ἦν ἅπαξ τισὶ πεπρᾶσθαι μᾶλλον ἢ μετὰ κενῶν ἐλευθερίας ὀνομάτων κατ' ἔτος λυτροῦσθαι; πόσῳ δὲ ἐσφάχθαι καὶ ἀπολωλέναι μᾶλλον ἢ κεφαλὰς ὑποτελεῖς περιφέρειν; καίτοι τί τοῦτο εἶπον; (4) οὐδὲ γὰρ τὸ τελευτῆσαι παρ' αὐτοῖς ἀζήμιόν ἐστιν, ἀλλ' ἴστε ὅσον καὶ ὑπὲρ τῶν νεκρῶν τελοῦμεν· παρὰ μὲν γὰρ τοῖς ἄλλοις ἀνθρώποις καὶ τοὺς δουλεύοντάς τισιν ὁ θάνατος ἐλευθεροῖ, Ῥωμαίοις δὲ δὴ μόνοις καὶ οἱ νεκροὶ ζῶσι πρὸς τὰ λήμματα. (5) τί δ' ὅτι, κἂν μὴ ἔχῃ τις ἡμῶν ἀργύριον (πῶς γὰρ ἢ πόθεν), ἀποδυόμεθα καὶ σκυλευόμεθα ὥσπερ οἱ φονευόμενοι; τί δ' ἂν προϊόντος τοῦ χρόνου μετριάσαιεν, οὕτως ἡμῖν κατὰ τὴν πρώτην εὐθύς, ὅτε πάντες καὶ τὰ θηρία τὰ νεάλωτα θεραπεύουσι, προσενηνεγμένοι;

(4.1) "ἡμεῖς δὲ δὴ πάντων τῶν κακῶν τούτων αἴτιοι, ὥς γε τἀληθὲς εἰπεῖν, γεγόναμεν, οἵτινες αὐτοῖς ἐπιβῆναι τὴν ἀρχὴν τῆς νήσου ἐπετρέψαμεν, καὶ οὐ παραχρῆμα αὐτούς, ὥσπερ καὶ τὸν Καίσαρα τὸν Ἰούλιον ἐκεῖνον, ἐξηλάσαμεν· οἵτινες οὐ πόρρωθέν σφισιν, ὥσπερ καὶ τῷ Αὐγούστῳ καὶ τῷ Γαΐῳ τῷ Καλιγόλᾳ, φοβερὸν τὸ καὶ πειρᾶσαι τὸν πλοῦν ἐποιήσαμεν. (2) τοιγαροῦν νῆσον τηλικαύτην, μᾶλλον δὲ ἤπειρον τρόπον τινὰ περίρρυτον νεμόμενοι καὶ ἰδίαν οἰκουμένην ἔχοντες, καὶ τοσοῦτον ὑπὸ τοῦ ὠκεανοῦ ἀφ' ἁπάντων τῶν ἄλλων ἀνθρώπων ἀφωρισμένοι ὥστε καὶ γῆν ἄλλην καὶ οὐρανὸν ἄλλον οἰκεῖν πεπιστεῦσθαι καί τινας αὐτῶν καὶ τοὺς σοφωτάτους γε μηδὲ τὸ ὄνομα ἡμῶν ἀκριβῶς πρότερον ἐγνωκέναι, κατεφρονήθημεν καὶ κατεπατήθημεν ὑπ' ἀνθρώπων μηδὲν ἄλλο ἢ πλεονεκτεῖν εἰδότων. (3) ἀλλ' εἰ καὶ μὴ πρότερον, νῦν ἔτι, ὦ πολῖται καὶ φίλοι καὶ συγγενεῖς (πάντας γὰρ ὑμᾶς συγγενεῖς, ἅτε καὶ μιᾶς νήσου οἰκήτορας ὄντας καὶ ἓν ὄνομα κοινὸν κεκλημένους, νομίζῳ), τὰ προσήκοντα πράξωμεν, ἕως ἔτι τῆς ἐλευθερίας μνημονεύομεν, ἵνα καὶ τὸ πρόσρημα καὶ τὸ ἔργον αὐτῆς τοῖς παισὶ καταλίπωμεν. ἂν γὰρ ἡμεῖς τῆς συντρόφου εὐδαιμονίας παντελῶς ἐκλαθώμεθα, τί ποτε ἐκεῖνοι ποιήσουσιν ἐν δουλείᾳ τραφέντες;

(5.1) "λέγω δὲ ταῦτα οὐχ ἵνα μισήσητε τὰ παρόντα (μεμισήκατε γάρ), οὐδ' ἵνα φοβηθῆτε τὰ μέλλοντα (πεφόβησθε γάρ), ἀλλ' ἵνα ἐπαινέσω τε ὑμᾶς ὅτι καὶ καθ' ἑαυτοὺς πάνθ' ὅσα δεῖ προαιρεῖσθε, καὶ χάριν ὑμῖν γνῶ ὅτι καὶ ἐμοὶ καὶ ἑαυτοῖς ἑτοίμως συναίρεσθε. φοβεῖσθε δὲ μηδαμῶς τοὺς Ῥωμαίους· **(2)** οὔτε γὰρ πλείους ἡμῶν εἰσιν οὔτ' ἀνδρειότεροι. τεκμήριον δὲ ὅτι καὶ κράνεσι καὶ θώραξι καὶ κνημῖσιν ἐσκέπασθε καὶ προσέτι καὶ σταυρώμασι καὶ τείχεσι καὶ τάφροις ἐσκεύασθε πρὸς τὸ μήτι πάσχειν ἐξ ἐπιδρομῆς τῶν πολεμίων. τοῦτο γὰρ αἱροῦνται μᾶλλον ὑπὸ τῶν φόβων ἢ τὸ καὶ δρᾶσαί τι προχείρως ὥσπερ ἡμεῖς. **(3)** τοσαύτῃ γὰρ περιουσίᾳ ἀνδρίας χρώμεθα ὥστε καὶ τὰς σκηνὰς ἀσφαλεστέρας τῶν τειχῶν καὶ τὰς ἀσπίδας πολυαρκεστέρας τῆς ἐκείνων πανοπλίας νομίζειν. ἐξ οὗπερ ἡμεῖς μὲν καὶ κρατοῦντες αἱροῦμεν αὐτοὺς καὶ βιασθέντες ἐκφεύγομεν, κἂν ἄρα καὶ ἀναχωρῆσαί ποι προελώμεθα, ἐς τοιαῦτα ἕλη καὶ ὄρη καταδυόμεθα ὥστε μήτε εὑρεθῆναι μήτε ληφθῆναι· **(4)** ἐκεῖνοι δὲ οὔτε διῶξαί τινα ὑπὸ τοῦ βάρους οὔτε φυγεῖν δύνανται, κἂν ἄρα καὶ ἐκδράμωσί ποτε, ἔς τε χωρία ἀποδεδειγμένα καταφεύγουσι, κἀνταῦθα ὥσπερ ἐς γαλεάγρας κατακλείονται. **(5)** ἔν τε οὖν τούτοις παρὰ πολὺ ἡμῶν ἐλαττοῦνται, καὶ ἐν ἐκείνοις, ὅτι οὔτε λιμὸν οὔτε δίψος, οὐ ψῦχος οὐ καῦμα ὑποφέρουσιν ὥσπερ ἡμεῖς, ἀλλ' οἱ μὲν καὶ σκιᾶς καὶ σκέπης σίτου τε μεμαγμένου καὶ οἴνου καὶ ἐλαίου δέονται, κἂν ἄρα τι τούτων αὐτοὺς ἐπιλίπῃ διαφθείρονται, ἡμῖν δὲ δὴ πᾶσα μὲν πόα καὶ ῥίζα σῖτός ἐστι, πᾶς δὲ χυμὸς ἔλαιον, πᾶν δὲ ὕδωρ οἶνος, πᾶν δὲ δένδρον οἰκία. **(6)** καὶ μὴν καὶ τὰ χωρία ταῦτα ἡμῖν μὲν συνήθη καὶ σύμμαχα, ἐκείνοις δὲ δὴ καὶ ἄγνωστα καὶ πολέμια· καὶ τοὺς ποταμοὺς ἡμεῖς μὲν γυμνοὶ διανέομεν, ἐκεῖνοι δὲ οὐδὲ πλοίοις ῥᾳδίως περαιοῦνται. ἀλλ' ἴωμεν ἐπ' αὐτοὺς ἀγαθῇ τύχῃ θαρροῦντες. δείξωμεν αὐτοῖς ὅτι λαγωοὶ καὶ ἀλώπεκες ὄντες κυνῶν καὶ λύκων ἄρχειν ἐπιχειροῦσιν."

Notes to Cassius Dio 62.3–5

(3.1) πέπεισθε. 2nd pl. pf. mid. ind. < πείθω. (*come to*) *believe.*
διαφέρω. *differ from, be superior to* + gen.: LSJ, s.v. III.4.
ὑπό + gen. *from, because of*: Smyth 1698.1.b.

ἐπαγωγός, -όν. *alluring.*

ἐπάγγελμα, -ατος (neu.). *promise.*

ἠπάτητο. 3rd sg. plupf. pass. ind. < ἀπατάω. *deceive.*

ἑκατέρου. i.e., how *both* the Romans and the natives operate.

πειράω. in mid., *test, experience* + gen.: LSJ, s.v. B.II.2.

ἐπισπαστός, -όν. *brought upon oneself, imported.*

πρό + gen. *rather than*: LSJ, s.v. A.III.1.

προτιμάω. *prefer, honor.*

ὅσῳ. dat. degree of difference: Smyth 1513.

(2) τί . . . τί. objects of πεπόνθαμεν.

τῶν αἰσχίστων . . . τῶν ἀλγίστων. The genitives are partitive. Boudicca employs the rhetorical device known as epiplexis; i.e., posing a series of questions meant to chastise one's opponent.

ἐξ οὗπερ. *from the very time when, ever since.*

παρακύπτω. *appear in*, with connotations of stealth or prurience: LSJ, s.v.

πεπόνθαμεν < πάσχω.

ἐστερήμεθα. 1st pl. pf. pass. ind. < στερέω. *deprive of* + gen.

τέλος, -ους (neu.). *tax*: LSJ, s.v. 8.

καταβάλλω. *pay*: LSJ, s.v. II.4.b.

(3) πρός + dat. *in addition to*: Smyth 1695.2.

τἄλλα πάντα = τὰ ἄλλα πάντα, the object of the articular infinitives.

σωμάτων αὐτῶν δασμὸν ἐτήσιον. i.e., each Briton is yearly subject to poll tax.

πόσῳ κρεῖττον ἦν. *how much better it would have been.* πόσῳ is dat. degree of difference; ἦν is impf. in an unfulfilled possibility in the past: Smyth 1774, 1776.

πεπρᾶσθαι. pf. pass. inf. < πιπράσκω. *sell.*

λυτρόω. *ransom, redeem.*

ἐσφάχθαι. pf. pass. inf. < σφάζω. *slaughter.*

ὑποτελής, -ές. *taxable, subject to taxes.*

καίτοι. *and yet*; often introduces a rhetorical question.

(4) ἀζήμιος, -ον. *free from payment, untaxed.*

ἴστε. ind. not impv.

τελοῦμεν. fut.

καί in this section is best translated as *even.*

λῆμμα, -ατος (neu.). *profit,* often in a negative sense: *unjust gain.*

(5) τί δ᾽ὅτι. *and why (is it) that.*

κἂν = καὶ ἐὰν, introducing a pres. general condition: this is not a one-time event, but a recurring practice.

σκυλεύω. *despoil, strip a dead soldier.* There are undertones of sexual violence in this section.

μετριάσαιεν. potential opt.

κατὰ τὴν πρώτην. *from the beginning.*

νεάλωτος, -ον. *newly caught.*

προσενηνεγμένοι < προσφέρω. in pass., *deal with, behave toward* + dat.: LSJ, s.v. B.4.

(4.1) τὴν ἀρχὴν. *at first.*

ἐπιτρέπω + dat. *allow, permit*: LSJ, s.v. II.

τὸν Καίσαρα τὸν Ἰούλιον. Julius Caesar (100–44 B.C.E.) twice invaded Britain, in 55 and 54 B.C.E., but did not reduce the island to a province.

πόρρωθεν (Attic) = πρόσωθεν. *from afar, far-off.*

σφισιν = αὐτοῖς.

Αὐγούστῳ. Augustus (reg. 27 B.C.E.–14 C.E.) did not in fact invade Britain, though Dio suggests that the emperor had planned military action on the island (e.g., 49.38.2, 53.22.5).

τῷ Γαΐῳ τῷ Καλιγόλᾳ. Gaius Caligula (reg. 37–41 C.E.; see C4) tried to invade Britain, to little result. His incursion is perhaps best remembered for the emperor's demand that his troops gather seashells on the beaches of northern Gaul: Dio

59.25.1–3, Suetonius *Gaius* 46. The rationale behind Gaius's order remains murky.

φοβερὸν. predicative with the following articular infinitive.

πλοῦν. contracted mas. sg. acc. < πλόος, -ος. *(sea) voyage.*

(2) τηλικ-οῦτος, -αύτη, -οῦτο. *so great*: LSJ, s.v. τηλικόσδε, II.

μᾶλλον δὲ. Boudicca "corrects" herself. Her sentiments here are similar to those expressed in John of Gaunt's "This Scepter'd Isle" speech in Shakespeare's *Richard II* (Act II, Scene 1).

τρόπον τινὰ. *in a way.*

νεμόμενοι, ἔχοντες. Translate as concessive.

ἰδίαν οἰκουμένην. *private world.*

πεπιστεῦσθαι. pf. pass. inf. in a result clause; sc. "we" as the subject.

ἐγνωκέναι. pf. act. inf. < γιγνώσκω.

καταπατέω. *trample, tread upon.*

πλεονεκτέω. *be greedy, overreaching.*

(3) συγγενεῖς. In reality, Britain was populated by a mosaic of tribes that had various relationships with one another and Rome.

ἅτε. *as, since.*

κεκλημένους. In the pass., καλέω may essentially function as a linking verb: LSJ, s.v. II.2. ἓν ὄνομα κοινὸν is thus in apposition with κεκλημένους: *called (by) one common name.*

προσήκω. *be at hand, fitting.*

μνημονεύομεν. Verbs of memory often take the gen.: Smyth 1356–57.

ἂν = ἐὰν.

σύντροφος, -ον. *innate.*

ἐκεῖνοι. i.e., future generations.

τραφέντες. mas. pl. nom., aor. pass. part. < τρέφω.

(5.1) καθ' ἑαυτοὺς. *individually.*

προαιρέω. *choose,* connoting a deliberate, strategic choice: LSJ, s.v. II.3.

χάριν γιγνώσκω. *thank* + dat.: LSJ, s.v. γιγνώσκω, IV.

γνῶ. 1st sg. aor. act. subj. < γιγνώσκω.

συναιρέω. in mid., *join with, cooperate with* + dat.

φοβεῖσθε. impv.

(2) τεκμήριον δέ ὅτι. *the proof of this (is) that*: LSJ, s.v. τεκμήριον, II.2.

κράνος, -εος (neu.). *helmet.*

ἐσκέπασθε. 2nd pl. pf. mid. ind. < σκεπάω. *protect.* The text is corrupt: logic suggests that the verbs ἐσκέπασθε and ἐσκεύασθε should be 3rd pl., and they should be translated as such.

σταύρωμα, -ατος (neu.). *palisade.*

μήτι = μή τι.

προχείρως. *rashly, offhandedly*; i.e., the Britons embrace a spontaneous, irregular approach to warfare that contrasts with the Romans' careful preparation for combat.

(3) περιουσία, -ας (fem.). *abundance.*

πολυαρκής, -ές. *helpful, effective.*

προελώμεθα < προαιρέω; see note on **(5.1)**.

ἕλος, -εος (neu.). *marsh.*

ληφθῆναι. aor. pass. inf. < λαμβάνω.

(4) ὑπὸ τοῦ βάρους. i.e., because of their heavy armor.

ἐκδράμωσί. 3rd pl. aor. act. subj. < ἐκτρέχω. *run off.*

κἀνταῦθα = καὶ ἐνταῦθα.

γαλεάγρα, -ας (fem.). *weasel-trap, cage.*

(5) παρὰ πολὺ. *by far*: LSJ, s.v. παρά, C.III.5.

μεμαγμένου. mas. sg. gen., pf. pass. part. < μάσσω. *knead.*

δέομαι. dep., *need, require* + gen.

ἐπιλείπω + acc. *fail X*; the subject is τι. In other words, if the Romans' supply of any of these products dries up, they perish.

χυμός, -οῦ (mas.). *juice, extract (of a plant).*

(6) συνήθη. neu. pl. nom. < συνήθης, ες. *familiar to* + dat.

πλοῖον, -ου (neu.). *(transport) ship.*

λαγωός, -οῦ (mas.). *hare.*

λύκων. Perhaps ironic? For Rome, of course, was identified with the wolf (A4, B5).

C6. ARISTIDES PRAISES ROME

Aelius Aristides *On Rome* 26 (14).96–101, 104

Publius Aelius Aristides (117–c. 185 C.E.) was a luminary of the Second Sophistic, a Greek literary movement centered in Greece and Asia Minor that reached its peak in the second century C.E. In the Second Sophistic, the highest form of verbal creativity was declamation, that is, the delivery of speeches not to sway a real-life assembly or jury, but as a form of public display. Master rhetors toured the world, speechifying before packed houses in the baroque, balanced style of classical sophists like Gorgias and Protagoras, who taught in Athens of the fifth and fourth centuries B.C.E. (see also C5). Eschewing the Greek commonly spoken in their day, orators of the Second Sophistic restricted themselves to the vocabulary and syntax of the "pure" and by then antiquated dialect of golden-age Athens; this linguistic phenomenon, called Atticism, reflected a growing interest and pride in the history and literature of classical Greece. It is debated whether this devotion to Attic dialect and reassertion of Greek identity during the high empire should be viewed as anti-Roman or as a cultural development more or less divorced from politics.

Aristides is a key figure in this debate. More than fifty of his speeches are extant. Some of them are encomiums, celebratory speeches of praise, which may be cloying to a modern palate, but which were well-respected in their day. Aristides delivered an encomium of Rome in the presence of the imperial family when he was visiting the capital. While the speech is grounded in rhetorical conventions about how a city ought to be praised (oratorical handbooks gave guidelines), it transcends them by praising Rome in Platonic terms: the Roman Empire is likened to Plato's ideal state, which, beloved by the gods, brings order, harmony, happiness, and freedom to its residents. But does Aristides's speech reflect the author's real feelings about Rome? If so, how prevalent were such views among Greeks of his time? Was his rosy picture geographically delimited? For Asia Minor and Greece in the second century were prosperous and culturally vibrant; would a provincial from elsewhere have so lauded the capital? Is there an anti-Roman subtext in the speech, as some have detected?

Further Reading

Aelius Aristides *On Rome* all; J. H. Oliver, *The Ruling Power: A Study of the Roman Empire in the Second Century after Christ through the Roman Oration of Aelius Aristides* (Philadelphia, 1953), 873–95; S. Swain, *Hellenism and Empire: Language, Classicism, and Power in the Greek World, A.D. 50–250* (Oxford, 1996), 254–97; L. Pernot, "Aelius Aristides and Rome," in *Aelius Aristides between Greece, Rome, and the Gods,* ed. W. V. Harris and B. Holmes, 175–201 (Leiden, 2008).

❧

(96) διατελεῖτε δὲ τῶν μὲν Ἑλλήνων ὥσπερ τροφέων ἐπιμελόμενοι, χεῖρά τε ὑπερέχοντες καὶ οἷον κειμένους ἀνιστάντες, τοὺς μὲν ἀρίστους καὶ πάλαι ἡγεμόνας ἐλευθέρους καὶ αὐτονόμους ἀφεικότες αὐτῶν, τῶν δ' ἄλλων μετρίως καὶ κατὰ πολλὴν φειδώ τε καὶ πρόνοιαν ἐξηγούμενοι, τοὺς δὲ βαρβάρους πρὸς τὴν ἑκάστοις αὐτῶν οὖσαν φύσιν παιδεύοντες πραότερόν τε καὶ σφοδρότερον, ὥσπερ εἰκὸς ἵππων ἐπιστατῶν μὴ εἶναι χείρους, ἀνδρῶν ὄντας ἄρχοντας, ἀλλ' ἐξητακέναι τὰς φύσεις, καὶ πρὸς ταύτας ἄγειν. **(97)** καὶ γὰρ ὥσπερ πανηγυρίζουσα πᾶσα ἡ οἰκουμένη τὸ μὲν παλαιὸν φόρημα τὸν σίδηρον κατέθετο, εἰς δὲ κόσμον καὶ πάσας εὐφροσύνας τέτραπται σὺν ἐξουσίᾳ. καὶ αἱ μὲν ἄλλαι πᾶσαι φιλονεικίαι τὰς πράξεις ἐπιλελοίπασι, μία δὲ αὕτη κατέχει πάσας ἔρις, ὅπως ὅτι καλλίστη καὶ ἡδίστη αὐτὴ ἑκάστη φανεῖται. πάντα δὲ μεστὰ γυμνασίων, κρηνῶν, προπυλαίων, νεῶν, δημιουργιῶν, διδασκάλων, ἐπιστημόνως τε ἔξεστιν εἰπεῖν οἷον πεπονηκυῖαν ἐξ ἀρχῆς ἀνακεκομίσθαι τὴν οἰκουμένην. **(98)** δωρεαὶ δ᾽ οὔποτε λείπουσιν εἰς ταύτας παρ᾽ ὑμῶν ἰοῦσαι, οὐδ᾽ ἔστιν εὑρεῖν τοὺς μειζόνων τετυχηκότας διὰ τὴν ὁμοίαν εἰς ἅπαντας ὑμῶν φιλανθρωπίαν. **(99)** πόλεις τε οὖν δή που λάμπουσιν αἴγλῃ καὶ χάριτι καὶ ἡ γῆ πᾶσα οἷον παράδεισος ἐγκεκόσμηται. καπνοὶ δ᾽ ἐκ πεδίων καὶ φρυκτοὶ φίλιοι καὶ πολέμιοι, οἷον πνεύματος ἐκριπίσαντος, φροῦδοι γῆς ἐπέκεινα καὶ θαλάττης· ἀντεισῆκται δὲ θέας πᾶσα χάρις καὶ ἀγώνων ἄπειρος ἀριθμός. ὥστε ὅλον πῦρ ἱερὸν καὶ ἄσβεστον οὐ διαλείπει τὸ πανηγυρίζειν, ἀλλὰ περίεισιν ἄλλοτε εἰς ἄλλους, ἀεὶ δὲ ἔστι που, πάντες γὰρ ἀξίως τούτου πεπράγασιν. ὥστε μόνους ἄξιον εἶναι κατοικτεῖραι τοὺς ἔξω τῆς ὑμετέρας, εἴ τινές που εἰσὶν ἄρα, ἡγεμονίας, οἵων ἀγαθῶν στέρονται. **(100)** καὶ μὴν τό γε ὑπὸ πάντων λεγόμενον, ὅτι γῆ πάντων μήτηρ καὶ πατρὶς κοινὴ πάντων, ἄριστα ὑμεῖς ἀπεδείξατε. νῦν γοῦν ἔξεστι καὶ Ἕλληνι καὶ βαρβάρῳ καὶ τὰ αὑτοῦ κομίζοντι καὶ χωρὶς τῶν αὑτοῦ βαδίζειν ὅποι βούλεται ῥᾳδίως, ἀτεχνῶς ὡς ἐκ πατρίδος εἰς πατρίδα ἰόντι· καὶ οὔτε Πύλαι Κιλίκιοι φόβον παρέχουσιν οὔτε στεναὶ καὶ ψαμμώδεις δι᾽ Ἀράβων ἐπ᾽ Αἴγυπτον πάροδοι, οὐκ ὄρη δύσβατα, οὐ ποταμῶν ἄπειρα μεγέθη, οὐ γένη βαρβάρων ἄμικτα, ἀλλ᾽ εἰς ἀσφάλειαν ἐξαρκεῖ Ῥωμαῖον εἶναι, μᾶλλον δὲ ἕνα τῶν ὑφ᾽ ὑμῖν. **(101)** καὶ τὸ Ὁμήρῳ λεχθὲν "γαῖα δ᾽ ἔτι ξυνὴ πάντων" ὑμεῖς ἔργῳ ἐποιήσατε, καταμετρήσαντες μὲν πᾶσαν τὴν οἰκουμένην, ζεύξαντες δὲ παντοδαπαῖς γεφύραις ποταμούς, καὶ ὄρη κόψαντες ἱππήλατον γῆν εἶναι, σταθμοῖς τε τὰ ἔρημα ἀναπλήσαντες, καὶ διαίτῃ καὶ τάξει πάντα ἡμερώσαντες. ὥστ᾽ ἔγωγε τὸν νομιζόμενον πρὸ Τριπτολέμου βίον τοῦτον εἶναι τὸν πρὸ ὑμῶν ἐπινοῶ, σκληρόν τινα καὶ ἄγροικον καὶ ὀρείου ὀλίγον ἀποκεχωρηκότα, ἀλλ᾽ ἄρξαι μὲν τοῦ ἡμέρου τε καὶ τοῦ νῦν τὴν Ἀθηναίων πόλιν, βεβαιωθῆναι δὲ καὶ τοῦτον ὑφ᾽ ὑμῶν δευτέρων, φασὶν, ἀμεινόνων.

[In section 102 through the beginning of 104, Aristides lauds Rome for uniting its subjects, who are now members of the same family and subject to a shared set of laws; he compares the advent of Roman rule to that of the orderly, pacific reign of Zeus, which ended the strife and violence of the Titans' age.]

(104) νῦν δὲ κοινὴ καὶ σαφὴς πᾶσι πάντων ἄδεια δέδοται αὐτῇ τε τῇ γῇ καὶ τοῖς ἐν αὐτῇ κατοικοῦσι, καὶ τοῦ μὲν κακῶς πάσχειν ἅπαντα ἀφεῖσθαι, τοῦ δὲ καλῶς ἄγεσθαι πολλὰς τὰς ἀφορμὰς εἰληφέναι μοι δοκοῦσι, καὶ οἱ θεοὶ καθορῶντες συγκατορθοῦν ὑμῖν εὐμενῶς τὴν ἀρχὴν καὶ διδόναι βέβαιον τὴν κτῆσιν αὐτῆς.

Notes to Aelius Aristides* On Rome *26 (14).96–101, 104

These notes are indebted to J. H. Oliver, *The Ruling Power: A Study of the Roman Empire in the Second Century after Christ through the Roman Oration of Aelius Aristides* (Philadelphia, 1953).

(96) διατελέω + part. *continue to X.* The Greek Aristides addresses the Romans.

τροφεύς, -έως (mas.). *adopted parent.* The Romans properly exhibit filial piety toward the Greeks who "reared" them.

ἐπιμελέομαι. *take care of* + gen. Cf. Plato, who writes that God, the caretaker of all (ὁ τοῦ πάντος ἐπιμελούμενος), has ordered all things "for the safety and excellence of the whole": *Laws* 10.903b, cited by Oliver, *Ruling Power,* 945.

ὑπερέχω χεῖρα. *hold a hand over (to protect)*: LSJ, s.v. ὑπερέχω, 2.

οἷον. *as it were.*

ἀνίστημι. *cause to stand up, raise (from the dead), resurrect*: LSJ, s.v. A.I.

ἀφεικότες < ἀφίημι. *release.*

φειδώ, -όος (contracting to -οῦς) (fem.). *consideration, sparing.* On the declension of this noun, see Smyth 267.

πρόνοια, -ας (fem.). *foresight, prudence, providence.*

πρός + acc. *according to, in accordance with*: Smyth 1695.3.c.

εἰκὸς . . . μὴ εἶναι χείρους. *(it is) likely (that you) are no worse* + gen. of comparison. εἰκὸς triggers additional complementary infinitives in the following lines.

ἐπιστατῶν. The horse-trainer metaphor is Platonic (e.g., *Gorgias* 516e); furthermore, the taming of horses is a common metaphor for the "domestication" of Greek women, who through marriage are changed from "wild" girls into "civilized" wives.

ὄντας. Translate as concessive.

ἐξητακέναι. pf. act. inf. < ἐξετάζω. *inspect, assess carefully.*

(97) τὸ . . . παλαιὸν φόρημα and τὸν σίδηρον are in apposition.

φιλονεικία, -ας (fem.). *(source of) contentiousness.*

μία . . . ἔρις. sc. πόλεις.

ἔρις. The word's use here is reminiscent of Hesiod's Good Eris: *Works and Days* 11–26.

ὅτι + superlative adj. *as X as possible*: Smyth 1086.

προπύλαια, -ων (neu. pl.). (*monumental*) *gateway.*

νεῶν. mas. pl. gen. < νεώς, νεώ. *temple*; for this noun's irregular declension: Smyth 238.

ἐπιστημόνως . . . εἰπεῖν. *speak in medical terms*: LSJ, s.v. ἐπιστήμων, II.

πονέω. *be sick,* perhaps with the implication that the illness was brought on by overwork: LSJ, s.v. A.I.2. Rome is the great physician; cf. Plato *Laws* 10.903c.

(98) λείπω. *be lacking, missing*: LSJ, s.v. II.2.

εἰς ταύτας. again, sc. πόλεις.

ἔστιν. *it is possible*; on the accent, see Smyth 187.b.

ὑμῶν. Take with φιλανθρωπίαν.

(99) φρυκτός, οῦ (mas.). *signal-fire, beacon*: LSJ, s.v. II.

ἐκριπίζω. *extinguish, blow out.*

ἐπέκεινα. *beyond* + gen.

ἀντεισῆκται. 3rd sg. pf. pass. ind. < ἀντεισάγω. *introduce instead*: LSJ, s.v.

θέας. Note accent < θέα, -ας (fem.). *sight, spectacle,* not θεά, *goddess.*

ὥστε. *just as, like.*

διαλείπω. *cease*; the verb's subject is τὸ πανηγυρίζειν.

τούτου. The gen. is triggered by ἀξίως.

μόνους . . . τοὺς ἔξω. object of κατοικτεῖραι.

ἄξιόν ἐστι + inf. impersonal: *it is appropriate.*

ἄρα heightens the improbability of the conditional: Smyth 2796.

(100) γοῦν. This particle often, as here, introduces particular evidence in support of a general contention that has just been made: Smyth 2830.

τὰ αὑτοῦ κομίζοντι. i.e., traveling with his possessions.

ἀτεχνῶς ὡς. *as if simply.*

Πύλαι Κιλίκιοι. The Cilician Gates are a pass from Anatolia to Cilicia through the Taurus Mountains that permits overland travel to the Near East. They are thus of great strategic importance.

ἐξαρκεῖ. impersonal: *it is enough, sufficient.*

(101) τὸ Ὁμήρῳ λεχθὲν = *Iliad* 15.193.

γέφυρα, -ας (fem.). *bridge*: LSJ, s.v. II.

ἱππήλατος, -ον. *traversable by horse.* ἱππήλατον γῆν is predicative with ὄρη.

σταθμός, -οῦ (mas.). *lodging, post-station.*

ἡμερόω. *tame, cultivate, civilize, subdue, conquer*; this is a verb with positive and negative connotations.

τὸν νομιζόμενον πρὸ Τριπτολέμου. *the (life) thought (to have existed) before Triptolemus,* Demeter's adopted son, who gave wheat-seed to the peoples of the earth and taught them about agriculture. In Sophocles's lost *Triptolemus,* the titular character is a symbol of Athens's beneficence toward other nations: Oliver, *Ruling Power,* 879–80.

ἀποχωρέω + gen. *be different from, distant from.*

ἄρξαι. inf. in indirect discourse introduced by φασὶν; the subject is τὴν Ἀθηναίων πόλιν.

τοῦ ἡμέρου . . . καὶ τοῦ νῦν. *the cultivated (way-of-life that exists) also now.*

(104) δέδοται. 3rd sg. pf. pass. ind. < δίδωμι.

ἀφεῖσθαι. pf. pass. inf. < ἀφίημι. *set free, release from* + gen.: LSJ, s.v. II.1.b.

εἰληφέναι. pf. act. inf. < λαμβάνω.

συγκατορθόω. *help succeed.*

C7. SERVING GREECE UNDER ROME

Plutarch *Political Precepts* 17, 19

In addition to more than fifty biographies (see B3–B4), Plutarch wrote numerous other works that treat all manner of subjects. Eighty or so of the latter are extant; they are collectively known as the *Moralia*. Especially germane here are those works that present Plutarch's views on the reasons for Rome's rise to power and the relationship between Greece and Rome. *On the Fortune of the Romans*, for example, assays the relative importance of Virtue (Ἀρετή) and Fortune (Τύχη) as factors contributing to Rome's success: surveying Rome's history, Plutarch, like the Roman historian Livy, argues that both played a role. Roman rule, then, was providential. For Plutarch, Rome was not founded by Greeks, as Dionysius of Halicarnassus would have it (see A3.2–A6); rather, in its early history, it developed independently. But later, when it encountered and eventually conquered Greece, many Romans were Hellenized, in that they absorbed Greek *paideia,* to their moral, aesthetic, and educational benefit.

Among the *Moralia,* perhaps the most illuminating political treatise is *Political Precepts,* which is addressed to a young, wealthy Greek named Menemachus from the city of Sardis in Asia Minor (17, 32). Menemachus had sought advice from Plutarch about the pursuit of a political career. In the treatise, Plutarch advises him to serve his πόλις. For if Greek cities are to retain a measure of autonomy, Plutarch says, their leaders must make sure that they are stable and their politics harmonious. When Greek leaders cultivate connections with but do not kowtow to powerful Romans, when they seek civic offices and honors but do not do so too ambitiously, when they firmly guide but do not dominate the people—then the Romans are more likely to leave the Greeks' well-governed cities alone.

Further Reading

C. P. Jones, *Plutarch and Rome* (Oxford, 1971), 110–30; C. Pelling, "The Moralism of Plutarch's Lives," in *Ethics and Rhetoric: Classical Essays for Donald Russell on His Seventy-Fifth Birthday,* ed. D. Innes, H. Hine, and C. Pelling, 205–20 (Oxford, 1995), reprinted in the author's *Plutarch and History: Eighteen Studies* (London, 2002), 237–51; S. Swain, *Hellenism and Empire: Language, Classicism, and Power in the Greek World, A.D. 50–250* (Oxford, 1996), 135–86, esp. 161–83; M. Trapp, "Statesmanship in a Minor Key?," in *The Statesman in Plutarch's Works,* ed. L. de Blois et al., 2 vols., 1:189–200 (Leiden, 2005); P. A. Stadter, "Competition and Its Costs: Φιλονικία in Plutarch's Society and Heroes," in *Virtues for the People: Aspects of Plutarchan Ethics,* ed. G. Roskam and L. Van der Stockt, 237–55 (Leuven, 2011), reprinted in the author's *Plutarch and His Roman Readers* (Oxford, 2015), 270–85.

❧

(17) φύσει μὲν οὖν ἄρχων ἀεὶ πόλεως ὁ πολιτικὸς ὥσπερ ἡγεμὼν ἐν μελίτταις, καὶ τοῦτο χρὴ διανοούμενον ἔχειν τὰ δημόσια διὰ χειρός· ἃς δ' ὀνομάζουσιν ἐξουσίας καὶ χειροτονοῦσιν ἀρχὰς μήτ' ἄγαν διώκειν καὶ πολλάκις, οὐ γὰρ σεμνὸν οὐδὲ δημοτικὸν ἡ φιλαρχία· μήτ' ἀπωθεῖσθαι, τοῦ δήμου κατὰ νόμον διδόντος καὶ καλοῦντος ἀλλὰ κἂν ταπεινότεραι τῆς δόξης ὦσι, δέχεσθαι καὶ συμφιλοτιμεῖσθαι· δίκαιον γὰρ ὑπὸ τῶν μειζόνων κοσμουμένους ἀρχῶν ἀντικοσμεῖν τὰς ἐλάττονας . . . εἰσιόντα δ' εἰς ἅπασαν ἀρχὴν οὐ μόνον ἐκείνους δεῖ προχειρίζεσθαι τοὺς λογισμούς, οὓς ὁ Περικλῆς αὐτὸν ὑπεμίμνησκεν ἀναλαμβάνων τὴν χλαμύδα, "πρόσεχε, Περίκλεις· ἐλευθέρων ἄρχεις, Ἑλλήνων ἄρχεις, πολιτῶν Ἀθηναίων"· ἀλλὰ κἀκεῖνο λέγειν πρὸς ἑαυτὸν, "ἀρχόμενος ἄρχεις, ὑποτεταγμένης πόλεως ἀνθυπάτοις, ἐπιτρόποις Καίσαρος· 'οὐ ταῦτα λόγχη πεδιάς,' οὐδ' αἱ παλαιαὶ Σάρδεις οὐδ' ἡ Λυδῶν ἐκείνη δύναμις"· εὐσταλεστέραν δεῖ τὴν χλαμύδα ποιεῖν, καὶ βλέπειν ἀπὸ τοῦ στρατηγίου πρὸς τὸ βῆμα, καὶ τῷ στεφάνῳ μὴ πολὺ φρονεῖν μηδὲ πιστεύειν, ὁρῶντα τοὺς καλτίους ἐπάνω τῆς κεφαλῆς· ἀλλὰ μιμεῖσθαι τοὺς ὑποκριτάς, πάθος μὲν ἴδιον καὶ ἦθος καὶ ἀξίωμα τῷ ἀγῶνι προστιθέντας, τοῦ δ' ὑποβολέως ἀκούοντας καὶ μὴ παρεκβαίνοντας τοὺς ῥυθμοὺς καὶ τὰ μέτρα τῆς διδομένης ἐξουσίας ὑπὸ τῶν κρατούντων. ἡ γὰρ ἔκπτωσις οὐ φέρει συριγμὸν οὐδὲ χλευασμὸν οὐδὲ κλωγμόν, ἀλλὰ πολλοῖς μὲν ἐπέβη, "δεινὸς κολαστὴς πέλεκυς αὐχένος τομεύς," ὡς τοῖς περὶ Παρδάλαν τὸν ὑμέτερον ἐκλαθομένοις τῶν ὅρων· ὁ δέ τις ἐκριφεὶς εἰς νῆσον γέγονε κατὰ τὸν Σόλωνα, "Φολεγάνδριος ἢ Σικινήτης, ἀντί γ' Ἀθηναίου πατρίδ' ἀμειψάμενος." τὰ μὲν γὰρ μικρὰ παιδία τῶν πατέρων ὁρῶντες ἐπιχειροῦντα τὰς κρηπῖδας ὑποδεῖσθαι καὶ τοὺς στεφάνους περιτίθεσθαι μετὰ παιδιᾶς γελῶμεν, οἱ δ' ἄρχοντες ἐν ταῖς πόλεσιν ἀνοήτως τὰ τῶν προγόνων ἔργα καὶ φρονήματα καὶ πράξεις ἀσυμμέτρους τοῖς παροῦσι καιροῖς καὶ πράγμασιν οὔσας μιμεῖσθαι κελεύοντες ἐξαίρουσι τὰ πλήθη, γέλωτά τε ποιοῦντες οὐκέτι γέλωτος ἄξια πάσχουσιν, ἂν μὴ πάνυ καταφρονηθῶσι.

[In the remainder of section 17, Plutarch advises Menemachus about which historical exemplars to employ and which to avoid in his speeches; he should use those that promote civic pride but not jingoism (don't bring up Marathon!). In section 18, he says that Menemachus should seek out powerful Romans who can benefit both him and his city; he cites several examples of Greeks, such as Polybius (A7.2–B2), who were blessed by Roman patrons. Relationships between Greek and Roman politicians, he says, ought to be characterized by equality and justice.]

(19) ποιοῦντα μέντοι καὶ παρέχοντα τοῖς κρατοῦσιν εὐπειθῆ τὴν πατρίδα δεῖ μὴ προσεκταπεινοῦν, μηδὲ τοῦ σκέλους δεδεμένου προσυποβάλλειν καὶ τὸν τράχηλον, ὥσπερ ἔνιοι, καὶ μικρὰ καὶ μείζω φέροντες ἐπὶ τοὺς ἡγεμόνας ἐξονειδίζουσι τὴν δουλείαν, μᾶλλον δ' ὅλως τὴν πολιτείαν ἀναιροῦσι, καταπλῆγα καὶ περιδεᾶ καὶ πάντων ἄκυρον ποιοῦντες. ὥσπερ γὰρ οἱ χωρὶς ἰατροῦ μήτε δειπνεῖν μήτε λούεσθαι συνεθισθέντες οὐδ᾽ ὅσον ἡ φύσις δίδωσι χρῶνται τῷ ὑγιαίνειν, οὕτως οἱ παντὶ δόγματι καὶ συνεδρίῳ καὶ χάριτι καὶ διοικήσει προσάγοντες ἡγεμονικὴν κρίσιν ἀναγκάζουσιν ἑαυτῶν μᾶλλον ἢ βούλονται δεσπότας εἶναι τοὺς ἡγουμένους. αἰτία δὲ τούτου μάλιστα πλεονεξία καὶ φιλονεικία τῶν πρώτων· ἢ γὰρ ἐν οἷς βλάπτουσι τοὺς ἐλάττονας ἐκβιάζονται φεύγειν τὴν πόλιν ἢ περὶ ὧν διαφέρονται πρὸς ἀλλήλους οὐκ ἀξιοῦντες ἐν τοῖς πολίταις ἔχειν ἔλαττον ἐπάγονται τοὺς κρείττονας· ἐκ τούτου δὲ καὶ βουλὴ καὶ δῆμος καὶ δικαστήρια καὶ ἀρχὴ πᾶσα τὴν ἐξουσίαν ἀπόλλυσι. δεῖ δὲ τοὺς μὲν ἰδιώτας ἰσότητι, τοὺς δὲ δυνατοὺς ἀνθυπείξει πραΰνοντα κατέχειν ἐν τῇ πολιτείᾳ καὶ διαλύειν τὰ πράγματα, πολιτικήν τινα ποιούμενον αὐτῶν ὥσπερ νοσημάτων ἀπόρρητον ἰατρείαν, αὐτόν τε μᾶλλον ἡττᾶσθαι βουλόμενον ἐν τοῖς πολίταις ἢ νικᾶν ὕβρει καὶ καταλύσει τῶν οἴκοι δικαίων, τῶν τ᾽ ἄλλων ἑκάστου δεόμενον καὶ διδάσκοντα τὴν φιλονεικίαν ὅσον ἐστὶ κακόν· νῦν δ᾽ ὅπως μὴ πολίταις καὶ φυλέταις οἴκοι καὶ γείτοσι καὶ συνάρχουσιν ἀνθυπείξωσι μετὰ τιμῆς καὶ χάριτος, ἐπὶ ῥητόρων θύρας καὶ πραγματικῶν χεῖρας ἐκφέρουσι σὺν πολλῇ βλάβῃ καὶ αἰσχύνῃ τὰς διαφοράς.

Notes to Plutarch **Political Precepts** ***17, 19***

(17) πολιτικός, -οῦ (mas.). *politician, statesman.* As this word suggests, Plutarch's advice is directed at the civically active citizen of a Greek πόλις.

ἐν μελίτταις. The beehive was a common metaphor for the state in antiquity: see, e.g., Plato *Republic* 7.520b and section **(12)** of E5.

τοῦτο χρὴ διανοούμενον. *it is necessary for (the politician), having this (principle) in mind.* χρὴ here triggers a string of complementary infinitives.

διὰ χειρός. *in hand*; i.e., under his control: LSJ, s.v. χείρ, II.6.c.

ἃς . . . ἀρχὰς. The antecedent, ἀρχὰς, is incorporated into the relative clause: Smyth 2536–37. Translate as *on the other hand, magistrates that they call "authorities"* (ἐξουσίας) *and that they elect.*

σεμνὸν . . . δημοτικὸν. These are predicative adjectives agreeing with φιλαρχία. A neu. predicate adj. may agree with a fem. or mas. noun in generalizing statements (Smyth 1048); such an adj. functions essentially as a substantive: *love of office is neither (a) respectable nor (a) popular (thing).*

ἀπωθέω. in mid., *decline, reject*: LSJ, s.v. 6.

κἂν = καὶ ἐὰν.

δόξης. i.e., the politician's reputation.

συμφιλοτιμέομαι. *zealously discharge.*

δίκαιον . . . ἐλάττονας. In other words, those who have served in prestigious offices should not thereafter hesitate to serve in lesser ones. In the omitted text, Plutarch further limns the benefits of such a scheme.

ἀντικοσμέω. *adorn in turn.*

προχειρίζω. in mid., *keep in mind, apply to oneself.*

Περικλῆς. This is the great Athenian statesman Pericles (c. 495–429 B.C.E.), who was repeatedly elected one of the city's generals (στρατηγοί).

χλαμύς, -ύδος (fem.). *cloak* worn by a general: LSJ, s.v. 3.

πρόσεχε. impv.: *keep in mind*; Pericles addresses himself.

κἀκεῖνο = καὶ ἐκεῖνο. i.e., what follows.

ἀνθύπατος, ου (mas.). *proconsul*: Mason, *Greek Terms,* 104–6.

οὐ ταῦτα λόγχη πεδιάς. *these are not spearmen of the plain,* a quotation from Sophocles *Trachiniae* 1058. The rest of the sentence sheds some light on this somewhat opaque phrase, which is meant to remind Menemachus that he lives not in the glory days of the past but under Roman rule.

Σάρδεις . . . δύναμις. Sardis was once the capital of the powerful and wealthy kingdom of Lydia, ruled most famously by Croesus (reg. c. 560–546 B.C.E.), as described in Herodotus (1.26–85).

εὐσταλής, -ές. *neat, proper*: LSJ, s.v. 4. The ancients were attuned to viewing a person's appearance as indicative of status, identity, and gender—even of the wearer's moral or intellectual worth.

στρατήγιον, -ου (neu.). *office* or *meeting-place* of a Greek magistrate known as a στρατηγός.

βῆμα, -ατος (neu.). *tribunal*; i.e., a dais (or, if on campaign, mound of earth) whence a politician might orate or, more specifically, a Roman magistrate such as a governor might preside: LSJ, s.v. II; BDAG, s.v. 3; see also note on section **(3.1)** of D7, s.v. The significance of Plutarch's advice here is unclear, in part because of textual problems. If the text printed here is correct, Plutarch is perhaps suggesting that a Greek magistrate such as a στρατηγός should keep an eye on the Roman official who literally rules over him from "on high"; i.e., from a βῆμα.

τῷ στεφάνῳ. i.e., the crown that the Greek politician wears as a sign of honor.

φρονέω. *think highly of, take pride in* + dat.: LSJ, s.v. II.2.b.

κάλτιος, -ου (mas.). *shoe,* quasi-transliteration of a Latin word for shoe (*calceus*); the word thus suggests Roman rather than Greek footwear.

ἀγῶνι. i.e., a (dramatic) contest, a play; the word may also refer to a public speech.

ὑποβολεύς, -έως (mas.). *prompter*; i.e., person in a theater who prompts actors to remember their lines.

μέτρον, -ου (neu.). The word is difficult to render in English, for the Greek word means both (poetic) *meter* and *measure, limit.*

ἔκπτωσις, -εως (fem.). *failure.*

κλωγμός, -οῦ (mas.). *hooting, clucking,* by which Greek theatergoers communicated disapproval.

ἐπέβη. The subsequent line of verse contains the subject of the verb.

δεινὸς . . . τομεύς. The line comes from an unknown play.

Παρδάλαν. Plutarch reports later in this treatise that feuding between two citizens of Sardis, Pardalas and Tyrrhenus, had once led to "rebellion and war" that nearly brought the city to ruin (32).

ὑμέτερον. i.e., your fellow Sardian.

ἐκλαθομένοις < ἐκλανθάνω. in mid., *entirely forget* + gen.

ὁ δέ τις. *many a(n).*

ἐκριφεὶς. mas. sg. nom., aor. pass. part. < ἐκρίπτω. *send forth, exile.*

Σόλωνα. Solon was a famous Athenian politician, lawgiver, and lyric poet active in the early sixth c. B.C.E.

Φολεγάνδριος ἢ Σικινήτης. *Pholegandrian or Sicenete*; i.e., a resident of Pholegandros or Sicinos, neighboring islets in the southern Aegean Sea.

ἐπιχειρέω. *try, attempt* + inf.

ὑποδέω. in mid., *lace up, tie.* The children are trying to wear their fathers' shoes.

παιδιά, -ᾶς (fem.). *(childish) amusement.* Note accent of nom. sg., which distinguishes the word from παιδία, found earlier in the section, < παιδίον, -ου (neu.), *child.*

ποιοῦντες. Translate as concessive.

οὐκέτι. Take closely with ἄξια.

ἂν (= ἐὰν) μὴ. *unless.* Politicians who rabble-rouse pay the ultimate price for their misdeeds—unless they are fortunate enough merely to be despised.

(19) ποιοῦντα, παρέχοντα. sc. "the politician."

προσεκταπεινόω. *further abase.* This is the verb's only appearance in Greek literature; its object is τὴν πατρίδα.

δεδεμένου. mas. sg. gen., pf. pass. part. < δέω. *bind.*

προσυποβάλλω. *further submit.*

ὥσπερ ἔνιοι. *just as some (do).*

ἐξονειδίζουσι τὴν δουλείαν. *they add the disgrace of slavery,* by referring matters both large and small to their overlords.

καταπλήξ, -ῆγος. *stricken, paralyzed.*

περιδεᾶ. fem. sg. acc. < περιδεής, -ές. *very fearful.*

χωρὶς ἰατροῦ. i.e., unless told by a doctor to do so.

ὅσον ἡ φύσις δίδωσι. *as much as nature permits.*

διοίκησις, -εως (fem.). *administrative matter.*

προσάγοντες ἡγεμονικὴν κρίσιν. *seeking a (Roman) official's judgment* + dat. In other words, the Greeks ought to enjoy what autonomy they do have, which they undermine by constantly seeking Roman approval of their internal affairs.

δεσπότας. predicative with τοὺς ἡγουμένους.

φιλονεικία. This is a key word in Plutarch's political vocabulary. It can be an admirable quality if directed toward a worthwhile end, but here, as often, it threatens to undermine the stability of the state.

τῶν πρώτων. i.e., the first citizens.

ἐν οἷς. *in (situations) which.*

διαφέρω πρὸς ἀλλήλους. in mid., *be at odds with one another*: LSJ, s.v. διαφέρω, IV.

οὐκ ἀξιοῦντες ἔχειν ἔλαττον. *not condescending* (LSJ, s.v. ἀξιόω, III.2) *to occupy a weaker position.*

ἀνθύπειξις, -εως (fem.). *exchange of concessions*; i.e., quid pro quo.

πολιτικήν . . . ἰατρείαν. *making a secret political cure for them* (= τὰ πράγματα), *as if (they were) diseases.*

ἡττᾶσθαι. *to be defeated.*

οἴκοι. adv., *at home*; i.e., in the affairs of his home city.

δεόμενον < δέομαι. dep., *beg, ask*: LSJ, s.v. δέω (B), II.2. The politician should implore others to follow Plutarch's advice.

ἀνθυπείκω. *make concessions in turn, compromise* (in a good sense). Cf. ἀνθύπειξις above. Here Plutarch describes the current state of affairs (νῦν), in which politicians fail to curb their φιλονεικία.

πραγματικός, -οῦ (mas.). *legal adviser*: LSJ, s.v. 2.

PART D

JEWS AND CHRISTIANS

This section begins with excerpts from the New Testament, dating to the first century C.E. In the first selection, three short passages—two from the gospel of Luke and one from Paul's letter to the Christians in Rome—explore the relationship between God and the state and the obligations owed to each (D1.1–2). A contrasting passage from Revelation portrays Rome as a whore drunk on the blood of her Christian subjects (D2). The next four selections come from the *Jewish War,* a history of the province Judaea's rebellion from Rome (66–73/74 C.E.), written by Josephus, a participant in many of the events he describes. In the first excerpt, Agrippa II, a client-king of Rome, urges the residents of Judaea not to make war with the Romans; his speech, an analytical showpiece within Josephus's narrative, dates to the spring of 66, just before hostilities break out in earnest (D3). In the second excerpt, Josephus dramatically describes the destruction of the Jewish Temple in 70, an event that had a profound impact on the future paths of Judaism and Christianity (D4). In the following year, the quashing of the rebellion was commemorated in a triumph, a military parade through Rome; Josephus's account of this spectacle is among the longest and richest that are extant (D5–D6). The final passage sees the state in 304 C.E. through the eyes of women persecuted for their Christian faith: Roman officials and martyrs-to-be engage in dramatic dialogue (D7).

D1. GOD AND STATE

Luke 2.1–7, 20.20–26; Romans 13.1–7

D1.1. LUKE 2.1–7, 20.20–26

Among our Greek sources for the Roman world, the writings of the New Testament (c. 51–c. 110 C.E.) represent something uncommon: literary texts written by authors who did not necessarily belong to the highest social strata. (Yet it should not be assumed that all early Christians were uneducated and destitute—indeed this assumption has been soundly disproven—just that they were not typically the crème de la crème.) The writings of the New Testament are germane to this volume in that they offer insight into what the earliest followers of Jesus thought of Rome.

Written toward the end of the first century C.E., Luke is one of the four gospels—accounts of Jesus's life—found in the New Testament. Luke is stylistically versatile, his prose ranging from the balanced periodicity favored by authors of the Second Sophistic (C6) to the idiom of the Septuagint, the Greek translation of the Old Testament that often imported the syntax and style of the Hebrew original. Of the evangelists—the authors of the gospels—Luke is often said to be the most sympathetic to Rome, and two passages relevant to this claim are reproduced below. The first is drawn from the story of Jesus's nativity, which connects the particular circumstances of his birth with the administrative workings of the empire: taxation and salvation go hand in hand. This account is not paralleled in the other gospels, suggesting that Luke is promoting his own perspective on events. The second passage appears later in Luke, when the relationship between Jesus, himself a Jew, and Jewish religious authorities, "the scribes and chief priests," is growing increasingly tense. This vignette reports a verbal duel between Jesus and his hostile interlocutors regarding their obligations to God and the state.

Further Reading

J. D. M. Derrett, "Luke's Perspective on Tribute to Caesar," in *Political Issues in Luke-Acts,* ed. R. J. Cassidy and P. J. Scharper, 38–48 (Maryknoll, 1983); F. F. Bruce, "Render to Caesar," in *Jesus and the Politics of His Day,* ed. E. Bammel and C. F. D. Moule, 249–63 (Cambridge, 1984); K. Wengst, Pax Romana *and the Peace of Jesus Christ,* trans. J. Bowden (Philadelphia, 1987), 58–61; J. L. Moles, "Accommodation, Opposition or Other? *Luke-Acts'* Stance Towards Rome," in *Roman Rule in Greek and Latin Writing: Double Vision,* ed. J. M. Madsen and R. Rees, 79–104 (Leiden, 2014).

❧

(2.1) Ἐγένετο δὲ ἐν ταῖς ἡμέραις ἐκείναις ἐξῆλθεν δόγμα παρὰ
Καίσαρος Αὐγούστου ἀπογράφεσθαι πᾶσαν τὴν οἰκουμένην· **(2)** (αὕτη
ἀπογραφὴ πρώτη ἐγένετο ἡγεμονεύοντος τῆς Συρίας Κυρηνίου·) **(3)**
καὶ ἐπορεύοντο πάντες ἀπογράφεσθαι, ἕκαστος εἰς τὴν ἑαυτοῦ πόλιν.

(4) Ἀνέβη δὲ καὶ Ἰωσὴφ ἀπὸ τῆς Γαλιλαίας ἐκ πόλεως Ναζαρὲθ εἰς
τὴν Ἰουδαίαν εἰς πόλιν Δαυὶδ ἥτις καλεῖται Βηθλέεμ, διὰ τὸ εἶναι
αὐτὸν ἐξ οἴκου καὶ πατριᾶς Δαυίδ, **(5)** ἀπογράψασθαι σὺν Μαριὰμ τῇ
ἐμνηστευμένῃ αὐτῷ, οὔσῃ ἐγκύῳ. **(6)** ἐγένετο δὲ ἐν τῷ εἶναι αὐτοὺς
ἐκεῖ ἐπλήσθησαν αἱ ἡμέραι τοῦ τεκεῖν αὐτήν, **(7)** καὶ ἔτεκεν τὸν υἱὸν
αὐτῆς τὸν πρωτότοκον, καὶ ἐσπαργάνωσεν αὐτὸν καὶ ἀνέκλινεν αὐτὸν
ἐν φάτνῃ, διότι οὐκ ἦν αὐτοῖς τόπος ἐν τῷ καταλύματι.

(20.20) Καὶ παρατηρήσαντες ἀπέστειλαν ἐγκαθέτους ὑποκρινομένους
ἑαυτοὺς δικαίους εἶναι, ἵνα ἐπιλάβωνται αὐτοῦ λόγου, ὥστε
παραδοῦναι αὐτὸν τῇ ἀρχῇ καὶ τῇ ἐξουσίᾳ τοῦ ἡγεμόνος. **(21)** καὶ
ἐπηρώτησαν αὐτὸν λέγοντες· "Διδάσκαλε, οἴδαμεν ὅτι ὀρθῶς λέγεις
καὶ διδάσκεις καὶ οὐ λαμβάνεις πρόσωπον, ἀλλ' ἐπ' ἀληθείας τὴν ὁδὸν

τοῦ θεοῦ διδάσκεις· **(22)** ἔξεστιν ἡμᾶς Καίσαρι φόρον δοῦναι ἢ οὔ;" **(23)** κατανοήσας δὲ αὐτῶν τὴν πανουργίαν εἶπεν πρὸς αὐτούς· **(24)** "Δείξατέ μοι δηνάριον· τίνος ἔχει εἰκόνα καὶ ἐπιγραφήν"; ἀποκριθέντες δὲ εἶπαν· "Καίσαρος." **(25)** ὁ δὲ εἶπεν πρὸς αὐτούς· "Τοίνυν ἀπόδοτε τὰ Καίσαρος Καίσαρι καὶ τὰ τοῦ θεοῦ τῷ θεῷ." **(26)** καὶ οὐκ ἴσχυσαν ἐπιλαβέσθαι τοῦ ῥήματος ἐναντίον τοῦ λαοῦ, καὶ θαυμάσαντες ἐπὶ τῇ ἀποκρίσει αὐτοῦ ἐσίγησαν.

Notes to Luke 2.1–7, 20.20–26

The notes on Luke 2 are indebted to R. E. Brown, *The Birth of the Messiah: A Commentary on the Infancy Narratives in the Gospels of Matthew and Luke*, updated ed., The Anchor Bible Reference Library (New York, 1993).

(2.1) Ἐγένετο often opens sentences in the Septuagint (the Greek translation of the OT) and the gospels. It is a Hebraism, that is, a Greek word, phrase, or grammatical construction that reflects the vocabulary or syntax of Hebrew; so authoritative are the Hebrew scriptures that their grammar and vocabulary are imported into Greek. In Luke, ἐγένετο is followed by a finite verb (as here) or by καί + finite verb. Translated *and it came to pass* in the King James Version, the verb is often omitted in contemporary translations: BDAG, s.v. γίνομαι, 4.f.

Καίσαρος Αὐγούστου. Rome's first emperor, Augustus (reg. 27 B.C.E.–14 C.E.).

ἀπογράφεσθαι. probably mid. rather than pass., in the light of ἀπογράψασθαι in **(5)**. The dating of the census is problematic and controversial. Quirinius (on whom see below) took a census of the residents of Judaea (excluding Galilee, where Joseph and Mary resided) in 6/7 C.E.: Josephus *Jewish Antiquities* 18.1.1, Acts 5.37. Such a date is very difficult to harmonize with indications elsewhere in Luke that Jesus was born no later than 4 B.C.E. (1.5) and that he was around thirty years old in 27/28 C.E. (3.1, 3.23). For our purposes, this difficulty is less important than the question of why Luke associates the birth of Jesus with the census.

(2) πρώτη. Some have suggested that this be translated not as *first* but adverbially as *before*, as part of an attempt to resolve the debate regarding the dating of the census.

Κυρηνίου. P. Sulpicius Quirinius (c. 51 B.C.E.–21 C.E.) was consul in 12 B.C.E. and later a triumphator. Furthermore, he served as governor of Syria, in which capacity he also had jurisdiction over Judaea, which had just been annexed as a province in 6 C.E. Quirinius's census was, essentially, a tax assessment, and it was met with some resistance.

(4) Ἀνέβη. The journey described spans about seventy miles as the crow flies. In the Hebrew of the OT, one "goes up" to Judaea; here the Greek again mimics the Hebrew.

Ἰωσήφ. Many non-Greek proper nouns do not decline in Greek: Smyth 284.

Βηθλέεμ. Bethlehem was the birthplace of David (whose indeclinable name is here gen.), the great king of Israel (1 Samuel 16); it was prophesied that one day another ruler of Israel would be born there (Micah 5.2).

(5) ἀπογράψασθαι. inf. of purpose, common in the NT, not unknown in classical Greek: Smyth 2008–10.

ἐμνηστευμένῃ. fem. sg. dat., pf. pass. part. < μνηστεύω. *be engaged* (to marry).

(6) ἐπλήσθησαν < πίμπλημι. *end, fulfill* (sometimes with reference to prophecy): BDAG, s.v. 1.

τεκεῖν. aor. act. inf. < τίκτω.

(7) σπαργανόω. *wrap in cloths, swaddle.*

(20.20) παρατηρέω. *observe closely,* often with negative connotations: *watch in order to trap*: BDAG, s.v. 1.

ἀπέστειλαν. sc. "the scribes and chief priests" (οἱ γραμματεῖς καὶ οἱ ἀρχιερεῖς) as the subject, as indicated in the previous verse. In the NT, a γραμματεύς is an expert in Jewish law:

BDAG, s.v. 2. Over the course of Luke, resistance to Jesus grows among the religious authorities.

ἐγκάθετος, -ου (mas.). *spy.*

ὑποκρίνω. *feign, pretend*: LSJ, s.v. 4. The verb may also mean *play a part* on stage, perhaps suggesting the dialogue to come is like a scene in a drama.

ἐπιλαμβάνομαι. dep., *grasp, catch* + gen. of person caught and another gen. of the thing by which he is caught: BDAG, s.v. 1, 3.

αὐτοῦ. i.e., Jesus.

ἡγεμόνος. i.e., Pontius Pilate, who governed Judaea 26–36 C.E.

(21) λαμβάνω πρόσωπον. Hebraism: *play favorites, show partiality*: BDAG, s.v. πρόσωπον, 1.b.

ἐπ' ἀληθείας. *truly, in accordance with truth*: BDAG, s.v. ἐπί, I.8.

(22) φόρος, -ου (mas.). *tribute, tax.* Three chapters later, when Jesus is accused before Pilate, he is said to have forbidden the payment of φόρους to the emperor (Luke 23.1–2).

(23) πανουργία, -ας (fem.). *cunning, chicanery.*

(24) δηνάριον. The Roman coin known as a *denarius* bore, at the time, a portrait of Tiberius with an inscription identifying him not just as emperor but also as son of the deified Augustus (*Augusti divi filius*). Jesus's responses are elegantly rendered with alliteration, parallel construction, and polyptoton (repetition of words with the same root but different endings).

Καίσαρος. sc. εἰκόνα καὶ ἐπιγραφήν.

(25) τοίνυν is usually postpositive (i.e., it does not stand as the first word in a sentence) in classical Greek; in later periods, this rule fades: LSJ, s.v. B.

(26) τοῦ λαοῦ. Luke repeatedly says that the religious authorities wanted to kill Jesus, but refrained from doing so out of fear of "the people" (e.g., 19.47–48, 20.19, 22.2).

D1.2. ROMANS 13.1–7

Paul, a saint in Christian tradition, was born Saul in the Greek city of Tarsus in Cilicia. An observant Jew, he at first persecuted those who embraced Jesus's teachings. But later, on the road to Damascus in Syria, he had a vision of Christ and thereafter traveled the Mediterranean as an "apostle" (< ἀποστέλλω), spreading the teachings that he had once rejected. Like Plato, Seneca, and other ancient philosophers, Paul expounded his ideas in letters, addressing them to Christian communities located in Greece and Asia Minor as well as in Rome; several of these epistles were incorporated into the New Testament. Written in the mid-50s C.E., before Luke (D1.1) and the other canonical gospels, Paul's letter to the Christians living in Rome is considered his masterpiece, a dense, sometimes dazzling theological treatise written by someone who is patently well-versed in both the Jewish scriptures and Greek rhetoric. The passage below expatiates on the nature of the relationship between Christians and the political authorities. Its contents have proven controversial. Indeed a few scholars, arguing on stylistic and thematic grounds, have claimed that the passage is an interpolation, that is, a text written by someone else that was incorporated into Paul's text. Even if it was not written by Paul, the passage offers an invaluable early Christian perspective on an individual's obligations to God and the state, one that is presented in a highly influential letter that was enshrined in the canon of Christian scripture.

Further Reading

J. D. G. Dunn, "Romans 13:1–7. A Charter for Political Quietism?," *Ex Auditu* 2 (1986): 55–68; K. Wengst, Pax Romana *and the Peace of Jesus Christ*, trans. J. Bowden (Philadelphia, 1987), 79–84; E. Bammel, "Romans 13," in *Jesus and the Politics of His Day*, ed. E. Bammel and C. F. D. Moule, 365–83 (Cambridge, 1984); N. Elliott, "Romans 13:1–7 in the Context of Imperial Propaganda," in *Paul and Empire: Religion and Power in Roman Imperial Society*, ed. R. A. Horsley, 184–204 (Harrisburg, 1997); S. Kim, *Christ and Caesar: The Gospel and the Roman Empire in the Writings of Paul and Luke* (Grand Rapids, 2008), 34–43; J. R. Harrison, "Paul among the Romans," in *All Things to All Cultures: Paul among Jews, Greeks, and Romans*, ed. M. Harding and A. Nobbs, 143–76 (Grand Rapids, 2013).

(1) Πᾶσα ψυχὴ ἐξουσίαις ὑπερεχούσαις ὑποτασσέσθω, οὐ γὰρ ἔστιν ἐξουσία εἰ μὴ ὑπὸ θεοῦ, αἱ δὲ οὖσαι ὑπὸ θεοῦ τεταγμέναι εἰσίν. (2) ὥστε ὁ ἀντιτασσόμενος τῇ ἐξουσίᾳ τῇ τοῦ θεοῦ διαταγῇ ἀνθέστηκεν, οἱ δὲ ἀνθεστηκότες ἑαυτοῖς κρίμα λήμψονται. (3) οἱ γὰρ ἄρχοντες οὐκ εἰσὶν φόβος τῷ ἀγαθῷ ἔργῳ ἀλλὰ τῷ κακῷ. θέλεις δὲ μὴ φοβεῖσθαι τὴν ἐξουσίαν; τὸ ἀγαθὸν ποίει, καὶ ἕξεις ἔπαινον ἐξ αὐτῆς· (4) θεοῦ γὰρ διάκονός ἐστιν σοὶ εἰς τὸ ἀγαθόν. ἐὰν δὲ τὸ κακὸν ποιῇς, φοβοῦ· οὐ γὰρ εἰκῇ τὴν μάχαιραν φορεῖ· θεοῦ γὰρ διάκονός ἐστιν, ἔκδικος εἰς ὀργὴν τῷ τὸ κακὸν πράσσοντι. (5) διὸ ἀνάγκη ὑποτάσσεσθαι, οὐ μόνον διὰ τὴν ὀργὴν ἀλλὰ καὶ διὰ τὴν συνείδησιν, (6) διὰ τοῦτο γὰρ καὶ φόρους τελεῖτε, λειτουργοὶ γὰρ θεοῦ εἰσιν εἰς αὐτὸ τοῦτο προσκαρτεροῦντες. (7) ἀπόδοτε πᾶσι τὰς ὀφειλάς, τῷ τὸν φόρον τὸν φόρον, τῷ τὸ τέλος τὸ τέλος, τῷ τὸν φόβον τὸν φόβον, τῷ τὴν τιμὴν τὴν τιμήν.

Notes to Romans 13.1–7

These notes are indebted to J. D. G. Dunn, *Romans 9–16,* Word Biblical Commentary 38B (Nashville, 1988).

(1) ὑποτασσέσθω. 3rd sg. pres. pass. impv. For this passage, it may be useful to list in full the principal parts of τάσσω (Attic τάττω): τάξω, ἔταξα, τέταχα, τέταγμαι, ἐτάχθην / ἐτάγην.

ἔστιν. *there is.* On the accent, see Smyth 187.b.

αἱ δὲ οὖσαι. sc. ἐξουσίαι.

τεταγμέναι εἰσίν. 3rd pl. pf. pass. ind. Repetition of τάσσω and related words reinforces the stepwise, interlocking logic of the author's argument.

(2) ἀνθεστηκότες. The pf. is significant because it implies a longstanding pattern of resistance that began at some point in the past and has repercussions that continue through the present: Dunn, *Romans,* ad loc.

κρίμα λαμβάνω. in mid., *bring judgment on* + dat. The phrase is a Hebraism: Dunn, *Romans,* ad loc.

λήμψονται = Attic λήψονται.

(3) ποίει. Note accent: 2nd sg. pres. act. impv.

(4) εἰς. *for* (the purpose of).

εἰκῇ. *in vain, without purpose.*

φορεῖ. Supply ἡ ἐξουσία as the subject.

ἔκδικος, -ου (mas.). *avenger, prosecutor, legal representative.*

(5) συνείδησις, -εως (fem.). *conscience*: LSJ, s.v. 5; BDAG, s.v. 2.

(6) τελεῖτε. not impv. but ind., as indicated by γὰρ.

λειτουργοὶ. In Greece, a λειτουργός was a wealthy donor who assumed the costs of a civic benefaction, e.g., paying the costs of a festival or underwriting the operating budget of a warship; in the Septuagint and NT, the term also describes a divine servant.

(7) τῷ τὸν φόρον τὸν φόρον. *tax to the one (owed) tax.*

D2. THE WHORE OF BABYLON

Revelation 17.1–18

Written in Asia Minor during the reign of Domitian (81–96 C.E.), Revelation (in Greek, Ἀποκάλυψις) is the last book of the New Testament and among the last to be accepted into the canon of scripture. Revelation belongs to the genre of apocalyptic literature, which flourished from roughly the third century B.C.E. through the second century C.E. in a variety of languages, including Greek, Hebrew, Aramaic, and Coptic, the late antique manifestation of the Egyptian language. Characteristic of this loosely defined genre are otherworldly visions and journeys; prophecies—often, paradoxically, of what has already taken place—that explore the wider significance of recent, sometimes traumatic, events; numerology and enigmatic, allegorical language; a dualistic worldview that seesaws from high optimism to dire pessimism; and a cosmic conflict that culminates in judgment, salvation, damnation, and a new world order under God's sovereignty. Apocalyptic literature is typically written from the perspective of a community that believes it is threatened by external forces.

Revelation records the visions of an apostle, John, now living on the isle of Patmos in the Aegean Sea. Accompanying John, the book's narrator, in the passage below is an angel—in fact, one of seven angels who hold gold bowls whence they pour God's wrath upon the earth (Revelation 16). Here the angel introduces John to the lurid Whore of Babylon. Scholars have convincingly argued that this passage is a grotesquely parodic ekphrasis of a Roman coin whose imagery offended Christians of the time. The attitude toward Rome here expressed may come as a surprise to those who have read the preceding excerpts from Luke and Romans (D1).

Further Reading

S. R. F. Price, *Rituals and Power: The Roman Imperial Cult in Asia Minor* (Cambridge, 1984), 170–206; E. Pagels, *Revelations: Visions, Prophecy, and Politics in the Book of Revelation* (New York, 2012), 1–35; S. J. Friesen, "Apocalypse and Empire," in *The Oxford Handbook of Apocalyptic Literature,* ed. J. J. Collins, 163–79 (Oxford, 2014).

(1) Καὶ ἦλθεν εἷς ἐκ τῶν ἑπτὰ ἀγγέλων τῶν ἐχόντων τὰς ἑπτὰ φιάλας,
καὶ ἐλάλησεν μετ' ἐμοῦ λέγων· "Δεῦρο, δείξω σοι τὸ κρίμα τῆς
πόρνης τῆς μεγάλης τῆς καθημένης ἐπὶ ὑδάτων πολλῶν, **(2)** μεθ' ἧς
ἐπόρνευσαν οἱ βασιλεῖς τῆς γῆς, καὶ ἐμεθύσθησαν οἱ κατοικοῦντες
τὴν γῆν ἐκ τοῦ οἴνου τῆς πορνείας αὐτῆς." **(3)** καὶ ἀπήνεγκέν με
εἰς ἔρημον ἐν πνεύματι. καὶ εἶδον γυναῖκα καθημένην ἐπὶ θηρίον
κόκκινον, γέμοντα ὀνόματα βλασφημίας, ἔχων κεφαλὰς ἑπτὰ καὶ
κέρατα δέκα. **(4)** καὶ ἡ γυνὴ ἦν περιβεβλημένη πορφυροῦν καὶ
κόκκινον, καὶ κεχρυσωμένη χρυσίῳ καὶ λίθῳ τιμίῳ καὶ μαργαρίταις,
ἔχουσα ποτήριον χρυσοῦν ἐν τῇ χειρὶ αὐτῆς γέμον βδελυγμάτων καὶ
τὰ ἀκάθαρτα τῆς πορνείας αὐτῆς, **(5)** καὶ ἐπὶ τὸ μέτωπον αὐτῆς ὄνομα
γεγραμμένον, μυστήριον, Βαβυλὼν ἡ μεγάλη, ἡ μήτηρ τῶν πορνῶν καὶ
τῶν βδελυγμάτων τῆς γῆς. **(6)** καὶ εἶδον τὴν γυναῖκα μεθύουσαν ἐκ τοῦ
αἵματος τῶν ἁγίων καὶ ἐκ τοῦ αἵματος τῶν μαρτύρων Ἰησοῦ.

Καὶ ἐθαύμασα ἰδὼν αὐτὴν θαῦμα μέγα· **(7)** καὶ εἶπέν μοι ὁ ἄγγελος· "Διὰ
τί ἐθαύμασας; ἐγὼ ἐρῶ σοι τὸ μυστήριον τῆς γυναικὸς καὶ τοῦ θηρίου
τοῦ βαστάζοντος αὐτήν, τοῦ ἔχοντος τὰς ἑπτὰ κεφαλὰς καὶ τὰ δέκα
κέρατα· **(8)** τὸ θηρίον ὃ εἶδες ἦν καὶ οὐκ ἔστιν, καὶ μέλλει ἀναβαίνειν
ἐκ τῆς ἀβύσσου, καὶ εἰς ἀπώλειαν ὑπάγει· καὶ θαυμασθήσονται οἱ
κατοικοῦντες ἐπὶ τῆς γῆς, ὧν οὐ γέγραπται τὸ ὄνομα ἐπὶ τὸ βιβλίον τῆς
ζωῆς ἀπὸ καταβολῆς κόσμου, βλεπόντων τὸ θηρίον ὅτι ἦν καὶ οὐκ ἔστιν
καὶ παρέσται."

(9) "Ὧδε ὁ νοῦς ὁ ἔχων σοφίαν. αἱ ἑπτὰ κεφαλαὶ ἑπτὰ ὄρη εἰσίν, ὅπου ἡ γυνὴ κάθηται ἐπ' αὐτῶν. καὶ βασιλεῖς ἑπτά εἰσιν· **(10)** οἱ πέντε ἔπεσαν, ὁ εἷς ἔστιν, ὁ ἄλλος οὔπω ἦλθεν, καὶ ὅταν ἔλθῃ ὀλίγον αὐτὸν δεῖ μεῖναι, **(11)** καὶ τὸ θηρίον ὃ ἦν καὶ οὐκ ἔστιν καὶ αὐτὸς ὄγδοός ἐστιν καὶ ἐκ τῶν ἑπτά ἐστιν, καὶ εἰς ἀπώλειαν ὑπάγει. **(12)** καὶ τὰ δέκα κέρατα ἃ εἶδες δέκα βασιλεῖς εἰσιν, οἵτινες βασιλείαν οὔπω ἔλαβον, ἀλλὰ ἐξουσίαν ὡς βασιλεῖς μίαν ὥραν λαμβάνουσιν μετὰ τοῦ θηρίου. **(13)** οὗτοι μίαν γνώμην ἔχουσιν, καὶ τὴν δύναμιν καὶ ἐξουσίαν αὐτῶν τῷ θηρίῳ διδόασιν. **(14)** οὗτοι μετὰ τοῦ ἀρνίου πολεμήσουσιν, καὶ τὸ ἀρνίον νικήσει αὐτούς, ὅτι κύριος κυρίων ἐστὶν καὶ βασιλεὺς βασιλέων, καὶ οἱ μετ' αὐτοῦ κλητοὶ καὶ ἐκλεκτοὶ καὶ πιστοί."

(15) Καὶ λέγει μοι· "Τὰ ὕδατα ἃ εἶδες, οὗ ἡ πόρνη κάθηται, λαοὶ καὶ ὄχλοι εἰσὶν καὶ ἔθνη καὶ γλῶσσαι. **(16)** καὶ τὰ δέκα κέρατα ἃ εἶδες καὶ τὸ θηρίον, οὗτοι μισήσουσι τὴν πόρνην, καὶ ἠρημωμένην ποιήσουσιν αὐτὴν καὶ γυμνήν, καὶ τὰς σάρκας αὐτῆς φάγονται, καὶ αὐτὴν κατακαύσουσιν ἐν πυρί· **(17)** ὁ γὰρ θεὸς ἔδωκεν εἰς τὰς καρδίας αὐτῶν ποιῆσαι τὴν γνώμην αὐτοῦ, καὶ ποιῆσαι μίαν γνώμην καὶ δοῦναι τὴν βασιλείαν αὐτῶν τῷ θηρίῳ, ἄχρι τελεσθήσονται οἱ λόγοι τοῦ θεοῦ. **(18)** καὶ ἡ γυνὴ ἣν εἶδες ἔστιν ἡ πόλις ἡ μεγάλη ἡ ἔχουσα βασιλείαν ἐπὶ τῶν βασιλέων τῆς γῆς."

Notes to Revelation 17.1–18

These notes are indebted to D. E. Aune, *Revelation 17–22,* Word Bible Commentary 52C (Nashville, 1998).

(1) εἷς. Note breathing and accent.

ἐλάλησεν. The pleonastic combination of this verb + λέγων introducing direct discourse is a Hebraism, frequently found in the Septuagint (the Greek translation of the Hebrew OT) and NT: BDAG, s.v. λαλέω, 3 and s.v. λέγω, 1.b.θ.

τῆς πόρνης. Objective gen.: Smyth 1331. In the OT, the relationship between God and Israel is likened to a marriage; when Israel is disobedient, "consorting" with other gods, it is sometimes cast as a prostitute or adulteress: see, e.g., Jeremiah 3.6–10, Hosea 4.12–13.

καθημένης ἐπὶ ὑδάτων πολλῶν. In both Hebrew and Greek writers, Babylon's watercourses are a defining feature of the city, which the woman represents: see verse **(5)**.

(3) πνεῦμα, -ατος (neu.). *vision, prophetic trance*: BDAG, s.v. 6.e.

κόκκινος, -η, -ον. *scarlet.* Revelation is full of vivid colors, many of them symbolic. κόκκινος dye was made from the kermes insect, and was very costly. The color thus indicates wealth. It is also the color of the cloak worn by a Roman general. And, of course, it is reminiscent of blood.

γέμοντα. The verb here takes an acc. (and is thus perhaps a Hebraism) instead of the usual gen. of what something is filled with (Smyth 1369); in verse **(4)** the same verb, curiously, takes both gen. *and* acc.

(4) περιβεβλημένη < περιβάλλω. in mid., *wear, clothe* + acc.

πορφυροῦν. Purple is associated with royalty, particularly the Roman emperor.

ποτήριον. This particular vessel was often used for drinking wine; indeed, in Christian literature it is often used of the cup employed in the Eucharist and comes to symbolize suffering and martyrdom: Lampe, s.v. 3–6.

βδέλυγμα, -ατος (neu.). *abomination,* often associated with paganism in the Septuagint: BDAG, s.v. 1.

(5) μυστήριον. Take either in apposition to ὄνομα γεγραμμένον—i.e., *a name written, a mystery*—or as part of the inscription itself: *a name written, "Mystery."* Disobedient slaves were sometimes punitively tattooed on their faces; the woman's inscribed forehead suggests that she is of servile status: Aune, *Revelation*, ad loc.

Βαβυλὼν is a coded reference to Rome; the two cities were identified with one another, in part because armies from both cities had conquered Jerusalem and destroyed the Jewish Temple: see D4.

(7) ἄγγελος. A divinely sent messenger who explains marvels to the protagonist is a topos in apocalyptic literature.

(8) ἦν καὶ οὐκ ἔστιν, καὶ μέλλει ἀναβαίνειν. This is a parodic reworking of the description of Jesus in Revelation as ὁ ὢν καὶ ὁ ἦν καὶ ὁ ἐρχόμενος vel sim. See, e.g., 1.4, 1.8, 4.8, 11.17, 16.5, as cited by Aune, *Revelation*, ad loc.

ἀπώλειαν. This is a play on words. At Revelation 9.11, the angel of the abyss is called Ἀπολλύων, likewise related to ἀπόλλυμι.

θαυμασθήσονται. 3rd pl. fut. dep. ind.: BDAG, s.v. θαυμάζω, 2.

βλεπόντων. gen. absolute; sc. τῶν κατοικούντων ἐπὶ τῆς γῆς.

(9) Ὧδε ὁ νοῦς ὁ ἔχων σοφίαν. This is not easily rendered in English: *the mind that has wisdom (understands things) in the following way.*

ἑπτὰ ὄρη. i.e., the seven hills of Rome.

βασιλεῖς. There is great debate about whether to interpret the seven kings as symbolic or historical figures; i.e., as Roman emperors. A "double interpretation" (heads = hills *and* kings) like this one is rare in apocalyptic literature, suggesting that the author may be drawing on multiple sources: Aune, *Revelation*, ad loc.

(10) ἔπεσαν = Attic ἔπεσον. In later Greek, alpha often replaces the thematic vowels epsilon and omicron in the strong aorist endings.

(11) ὄγδοός. While there is no consensus about the identity of the first seven kings, it is generally agreed that the eighth king is Nero, who elsewhere in Revelation appears as the Antichrist. This text shows similarities to the folkloric "Nero *redux*" legends that maintained that the emperor had not died in 68 but, having fled beyond Rome's eastern frontier, was there assembling a massive army with which to invade the empire. Furthermore, in the first century C.E., three faux Neros popped up as pretenders to the throne.

(12) δέκα βασιλεῖς. Here the author seems to refer to client-kings, local regents under Rome's patronage.

(13) μίαν γνώμην. i.e., among the authorities there will be ὁμόνοια, a political concept with a long history in Greek culture.

(14) μετά + gen. *with,* but in the sense of *against,* as is common with verbs of fighting in the NT: BDAG, s.v. A.2.c.β.

κύριος κυρίων, βασιλεὺς βασιλέων. Such double titles were prevalent in Hebrew and other ancient Near Eastern languages: Aune, *Revelation,* ad loc.

(16) ἠρημωμένην. i.e., depopulated, which is especially significant when it is recalled that the woman represents Babylon/Rome.

φάγονται. 3rd pl. fut. dep. ind. < ἐσθίω. On the form, see BDAG, s.v.

(17) ἔδωκεν εἰς τὰς καρδίας. Hebraism: see, e.g., Ezra 7.27.

ποιῆσαι τὴν γνώμην αὐτοῦ. *to carry out his plan.*

D3. PERILS OF WAR WITH ROME

Josephus *Jewish War* 2.355–357, 361, 390–402

Titus Flavius Josephus, born Yosef ben Matityahu (son of Mattathias), bridged three worlds: Jewish, Greek, and Roman. Born in Jerusalem in 37 C.E., Josephus descended from the Hasmoneans, the family that had once ruled over an independent Judaea (142–63 B.C.E.; see B6); like others of his lineage, he was a priest at the Jewish Temple in Jerusalem. Versed in Greek literature and philosophy, Josephus wrote several works in the language, including a gripping account of the rebellion of Judaea from Rome (66–73/74 C.E.). In English, this work has been traditionally titled *Jewish War,* though some prefer *Judaean War* since the adjective Ἰουδαϊκός found in many of the Greek titles for the work (there are many variants, and the work's original title is unclear) may refer both to the Jewish people and to the province of Judaea. Josephus participated in many of the events narrated in this work. Appointed a general charged with defending the Galilee, he failed to save the city of Jotapata from a Roman siege and surrendered in July 67 C.E. About to be sent to Rome as a prisoner, he prophesied that the commander of the Roman expedition, Titus Flavius Vespasianus (reg. 69–79 C.E.), would ascend the throne; this prediction brought Josephus into favor with the future emperor and his son, Titus (reg. 79–81 C.E.). After Vespasian was acclaimed as emperor by his troops on July 1, 69, he freed Josephus, who remained in the Roman camp and witnessed the siege of Jerusalem.

After the fall of the city, Josephus traveled to Rome with Titus in 71. In the city, benefitting from imperial patronage, he dedicated himself to writing.

In the late spring of 66, many Judaeans were growing increasingly wroth with the predacious Roman governor, Gessius Florus, and were demanding that the chief priests and Marcus Julius Agrippa II (reg. 50–c. 93 C.E.), the Roman client-king of territory that bordered Judaea and the supervisor of the Temple, send envoys to the emperor Nero in search of redress. In response, Agrippa delivers the first and, arguably, most important speech in the *Jewish War.* According to the categories of ancient rhetorical theory, it is a deliberative speech, one in which a speaker argues for or against a course of action on the grounds of expediency: here the king warns against war with Rome. Although Josephus corresponded with Agrippa, even sharing with him drafts of the *Jewish War,* this speech should be read not as a precise rendering of the king's actual words but as a confection of the author. Like the speeches found in other Greek and Roman historical works, this oration represents the author's own complex and rhetorically sophisticated analysis of broader issues raised in the narrative.

Further Reading

Josephus *Jewish War* 1.1–30; T. Rajak, "Friends, Romans, Subjects: Agrippa II's Speech in Josephus's *Jewish War,*" in *Images of Empire,* ed. L. Alexander, 122–34 (Sheffield, 1991); D. R. Runnalls, "The Rhetoric of Josephus," in *Handbook of Classical Rhetoric in the Hellenistic Period, 330 B.C.–A.D. 400,* ed. S. E. Porter, 737–54 (Leiden, 1997); M. Goodman, *Rome and Jerusalem: The Clash of Ancient Civilizations* (New York, 2007), 3–25.

(355) "ἀλλὰ μὴν τό γε νῦν ἐλευθερίας ἐπιθυμεῖν ἄωρον, δέον ὑπὲρ τοῦ μηδὲ ἀποβαλεῖν αὐτὴν ἀγωνίζεσθαι πρότερον· ἡ γὰρ πεῖρα τῆς δουλείας χαλεπή, καὶ περὶ τοῦ μηδ' ἄρξασθαι ταύτης ὁ ἀγὼν δίκαιος. **(356)** ὁ δ' ἅπαξ χειρωθείς, ἔπειτα ἀφιστάμενος, αὐθάδης δοῦλός ἐστιν, οὐ φιλελεύθερος. τότε τοιγαροῦν ἐχρῆν πάνθ' ὑπὲρ τοῦ μὴ δέξασθαι Ῥωμαίους ποιεῖν, ὅτε ἐπέβαινεν τῆς χώρας Πομπήιος. **(357)** ἀλλ' οἱ μὲν ἡμέτεροι πρόγονοι καὶ οἱ βασιλεῖς αὐτῶν καὶ χρήμασιν καὶ σώμασιν καὶ ψυχαῖς ἄμεινον ὑμῶν πολλῷ διακείμενοι πρὸς μοῖραν ὀλίγην τῆς Ῥωμαίων δυνάμεως οὐκ ἀντέσχον· ὑμεῖς δὲ οἱ τὸ μὲν ὑπακούειν ἐκ διαδοχῆς παρειληφότες, τοῖς πράγμασιν δὲ τῶν πρώτων ὑπακουσάντων τοσοῦτον ἐλαττούμενοι, πρὸς ὅλην ἀνθίστασθε τὴν Ῥωμαίων ἡγεμονίαν;

[In the remainder of 357 through 360, Agrippa offers examples of great states—Athens, Sparta, and Macedon—which, though once powerful, now submit to Rome].

(361) "ἄλλα τε ἔθνη μυρία πλείονος γέμοντα πρὸς ἐλευθερίαν παρρησίας εἴκει· μόνοι δ' ὑμεῖς ἀδοξεῖτε δουλεύειν οἷς ὑποτέτακται τὰ πάντα. ποίᾳ στρατιᾷ, ποίοις πεποιθότες ὅπλοις; ποῦ μὲν ὁ στόλος ὑμῖν διαληψόμενος τὰς Ῥωμαίων θαλάσσας; ποῦ δ' οἱ ταῖς ἐπιβολαῖς ἐξαρκέσοντες θησαυροί;

[In 362–89, Agrippa reviews, region by region, the extent of Rome's conquests in the Mediterranean and beyond. The Judaeans would have to fight the Romans alone, for no other peoples of the earth would dare to ally with them.]

(390) "λοιπὸν οὖν ἐπὶ τὴν τοῦ θεοῦ συμμαχίαν καταφευκτέον. ἀλλὰ καὶ τοῦτο παρὰ Ῥωμαίοις τέτακται· δίχα γὰρ θεοῦ συστῆναι τηλικαύτην ἡγεμονίαν ἀδύνατον. **(391)** σκέψασθε δ' ὡς ὑμῖν τὸ τῆς θρησκείας ἄκρατον, εἰ καὶ πρὸς εὐχειρώτους πολεμοίητε, δυσδιοίκητον, καὶ δι' ἃ μᾶλλον τὸν θεὸν ἐλπίζετε σύμμαχον, ταῦτ' ἀναγκαζόμενοι παραβαίνειν ἀποστρέψετε. **(392)** τηροῦντές γε μὴν τὰ τῶν ἑβδομάδων ἔθη καὶ πρὸς μηδεμίαν πρᾶξιν κινούμενοι ῥᾳδίως ἁλώσεσθε, καθάπερ οἱ πρόγονοι Πομπηίῳ ταύτας μάλιστα τὰς ἡμέρας ἐνεργοὺς ποιησαμένῳ τῆς πολιορκίας, ἐν αἷς ἤργουν οἱ πολιορκούμενοι· **(393)** παραβαίνοντες δὲ ἐν τῷ πολέμῳ τὸν πάτριον νόμον οὐκ οἶδ' ὑπὲρ ὅτου λοιπὸν ποιήσεσθε τὸν ἀγῶνα· σπουδὴ γὰρ ὑμῖν μία τὸ μὴ τῶν πατρίων τι καταλῦσαι. **(394)** πῶς δὲ ἐπικαλέσεσθε τὸ θεῖον πρὸς τὴν ἄμυναν οἱ παραβάντες ἑκουσίως τὴν εἰς αὐτὸ θεραπείαν; ἐπαναιροῦνται δὲ ἕκαστοι πόλεμον ἢ θείᾳ πεποιθότες ἢ ἀνθρωπίνῃ βοηθείᾳ· ὅταν δὲ τὴν παρ' ἀμφοῖν τὸ εἰκὸς ἀποκόπτῃ, φανερὰν ἅλωσιν οἱ πολεμοῦντες αἱροῦνται. **(395)** τί δὴ κωλύει ταῖς ἑαυτῶν χερσὶν διαχρήσασθαι τέκνα καὶ γυναῖκας καὶ τὴν περικαλλεστάτην πατρίδα ταύτην καταφλέξαι; μανέντες γὰρ οὕτως τό γε τῆς ἥττης ὄνειδος κερδήσετε. **(396)** καλόν, ὦ φίλοι, καλόν, ἕως ἔτι ἐν ὅρμῳ τὸ σκάφος προσκέπτεσθαι τὸν μέλλοντα χειμῶνα μηδ' εἰς μέσας τὰς θυέλλας ἀπολουμένους ἀναχθῆναι· τοῖς μὲν γὰρ ἐξ ἀδήλων ἐπιπεσοῦσιν δεινοῖς τὸ γοῦν ἐλεεῖσθαι περίεστιν, ὁ δ' εἰς πρόδηλον ἀπώλειαν ὁρμήσας καὶ προσονειδίζεται. **(397)** πλὴν εἰ μή τις ὑπολαμβάνει κατὰ συνθήκας πολεμήσειν καὶ Ῥωμαίους κρατήσαντας ὑμῶν μετριάσειν, ἀλλ' οὐκ εἰς ὑπόδειγμα τῶν ἄλλων ἐθνῶν καταφλέξειν μὲν τὴν ἱερὰν πόλιν, ἀναιρήσειν δὲ πᾶν ὑμῶν τὸ φῦλον· οὐδὲ γὰρ περιλειφθέντες φυγῆς εὑρήσετε τόπον ἁπάντων ἐχόντων Ῥωμαίους δεσπότας ἢ δεδοικότων σχεῖν. **(398)** ὁ δὲ κίνδυνος οὐ τῶν ἐνθάδε μόνον, ἀλλὰ καὶ τῶν κατὰ τὰς ἄλλας κατοικούντων πόλεις· οὐ γὰρ ἔστιν ἐπὶ τῆς οἰκουμένης δῆμος ὁ μὴ μοῖραν ἡμετέραν ἔχων. **(399)** οὓς ἅπαντας πολεμησάντων ὑμῶν κατασφάξουσιν οἱ διάφοροι, καὶ δι' ὀλίγων ἀνδρῶν κακοβουλίαν πᾶσα πλησθήσεται πόλις Ἰουδαϊκοῦ φόνου. καὶ συγγνώμη μὲν τοῖς τοῦτο πράξασιν· ἂν δὲ μὴ πραχθῇ, λογίσασθε, πῶς πρὸς οὕτω φιλανθρώπους ὅπλα κινεῖν ἀνόσιον. **(400)** εἰσελθέτω δ' οἶκτος ὑμᾶς εἰ καὶ μὴ τέκνων καὶ γυναικῶν, ἀλλὰ τῆς γε μητροπόλεως ταύτης καὶ τῶν ἱερῶν περιβόλων. φείσασθε τοῦ ἱεροῦ καὶ τὸν ναὸν ἑαυτοῖς μετὰ τῶν ἁγίων τηρήσατε· ἀφέξονται γὰρ οὐκέτι Ῥωμαῖοι τούτων κρατήσαντες, ὧν φεισάμενοι πρότερον ἠχαρίστηνται. **(401)** μαρτύρομαι δὲ ἐγὼ μὲν ὑμῶν τὰ ἅγια καὶ τοὺς ἱεροὺς ἀγγέλους τοῦ θεοῦ καὶ πατρίδα τὴν κοινήν, ὡς οὐδὲν τῶν σωτηρίων ὑμῖν καθυφηκάμην, ὑμεῖς δὲ βουλευσάμενοι μὲν τὰ δέοντα κοινὴν σὺν ἐμοὶ τὴν εἰρήνην ἕξετε, προαχθέντες δὲ τοῖς θυμοῖς χωρὶς ἐμοῦ κινδυνεύσετε."

(402) Τοσαῦτα εἰπὼν ἐπεδάκρυσέν τε μετὰ τῆς ἀδελφῆς καὶ πολὺ τῆς ὁρμῆς αὐτῶν ἔπαυσεν τοῖς δακρύοις. ἀνεβόων δὲ οὐ Ῥωμαίοις, ἀλλὰ Φλώρῳ δι' ἃ πεπόνθασιν πολεμεῖν.

Notes to Josephus Jewish War *2.355–357, 361, 390–402*

These notes are indebted to S. Mason, *Flavius Josephus: Translation and Commentary,* vol. 1b, *Judean War 2* (Leiden, 2008).

(355) ἐλευθερίας. ἐλευθερία is a key theme in the speech, the *Jewish War,* and this reader as a whole. The language here echoes that of Herodotus, who casts the Persian Wars as a struggle for the preservation of a people's freedom (Greece ~ Judaea) under threat of enslavement by an invading army (Persia ~ Rome).

ἄωρον. predicative adj. modifying the articular inf.

δέον < δεῖ. acc. absolute: *since (it was) necessary* + inf.: Smyth 2076. πρότερον indicates that the form of "to be" supplied when translating the acc. absolute should be past rather than present.

αὐτὴν = ἐλευθερίαν = object of ὑπὲρ τοῦ μηδὲ ἀποβαλεῖν.

(356) ἀφίστημι. *rebel, revolt*: LSJ, s.v. B.2.

αὐθάδης, -ες. *stubborn.*

Πομπήιος. In 63 B.C.E., the Roman general and statesman Gnaeus Pompeius, a.k.a. Pompey, settled the claims of two rivals to the Hasmonean throne (B6) in Judaea; in the end, he compelled the residents of the region, though it remained nominally autonomous, to pay tribute to Rome and be subject to the oversight of its officials. Josephus narrates these events in the first book of the *Jewish War.*

(357) πολλῷ. dat. degree of difference: Smyth 1513.

πρός + acc. *against,* esp. in military contexts: Smyth 1695.3.c.

ἐκ διαδοχῆς. i.e., submission had been "handed down" from generation to generation, thus acclimating the people to subservience.

παρειληφότες. mas. pl. nom., pf. act. part. < παραλαμβάνω.

τοῖς πράγμασιν. dat. of respect: Smyth 1516.

(361) ἄλλα. Note accent.

γέμω. *be full of* + gen.; on verbs of filling, see Smyth 1369.

πρός + acc. *with respect to.*

παρρησία, -ας (fem.). *bold, forthright speech.* In Greek political discourse, παρρησία is often tied to ἐλευθερία: Mason, *Josephus*, ad loc.

οἷς. As often, the antecedent to the relative, presumably the demonstrative pronoun τούτοις, is omitted: Smyth 2509.

ὑποτέτακται. The tense is important: not only have all the other states (τὰ πάντα) submitted to Rome, they have remained in a state of submission ever since.

πεποιθότες < πείθω.

διαληψόμενος. Note tense: fut. part. indicating purpose < διαλαμβάνω. *conquer, divide.*

(390) λοιπὸν. *finally*; i.e., only one option remains.

καταφευκτέον. impersonal verbal adj. < καταφεύγω. *it is necessary to flee to, seek recourse in* + ἐπί. Verbal adjectives that end in -τέος, -τέα, -τέον connote necessity: Smyth 473.

τάσσω (Attic τάττω). The verb has martial overtones: *station, post, deploy.*

δίχα γὰρ θεοῦ. Not only Agrippa, but also the narrator and various speakers in the *Jewish War* express this opinion.

τηλικ-οῦτος, -αύτη, -οῦτο. *so great*: LSJ, s.v. τηλικόσδε, II.

(391) σκέψασθε. 2nd pl. aor. dep. impv.

θρησκεία, -ας (fem.). *worship, cult.*

δυσδιοίκητος, -ον. a rare word: *unmanageable, unworkable.* In medical writers, it means *indigestible*; Josephus may hint at the difficulty of observing Jewish dietary law in wartime: Mason, *Josephus*, ad loc.

δι' ἅ. The antecedent, ταῦτ', is incorporated into the relative clause: Smyth 2536–37. Agrippa is referring here to the traditional practices of Jewish law. He argues that the rebels face a Catch-22: by observing the law, the rebels hope for God's support in a war during which they will be compelled to transgress the law and thus alienate their divine ally.

ἀποστρέψετε. sc. τὸν θεὸν as object.

(392) τὰ τῶν ἑβδομάδων ἔθη. i.e., the Sabbath. Elsewhere Josephus approves of observing the Sabbath rest in times of war: *Against Apion* 1.209–12.

ἁλώσεσθε. 2nd pl. fut. dep. ind. < ἁλίσκομαι. *be conquered.*

καθάπερ οἱ πρόγονοι. sc. "were conquered."

Πομπηίῳ. dat. of agent. While the defenders were observing the Sabbath, Pompey took the opportunity to enhance his siege-works: *Jewish War* 1.145–47.

ἤργουν. 3rd pl. impf. act. ind. < ἀργέω. Antithetical words sharing the same root, ἔργον, draw attention to the contrast between the inactivity of the defenders (ἤργουν) and the heightened activity (ἐνεργοὺς) of the attackers.

(393) ὑπὲρ ὅτου (= οὗτινος). *on what basis*: Mason, *Josephus*, ad loc. The indefinive relative pronoun here introduces an indirect question: Smyth 1263, 2663.

τῶν πατρίων. partitive gen. after τι.

(394) παραβάντες. Repetition of the verb παραβαίνω in this passage hammers home Agrippa's point: resistance will require violating the law.

ἐπαναιρέω. in mid., *enter into* + acc.: LSJ, s.v. II. These sentiments recall the Melian Dialogue (Thucydides 5.104–5): Mason, *Josephus*, ad loc.

ὅταν . . . ἀποκόπτῃ. *whenever probability cuts off (help) from both.*

ἅλωσιν. There is suggestive evidence that ἅλωσις was the original title of Josephus's work: Mason, *Josephus*, ad loc.

αἱροῦνται. Josephus is deeply interested in the question of who is responsible for the Jewish War; note here the mid. voice: the Judaeans *choose* capture *for themselves*: LSJ, s.v. αἱρέω, B.

(395) κωλύει. Verbs of hindering like κωλύω regularly take inf. and acc.: Smyth 2739. The acc. must here be supplied: sc. ὑμᾶς.

διαχράομαι. *kill*: LSJ, s.v. I.2.

καταφλέξαι. aor. act. inf. < καταφλέγω. *burn down.*

μανέντες. mas. pl. nom., aor. dep. part. < μαίνομαι. *be mad, insane.*

κερδήσετε. 2nd pl. fut. act. ind. < κερδαίνω. *avoid*: LSJ, s.v. III.

(396) καλόν. diacope, repetition of a word with one or more others in between; the figure adds pathos and emphasis to Agrippa's argument. Agrippa is countering the suggestion that rebellion is the nobler path; he argues that refraining from revolt is not just expedient, as he has maintained throughout the speech, but also noble. In deliberative speeches, it is usual to weigh the expediency vs. the nobility or justice of different courses of action.

σκάφος, -εος (neu.). *ship.* The ship of state was a common metaphor in Greek and Roman literature.

ἀπολουμένους. mas. pl. acc., fut. mid. part. < ἀπόλλυμι.

ἀναχθῆναι. aor. pass. inf. < ἀνάγω. Here the pass. has an act. meaning. *set sail, put to sea*: LSJ, s.v. B.

ἐπιπεσοῦσιν. mas. pl. dat., aor. act. part < ἐπιπίπτω.

τὸ . . . ἐλεεῖσθαι is the subject of περίεστιν.

ὁρμάω. *rush headlong*: LSJ, s.v. A.II.2.

προσονειδίζω. *suffer reproach.* Cf. ὄνειδος in the previous section.

(397) ὑπολαμβάνω. *suppose, assume*: LSJ, s.v. III. The verb often implies that the supposition or assumption is erroneous. Agrippa employs dialogismus: he has an imaginary interlocutor (τις) raise an objection in order to quash it.

μετριάσειν. The warrior-queen Boudicca employs the same verb to question the Romans' restraint: see section **(3.5)** of C5.

φῦλον, -ου (neu.). *nation, people, tribe, race*; in Josephus, this word is equivalent to ἔθνος: Mason, *Josephus,* s.v. 2.366.

περιλείπομαι. dep., *survive*; translate the participle as conditional and οὐδὲ with the main verb.

σχεῖν. aor. act. inf. < ἔχω.

(398) τῶν κατὰ τὰς ἄλλας κατοικούντων πόλεις. Here, as the speech approaches its conclusion, Agrippa, as recommended by rhetorical theorists (e.g., *Rhetorica ad Herennium* 2.47–48), rouses his audience's pity and broadens the scope of his argument: resistance to Rome in this *particular* case is futile and will have *universal* repercussions.

ἔστιν. *there is*; on the accent, see Smyth 187.b. There were indeed many Jewish communities in the cities of the Mediterranean littoral.

(399) πλησθήσεται. 3rd sg. fut. pass. ind. < πίμπλημι. *fill* + gen. After Agrippa's speech, there were waves of reciprocal killings of Jews by non-Jews and vice versa in Syria and Judaea: Mason, *Josephus*, ad loc.

πράξασιν. i.e., those who attack the rebels' coreligionists.

πρὸς οὕτω φιλανθρώπους. Agrippa predicts that the rebels will visit violence even on those cities that had not attacked their own Jewish populations.

(400) εἰσελθέτω. 3rd sg. aor. dep. impv. < εἰσέρχομαι.

τέκνων καὶ γυναικῶν. These and the following genitives are objective (Smyth 1331), triggered by οἶκτος.

τοῦ ἱεροῦ καὶ τὸν ναὸν. τοῦ ἱεροῦ refers to the structures on the Temple Mount as a whole; τὸν ναὸν refers to the Temple itself, which houses inter alia the Sanctuary (Holy Place) and the Holy of Holies. The destruction of the Temple is narrated in D4.

ἠχαρίστηνται. 3rd pl. pf. pass. ind. < ἀχαριστέω. *be treated with ingratitude,* even though the Romans had refrained from despoiling the Temple up to this point.

(401) σωτήριος, -ον. *saving, bringing safety.*

καθυφίημι. *compromise, betray.*

προαχθέντες < προάγω. *induce, provoke.*

(402) ἀδελφῆς. i.e., the princess Berenice, who was next to Agrippa as he spoke.

ὁρμή, -ῆς (fem.). *impulse, rage, desire, zeal*—a key word in Josephus; look for it again in D4.

ἀνεβόων. The impf. here indicates repeated action: Smyth 1893.

πολεμεῖν. The complementary inf. is dramatically delayed until the sentence's end.

D4. THE TEMPLE IS BURNED

Josephus *Jewish War* 6.249–270

In April 70 C.E., Titus, son of the emperor Vespasian (reg. 69–79), besieged Jerusalem with a massive army of four Roman legions and numerous allied troops. (Among the allies were forces sent by Agrippa II; see D3.) Titus sought a quick capitulation. But Jerusalem held on for five months, making this the longest siege in Roman imperial history. Not only was Josephus (D3) an eyewitness to Titus's campaign, but he also had access to the commander's field diary and the testimony of Judaeans who had joined the Roman side. His account thus has a strong evidentiary basis; moreover, it is told in an arresting style that draws on the vocabulary of epic and tragedy.

During the final stages of the siege in July 70, Roman forces surrounded the Temple Mount. Atop this plateau was the Jewish Temple, a center of cultic activity and, for many Jews, a touchstone of their identity. To follow Josephus's account below, some additional topographical information is needed. Herod the Great, client-king of Judaea (reg. 40–4 B.C.E.), had enlarged, paved, and enclosed the Temple Mount with a huge rectangular wall pierced by gates. In the middle of this enclosed space, referred to below as "the outer court," lay the Temple proper, a splendid structure that was surrounded by another gated wall that enclosed "the inner court." To the northwest, just outside the outer wall, lay the Antonia, a tower or towered fortress (its design is unclear) that the Romans had taken and were employing as a staging ground for the siege. In the passage below, Josephus tells of the Temple's destruction on a day already inauspicious in the building's history. Who or what is ultimately responsible for this tragedy, which had profound effects on the future path of both Judaism and Christianity? Josephus offers a many-layered answer to this question of agency.

Further Reading

T. Rajak, *Josephus: The Historian and His Society,* 2nd ed. (London, 2002), 78–103; T. D. Barnes, "The Sack of the Temple in Josephus and Tacitus," in *Flavius Josephus and Flavian Rome,* ed. J. Edmondson, S. Mason, and J. Rives, 129–44 (Oxford, 2005).

(249) Τίτος δὲ ἀνεχώρησεν εἰς τὴν Ἀντωνίαν διεγνωκὼς τῆς ἐπιούσης ἡμέρας ὑπὸ τὴν ἕω μετὰ πάσης ἐμβαλεῖν τῆς δυνάμεως καὶ τὸν ναὸν περικατασχεῖν. **(250)** τοῦ δ' ἄρα κατεψήφιστο μὲν τὸ πῦρ ὁ θεὸς πάλαι, παρῆν δ' ἡ εἱμαρμένη χρόνων περιόδοις ἡμέρα δεκάτη Λώου μηνός, καθ' ἣν καὶ πρότερον ὑπὸ τοῦ τῶν Βαβυλωνίων βασιλέως ἐνεπρήσθη. **(251)** λαμβάνουσι δ' αἱ φλόγες ἐκ τῶν οἰκείων τὴν ἀρχὴν καὶ τὴν αἰτίαν· ὑποχωρήσαντος γὰρ τοῦ Τίτου πρὸς ὀλίγον λωφήσαντες οἱ στασιασταὶ πάλιν τοῖς Ῥωμαίοις ἐπιτίθενται, καὶ τῶν τοῦ ναοῦ φρουρῶν γίνεται συμβολὴ πρὸς τοὺς σβεννύντας τὸ πῦρ τοῦ ἔνδοθεν ἱεροῦ, οἳ τρεψάμενοι τοὺς Ἰουδαίους μέχρι τοῦ ναοῦ παρηκολούθουν. **(252)** ἔνθα δὴ τῶν στρατιωτῶν τις οὔτε παράγγελμα περιμείνας οὔτ' ἐπὶ τηλικούτῳ δείσας ἐγχειρήματι, δαιμονίῳ ὁρμῇ τινι χρώμενος ἁρπάζει μὲν ἐκ τῆς φλεγομένης † φλογός, ἀνακουφισθεὶς δὲ ὑπὸ συστρατιώτου τὸ πῦρ ἐνίησι θυρίδι χρυσῇ, καθ' ἣν εἰς τοὺς περὶ τὸν ναὸν οἴκους εἰσιτὸν ἦν ἐκ τοῦ βορείου κλίματος. **(253)** αἰρομένης δὲ τῆς φλογὸς Ἰουδαίων μὲν ἐγείρεται κραυγὴ τοῦ πάθους ἀξία, καὶ πρὸς τὴν ἄμυναν συνέθεον, οὔτε τοῦ ζῆν ἔτι φειδὼ λαμβάνοντες οὔτε ταμιευόμενοι τὴν ἰσχύν, δι' ὃ φυλακτικοὶ πρότερον ἦσαν οἰχομένου.

(254) Δραμὼν δέ τις ἀγγέλλει Τίτῳ· κἀκεῖνος, ἔτυχεν δὲ κατὰ σκηνὴν ἀναπαυόμενος ἐκ τῆς μάχης, ὡς εἶχεν ἀναπηδήσας ἔθει πρὸς τὸν ναὸν εἴρξων τὸ πῦρ. **(255)** κατόπιν δὲ οἵ τε ἡγεμόνες εἵποντο πάντες, καὶ

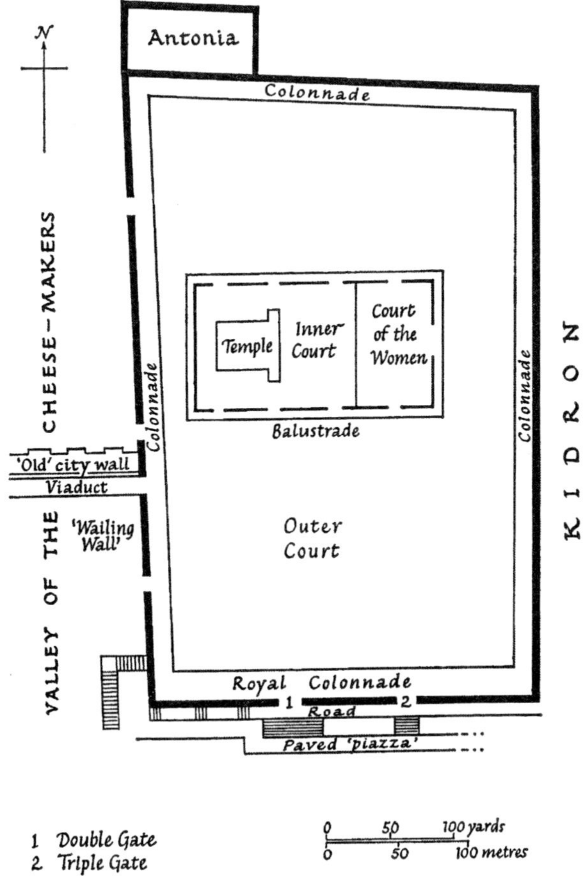

"Herod's Temple Enclosure." This is a plan of the Jewish Temple in Jerusalem and its environs as renovated and expanded by Herod the Great (reg. 40–4 B.C.E.), king of Judaea. Josephus narrates the destruction of the Temple in *Jewish War* 6.249–270 (D4). *From Josephus,* The Jewish War, *translated by G. A. Williamson, revised with an introduction, notes and appendixes by E. Mary Smallwood (Penguin Classics 1959, Revised edition 1981). Copyright © G. A. Williamson, 1959, 1969. Introduction and editorial matter copyright © E. M. Smallwood, 1981. Reproduced by permission of Penguin Books, Ltd.*

πτοηθέντα τούτοις ἠκολούθει τὰ τάγματα· βοὴ δὲ ἦν καὶ θόρυβος ἅτε τηλικαύτης δυνάμεως ἀτάκτως κεκινημένης. **(256)** ὁ μὲν οὖν Καῖσαρ τῇ τε φωνῇ καὶ τῇ δεξιᾷ διεσήμαινε τοῖς μαχομένοις τὸ πῦρ σβεννύειν, οὔτε δὲ βοῶντος ἤκουον μείζονι κραυγῇ τὰς ἀκοὰς προκατειλημμένοι καὶ τοῖς νεύμασι τῆς χειρὸς οὐ προσεῖχον, οἱ μὲν τῷ πολεμεῖν, οἱ δὲ ὀργῇ περισπώμενοι. **(257)** τῶν δὲ ταγμάτων εἰσθεόντων οὔτε παραίνεσις οὔτ᾽ ἀπειλὴ κατεῖχεν τὰς ὁρμάς, ἀλλ᾽ ὁ θυμὸς ἁπάντων ἐστρατήγει· καὶ περὶ τὰς εἰσόδους συνωθούμενοι πολλοὶ μὲν ὑπ᾽ ἀλλήλων κατεπατοῦντο, πολλοὶ δὲ θερμοῖς ἔτι καὶ τυφομένοις τοῖς ἐρειπίοις τῶν στοῶν ἐμπίπτοντες ἡττωμένων συμφοραῖς ἐχρῶντο. **(258)** πλησίον δὲ τοῦ ναοῦ γινόμενοι τῶν μὲν τοῦ Καίσαρος παραγγελμάτων προσεποιοῦντο μηδὲ κατακούειν, τοῖς πρὸ αὐτῶν δὲ τὸ πῦρ ἐνιέναι παρεκελεύοντο. **(259)** τῶν δὲ στασιαστῶν ἀμηχανία μὲν ἦν ἤδη τοῦ βοηθεῖν, φόνος δὲ πανταχοῦ καὶ τροπή. τὸ δὲ πλέον ἀπὸ τοῦ δήμου λαὸς ἀσθενὴς καὶ ἄνοπλος ὅπου καταληφθείη τις ἀπεσφάττετο, καὶ περὶ μὲν τὸν βωμὸν πλῆθος ἐσωρεύετο νεκρῶν, κατὰ δὲ τῶν τοῦ ναοῦ βάθρων αἷμά τ᾽ ἔρρει πολὺ καὶ τὰ τῶν ἄνω φονευομένων σώματα κατωλίσθανε.

(260) Καῖσαρ δ᾽ ὡς οὔτε τὰς ὁρμὰς ἐνθουσιώντων τῶν στρατιωτῶν κατασχεῖν οἷός τε ἦν καὶ τὸ πῦρ ἐπεκράτει, παρελθὼν μετὰ τῶν ἡγεμόνων ἔνδον ἐθεάσατο τοῦ ναοῦ τὸ ἅγιον καὶ τὰ ἐν αὐτῷ, πολὺ μὲν τῆς παρὰ τοῖς ἀλλοφύλοις φήμης ἀμείνω, τοῦ δὲ κόμπου καὶ τῆς παρὰ τοῖς οἰκείοις δόξης οὐκ ἐλάττω. **(261)** τῆς φλογὸς δὲ οὐδέπω διικνουμένης οὐδαμόθεν εἴσω, τοὺς δὲ περὶ τὸν ναὸν οἴκους νεμομένης, νομίσας, ὅπερ ἦν, ἔτι σώζεσθαι τὸ ἔργον δύνασθαι προπηδᾷ, **(262)** καὶ αὐτός τε παρακαλεῖν τοὺς στρατιώτας ἐπειρᾶτο τὸ πῦρ σβεννύειν καὶ Λιβεράλιον ἑκατοντάρχην τῶν περὶ αὐτὸν λογχοφόρων ξύλοις παίοντα τοὺς ἀπειθοῦντας ἐκέλευσεν εἴργειν. **(263)** τῶν δὲ καὶ τὴν πρὸς τὸν Καίσαρα αἰδῶ καὶ τὸν ἀπὸ τοῦ κωλύοντος φόβον ἐνίκων οἱ θυμοὶ καὶ τὸ πρὸς Ἰουδαίους μῖσος, καὶ πολεμική τις ὁρμὴ λαβροτέρα· **(264)** τοὺς δὲ πολλοὺς ἐνῆγεν ἁρπαγῆς ἐλπίς, δόξαν τε ἔχοντας ὡς τὰ ἔνδον ἅπαντα χρημάτων μεστὰ εἴη, καὶ τὰ πέριξ ὁρῶντας χρυσοῦ πεποιημένα. **(265)** φθάνει δέ τις καὶ τῶν εἴσω παρεληλυθότων ἐκπηδήσαντος τοῦ Καίσαρος πρὸς ἐποχὴν τῶν στρατιωτῶν πῦρ εἰς τοὺς στροφέας ἐμβαλὼν τῆς πύλης † ἐν σκότῳ· (266) τότε γὰρ ἐξαπίνης ἔνδοθεν ἐκφανείσης φλογὸς οἵ τε ἡγεμόνες μετὰ τοῦ Καίσαρος ἀνεχώρουν, καὶ τοὺς ἔξωθεν οὐδεὶς ὑφάπτειν ἐκώλυεν. ὁ μὲν οὖν ναὸς οὕτως ἄκοντος Καίσαρος ἐμπίπραται.

(267) Πολλὰ δ' ἄν τις ἐπολοφυράμενος ἔργῳ πάντων ὧν ὄψει καὶ ἀκοῇ παρειλήφαμεν θαυμασιωτάτῳ κατασκευῆς τε ἕνεκα καὶ μεγέθους ἔτι τε τῆς καθ' ἕκαστον πολυτελείας καὶ τῆς περὶ τὰ ἅγια δόξης, μεγίστην λάβοι παραμυθίαν τὴν εἱμαρμένην ἄφυκτον οὖσαν ὥσπερ ἐμψύχοις οὕτω καὶ ἔργοις καὶ τόποις. (268) θαυμάσαι δ' ἄν τις ἐν αὐτῇ τῆς περιόδου τὴν ἀκρίβειαν· καὶ μῆνα γοῦν, ὡς ἔφην, καὶ ἡμέραν ἐτήρησεν τὴν αὐτήν, ἐν ᾗ πρότερον ὑπὸ Βαβυλωνίων ὁ ναὸς ἐνεπρήσθη. (269) καὶ ἀπὸ μὲν τῆς πρώτης αὐτοῦ κτίσεως, ἣν κατεβάλετο Σολομὼν ὁ βασιλεύς; μέχρι τῆς νῦν ἀναιρέσεως, ἣ γέγονεν ἔτει δευτέρῳ τῆς Οὐεσπασιανοῦ ἡγεμονίας, ἔτη συνάγεται χίλια ἑκατὸν τριάκοντα, πρὸς δὲ μῆνες ἑπτὰ καὶ πεντεκαίδεκα ἡμέραι· (270) ἀπὸ δὲ τῆς ὕστερον, ἣν ἔτει δευτέρῳ Κύρου βασιλεύοντος ἐποιήσατο Ἀγγαῖος, ἔτη μέχρι τῆς ὑπὸ Οὐεσπασιανοῦ ἁλώσεως τριακονταεννέα πρὸς ἑξακοσίοις καὶ ἡμέραι τεσσαρακονταπέντε.

Notes to Josephus Jewish War *6.249–270*

(249) διεγνωκὼς < διαγιγνώσκω. *decide, determine.*

ἕω. acc. sg. < ἕως, ἕω (fem.), *dawn*; on the word's declension, see Smyth 238.

περικατέχω. *surround, envelop.*

(250) κατεψήφιστο. 3rd sg. plupf. dep. ind. < καταψηφίζομαι. *pronounce sentence of X* (+ acc.) *against Y* (+ gen.). Note the tense of the verb—judgment had been passed long ago—and the dramatic word order.

εἱμαρμένη. fem. sg. nom., pf. dep. part. < μείρομαι. in pf., *be allotted, decreed by fate*: LSJ, s.v. III.

δεκάτη Λώου μηνός. In 586 B.C.E., under King Nebuchadnezzar II (reg. c. 605–c. 562), the Babylonians had razed the first

Temple on the 7th or 10th day of Ab, the Jewish month equivalent to the Macedonian month of Loös. The second Temple was built 538–515 B.C.E., under the aegis of Cyrus the Great, the Persian emperor (reg. 559–530). In the OT, Cyrus was thus celebrated as a deliverer of the Jews: e.g., Ezra 1, Isaiah 45:1–8.

ἐνεπρήσθη. 3rd sg. aor. pass. ind. < ἐμπίμπρημι. *burn down.*

(251) οἰκείων. i.e., Josephus's fellow Jews.

οἱ στασιασταὶ. Throughout the *Jewish War,* Josephus argues that factional infighting (στάσις) among the residents of Judaea had hamstrung the rebellion; the crippling effects of στάσις were commonly decried in Greek historiography: e.g., Thucydides 3.82–84.

ἐπιτίθημι. in mid., *attack* + dat.: LSJ, s.v. B.III.2.

τῶν τοῦ ναοῦ φρουρῶν. A group of Jews had retreated within the inner court of the temple (6.248).

συμβολή, -ῆς (fem.). *melee, engagement*: LSJ, s.v. II.

τοὺς σβεννύντας . . . ἱεροῦ. *the men extinguishing the fire (burning) within the inner (court of the) Temple.* Titus had ordered his troops to set fire to the gates of the Temple (6.228) but then reversed himself (6.243), for he did not want to destroy the structure, as Josephus reiterates (e.g., 6.241, 254, 266). Yet Josephus seems to suggest elsewhere that Titus bore more responsibility for what happened: *Jewish Antiquities* 20.250.

(252) τηλικ-οῦτος, -αύτη, -οῦτο. *so great*: LSJ, s.v. τηλικόσδε, II.

ἐγχείρημα, -ατος (neu.). *undertaking, endeavor.*

ὁρμή, -ῆς (fem.). *rage, impulse*: LSJ, s.v. II.

ἁρπάζει. Note the dramatic shift to the historical present: Smyth 1883.

† φλογός. A single obelus (dagger) indicates that the word following it is corrupt and that the editor cannot determine how to emend (i.e., replace the word with a conjecture) the

text satisfactorily. Although this occurs at a crucial moment in Josephus's narrative, the general meaning of the passage is clear.

ἀνακουφίζω. *lift, raise up.*

ναὸν. See note on section (400) of D3, s.v. τοῦ ἱεροῦ καὶ τὸν ναὸν.

οἶκος, -ου (mas.). *chamber, room*: LSJ, s.v. 2.

(253) φειδὼ. contracted acc. sg. < φειδώ, -όος (contracting to -οῦς) (fem.). *consideration for* + gen. On the declension of this noun, see Smyth 266.

ταμιεύω. *store up, keep in reserve.*

οἰχομένου. mas. sg. gen., pres. dep. part < οἴχομαι. *vanish, go away*; sc. ναοῦ.

(254) ὡς εἶχεν. *just as he was.* Titus's rapid response characterizes him as a capable commander.

ἔθει. 3rd sg. impf. act. ind. < θέω. *run.*

εἴρξων. fut. part. expressing purpose < ἔργω. *contain.* This verb is common in epic and tragedy, as is much of the vocabulary in these sections, reflecting their content.

(255) πτοέω. *be agitated, stirred up, excited, scared.*

ἅτε. *since, as* + gen. absolute: Smyth 2085.

(256) μείζονι κραυγῇ. dat. of cause.

τὰς ἀκοὰς προκατειλημμένοι. *prevented from hearing.*

ὀργή, -ῆς (fem.). *temperment, anger, passion*; a poetic word found often in tragedy. The men are driven by both ὀργή and ὁρμή (252, 257, 260, 263). Josephus effectively conveys the mindset of the soldiers.

περισπάω. *divert, distract.*

(257) συνωθέω. *jam together, cram.*

ἡττάομαι. dep., *be defeated*: LSJ, s.v. ἡσσάομαι, 2. That is, soldiers who succumbed to the flames suffered the same fate as those who died in combat.

συμφορά, -ᾶς (fem.). *misfortune*: LSJ, s.v. II.2.

(258) προσποιέω. *pretend, feign* + inf.: LSJ, s.v. II.4.

τοῖς πρὸ αὐτῶν. i.e., the soldiers in front of them.

(259) ἀμηχανία, -ας (fem.). *inability* + gen.

τροπή, -ῆς (fem.). *rout, forcing of the enemy to flee*: LSJ, s.v. II.

τὸ δὲ πλέον. adverbial: *mostly, for the most part.*

λαὸς. another poetic word.

καταληφθείη. 3rd sg. aor. pass. opt. < καταλαμβάνω. This is opt. because the verb appears in an indirect question (introduced by the indefinite relative pronoun ὅπου) in secondary sequence.

ἀποσφάττω. *cut the throat, slay.*

βωμὸν. The altar where animal sacrifices were offered is now tragically associated with sacrifices of a different kind.

(260) ἐνθουσιάω. *be inspired, possessed by a god.* Is the verb here used metaphorically to capture the soldiers' frenzied state? Or is it meant to be taken literally, indicating that the soldiers are divine agents? Cf. section **(250)** above.

οἷός τε ἦν. *it was possible*: LSJ, s.v. οἷος, III.2.

τὸ πῦρ is the subject of ἐπεκράτει.

θεάομαι. *view as a spectactor.* The verb implies that Titus (and by extension the reader) witnesses these events like a theatergoer, except that he is witnessing a *real* tragedy that he is powerless to avert.

τὸ ἅγιον. Perhaps the "Holy of Holies," the chamber at the heart of the Temple that no one but the high priest was supposed to enter, and even he was to enter it but once a year, on Yom Kippur.

(261) οὐδαμόθεν εἴσω. i.e., the flames had not yet reached the Temple itself.

νέμω. *graze, feed on.*

ὅπερ ἦν. *what (the situation) was.*

ἑκατοντάρχης, -ου (mas.). *centurion.*

(263) αἰδῶ. contracted acc. sg. < αἰδώς, -όος (contracting to -οῦς) (fem.). *respect.*

λάβρος, -ον. *turbulent, violent*; another poetic word, used frequently of wind and water and thus indicating the elemental nature of the soldiers' ὁρμή.

(265) φθάνω. *act first*: LSJ, s.v. II. In other words, one soldier takes action *before* the other soldiers are able to sate their desire to loot.

ἐκπηδήσαντος τοῦ Καίσαρος. Translate as concessive.

πρός + acc. here expresses purpose: Smyth 1695.3.c.

στροφεύς, -έως (mas.). *hinge.*

† ἐν σκότῳ. The text is again corrupt; see further note on **(252)** above, s.v. † φλογός.

(266) ὑφάπτω. *light a fire.*

(267) ἐπολοφύρομαι. *lament, mourn* + dat.

ὧν. The relative pronoun, as often, is attracted into the case of its gen. antecedent: Smyth 2522.

παρειλήφαμεν < παραλαμβάνω. *ascertain.*

κατασκευή, -ῆς (fem.). *construction, decoration.*

καθ' ἕκαστον. *in every part.*

λάβοι. The subject is τις.

παραμυθία, -ας (fem.). *consolation.*

τὴν εἱμαρμένην (sc. μοῖραν: Smyth 1027.b) ἄφυκτον οὖσαν. *Fate is inescapable.* Cf. section **(250)** above.

(268) θαυμάσαι. 3rd sg. aor. act. opt.

γοῦν. On this particle, see note on section **(100)** of C6.

ἐτήρησεν. sc. "Fate" as the subject.

(269) Οὐεσπασιανοῦ. Vespasian ruled 69–79 C.E.

πρὸς. adverbial: *as well as.*

(270) ἀπὸ δὲ τῆς ὕστερον. i.e., from the building of the second Temple; see note on section (250), s.v. δεκάτη Λώου μηνός.

Ἀγγαῖος. Haggai rebuilds the Temple, as described in the prophet's eponymous book in the Old Testament.

τριακονταεννέα πρὸς ἑξακοσίοις. *639.*

D5. FLAVIAN TRIUMPH I

Josephus *Jewish War* 7.123–141

In 70 C.E., the Temple burned (D4), Jerusalem fell, and the rebellion was quashed, save for a small band occupying the mountain fortress of Masada, whence they fended off the Romans until 73 or 74. Back at Rome, in 71, Vespasian (reg. 69–79 C.E.) celebrated a triumph—though the term's use is somewhat problematic, for the parade glorified not the conquest of a foreign enemy, its usual raison d'être, but the suppression of renegade provincials. This irony should not detract from the importance of the event, for it legitimated the rule of the upstart Vespasian. After the instability of the year 69, in which Vespasian and three other claimants fought for the throne, the triumph also advertised the dynastic stability promised by his accession: the emperor's sons Titus (reg. 79–81 C.E.) and Domitian (reg. 81–96 C.E.) shadowed the emperor during the triumph.

The first part of Josephus's eyewitness account of the triumph appears below. It is one of the fullest and most vivid descriptions of this spectacle in our sources. Some motifs found here are paralleled in other accounts of the event: by replaying before the capital's populace events that took place in the provinces, the triumph advertises Roman imperialism, blurs the line between representation and reality, and connects the empire's center with its periphery. Yet the passage is unique. For it is a firsthand account written by a former leader of the people whose defeat was celebrated in the very triumph he is describing.

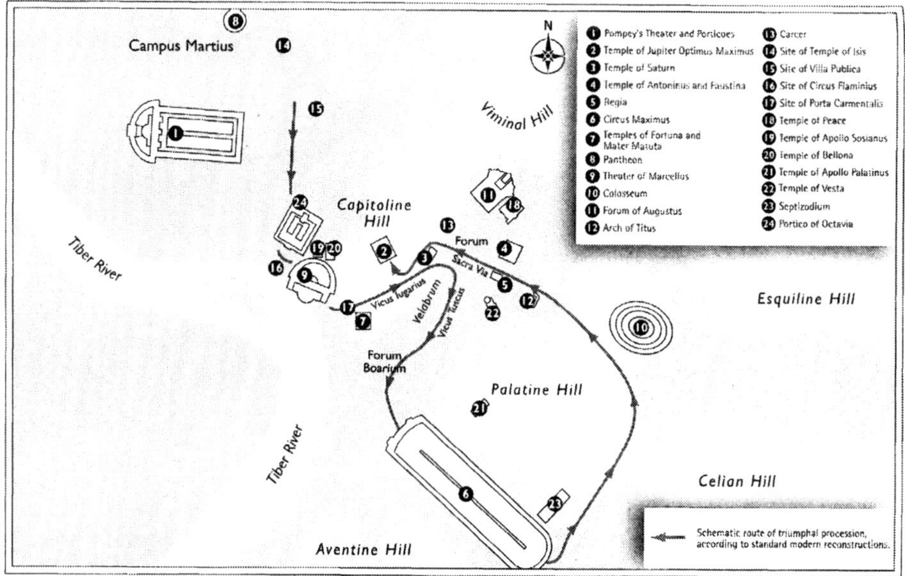

"Schematic Plan of Triumphal Rome." This plan traces the approximate route of the triumphal processions through Rome. Josephus describes the Flavians' triumph in *Jewish War* 7.123–141 (D5) and 7.142–162 (D6). *From Mary Beard,* The Roman Triumph *(Cambridge, Mass., 2007). Copyright © 2007 by the President and Fellows of Harvard College. Reproduced by permission of Harvard University Press.*

Further Reading

M. Beard, "The Triumph of Flavius Josephus," in *Flavian Rome: Culture, Image, Text,* ed. A. J. Boyle and W. J. Dominik, 543–58 (Leiden, 2003); F. Millar, "Last Year In Jerusalem: Monuments of the Jewish War in Rome," in *Flavius Josephus and Flavian Rome,* ed. J. Edmondson, S. Mason, and J. Rives, 101–28 (Oxford, 2005); M. Beard, *The Roman Triumph* (Cambridge, Mass., 2007), 92–106; M. Goodman, *Rome and Jerusalem: The Clash of Ancient Civilizations* (New York, 2007), 424–87; F. Coarelli, *Rome and Environs: An Archaeological Guide,* trans. J. J. Clauss and D. P. Harmon, new ed. (Berkeley, 2014), on the buildings mentioned below.

❧

(123) Τοῦ δὲ στρατιωτικοῦ παντὸς ἔτι νύκτωρ κατὰ λόχους καὶ τάξεις ὑπὸ τοῖς ἡγεμόσι διεξωδευκότος καὶ περὶ θύρας ὄντος οὐ τῶν ἄνω βασιλείων ἀλλὰ πλησίον τοῦ τῆς Ἴσιδος ἱεροῦ, ἐκεῖ γὰρ ἀνεπαύοντο τῆς νυκτὸς ἐκείνης οἱ αὐτοκράτορες, (124) περὶ αὐτὴν ἀρχομένην ἤδη τὴν ἕω προΐασιν Οὐεσπασιανὸς καὶ Τίτος δάφνῃ μὲν ἐστεφανωμένοι, πορφυρᾶς δ' ἐσθῆτας πατρίους ἀμπεχόμενοι, καὶ παρίασιν εἰς τοὺς Ὀκταουίας περιπάτους· (125) ἐνταῦθα γὰρ ἥ τε βουλὴ καὶ τὰ τέλη τῶν ἀρχόντων οἵ τε ἀπὸ τῶν τιμημάτων ἱππεῖς τὴν ἄφιξιν αὐτῶν ἀνέμενον. (126) πεποίητο δὲ βῆμα πρὸ τῶν στοῶν δίφρων αὐτοῖς ἐλεφαντίνων ἐπ' αὐτοῦ κειμένων, ἐφ' οὓς παρελθόντες ἐκαθέσθησαν, καὶ τὸ στρατιωτικὸν εὐθέως ἐπευφήμει πολλὰς αὐτοῖς τῆς ἀρετῆς μαρτυρίας ἀποδιδόντες ἅπαντες· κἀκεῖνοι χωρὶς ὅπλων ἦσαν ἐν ἐσθήσεσιν σηρικαῖς ἐστεφανωμένοι δάφναις. (127) δεξάμενος δ' αὐτῶν τὴν εὐφημίαν Οὐεσπασιανὸς ἔτι βουλομένων λέγειν τὸ τῆς σιγῆς ἐποιήσατο σύμβολον, (128) καὶ πολλῆς ἐκ πάντων ἡσυχίας γενομένης ἀναστὰς καὶ τῷ περιβλήματι τὸ πλέον τῆς κεφαλῆς μέρος ἐπικαλυψάμενος εὐχὰς ἐποιήσατο τὰς νενομισμένας· ὁμοίως δὲ καὶ Τίτος ηὔξατο. (129) μετὰ δὲ τὰς εὐχὰς εἰς κοινὸν ἅπασιν Οὐεσπασιανὸς βραχέα διαλεχθεὶς τοὺς μὲν στρατιώτας ἀπέλυσεν ἐπὶ τὸ νενομισμένον ἄριστον αὐτοῖς ὑπὸ τῶν αὐτοκρατόρων εὐτρεπίζεσθαι, (130) πρὸς δὲ τὴν πύλην αὐτὸς ἀνεχώρει τὴν ἀπὸ τοῦ πέμπεσθαι δι' αὐτῆς αἰεὶ τοὺς θριάμβους τῆς προσηγορίας ἀπ' αὐτῶν τετυχυῖαν. (131) ἐνταῦθα τροφῆς τε προαπογεύονται καὶ τὰς θριαμβικὰς ἐσθῆτας ἀμφιασάμενοι τοῖς τε παριδρυμένοις τῇ πύλῃ θύσαντες θεοῖς ἔπεμπον τὸν θρίαμβον διὰ τῶν θεάτρων διεξελαύνοντες, ὅπως εἴη τοῖς πλήθεσιν ἡ θέα ῥᾴων.

(132) Ἀμήχανον δὲ κατὰ τὴν ἀξίαν εἰπεῖν τῶν θεαμάτων ἐκείνων τὸ πλῆθος καὶ τὴν μεγαλοπρέπειαν ἐν ἅπασιν οἷς ἄν τις ἐπινοήσειεν ἢ τεχνῶν ἔργοις ἢ πλούτου μέρεσιν ἢ φύσεως σπανιότησιν· (133) σχεδὸν γὰρ ὅσα τοῖς πώποτε ἀνθρώποις εὐδαιμονήσασιν ἐκτήθη κατὰ μέρος ἄλλα παρ' ἄλλοις θαυμαστὰ καὶ πολυτελῆ, ταῦτα ἐπὶ τῆς ἡμέρας ἐκείνης

ἀθρόα τῆς Ῥωμαίων ἡγεμονίας ἔδειξε τὸ μέγεθος. **(134)** ἀργύρου γὰρ καὶ χρυσοῦ καὶ ἐλέφαντος ἐν παντοίαις ἰδέαις κατασκευασμάτων ἦν ὁρᾶν οὐχ ὥσπερ ἐν πομπῇ κομιζόμενον πλῆθος, ἀλλ᾽ ὡς ἂν εἴποι τις ῥέοντα ποταμόν, καὶ τὰ μὲν ἐκ πορφύρας ὑφάσματα τῆς σπανιωτάτης φερόμενα, τὰ δ᾽ εἰς ἀκριβῆ ζωγραφίαν πεποικιλμένα τῇ Βαβυλωνίων τέχνῃ· **(135)** λίθοι τε διαφανεῖς, οἱ μὲν χρυσοῖς ἐμπεπλεγμένοι στεφάνοις, οἱ δὲ κατ᾽ ἄλλας ποιήσεις, τοσοῦτοι παρηνέχθησαν, ὥστε μαθεῖν ὅτι μάτην εἶναί τι τούτων σπάνιον ὑπειλήφαμεν. **(136)** ἐφέρετο δὲ καὶ θεῶν ἀγάλματα τῶν παρ᾽ αὐτοῖς μεγέθεσι θαυμαστὰ καὶ κατὰ τὴν τέχνην οὐ παρέργως πεποιημένα, καὶ τούτων οὐδέν, ὅ τι μὴ τῆς ὕλης τῆς πολυτελοῦς, ζῴων τε πολλαὶ φύσεις παρήγοντο κόσμον οἰκεῖον ἁπάντων περικειμένων. **(137)** ἦν δὲ καὶ τὸ κομίζον ἕκαστα τούτων πλῆθος ἀνθρώπων ἁλουργαῖς ἐσθῆσι καὶ διαχρύσοις κεκοσμημένον, οἵ τ᾽ εἰς αὐτὸ τὸ πομπεύειν διακριθέντες ἐξαίρετον εἶχον καὶ καταπληκτικὴν περὶ αὐτοὺς τοῦ κόσμου τὴν πολυτέλειαν. **(138)** ἐπὶ τούτοις οὐδὲ τὸν αἰχμάλωτον ἦν ἰδεῖν ὄχλον ἀκόσμητον, ἀλλ᾽ ἡ τῶν ἐσθήτων ποικιλία καὶ τὸ κάλλος αὐτοῖς τὴν ἀπὸ τῆς κακώσεως τῶν σωμάτων ἀηδίαν ἔκλεπτε τῆς ὄψεως. **(139)** θαῦμα δ᾽ ἐν τοῖς μάλιστα παρεῖχεν ἡ τῶν φερομένων πηγμάτων κατασκευή· καὶ γὰρ διὰ μέγεθος ἦν δεῖσαι τῷ βεβαίῳ τῆς φορᾶς ἀπιστήσαντα, **(140)** τριώροφα γὰρ αὐτῶν πολλὰ καὶ τετρώροφα πεποίητο, καὶ τῇ πολυτελείᾳ τῇ περὶ τὴν κατασκευὴν ἦν ἡσθῆναι μετ᾽ ἐκπλήξεως. **(141)** καὶ γὰρ ὑφάσματα πολλοῖς διάχρυσα περιβέβλητο, καὶ χρυσὸς καὶ ἐλέφας οὐκ ἀποίητος πᾶσι περιεπεπήγει.

Notes to Josephus Jewish War *7.123–141*

(123) λόχος, -ου (mas.). *band, division*; *century,* the smallest unit in the Roman army, a company of one hundred men: LSJ, s.v. I.3; Mason, *Greek Terms,* 66–67.

ὑπὸ. *under,* the dat. implying subjection or submission: Smyth 1698.2.b.

διεξοδεύω. *march out.*

τῶν ἄνω βασιλείων. i.e., the imperial palace located high (ἄνω) on the Palatine Hill.

Ἴσιδος. Vespasian and the other Flavians cultivated a connection to the cult of Isis. The Temple of Isis was located in the Campus Martius near the beginning of the triumphal route.

(124) ἕω. acc. sg. < ἕως, ἕω (fem.). *dawn*; on the word's declension, see Smyth 238.

προΐασιν. Josephus switches to historical present for vividness: Smyth 1883.

δάφνῃ. Laurel was associated with victory: see notes on sections **(16.4)** of C2 and **(34)** of C3.

πορφυρᾶς. Triumphators wore purple garments embroidered with golden thread: see also note on section **(53.7)** of B2, s.v. θριαμβεύω.

Ὀκταουίας περιπάτους. Located in the eastern Campus Martius, the Porticus Octaviae, a quadroporticus (four covered colonnades forming a rectangle) that enclosed two temples, was built in honor of Augustus's sister, Octavia.

(125) τέλος, -εος (neu.). *magistrate*: LSJ, s.v. τέλος, 3.

τίμημα, -ατος (neu.). *property valuation, census*: LSJ, s.v. 6. Senators and equestrians had to maintain a certain level of wealth to be eligible for membership in their respective orders.

ἱππεῖς. i.e., the equestrians.

(126) πεποίητο. 3rd sg. plupf. pass. ind. < ποιέω. The plupf. is not always augmented in later Greek.

δίφρων . . . ἐλεφαντίνων . . . κειμένων. gen. absolute. Certain "curule" magistrates were permitted to sit on ivory chairs known in Latin as *sellae curules*.

τὸ στρατιωτικὸν . . . ἀποδιδόντες ἅπαντες. A collective singular noun may take a plural part. as a predicate: Smyth 1044.

εὐθέως = εὐθύς.

χωρὶς ὅπλων. i.e., they were unarmed.

(128) ἐπικαλυψάμενος. It was typical, when performing religious acts, for a Roman man to cover his head in this fashion.

Τίτος ηὔξατο. Titus's doubling of his father's prayer advertises their family's dynastic aspirations, which are also showcased elsewhere in the triumph: e.g., section **(152)** of D6.

(129) ἄριστον. Note the accent: not the superlative adjective ἀριστόν but the noun ἄριστον, -ου (neu.), which may mean either *breakfast* or *lunch*; even perhaps, considering the time of day and the festive atmosphere, *brunch*, a definition not envisioned by LSJ.

εὐτρεπίζεσθαι. complementary inf. triggered by νενομισμένον.

(130) πύλην. The precise location and design of the Triumphal Gate (Latin, Porta Triumphalis) is unclear.

ἀπὸ τοῦ πέμπεσθαι . . . τετυχυῖαν. *that received its name from the triumphs always sent through it.*

(131) προαπογεύομαι. *eat beforehand* (i.e., before the parade proceeds); sc. "triumphators" as subject.

παριδρύω. *set up beside*; i.e., the triumphators sacrifice to the gods culted near the gate.

διὰ τῶν θεάτρων. On the topographical difficulties raised by the phrase, see Millar, "Last Year in Jerusalem," 104–7.

θέα, -ας (fem.). *sight, spectacle,* not θεά, *goddess.*

(132) οἷς, the object of ἐπινοήσειεν, is attracted into the case of its dat. antecedent, as commonly occurs with the relative pronoun: Smyth 2522.

ἐπινοέω. *conceive of, contrive, invent.* Here is introduced a theme commonly found in accounts of the triumph: the spectacle blurs the line between representation and reality, between the artificial and the natural.

σπανιότης, -ητος (fem.). in pl., *rarities.*

(133) τοῖς . . . ἀνθρώποις εὐδαιμονήσασιν. dat. of agent.

ἐκτήθη < κτάομαι. In aor. pass., this usually dep. verb is a true pass.: LSJ, s.v. III.

κατὰ μέρος. *separately, individually*: LSJ, s.v. μέρος, II.2.

ἄλλα παρ' ἄλλοις. *one next to another*; for double ἄλλος, see Smyth 1274. In Josephus's account of the superabundant spoils on display, is there an undercurrent of criticism?

(134) ἀργύρου . . . χρυσοῦ . . . ἐλέφαντος. genitives of material (Smyth 1323–24) dependent on κατασκευασμάτων, itself a gen. dependent on πλῆθος.

ἦν. *it was possible* + inf.

κομίζω. *carry (off as booty), gather*: LSJ, s.v. II.

ἐκ πορφύρας. i.e., very costly purple dye made from the mollusk known as the murex.

(135) ἐμπλέκω. *set in, entwine.*

ποίησις, -εως (fem.). *setting.*

παρηνέχθησαν < παραφέρω. lit. *carry by*; i.e., *display, exhibit.*

μαθεῖν . . . ὑπειλήφαμεν. *we knew that we supposed in vain that any of these (jewels) was rare.*

(136) οὐ παρέργως. litotes (Smyth 3032): *not shoddily.*

τῆς ὕλης τῆς πολυτελοῦς. gen. of material: Smyth 1323–24.

φύσις, -εως (fem.). *kind, species*: LSJ, s.v. VI.

(137) ἦν. sc. ὁρᾶν vel sim.

ἁλουργός, -όν. *dyed purple.*

καταπληκτικός, -ή,-όν. *astonishing, marvelous.*

(138) ἐπὶ τούτοις. *furthermore.*

(139) πῆγμα, -ατος (neu.). *moving stage, float* (in a parade).

ἦν . . . ἀπιστήσαντα. *it was possible for someone who didn't trust in* + dat.

(140) τριώροφα . . . τετρώροφα. *three-tiered . . . four-tiered.*

ἡσθῆναι. aor. dep. inf. < ἥδομαι + dat.

(141) περιεπεπήγει. 3rd sg. plupf. act. ind. < περιπήγνυμι. *cover.*

D6. FLAVIAN TRIUMPH II

Josephus *Jewish War* 7.142–162

This passage continues Josephus's account of the Flavian triumph (D5). He describes prodigious floats that portray with amazing verisimilitude the events of the Jewish War; then he details the booty plundered from the Temple. Finally, he tells of the construction of the Temple of Peace, in whose precincts are displayed many of the spoils, save a few choice items reserved for the imperial palace.

Further Reading

Further reading may be found in the introduction to D5.

(142) διὰ πολλῶν δὲ μιμημάτων ὁ πόλεμος ἄλλος εἰς ἄλλα μεμερισμένος ἐναργεστάτην ὄψιν αὑτοῦ παρεῖχεν· **(143)** ἦν γὰρ ὁρᾶν χώραν μὲν εὐδαίμονα δῃουμένην, ὅλας δὲ φάλαγγας κτεινομένας πολεμίων, καὶ τοὺς μὲν φεύγοντας τοὺς δ' εἰς αἰχμαλωσίαν ἀγομένους, τείχη δ' ὑπερβάλλοντα μεγέθει μηχαναῖς ἐρειπόμενα καὶ φρουρίων ἁλισκομένας ὀχυρότητας καὶ πόλεων πολυανθρώπους περιβόλους κατ' ἄκρας ἐχομένους, **(144)** καὶ στρατιὰν ἔνδον τειχῶν εἰσχεομένην, καὶ πάντα φόνου πλήθοντα τόπον, καὶ τῶν ἀδυνάτων χεῖρας ἀνταίρειν ἱκεσίας, πῦρ τε ἐνιέμενον ἱεροῖς καὶ κατασκαφὰς οἴκων ἐπὶ τοῖς δεσπόταις, **(145)** καὶ μετὰ πολλὴν ἐρημίαν καὶ κατήφειαν

Giovanni Battista Piranesi, "Veduta dell'Arco di Tito," c. 1748–1778. Piranesi portrays the Arch of Titus, which commemorates Rome's victory in the Jewish War and the Flavians' subsequent triumphal procession through the city. Josephus describes the triumph in *Jewish War* 7.123–141 (D5) and 7.142–162 (D6). *Reproduced by permission of Greenslade Special Collections and Archives, Kenyon College, Gambier, Ohio.*

ποταμοὺς ῥέοντας οὐκ ἐπὶ γῆν γεωργουμένην, οὐδὲ ποτὸν ἀνθρώποις ἢ βοσκήμασιν, ἀλλὰ διὰ τῆς ἐπιπανταχόθεν φλεγομένης· ταῦτα γὰρ Ἰουδαῖοι πεισομένους αὐτοὺς τῷ πολέμῳ παρέδοσαν. **(146)** ἡ τέχνη δὲ καὶ τῶν κατασκευασμάτων ἡ μεγαλουργία τοῖς οὐκ ἰδοῦσι γινόμενα τότ' ἐδείκνυεν ὡς παροῦσι. **(147)** τέτακτο δ' ἐφ' ἑκάστῳ τῶν πηγμάτων ὁ τῆς ἁλισκομένης πόλεως στρατηγὸς ὃν τρόπον ἐλήφθη. πολλαὶ δὲ καὶ νῆες εἵποντο. **(148)** λάφυρα δὲ τὰ μὲν ἄλλα χύδην ἐφέρετο, διέπρεπε δὲ πάντων τὰ ἐγκαταληφθέντα τῷ ἐν Ἱεροσολύμοις ἱερῷ, χρυσῆ τε τράπεζα τὴν ὁλκὴν πολυτάλαντος καὶ λυχνία χρυσῆ μὲν ὁμοίως πεποιημένη, τὸ δ' ἔργον ἐξήλλακτο τῆς κατὰ τὴν ἡμετέραν χρῆσιν συνηθείας. **(149)** ὁ μὲν γὰρ μέσος ἦν κίων ἐκ τῆς βάσεως πεπηγώς, λεπτοὶ δ' ἀπ' αὐτοῦ μεμήκυντο καυλίσκοι τριαίνης σχήματι παραπλησίαν τὴν θέσιν ἔχοντες, λύχνον ἕκαστος αὐτῶν ἐπ' ἄκρον κεχαλκευμένος· ἑπτὰ δ' ἦσαν οὗτοι τῆς παρὰ τοῖς Ἰουδαίοις ἑβδομάδος τὴν τιμὴν ἐμφανίζοντες. **(150)** ὅ τε νόμος ὁ τῶν Ἰουδαίων ἐπὶ τούτοις ἐφέρετο τῶν λαφύρων τελευταῖος. **(151)** ἐπὶ τούτοις παρῄεσαν πολλοὶ Νίκης ἀγάλματα κομίζοντες· ἐξ ἐλέφαντος δ' ἦν πάντων καὶ χρυσοῦ ἡ κατασκευή. **(152)** μεθ' ἃ Οὐεσπασιανὸς ἤλαυνε πρῶτος καὶ Τίτος εἵπετο, Δομετιανὸς δὲ παρίππευεν, αὐτός τε διαπρεπῶς κεκοσμημένος καὶ τὸν ἵππον παρέχων θέας ἄξιον.

(153) Ἦν δὲ τῆς πομπῆς τὸ τέλος ἐπὶ τὸν νεὼ τοῦ Καπετωλίου Διός, ἐφ' ὃν ἐλθόντες ἔστησαν· ἦν γὰρ παλαιὸν πάτριον περιμένειν, μέχρις ἂν τὸν τοῦ στρατηγοῦ τῶν πολεμίων θάνατον ἀπαγγείλῃ τις. **(154)** Σίμων οὗτος ἦν ὁ Γιώρα, τότε πεπομπευκὼς ἐν τοῖς αἰχμαλώτοις, βρόχῳ δὲ περιβληθεὶς εἰς τὸν ἐπὶ τῆς ἀγορᾶς ἐσύρετο τόπον αἰκιζομένων αὐτὸν ἅμα τῶν ἀγόντων· νόμος δ' ἐστὶ Ῥωμαίοις ἐκεῖ κτείνειν τοὺς ἐπὶ κακουργίᾳ θάνατον κατεγνωσμένους. **(155)** ἐπεὶ δ' ἀπηγγέλθη τέλος ἔχων καὶ πάντες εὐφήμησαν, ἤρχοντο τῶν θυσιῶν, ἃς ἐπὶ ταῖς νομιζομέναις καλλιερήσαντες εὐχαῖς ἀπῄεσαν εἰς τὸ βασίλειον. **(156)** καὶ τοὺς μὲν αὐτοὶ πρὸς εὐωχίαν ὑπεδέχοντο, τοῖς δ' ἄλλοις ἅπασιν εὐτρεπεῖς κατὰ τὸ οἰκεῖον αἱ τῆς ἑστιάσεως ἦσαν παρασκευαί. **(157)** ταύτην γὰρ τὴν ἡμέραν ἡ Ῥωμαίων πόλις ἑώρταζεν ἐπινίκιον μὲν τῆς κατὰ τῶν πολεμίων στρατείας, πέρας δὲ τῶν ἐμφυλίων κακῶν, ἀρχὴν δὲ τῶν ὑπὲρ τῆς εὐδαιμονίας ἐλπίδων.

(158) Μετὰ δὲ τοὺς θριάμβους καὶ τὴν βεβαιοτάτην τῆς Ῥωμαίων ἡγεμονίας κατάστασιν Οὐεσπασιανὸς ἔγνω τέμενος Εἰρήνης κατασκευάσαι· ταχὺ δὲ δὴ μάλα καὶ πάσης ἀνθρωπίνης κρεῖττον ἐπινοίας ἐτετελείωτο. **(159)** τῇ γὰρ ἐκ τοῦ πλούτου χορηγίᾳ δαιμονίῳ χρησάμενος ἔτι καὶ τοῖς ἔκπαλαι κατωρθωμένοις γραφῆς τε καὶ πλαστικῆς ἔργοις αὐτὸ κατεκόσμησεν· **(160)** πάντα γὰρ εἰς ἐκεῖνον τὸν νεὼ συνήχθη καὶ κατετέθη, δι' ὧν τὴν θέαν ἄνθρωποι πρότερον περὶ πᾶσαν ἐπλανῶντο τὴν οἰκουμένην, ἕως ἄλλο παρ' ἄλλοις ἦν κείμενον ἰδεῖν ποθοῦντες. **(161)** ἀνέθηκε δὲ ἐνταῦθα καὶ τὰ ἐκ τοῦ ἱεροῦ τῶν Ἰουδαίων χρυσᾶ κατασκευάσματα σεμνυνόμενος ἐπ' αὐτοῖς. **(162)** τὸν δὲ νόμον αὐτῶν καὶ τὰ πορφυρᾶ τοῦ σηκοῦ καταπετάσματα προσέταξεν ἐν τοῖς βασιλείοις ἀποθεμένους φυλάττειν.

Notes to Josephus Jewish War *7.142–162*

(142) ὁ πόλεμος ἄλλος εἰς ἄλλα μεμερισμένος. *the war, divided into many (scenes).* Josephus is referring to the floats or moving stages (πήγματα: section **[139]** of D5) on which are portrayed scenes from the war. In his description below, polysyndeton and paratactic syntax (when subordinate clauses are minimized and phrases and clauses are linked by conjunctions like pearls on a string) recreate the viewer's experience of seeing the floats as they pass by one by one, creating serially a slideshow of the war.

ἐναργεστάτην ὄψιν. The spectacle transcends time and space: the war in Jerusalem is brought before the Roman viewer's, and the reader's, eye. By employing an adjective related to ἐνάργεια—in the vocabulary of rhetoric, *vivid description* (LSJ, s.v. 3)—Josephus also draws attention to the fact that his *verbal* account brings to life a *visual* spectacle.

(143) δῃουμένην < δηϊόω. *ravage.*

πολεμίων. For a moment, the reader may wonder: does Josephus mean the Romans or the Judaeans? Yet he must be referring to the latter, an indication that Josephus is narrating the scene from the perspective of a Roman viewer. It is worth emphasizing that at no point does Josephus explicitly insert himself into the narrative; the reader can only speculate about Josephus's *personal* reaction to the spectacle.

ὀχυρότης, -ητος (fem.). lit. *strength*; here, *stronghold.*

περίβολος, -ον. adj. as substantive: *walled environs*: LSJ, s.v. II.2.

κατ'. *on, throughout.*

(144) πλήθοντα. Verbs of filling may take a gen.: Smyth 1369.

ἐνιέμενον < ἐνίημι. Similar language is used in Josephus's description of the burning of the Temple: see section **(252)** of D4.

(145) ποταμοὺς. The triumph, which flows by like a river **(134)**, portrays the watercourses of Judaea.

τῆς ἐπιπανταχόθεν φλεγομένης. sc. γῆς. Smyth 1027.b, 1302.

πεισομένους. mas. pl. acc., fut. mid. part. < πάσχω. i.e., the devastation had been predicted.

(147) τέτακτο. 3rd sg. plupf. pass. ind. < τάσσω (Attic τάττω). The plupf. is not always augmented in later Greek.

ὃν τρόπον. *in which fashion.* Again one must wonder about how Josephus reacted when he saw the representations of a war in which he had served as a general on the losing side.

ἐλήφθη. 3rd sg. aor. pass. ind. < λαμβάνω.

(148) λάφυρα, -ων (neu. pl.). *booty.*

διέπρεπε . . . πάντων. *were most conspicuous of all.*

τράπεζα. This was the table of the "shewbread" or "bread of the presence," on which were perpetually offered twelve cakes made from fine flour; they were replaced each week on the Sabbath. The table was made either of solid gold or acacia wood plated with gold. Like the Romans, Antiochus IV Epiphanes (reg. 175–164 B.C.E.), king of the Seleucids, plundered the table and menorah from the Temple; this was one of the many acts that prompted the Maccabean revolt (B6).

τὴν ὁλκὴν. acc. of respect.

ἐξήλλακτο. 3rd sg. plupf. mid. ind. < ἐξαλλάσσω. *change completely from* + gen.: LSJ, s.v. II.2. The Temple lampstand (menorah), made of solid gold, had seven branches (Exodus 25.31–40); the menorah used at Hanukkah in Josephus's day had nine (as it still does today).

(149) κίων, -ονος (mas.). *column, shaft.*

μεμήκυντο. 3rd pl. plupf. mid. ind. < μηκύνω. *extend.*

καυλίσκος, -ου (mas.). *branch* (of a candelabrum).

παραπλήσιος, -α, -ον or -ος, -ον. *resembling, similar to* + dat.

ἕκαστος. sc. ἔχων.

οὗτοι. sc. λύχνοι.

ἑβδομάς, -άδος (fem.). *the number seven.* On the seventh day of creation, God rested, thus hallowing the number seven. Josephus elsewhere offers another explanation for the seven branches, saying that they represent the seven planets: *Jewish War* 5.217, *Jewish Antiquities* 3.144–45, 182.

(150) νόμος. i.e., scrolls on which were written the Torah or Pentateuch, the first five books of the OT.

(151) ἐπὶ τούτοις. *after these things*; i.e., *next.* The Law, which forbids graven images of gods (Exodus 20.4–6), is followed in the procession by statues of Victory.

(152) θέας. See note on section **(131)** of D5.

(153) τὸν νεὼ τοῦ Καπετωλίου Διός = the Temple of Jupiter Optimus Maximus on the Capitoline Hill.

νεὼ. mas. sg. acc. < νεώς, νεώ. *temple.* On the word's declension, see Smyth 238.

(154) ὁ Γιώρα. *the son of Giora,* which, like many non-Greek names, does not decline: Smyth 284. Simon bar (Hebrew for "son of") Giora was a Judaean populist revolutionary prone to extremism who led one of the factions that destabilized Jerusalem during Titus's siege.

ἐκεῖ. i.e., in the ancient Tullianum, a.k.a. the Mamertine prison, which was located toward the northern edge of the Roman Forum (ἐπὶ τῆς ἀγορᾶς) at the foot of the Capitoline Hill.

καταγιγνώσκω. *condemn, sentence to* + acc. of punishment: LSJ, s.v. III.

(155) ἀπηγγέλθη τέλος ἔχων. lit., *when Simon having an end was announced*; i.e., *when it was announced that Simon had met his end*; on the Greek construction, see Smyth 1982.

καλλιερέω. *sacrifice X* (+ acc.) *with good omens.*

βασίλειον. i.e., the imperial palace on the Palatine Hill.

(156) αὐτοὶ. i.e., the emperor and his family feasted select guests.

(157) ἐπινίκιον, -ου (neu.). *victory.*

πέρας, -ατος (neu.). *end.*

(158) γιγνώσκω. *determine, decide*: LSJ, s.v. II.

τέμενος Εἰρήνης. Completed as early as 75 C.E., the Temple of Peace was sited southeast of the Forum of Augustus. It consisted of a square quadroporticus (for the term, see note on section [124] of D5) about 325 feet on each side; abutting the southeast colonnade was the shrine proper, a rectangular chamber with an apse, flanked by rooms that housed libraries and (later) the Severan Marble Plan of Rome.

(159) τῇ γὰρ ἐκ τοῦ πλούτου χορηγίᾳ δαιμονίῳ. i.e., through the wealth obtained from the conquest of Judaea, with which providence had provided him.

(160) δι'. The preposition governs τὴν θέαν.

ἕως . . . ποθοῦντες. *while they were eager to see (the artworks), one after another, where(ever) they were.*

(161) σεμνυνόμενος ἐπ' αὐτοῖς. *(he himself) being exalted by them*; i.e., the splendid items seized and dedicated by Vespasian redounded to his glory.

(162) τοῦ σηκοῦ. i.e., of the Temple's precincts.

προστάσσω. *order, command* + inf.: LSJ, s.v. II.3.

D7. MAKING MARTYRS

Martyrdom of Agape, Irene, and Chione 1.2–2.1, 3–4

Of the ancient sources that offer views of the Romans, none may be more dramatic than the accounts of martyrs (in Greek, μάρτυρες), whose public deaths at the hands of Roman officials "witnessed" to the sufferers' faith. With their defiant responses to the imperial authorities, who tended to grow exasperated by the defendants' willfulness, and their stagy embrace of debasing and even eroticized torture, the martyrs subverted the intended meanings of their deaths: blood became baptismal water, humiliation became pleasure, victim became victor. The wildly popular accounts of the martyrs' deaths, ranging in form from transcripts of legal proceedings to quasi-historical narratives to fanciful legends, circulated widely in the Christian communities of the Mediterranean. Martyrs came to be culted, especially in the cities and regions in which they had died, where the anniversaries of their deaths were commemorated with special services. Their power even transcended the grave in that their relics—parts of their bodies or objects they had touched—could heal sickness and ward off evil.

The persecution of Christians was localized and sporadic until the reign of Decius (249–51 C.E.). Beginning in February 303, the emperor Diocletian (reg. 284–305 C.E.) issued four anti-Christian edicts, thereby initiating what is often termed the "Great Persecution," which did not cease until about a decade later. The last of the edicts, issued in the winter of 304, required all residents of the empire to sacrifice to the gods. In March of that same year, seven Christian women fled persecution in their home city of Thessalonica and decided to live together on a nearby mountain. Thence they were summoned before the Roman governor, Dulcitius, and asked to sacrifice in accordance with the edict. In the passage below, the protagonists are introduced, and then, as in many martyr accounts, their dramatic exchange with the Roman authorities is presented. For the reader's convenience, this exchange is printed below not as continuous text but as dialogue.

Further Reading

Martyrdom of Agape, Irene, and Chione all, trans. in H. Musurillo, *The Acts of the Christian Martyrs* (Oxford, 1972), 280–93; G. E. M. de Ste Croix, "Why Were the Early Christians Persecuted?," *Past and Present* 26 (1963): 6–38, reprinted in *Studies in Ancient Society,* ed. M. I. Finley, 210–49 (London, 1974), in which volume A. N. Sherwin-White's "amendment" to de Ste Croix is also reproduced (250–55) as well as the latter's "rejoinder" to the "amendment" (256–62); G. W. Bowersock, *Martyrdom and Rome* (Cambridge, 1995), 23–39; G. Clark, *Christianity and Roman Society* (Cambridge, 2004), 38–59.

(1.2) διωγμοῦ καταλαβόντος τοῦ κατὰ Μαξιμιανόν, καὶ αὗται ἑαυτὰς ταῖς ἀρεταῖς κοσμήσασαι καὶ τοῖς εὐαγγελικοῖς νόμοις πειθόμεναι, καταλείπουσι μὲν τὴν πατρίδα καὶ γένος καὶ περιουσίαν καὶ κτῆσιν διὰ τὴν περὶ τὸν θεὸν ἀγάπην καὶ προσδοκίαν τῶν ἐπουρανίων ἀγαθῶν, ἄξια τοῦ πατρὸς Ἀβραὰμ διαπραττόμεναι. καὶ φεύγουσι μὲν τοὺς διώκοντας κατὰ τὴν ἐντολήν, καὶ καταλαμβάνουσιν ὄρος τι ὑψηλόν. **(3)** κἀκεῖ ταῖς προσευχαῖς ἐσχόλαζον, καὶ τὸ μὲν σῶμα τῷ ὕψει τοῦ ὄρους προσῆπτον, τὴν δὲ ψυχὴν ἐν οὐρανοῖς εἶχον πολιτευομένην.

(2.1) Ἐκ τούτου τοίνυν τοῦ τόπου συλληφθεῖσαι, προσάγονται τῷ διωγμίτῃ ἄρχοντι, ἵνα τὸ λεῖπον τῶν ἐντολῶν ἐπιτελέσασαι καὶ μέχρι θανάτου τὸν δεσπότην ἀγαπήσασαι τὸν τῆς ἀφθαρσίας ἀναδήσωνται στέφανον.

[In 2.2–2.3, Chione, Irene, and Agape are introduced; the significance of their names is explained. The author then offers the following account of their appearance before the authorities.]

(3.1) Προκαθίσαντος Δουλκητίου ἡγεμόνος ἐπὶ τοῦ βήματος, Ἀρτεμήσιος κομενταρήσιος εἶπεν· "Ὁποίαν νοτωρίαν περὶ τῶν παρεστώτων τούτων ὁ ἐνθάδε στατιωνάριος ἀπέστειλεν πρὸς τὴν σὴν Τύχην, εἰ κελεύεις, ἀναγινώσκω."

Δουλκήτιος ἡγεμὼν εἶπεν· "Ἀνάγνωθι."

καὶ ἐκ τῆς τάξεως ἀνεγνώσθη. "Σοὶ τῷ ἐμῷ δεσπότῃ Κάσσανδρος βενεφικιάριος. γίνωσκε, κύριε, Ἀγάθωνα καὶ Εἰρήνην καὶ Ἀγάπην καὶ Χιόνην καὶ Κασσίαν καὶ Φιλίππαν καὶ Εὐτυχίαν μὴ βούλεσθαι ἱερόθυτον φαγεῖν, ἅστινας προσάγω σου τῇ Τύχῃ."

(2) Δουλκήτιος ἡγεμὼν εἶπεν πρὸς αὐτούς· "Τίς ἡ τοσαύτη μανία τὸ μὴ πείθεσθαι ὑμᾶς τῇ κελεύσει τῶν θεοφιλεστάτων βασιλέων ἡμῶν καὶ Καισάρων;"

καὶ πρὸς Ἀγάθωνα εἶπεν· "Διὰ τί παραγενόμενος εἰς τὰ ἱερά, καθὼς οἱ καθωσιωμένοι, τοῖς ἱεροῖς οὐκ ἐχρήσω;"

Ἀγάθων εἶπεν· "Ὅτι Χριστιανός εἰμι."

(3) Δουλκήτιος ἡγεμὼν εἶπεν· "Ἔτι καὶ σήμερον τοῖς αὐτοῖς ἐπιμένεις;"

Ἀγάθων εἶπεν· "Ναί."

Δουλκήτιος εἶπεν· "Σὺ τί λέγεις, ἡ Ἀγάπη;"

Ἀγάπη εἶπεν· "Θεῷ ζῶντι πεπίστευκα, καὶ οὐ βούλομαι τὴν συνείδησίν μου ἀπολέσαι."

(4) Δουλκήτιος ἡγεμὼν εἶπεν·"Σὺ τί λέγεις, Εἰρήνη; διὰ τί οὐκ ἐπείσθης τῇ κελεύσει τῶν δεσποτῶν ἡμῶν τῶν βασιλέων καὶ Καισάρων;"

Εἰρήνη εἶπεν· "Διὰ φόβον θεοῦ."

ὁ ἡγεμὼν εἶπεν· "Σὺ τί λέγεις, Χιόνη;"

Χιόνη εἶπεν· "Θεῷ ζῶντι πεπίστευκα καὶ οὐ ποιῶ τοῦτο."

ὁ ἡγεμὼν λέγει· "Σὺ τί λέγεις, Κασσία;"

Κασσία εἶπεν· "Τὴν ψυχήν μου σῶσαι θέλω."
ὁ ἡγεμὼν εἶπεν· "Τῶν ἱερῶν μεταλαβεῖν θέλεις;"
Κασσία εἶπεν· "Οὐ θέλω."

(5) ὁ ἡγεμὼν εἶπεν· "Σὺ τί λέγεις, ἡ Φιλίππα;"
Φιλίππα εἶπεν· "Τὸ αὐτὸ λέγω."
ὁ ἡγεμὼν εἶπεν· "Τί ἐστι τὸ αὐτό;"
Φιλίππα εἶπεν· "Ἀποθανεῖν θέλω μᾶλλον ἢ φαγεῖν."
ὁ ἡγεμὼν εἶπεν· "Σὺ τί λέγεις, Εὐτυχία;"
Εὐτυχία εἶπεν· "Τὸ αὐτὸ λέγω, ἀποθανεῖν μᾶλλον θέλω."

(6) ὁ ἡγεμὼν εἶπεν· "Ἄνδρα ἔχεις;"
Εὐτυχία εἶπεν· "Ἐτελεύτησεν."
ὁ ἡγεμὼν εἶπεν· "Πότε ἐτελεύτησεν;"
Εὐτυχία εἶπεν· "Πρὸ μηνῶν τάχα ἑπτά."
ὁ ἡγεμὼν εἶπεν· "Πόθεν οὖν ἐγκύμων εἶ;"
Εὐτυχία εἶπεν· "Ἐξ οὗ ἔδωκέν μοι ὁ θεὸς ἀνδρός."

(7) ὁ ἡγεμὼν εἶπεν· "Πῶς οὖν ἐγκύμων τυγχάνεις, ὁπότε λέγεις τὸν ἄνδρα σου τετελευτηκέναι;"
Εὐτυχία εἶπεν· "Τὴν βούλησιν τοῦ παντοκράτορος θεοῦ οὐδεὶς δύναται εἰδέναι. οὕτως ἠθέλησεν ὁ θεός."
ὁ ἡγεμὼν εἶπεν· "Παύσασθαι τὴν Εὐτυχίαν τῆς μανίας προτρέπομαι μετελθεῖν τε ἐπὶ τὸν ἀνθρώπινον λογισμόν. τί λέγεις; πείθῃ τῇ βασιλικῇ κελεύσει;"
Εὐτυχία εἶπεν· "Οὐ πείθομαι, Χριστιανή εἰμι, θεοῦ δούλη παντοκράτορος."
ὁ ἡγεμὼν εἶπεν· "Εὐτυχία, διὰ τὸ ἐγκύμονα αὐτὴν εἶναι, τέως ἀναληφθήσεται εἰς τὸ δεσμωτήριον."

(4.1) Καὶ προσέθηκεν· "Σὺ τί λέγεις, Ἀγάπη; ποιεῖς ταῦτα πάντα ὅσα ἡμεῖς οἱ καθωσιωμένοι τοῖς δεσπόταις ἡμῶν βασιλεῦσι καὶ Καίσαρσι ποιοῦμεν;"

Ἀγάπη εἶπεν· "Οὐκ ἔνι καλῶς τῷ σατανᾷ. οὐκ ἄγει μου τὸν λογισμόν. ἀνίκητος ὁ λογισμὸς ἡμῶν."
ὁ ἡγεμὼν εἶπεν· "Σὺ τί λέγεις, Χιόνη;"
Χιόνη εἶπεν· "Τὸν λογισμὸν ἡμῶν οὐδεὶς δύναται μεταγαγεῖν."

(2) ὁ ἡγεμὼν εἶπεν· "Μή τινά ἐστιν παρ' ὑμῖν τῶν ἀνοσίων Χριστιανῶν ἢ ὑπομνήματα ἢ διφθέραι ἢ βιβλία;"
Χιόνη εἶπεν· "Οὐκ ἔστιν, κύριε· ἅπαντα γὰρ οἱ νῦν αὐτοκράτορες ἐξεφόρησαν."
ὁ ἡγεμὼν εἶπεν· "Τίνες ὑμῖν τὴν γνώμην ταύτην ἔδωκαν;"
Χιόνη εἶπεν· "Ὁ παντοκράτωρ θεός."
ὁ ἡγεμὼν εἶπεν· "Τίνες εἰσὶν οἱ συμβουλεύσαντες ὑμῖν εἰς ταύτην τὴν ἀπόνοιαν ἐλθεῖν;"
Χιόνη εἶπεν· "Ὁ θεὸς ὁ παντοκράτωρ καὶ ὁ υἱὸς αὐτοῦ ὁ μονογενής, ὁ κύριος ἡμῶν Ἰησοῦς Χριστός."

(3) Δουλκήτιος ἡγεμὼν εἶπεν· "Πάσας ὑποκεῖσθαι τῇ καθοσιώσει τῶν δεσποτῶν ἡμῶν τῶν βασιλέων καὶ Καισάρων πᾶσι πρόδηλόν ἐστιν. ἐπειδὴ δὲ ἀπονοίᾳ τινὶ χρησάμεναι ἀπὸ τοσούτου χρόνου καὶ τοσαύτης παραγγελίας γενομένης καὶ τοσούτων διαταγμάτων προτεθέντων, τηλικαύτης ἀπειλῆς ἐπηρτημένης, κατεφρονήσατε τῆς κελεύσεως τῶν δεσποτῶν ἡμῶν τῶν βασιλέων καὶ Καισάρων, ἐπιμένουσαι τῷ ἀνοσίῳ ὀνόματι τῶν Χριστιανῶν, ἔτι τε μὴν καὶ τήμερον ἀναγκαζόμεναι ὑπό τε τῶν στατιωνιζόντων καὶ τῶν πρωτευόντων ἀρνήσασθαι καὶ ἐγγράφως ποιῆσαι τὰ κελευσθέντα, οὐ βούλεσθε. τούτου ἕνεκεν τὴν δέουσαν εἰς ἑαυτὰς τιμωρίαν ἐκδέξασθε." (4) καὶ τὴν ἀπόφασιν ἔγγραφον ἐκ χάρτου ἀνέγνω· "Ἀγάπην καὶ Χιόνην, ἐπειδὴ ἀκαθοσιώτῳ διανοίᾳ ἐναντία ἐφρόνησαν τῷ θείῳ θεσπίσματι τῶν δεσποτῶν ἡμῶν Αὐγούστων καὶ Καισάρων, ἔτι εἰκαίαν καὶ ἕωλον καὶ στυγητὴν πᾶσι τοῖς καθωσιωμένοις σέβουσαι τὴν τῶν Χριστιανῶν θρησκείαν, πυρὶ ἐκέλευσα παραδοθῆναι." καὶ προσέθηκεν· "Ἀγάθων καὶ Εἰρήνη καὶ Κασσία καὶ Φιλίππα καὶ Εὐτυχία διὰ τὸ νέον τῆς ἡλικίας τέως ἐμβληθήσονται εἰς τὸ δεσμωτήριον."

[On the next day, Irene alone is questioned by Dulcitius; she stands her ground, and the governor orders her to be confined naked in a brothel. There she is protected by the Holy Spirit; none of the customers dares even to go near her. Dulcitius summons her again; seeing that Irene still refuses to sacrifice, Dulcitius sentences her to be burned alive. She is martyred on April 1, 304.]

Notes to Martyrdom of Agape, Irene, and Chione *1.2–2.1, 3–4*

(1.2) διωγμός, -οῦ (mas.). *persecution.*

καταλαμβάνω. *happen,* usually used of something dire: LSJ, s.v. IV.

Μαξιμιανόν. Diocletian (reg. 284–305 C.E.) divided the empire among four tetrarchs: two senior emperors or Augusti (referred to in this text as βασιλεῖς) and two junior emperors or Caesars (in this text, Καίσαρες). Here the author is presumably referring *not* to the emperor we call Maximian (Marcus Aurelius Valerius Maximianus), who was in 304 Augustus of the western empire, but to Galerius (Gaius Galerius Valerius Maximianus), then Caesar of the eastern empire. Galerius is frequently called Μαξιμιανός in the sources; a fervent persecutor, he erected a palace, rotunda, and triumphal arch in Thessalonica.

αὗται. i.e., the women from Thessalonica.

εὐαγγελικοῖς. i.e., found in the gospels (εὐαγγέλια).

προσδοκία, -ας (fem.). *expectation.*

Ἀβραὰμ. Many non-Greek proper nouns do not decline: Smyth 284.

ἐντολήν. cf. Matthew 10.23: "ὅταν δὲ διώκωσιν ὑμᾶς ἐν τῇ πόλει ταύτῃ, φεύγετε εἰς τὴν ἑτέραν."

(3) σχολάζω + dat. *devote oneself to,* usually educational or spiritually edifying activities: Lampe, s.v. 3. The fugitive women essentially form a monastic community.

(2.1) συλληφθεῖσαι. fem. pl. nom., aor. pass. part. < συλλαμβάνω. *seize, arrest.*

διωγμίτης, -ου (mas.). *persecutor*; i.e., a civil official enforcing the edicts against the Christians; see note on διωγμός in **(2)** above.

τὸ λεῖπον. *the rest of* + partitive gen.

τῆς ἀφθαρσίας . . . στέφανον. cf. 1 Peter 5.4: "And when the head shepherd has appeared, you will receive the imperishable crown of glory (τὸν ἀμαράντινον τῆς δόξης στέφανον)."

(3.1) βῆμα, -ατος (neu.). *tribunal*; i.e., the dais from which a Roman magistrate presided: LSJ, s.v. II, BDAG, s.v. 3; see also note on section **(17)** of C7, s.v.

Δουλκητίου. Several Roman officials bore the name Dulcitius in the fourth century.

ἡγεμών, -όνος (mas.). here, *governor.*

κομενταρήσιος, -ου (mas.) = Latin *commentariensis,* a judicial clerk serving immediately under the governor's chief-of-staff. It is common, especially in late antique Greek, to transliterate the Latin titles of specialized public officials rather than translate them or use calques: Mason, *Greek Terms,* 4. The technical language often employed in the passage also lends verisimilitude to the proceedings.

νοτωρία, -ας (fem.) = Latin *notoria. written statement attesting to a crime.* Note the formal, bureaucratic Greek with which the official speaks to the governor.

παρεστώτων. mas. pl. gen., pf. act. part. < παρίστημι.

στατιωνάριος = Latin *stationarius,* essentially a military policeman.

πρὸς τὴν σὴν Τύχην. *to your Genius*: Mason, *Greek Terms,* 94. The *Genius* was the deified essence of an individual, his spiritual double.

ἀναγιγνώσκω. *read aloud*: LSJ, s.v. II.

Ἀνάγνωθι. 2nd sg. aor. act. impv.: Smyth 684.

ἐκ τῆς τάξεως. *in an orderly fashion.*

βενεφικιάριος = Latin *beneficiarius*, another Roman official, this one much lower on the food chain than those already mentioned.

ἱερόθυτον. i.e., food that had been offered to the gods, such as sacrificial meat; cf. Paul's first letter to the Christians of Corinth, which tackles the question of whether such food may be eaten: 8.1–13.

(2) τὸ μὴ πείθεσθαι . . . . The articular inf. is nom., in apposition with ἡ τοσαύτη μανία.

παραγίγνομαι. *be present at.*

καθοσιόω. *devote, dedicate.* Hence οἱ καθωσιωμένοι = *the devoted ones, the pious.*

(3) ἐπιμένω. *persist in* + dat.: LSJ, s.v. 3.

συνείδησις, -εως (fem.). *conscience*: LSJ, s.v. 5; BDAG, s.v. 2.

(6) τάχα. *maybe, perhaps.*

οὗ. As often, the relative pronoun is attracted into the case of its gen. antecedent (ἀνδρός): Smyth 2522. Moreover, here the antecedent appears not before but after the relative pronoun, a phenomenon known as "incorporation": Smyth 2536.

(7) παντοκράτωρ, -ορος. *almighty.* By using this adjective, is Eutychia taking a jab at the emperors (αὐτοκράτορες)?

πείθῃ. 2nd sg. pres. mid. ind., with a future sense: Smyth 1579.

ἀναληφθήσεται. 3rd sg. fut. pass. ind. < ἀναλαμβάνω.

(4.1) ἔνι = ἔνεστι. impersonal: *it is in the power of* + dat.: LSJ, s.v. ἔνειμι, s.v. II.2.

καλῶς. *altogether*: LSJ, s.v. καλός, C.II.3.

(2) Μή. This interrogative particle indicates that the governor is expecting "no" as an answer: LSJ, s.v. C.I.1.

ἢ ὑπομνήματα ἢ διφθέραι ἢ βιβλία. The first edict against the Christians, dating to February 24, 303, mandated inter alia the confiscation and burning of copies of the scriptures and liturgical books.

(3) ὑπόκειμαι. *be subject to, liable to a charge of* + dat.: LSJ, s.v. II.6; Lampe, s.v. 1.

καθοσίωσις, -εως (fem.) = Latin *crimen maiestatis. treason*, here + dat.: Lampe, s.v. 4.

τοσαύτης παραγγελίας γενομένης. gen. absolute. Translate this and the subsequent gen. absolutes as concessive.

προτεθέντων. neu. pl. gen., aor. pass. part.

τηλικ-οῦτος, -αύτη, -οῦτο. *so great*: LSJ, s.v. τηλικόσδε, II.

ἐπηρτημένης. fem. sg. gen., pf. pass. part. < ἐπαρτάω. in pass., *loom, threaten.*

καταφρονέω. *look down on, disdain* + gen.

στατιωνίζω. *be on duty* (as a soldier): Lampe, s.v. cf. Latin *stationarius.*

ἀρνέομαι. *apostasize; deny*, in this case, the Christian faith.

δέουσαν < δεῖ.

(4) χάρτης, -ου (mas.). *papyrus* (document); cf. Latin *charta.*

Ἀγάπην καὶ Χιόνην. acc. subject in indirect discourse after ἐκέλευσα below.

ἀκαθοσίωτος, -ον. *impious*: Lampe, s.v. 2.

ἐναντία φρονέω. *have thoughts against, be ill-intentioned toward* + dat.

θρησκεία, -ας (fem.). *worship, cult.*

ἐμβληθήσονται. 3rd pl. fut. pass. ind. < ἐμβάλλω.

PART E

LATE ANTIQUITY

This section presents passages from late antiquity, the period bridging the classical world and the Middle Ages. The first three excerpts derive from Eusebius's panegyrical biography of Constantine (reg. 306–37 C.E.), the first Christian emperor. In the opening excerpt, Constantine contemplates a campaign against the usurper Maxentius and considers with which deity he should align himself to ensure victory. He decides on the Christian God and then has a vision of a cross above the sun (E1). In a dream, Christ interprets this sign for the emperor, who, in the light of what he has seen, fashions the *labarum,* a sort of Christianized military standard that is carried before his armies (E2). Constantine then marches on Rome, where he defeats Maxentius at the Battle of the Milvian Bridge on October 28, 312. After triumphantly entering the city, Constantine erects a statue of himself with an inscription that commemorates his victory (E3). Eusebius's encomiastic account of Constantine is undercut by a selection from the emperor Julian's (reg. 361–63 C.E.) *Caesars,* a seriocomic account of a banquet above Mount Olympus where Roman emperors compete to see who ruled best. Constantine does poorly, to put it mildly (E4). With the exception of Julian, all the emperors after Constantine were Christian, and many of them restricted the practice of paganism. According to the pagan rhetorician Libanius, marauding monks were taking the law into their own hands, destroying temples and plundering their property. Libanius urges the emperor Theodosius I (reg. 379–95 C.E.) to put an end to this vigilantism (E5–E6), arguing that the ongoing practice of traditional religion was crucial to the empire's welfare. The final selection in this reader is set during the wars through which the emperor Justinian (reg. 527–65 C.E.) sought to (re)conquer Italy. Justinian's general Belisarius urges a Gothic king who had seized Rome not to raze the city and thereby destroy all that it represented (E7).

E1. CONSTANTINE'S VISION I

Eusebius *Life of Constantine* 1.26–28

Eusebius (c. 260–339 C.E.) was a prelate and writer. From c. 313 until his death, Eusebius was bishop of Caesarea, a coastal city in the Levant. In 325, he participated in the Council of Nicaea, where one of the seminal summaries of Christian belief, the Nicene Creed, was written. (In modified form it is still recited regularly by many Christians today.) Eusebius was also a prolific author whose extant writings include commentaries on scripture; polemical, chronological, geographical, and apologetic works; and orations, including one delivered to celebrate the thirtieth anniversary of the emperor Constantine's accession (reg. 306–37 C.E.). His understanding of the relationship between temporal and spiritual authority would prove foundational to Byzantine political thought. Eusebius also wrote the first history of Christianity, covering the life of Jesus through 324. It was highly influential, and, as a pioneering writer of ecclesiastical historiography, Eusebius was a kind of Christian Herodotus.

Influential, too, was Eusebius's biography of the first Christian emperor, Constantine, which appeared soon after its subject's death on May 22, 337. (It may have been unfinished, for Eusebius himself died in May 339.) Drawing on imperial laws and letters, a deep knowledge of the Bible, his own earlier works, and his acquaintance with the emperor—Eusebius met Constantine more than once, and the two corresponded—Eusebius produced a text that was, again, pioneering and sui generis, blending elements of panegyric, history, biography, and hagiography. It is written in an elevated, pleonastic style, suggesting that it was aimed at the political and ecclesiastical elite, including, perhaps, Constantine's own sons, who jointly ruled the empire after their father's death. The excerpt below is taken from Eusebius's account of Constantine's preparations to fight Maxentius in 312, for which some background should be provided. Since 293, the empire, divided into eastern and western halves, had been ruled by a "tetrarchy" of two senior emperors and two junior emperors, each of them responsible for particular provinces. From May 1, 305, Constantine's father, Constantius I (a.k.a. Constantius Chlorus), was the senior emperor of the west; when Constantius I died on July 25, 306, Constantine assumed control of his father's territory, namely, Britain, Spain, and Gaul. That same year, Maxentius, himself the son of a former senior emperor, was declared emperor in Rome; in 312, he controlled Italy and Africa, though he was a usurper, that is, not a member of the tetrarchy. Contrary to the hostile treatment of him in pro-Constantinian sources, Maxentius portrayed himself as an equitable, even Augustan, ruler; as the defender of Rome, he cultivated the loyalty of the Senate and people. In the passage below, Constantine contemplates his campaign against Maxentius as well as his religious allegiances. And he sees a vision.

Further Reading

Eusebius *Life of Constantine* 1.1–25; A. Momigliano, "Pagan and Christian Historiography in the Fourth Century A.D.," in *The Conflict between Paganism and Christianity in the Fourth Century,* ed. A. Momigliano, 79–99 (Oxford, 1963); R. A. Markus, "The Roman Empire in Early Christian Historiography," *The Downside Review* 81 (1963): 340–53, reprinted as chapter 4 in the author's *From Augustine to Gregory the Great: History and Christianity in Late Antiquity* (London, 1983); A. Cameron, "Eusebius' *Vita Constantini* and the Construction of Constantine," in *Portraits: Biographical Representation in the Greek and Latin Literature of the Roman Empire,* ed. M. J. Edwards and S. Swain, 145–74 (Oxford, 1997).

(26) Εἶθ' ὥσπερ μέγα σῶμα τὸ πᾶν τῆς γῆς ἐννοήσας στοιχεῖον, κἄπειτα τὴν τοῦ παντὸς κεφαλήν, τῆς Ῥωμαίων ἀρχῆς τὴν βασιλεύουσαν πόλιν, τυραννικῇ δουλείᾳ συνιδὼν καθυπηγμένην, παρεχώρει μὲν τὰ πρῶτα τὴν ὑπὲρ αὐτῆς ἄμυναν τοῖς τῶν λοιπῶν κρατοῦσι μερῶν ἅτε δὴ χρόνῳ προάγουσιν, ἐπεὶ δὲ τούτων οὐδεὶς οἷός τ' ἦν ἐπικουρεῖν, ἀλλὰ καὶ οἱ πεῖραν λαβεῖν ἐθελήσαντες αἰσχρὸν ὑπέμειναν τέλος, οὐδὲ βιωτὸν αὐτῷ τὴν ζωὴν εἶναι εἰπών, εἰ τὴν βασιλίδα πόλιν οὕτω κάμνουσαν παρίδοι, παρεσκευάζετο τὰ πρὸς τὴν καθαίρεσιν τῆς τυραννίδος.

(27.1) Εὖ δ' ἐννοήσας ὡς κρείττονος ἢ κατὰ στρατιωτικὴν δέοι αὐτῷ βοηθείας διὰ τὰς κακοτέχνους καὶ γοητικὰς μαγγανείας τὰς παρὰ τῷ τυράννῳ σπουδαζομένας, θεὸν ἀνεζήτει βοηθόν, τὰ μὲν ἐξ ὁπλιτῶν καὶ στρατιωτικοῦ πλήθους δεύτερα τιθέμενος (τῆς γὰρ παρὰ θεοῦ βοηθείας ἀπούσης τὸ μηθὲν ταῦτα δύνασθαι ἡγεῖτο), τὰ δ' ἐκ θεοῦ συνεργίας ἄμαχα εἶναι καὶ ἀήττητα λέγων. **(2)** ἐννοεῖ δῆτα ὁποῖον δέοι θεὸν βοηθὸν ἐπιγράψασθαι, ζητοῦντι δ' αὐτῷ ἔννοιά τις ὑπεισῆλθεν, ὡς πλειόνων πρότερον τῆς ἀρχῆς ἐφαψαμένων οἱ μὲν πλείοσι θεοῖς τὰς σφῶν αὐτῶν ἀναρτήσαντες ἐλπίδας, λοιβαῖς τε καὶ θυσίαις καὶ ἀναθήμασι τούτους θεραπεύσαντες, ἀπατηθέντες τὰ πρῶτα διὰ μαντειῶν κεχαρισμένων χρησμῶν τε τὰ αἴσια ἀπαγγελλομένων αὐτοῖς τέλος οὐκ αἴσιον εὕραντο, οὐδέ τις θεῶν πρὸς τὸ μὴ θεηλάτοις ὑποβληθῆναι καταστροφαῖς δεξιὸς αὐτοῖς παρέστη, μόνον δὲ τὸν ἑαυτοῦ πατέρα τὴν ἐναντίαν ἐκείνοις τραπέντα τῶν μὲν πλάνην καταγνῶναι, αὐτὸν δὲ τὸν ἐπέκεινα τῶν ὅλων θεόν, διὰ πάσης τιμήσαντα ζωῆς, σωτῆρα καὶ φύλακα τῆς βασιλείας ἀγαθοῦ τε παντὸς χορηγὸν εὕρασθαι. **(3)** ταῦτα παρ' ἑαυτῷ διακρίνας εὖ τε λογισάμενος, ὡς οἱ μὲν πλήθει θεῶν ἐπιθαρρήσαντες καὶ πλείοσιν ἐπιπεπτώκασιν ὀλέθροις, ὡς μηδὲ γένος μηδὲ φυὴν μὴ ῥίζαν αὐτοῖς, μηδ' ὄνομα μηδὲ μνήμην ἐν ἀνθρώποις ἀπολειφθῆναι, ὁ δὲ πατρῷος αὐτῷ θεὸς τῆς αὐτοῦ δυνάμεως ἐναργῆ καὶ πάμπολλα δείγματα εἴη δεδωκὼς τῷ αὐτοῦ πατρί, ἀλλὰ καὶ τοὺς ἤδη καταστρατεύσαντας πρότερον τοῦ τυράννου διασκεψάμενος σὺν πλήθει μὲν θεῶν τὴν παράταξιν πεποιημένους αἰσχρὸν δὲ τέλος ὑπομείναντας· ὁ μὲν γὰρ αὐτῶν σὺν αἰσχύνῃ τῆς συμβολῆς ἄπρακτος ἀνεχώρει, ὁ δὲ καὶ μέσοις αὐτοῖς τοῖς στρατεύμασι κατασφαγεὶς πάρεργον ἐγένετο θανάτου· ταῦτ' οὖν πάντα συναγαγὼν τῇ διανοίᾳ, τὸ μὲν περὶ τοὺς μηθὲν ὄντας θεοὺς ματαιάζειν καὶ μετὰ τοσοῦτον ἔλεγχον ἀποπλανᾶσθαι μωρίας ἔργον ὑπελάμβανε, τὸν δὲ πατρῷον τιμᾶν μόνον ᾤετο δεῖν θεόν.

(28.1) Ἀνεκαλεῖτο δῆτα ἐν εὐχαῖς τοῦτον, ἀντιβολῶν καὶ ποτνιώμενος φῆναι αὐτῷ ἑαυτὸν ὅστις εἴη καὶ τὴν ἑαυτοῦ δεξιὰν χεῖρα τοῖς προκειμένοις ἐπορέξαι. εὐχομένῳ δὲ ταῦτα καὶ λιπαρῶς ἱκετεύοντι τῷ βασιλεῖ θεοσημεία τις ἐπιφαίνεται παραδοξοτάτη, ἣν τάχα μὲν ἄλλου λέγοντος οὐ ῥᾴδιον ἦν ἀποδέξασθαι, αὐτοῦ δὲ τοῦ νικητοῦ βασιλέως τοῖς τὴν γραφὴν διηγουμένοις ἡμῖν μακροῖς ὕστερον χρόνοις, ὅτε ἠξιώθημεν τῆς αὐτοῦ γνώσεώς τε καὶ ὁμιλίας, ἐξαγγείλαντος ὅρκοις τε πιστωσαμένου τὸν λόγον, τίς ἂν ἀμφιβάλοι μὴ οὐχὶ πιστεῦσαι τῷ διηγήματι; μάλισθ᾽ ὅτε καὶ ὁ μετὰ ταῦτα χρόνος ἀληθῆ τῷ λόγῳ παρέσχε τὴν μαρτυρίαν. **(2)** ἀμφὶ μεσημβρινὰς ἡλίου ὥρας, ἤδη τῆς ἡμέρας ἀποκλινούσης, αὐτοῖς ὀφθαλμοῖς ἰδεῖν ἔφη ἐν αὐτῷ οὐρανῷ ὑπερκείμενον τοῦ ἡλίου σταυροῦ τρόπαιον ἐκ φωτὸς συνιστάμενον, γραφήν τε αὐτῷ συνῆφθαι λέγουσαν· "τούτῳ νίκα." θάμβος δ᾽ ἐπὶ τῷ θεάματι κρατῆσαι αὐτόν τε καὶ τὸ στρατιωτικὸν ἅπαν, ὃ δὴ στελλομένῳ ποι πορείαν συνείπετό τε καὶ θεωρὸν ἐγίνετο τοῦ θαύματος.

Notes to Eusebius Life of Constantine *1.26–28*

These notes are indebted to A. Cameron and S. G. Hall, *Eusebius: Life of Constantine* (Oxford, 1999) and F. Winkelmann, L. Pietri, and M.-J. Rondeau, *Eusèbe de Césarée, Vie de Constantin,* Sources chrétiennes 559 (Paris, 2013).

(26) Εἶθ᾽ = Εἶτα. *then.*

πᾶν. When πᾶς appears in the attributive position, it indicates a whole as the sum of its collective parts: Smyth 1174.

ἐννοήσας. The subject is Constantine.

στοιχεῖον, -ου (neu.). *part, component.*

τυραννικῇ. i.e., by Maxentius, son of the former emperor Maximian (reg. 285–305), who was acclaimed emperor by the people and soldiers of Rome on October 28, 306. Eusebius characterizes Maxentius as a tyrant, yet Maxentius cast himself as Rome's guardian, a patron of the Senate, and a conservative Augustan alternative to the un-Roman, crude, and distant tetrarchs.

καθυπαγάομαι. *be subjected to* + dat.: Lampe, s.v., citing this passage.

παραχωρέω. *yield X* (+ acc.) *to Y* (+ dat.), often as a sign of respect: LSJ, s.v. b, 3.

τὰ πρῶτα. adverbial: *at first.*

τοῖς τῶν λοιπῶν κρατοῦσι μερῶν. Eusebius may introduce this act of "courtesy" by Constantine, giving way to the older tetrarchs, to account for the years-long delay between his accession in 306 and his campaign against Maxentius in 312: cf. Cameron and Hall, *Life of Constantine*, ad loc.

τούτων οὐδεὶς οἷός τ' ἦν. *none of these men* (i.e., the other emperors) *was able* + inf. LSJ, s.v. οἷος, III.2.

αἰσχρὸν . . . τέλος. Eusebius provides further detail about the other emperors' attempts to defeat Maxentius in **(27.3)**.

(27.1) δέοι. *there might be need of* + gen. 3rd sg. pres. act. opt. < δεῖ. Opt. in secondary sequence after aor. ἐννοήσας.

γοητικός, -ή, -όν. *magical.* Eusebius later details Maxentius's superstitious sorcery (1.33–36), which contrasts with Constantine's piety, but elsewhere admits that Maxentius also proclaimed tolerance of Christianity in the lands over which he held sway (*Ecclesiastical History* 8.14.1).

μαγγανεία, -ας (fem.). *trickery,* esp. associated with magic.

βοηθός, -οῦ (mas.). *helper, ally,* esp. in military contexts.

δεύτερα. *of secondary importance*; take as adverbial or predicative with τὰ μὲν . . . πλήθους.

τίθημι. *consider, reckon*: LSJ, s.v. B.II.

τὸ μηθὲν = τὸ μηδὲν. *not at all, by no means.*

ἀήττητος, -ον. *invincible,* an adj. often associated with Christ in early Christian writers: Lampe, s.v. 2.

(2) δῆτα, one of Eusebius' favorite particles, is an emphatic form of δή.

ἐπιγράφω. lit., *write upon, inscribe*; also a verb, esp. in the mid., associated with politics and the law: *register, claim, choose as patron*: LSJ and Lampe, s.v. As the narrative will soon make clear, both the literal and politico-legal meanings may be appropriate here.

ὡς introduces indirect discourse.

πλειόνων . . . ἐφαψαμένων. partitive gen. dependent on οἱ μὲν.

ἐφάπτω. in later Greek, usually dep.: *lay hold of, grasp at* + gen. τῆς ἀρχῆς; verbs of touching take a gen.: Smyth 1345.

ἀναρτάω. *hang X* (+ acc.) *on Y* (+ dat.).

τούτους. i.e., the gods.

κεχαρισμένων. *favorable.*

αὐτοῖς. complement of ἀπαγγελλομένων.

οὐκ αἴσιον. delicate irony marked by litotes (Smyth 3032).

εὕραντο. 3rd pl. aor. mid. ind. < εὑρίσκω. In later Greek, alpha often replaces the thematic vowels epsilon and omicron in the strong aorist endings.

πρὸς τὸ μὴ θεηλάτοις ὑποβληθῆναι καταστροφαῖς. *from being cast down by divinely sent catastrophes*; the redundant μὴ, used after a main verb of hindering (οὐδέ . . . παρέστη), is not translated: Smyth 2739.

παρίστημι. in 2nd aor., *protect, prevent X* (+ dat.): LSJ, s.v. B.1.

μόνον δὲ balances the οἱ μὲν above. The transition from the "many" to the "one" is also flagged syntactically, for Eusebius switches from indirect discourse constructed with ὡς + ind. to acc. + inf., a not uncommon phenomenon in Greek: Smyth 2628.

τὸν ἑαυτοῦ πατέρα. i.e., Constantine's father, Constantius I, a.k.a. Constantius Chlorus (reg. 293–306 C.E.).

τὴν ἐναντίαν (sc. ὁδόν: Smyth 1027.b) ἐκείνοις τραπέντα. *having taken the road contrary to them*; i.e., they took one path, while he alone took the other.

καταγιγνώσκω. *condemn, despise.*

αὐτὸν. i.e., Constantius, the acc. subject in indirect discourse.

ἐπέκεινα + gen. *above, beyond.*

χορηγός, -οῦ (mas.). *sponsor, patron,* one who in classical Athens paid the costs of a chorus. The word belongs to the vocabulary of euergetism or civic benefaction, on which see also notes on section **(10.2)** of B3 and verse **(6)** of D1.2.

(3) ἐπιθαρρέω. *trust in* + dat.

ἐπιπεπτώκασιν < ἐπιπίπτω.

ὡς (= ὥστε) . . . ἀπολειφθῆναι is a result clause.

ῥίζα, -ης (fem.). *family*: LSJ, s.v. II.

εἴη δεδωκὼς. 3rd sg. pf. act. opt. < δίδωμι. Opt. in indirect discourse, secondary sequence introduced by διακρίνας εὖ τε λογισάμενος.

ὁ μὲν. i.e., Galerius, senior emperor of the east, who attacked his son-in-law Maxentius, ensconced in Rome, in fall 307. Finding the city larger and better fortified than he anticipated and heading a reluctant, too-small force, Galerius abandoned his campaign. Like Augustus in the *Res Gestae* (C3), Eusebius does not name the emperor's rivals even as he describes their defeat.

συμβολή, -ῆς (fem.). *(military) engagement, battle*: LSJ, s.v. II.

ἄπρακτος, -ον. *not taking part in* + gen.; i.e., Galerius never actually fought Maxentius.

ὁ δὲ. i.e., Severus, senior emperor of the west, who attacked Maxentius in spring 307. His troops defected to Maxentius's side and he fled to Ravenna; later he was executed or permitted to commit suicide by Maxentius. Eusebius's account of Severus's death thus appears to be specious.

τὸ . . . ματαιάζειν καὶ . . . ἀποπλανᾶσθαι. These articular infinitives are predicative with μωρίας ἔργον.

ματαιάζω. *fool around with* + περί.

ἔλεγχος, -εος (neu.). *examination, scrutiny,* drawn from the vocabulary of logic and the courts.

ᾤετο. 3rd sg. impf. dep. ind. < οἴομαι.

οἴομαι δεῖν. lit. *think it is necessary*; i.e., *decide, intend*: LSJ, s.v. οἴομαι, VI.2.

(28.1) Ἀνεκαλεῖτο. Note the impf.: this was not a one-time act.

φῆναι. aor. act. inf. < φαίνω.

πρόκειμαι. *be set before (someone).* The language echoes that of the Psalms: "you have stretched out your hands against the wrath of my enemies, and your right hand has saved me," Psalm 137.7 (Septuagint), as cited by Winkelmann, Pietri, and Rondeau, *Vie de Constantin,* ad loc.

ἐπιφαίνεται. The switch to historical present heightens the drama: Smyth 1883.

τάχα. *perhaps*: LSJ, s.v. II.

ἄλλου λέγοντος. Translate as conditional.

βασιλέως. sc. λέγοντος.

μακροῖς ὕστερον χρόνοις. Eusebius may have heard this story from Constantine at the Council of Nicaea in 325 or in 336, when both were in Constantinople.

ἠξιώθημεν. 1st pl. aor. pass. ind. < ἀξιόω. *consider worthy of* + gen.

μὴ οὐχὶ. These double negatives yield a positive, a not unusual construction after a verb of doubting: Smyth 2743.

(2) μεσημβρινὰς ἡλίου ὥρας. In the ancient world, supernatural phenomena often appeared around midday: see section **(4)** of B5 for another example of a daytime apparition. It is also worth noting that Constantine associated himself with

Apollo / Sol Invictus (Unconquered Sun), and continued to do so well after his defeat of Maxentius, as late as 325.

τρόπαιον. For Eusebius and many early Christians, the cross was a symbol of triumph, not suffering: Lampe, s.v. The cross's association with victory must have been especially meaningful to Constantine as a general on campaign.

αὐτῷ. i.e., to the trophy.

συνῆφθαι. aor. pass. inf. < συνάπτω.

νίκα. 2nd sg. pres. act. impv. < νικάω.

θάμβος. neu. sg. acc., the subject (in indirect discourse) of κρατῆσαι.

ποι. This word's importance has often been overlooked; the vision happened *somewhere* on campaign and not just before the Battle of the Milvian Bridge. For Constantine has not yet even marched into Italy.

E2. CONSTANTINE'S VISION II

Eusebius *Life of Constantine* 1.29–32

The passage below follows directly on E1, where Eusebius and the historical context are more fully introduced. The emperor Constantine (reg. 306–337 C.E.) has just seen a vision somewhere on campaign—not just before the Battle of the Milvian Bridge against Maxentius on October 28, 312, as has been often assumed. This battle is treated in many sources. Two panegyric speeches, dating 313 and 321, offer accounts thereof, but neither mentions a vision (*Panegyrici Latini* 9 [12].16–18, 4 [10].27–32). Nor does Eusebius mention it in his earlier version of the battle, found in his *Ecclesiastical History* (9.9.2–8). Only the Latin author Lactantius, in his *On the Deaths of the Persecutors* (44), which dates to 314/15, speaks of a supernatural sight, but his version differs significantly from Eusebius's in *Life of Constantine.* In short, the sources for the vision and the battle are difficult to interpret; it is not possible to harmonize them convincingly into a "master narrative."

In the passage below, Constantine dreams of Christ, who helps him interpret his vision of the solar cross. In response, the emperor commissions craftsmen to build a representation of what he has seen. This is the *labarum,* a sort of Christianized military standard. Then the emperor summons clergymen so that he may learn more about the deity who has so dramatically made himself known. What makes this and the previous passage (E1) so fascinating is Eusebius's knack for dramatizing Constantine's thought process, as he mulls over what he has seen and its implications.

Bronze coin issued by the emperor Constantine in 327 C.E. On the obverse (*left*) appears a laureate bust of the emperor, identified as "CONSTANTINVS, MAX(IMVS) AVG(VSTVS)." The reverse (*right*) bears the motto "Public Hope" (SPES PVBLIC[A]) and, at bottom, a mint-mark indicating that the coin was struck in Constantinople. The reverse also portrays a snake speared by a *labarum,* the ensign pioneered by Constantine. Eusebius describes the *labarum's* design in *Life of Constantine* 1.29–32 (E2). *Image courtesy Wikimedia Commons.*

Further Reading

Exodus 3.1–22, an important model for Eusebius's account; Lactantius *On the Deaths of the Persecutors* 44; P. Weiss, "The Vision of Constantine," *Journal of Roman Archaeology* 16 (2003): 237–59; R. Van Dam, *Remembering Constantine at the Milvian Bridge* (Cambridge, 2011), 1–18, 82–100.

(29) καὶ δὴ διαπορεῖν, πρὸς ἑαυτὸν ἔλεγε, τί ποτε εἴη τὸ φάσμα. ἐνθυμουμένῳ δ' αὐτῷ καὶ ἐπὶ πολὺ λογιζομένῳ νὺξ ἐπῄει καταλαβοῦσα. ἔνθα δὴ ὑπνοῦντι αὐτῷ τὸν Χριστὸν τοῦ θεοῦ σὺν τῷ φανέντι κατ' οὐρανὸν σημείῳ ὀφθῆναί τε καὶ παρακελεύσασθαι, μίμημα ποιησάμενον τοῦ κατ' οὐρανὸν ὀφθέντος σημείου τούτῳ πρὸς τὰς τῶν πολεμίων συμβολὰς ἀλεξήματι χρῆσθαι. **(30)** ἅμα δ' ἡμέρᾳ διαναστὰς τοῖς φίλοις ἐξηγόρευε τὸ ἀπόρρητον. κἄπειτα χρυσοῦ καὶ λίθων πολυτελῶν δημιουργοὺς συγκαλέσας μέσος αὐτὸς καθιζάνει καὶ τοῦ σημείου τὴν εἰκόνα φράζει, ἀπομιμεῖσθαί τε αὐτὴν χρυσῷ καὶ πολυτελέσι λίθοις διεκελεύετο. ὃ δὴ καὶ ἡμᾶς ὀφθαλμοῖς ποτε παραλαβεῖν αὐτὸς βασιλεύς, θεοῦ καὶ τοῦτο χαρισαμένου, ἠξίωσεν.

(31) Ἦν δὲ τοιῷδε σχήματι κατεσκευασμένον. ὑψηλὸν δόρυ χρυσῷ κατημφιεσμένον κέρας εἶχεν ἐγκάρσιον σταυροῦ σχήματι πεποιημένον, ἄνω δὲ πρὸς ἄκρῳ τοῦ παντὸς στέφανος ἐκ λίθων πολυτελῶν καὶ χρυσοῦ συμπεπλεγμένος κατεστήρικτο, καθ᾽ οὗ τῆς σωτηρίου ἐπηγορίας τὸ σύμβολον δύο στοιχεῖα τὸ Χριστοῦ παραδηλοῦντα ὄνομα διὰ τῶν πρώτων ὑπεσήμαινον χαρακτήρων, χιαζομένου τοῦ ῥῶ κατὰ τὸ μεσαίτατον· ἃ δὴ καὶ κατὰ τοῦ κράνους φέρειν εἴωθε κἀν τοῖς μετὰ ταῦτα χρόνοις ὁ βασιλεύς. **(2)** τοῦ δὲ πλαγίου κέρως τοῦ κατὰ τὸ δόρυ πεπαρμένου ὀθόνη τις ἐκκρεμὴς ἀπῃώρητο, βασιλικὸν ὕφασμα ποικιλίᾳ συνημμένων πολυτελῶν λίθων φωτὸς αὐγαῖς ἐξαστραπτόντων καλυπτόμενον σὺν πολλῷ τε καθυφασμένον χρυσῷ, ἀδιήγητόν τι χρῆμα τοῖς ὁρῶσι παρέχον τοῦ κάλλους. τοῦτο μὲν οὖν τὸ φᾶρος τοῦ κέρως ἐξημμένον σύμμετρον μήκους τε καὶ πλάτους περιγραφὴν ἀπελάμβανε· τὸ δ᾽ ὄρθιον δόρυ, τῆς κάτω ἀρχῆς ἐπὶ πολὺ μηκυνόμενον ἄνω μετέωρον, ὑπὸ τῷ τοῦ σταυροῦ τροπαίῳ πρὸς αὐτοῖς ἄκροις τοῦ διαγραφέντος ὑφάσματος τὴν τοῦ θεοφιλοῦς βασιλέως εἰκόνα χρυσῆν μέχρι στέρνων τῶν τ᾽ αὐτοῦ παίδων ὁμοίως ἔφερε. **(3)** τούτῳ μὲν οὖν τῷ σωτηρίῳ σημείῳ πάσης ἀντικειμένης καὶ πολεμίας δυνάμεως ἀμυντηρίῳ διὰ παντὸς ἐχρῆτο βασιλεύς, τῶν τε στρατοπέδων ἁπάντων ἡγεῖσθαι τὰ τούτου ὁμοιώματα προσέταττεν.

(32.1) Ἀλλὰ ταῦτα σμικρὸν ὕστερον. κατὰ δὲ τὸν δηλωθέντα χρόνον τὴν παράδοξον καταπλαγεὶς ὄψιν, οὐδ᾽ ἕτερον θεὸν ἢ τὸν ὀφθέντα δοκιμάσας σέβειν, τοὺς τῶν αὐτοῦ λόγων μύστας ἀνεκαλεῖτο, καὶ τίς εἴη θεὸς οὗτος ἠρώτα τίς τε ὁ τῆς ὀφθείσης ὄψεως τοῦ σημείου λόγος. **(2)** οἱ δὲ τὸν μὲν εἶναι θεὸν ἔφασαν θεοῦ τοῦ ἑνὸς καὶ μόνου μονογενῆ παῖδα, τὸ δὲ σημεῖον τὸ φανὲν σύμβολον μὲν ἀθανασίας εἶναι, τρόπαιον δ᾽ ὑπάρχειν τῆς κατὰ τοῦ θανάτου νίκης, ἣν ἐποιήσατό ποτε παρελθὼν ἐπὶ γῆς, ἐδίδασκόν τε τὰς τῆς παρόδου αἰτίας, τὸν ἀκριβῆ λόγον αὐτῷ τῆς κατ᾽ ἀνθρώπους οἰκονομίας ὑποτιθέμενοι. **(3)** ὁ δὲ καὶ τούτοις μὲν ἐμαθητεύετο τοῖς λόγοις, θαῦμα δ᾽ εἶχε τῆς ὀφθαλμοῖς αὐτῷ παραδοθείσης θεοφανείας, συμβάλλων τε τὴν οὐράνιον ὄψιν τῇ τῶν λεγομένων ἑρμηνείᾳ τὴν διάνοιαν ἐστηρίζετο, θεοδίδακτον αὐτῷ τὴν τούτων γνῶσιν παρεῖναι πειθόμενος. καὶ αὐτὸς δ' ἤδη τοῖς ἐνθέοις ἀναγνώσμασι προσέχειν ἠξίου. καὶ δὴ τοὺς τοῦ θεοῦ ἱερέας παρέδρους αὐτῷ ποιησάμενος τὸν ὀφθέντα θεὸν πάσαις δεῖν ᾤετο θεραπείαις τιμᾶν. κἄπειτα φραξάμενος ταῖς εἰς αὐτὸν ἀγαθαῖς ἐλπίσιν ὡρμᾶτο λοιπὸν τοῦ τυραννικοῦ πυρὸς τὴν ἀπειλὴν κατασβέσων.

Notes to Eusebius Life of Constantine *1.29–32*

These notes are indebted to A. Cameron and S. G. Hall, *Eusebius: Life of Constantine* (Oxford, 1999) and F. Winkelmann, L. Pietri, and M.-J. Rondeau, *Eusèbe de Césarée, Vie de Constantin,* Sources chrétiennes 559 (Paris, 2013).

(29) ἔλεγε. The subject is Constantine.

ἐπὶ πολύ. *for a long time*: LSJ, s.v. πολύς, IV.4.b.

ἐπῄει. 3rd sg. impf. act. ind. < ἔπειμι (εἰμί).

ὑπνοῦντι. A daytime vision (E1) is followed by a nighttime dream.

παρακελεύσασθαι triggers a fresh round of indirect discourse, with Constantine as the acc. subject.

μίμημα, -ατος (neu.). *copy,* esp. an artistic representation of something.

σημεῖον, -ου (neu.). *sign, (military) standard, miracle*: Lampe, s.v. Eusebius often denominates the cross a σωτήριον σημεῖον: see, e.g., section **(37.1)** of E3.

συμβολή, -ῆς (fem.). *(military) engagement, battle*: LSJ, s.v. II.

ἀλεξήματι. The shields of Roman soldiers often bore apotropaic symbols.

(30) αὐτὴν. This is the *labarum,* which appears on the emperor's coins from 327. Although its representation thereon varies in the details, it generally resembles a military standard. The coins also suggest that the design of the *labarum* may have evolved over time; Eusebius's description in the following section is based on a later form, as made clear in **(32.1)**. The account here recalls Exodus (25–27, 35–39), where God reveals the design of the Ark of the Covenant and other sacred objects to Moses, who thereafter summons the people, relates what he has heard, and commissions artisans to build what God has described. See further Cameron and Hall, *Life of Constantine*, s.v. 1.29.

χαρίζω. in mid., *grant, allow*, with a sense of doing so benevolently.

(31) κατημφιεσμένον. neu. sg. nom., pf. pass. part. < καταμφιέννυμι. lit. *clothe round-about*; here, *cover, plate*.

κέρας, -αος (contracting to -ως) (neu.). *bar*.

ἐγκάρσιος, -α, -ον or -ος, -ον. *perpendicular*.

συμπεπλεγμένος < συμπλέκω. *weave*.

κατεστήρικτο. 3rd sg. plupf. pass. ind. < καταστηρίζω. *firmly attach*.

ἐπηγορία, -ας (fem.). *name, appellation*.

σύμβολον, -ου (neu.). *symbol*. Here the word is acc. sg., the object of ὑπεσήμαινον.

στοιχεῖον, -ου (neu.). *letter*.

παραδηλοῦντα. neu. pl. nom., agreeing with δύο στοιχεῖα; the object of the part. is τὸ Χριστοῦ . . . ὄνομα.

χιαζομένου τοῦ ῥῶ κατὰ τὸ μεσαίτατον. i.e., a chi and a rho superimposed. The earliest example of the chi-rho or christogram is found on an epitaph from Rome dating to 268: Winkelmann, Pietri, and Rondeau, *Vie de Constantin*, ad loc.

ἅ. The antecedent is χαρακτήρων.

κατὰ τοῦ κράνους. During Constantine's reign, medallions were minted in Ticinum and Siscia that seem to portray the chi-rho on the crest of the emperor's helmet: Winkelmann, Pietri, and Rondeau, *Vie de Constantin*, 70.

εἴωθε. 3rd sg. pf. act. ind. < ἔθω. *be accustomed to* + inf. The pf. of this defective verb should be translated as pres.: LSJ, s.v.

κἀν = καὶ ἐν.

(2) πλάγιος, -α, -ον or -ος, -ον. *transverse, perpendicular.*

κέρως. See note on κέρας in **(31.1)**.

πεπαρμένου. neu. sg. gen., pf. pass. part. < πείρω. *transfix, criss-cross.*

ἐκκρεμής, -ές. *suspended, pendent.*

ἀπῃώρητο. 3rd sg. plupf. dep. ind. < ἀπαιωρέομαι + gen. *hang from.*

βασιλικὸν ὕφασμα . . . καλυπτόμενον . . . καθυφασμένον are in apposition with ὀθόνη τις ἐκκρεμὴς.

ποικιλία, -ας (fem.). *decoration, embroidery,* often of a polychromatic kind. The word here is dat. of means triggered by καλυπτόμενον. The complex, pleonastic (Smyth 3042) language conveys the overwhelming splendor of the work described.

συνημμένων. mas. pl. gen., pf. pass. part. < συνάπτω. It may be useful here to review the principal parts of ἅπτω, ἅψω, ἧψα, —, ἧμμαι, ἥφθην.

ἐξαστράπτω. *twinkle* (like a star).

καθυφαίνω. *interweave.*

παρέχον agrees with ὕφασμα; ἀδιήγητόν τι χρῆμα is the part.'s object.

σύμμετρον modifies περιγραφὴν.

περιγραφή, -ῆς (fem.). *shape, appearance.*

ἀπολαμβάνω. here, *have.*

μηκύνω. *extend.*

μετέωρος, -ον. *high in the air.*

διαγραφέντος. neu. sg. gen., aor. pass. part. < διαγράφω. The part. could here mean either *decorated* or *(just) described.* To clarify: below the cross formed by the intersection of the vertical pole and the horizontal crossbar hangs a square tapestry, toward the top of which appear busts of Constantine and his sons.

(3) ἀμυντήριον, -ου (neu.). *bulwark, defense against* + gen. This noun makes explicit the apotropaic function of the *labarum*.

διὰ παντὸς. *continually*: LSJ, s.v. πᾶς, IV.

(32.1) Ἀλλὰ ταῦτα σμικρὸν ὕστερον. The implication is that the *labarum* just described, which the emperor showed Eusebius at a later date, may not have looked exactly like the *labarum* as it appeared to Constantine in his dream.

καταπλαγεὶς. mas. sg. nom., aor. pass. part. < καταπλήσσω. in pass., *be amazed at, terrified by* + cognate acc.

δοκιμάζω. *decide,* with the implication of doing so after careful calculation.

μύστης, -ου (mas.). *expert, confidant; initiate,* i.e., someone initiated into the mysteries: Lampe, s.v. The language may be meant to help the reader see things as Constantine did at the time: to the emperor, the clergy are mystagogues, privy to esoteric knowledge of the deity. Like a catechumen—someone being educated in the faith as preparation for baptism—Constantine now receives a crash course in Christian theology.

(2) μονογενής, -ές. *only-begotten*: Lampe, s.v. B. The language is credal. In the first part of this section, Constantine learns of Jesus's divine nature; toward the end, he learns of Jesus's human nature: Winkelmann, Pietri and Rondeau, *Vie de Constantin,* s.v. 1.32.

τρόπαιον. See note on section **(28.2)** of E1, s.v.

πάροδος, -ου (fem.). *appearance, coming*: LSJ, s.v. III; Lampe, s.v. 2.

οἰκονομία, -ας (fem.). *self-accommodation*; i.e., his incarnation: Cameron and Hall, *Life of Constantine,* ad loc.; Lampe, s.v. C.6.

(3) μαθητεύω. in pass., *become a disciple*: BDAG, s.v. 2; Lampe, s.v. 3.

τῆς . . . θεοφανείας. objective gen. (Smyth 1331) after θαῦμα.

στηρίζω. *hold fast to* + acc.

θεοδίδακτον. predicative with τὴν . . . γνῶσιν.

προσέχω. *devote oneself to* + dat.: LSJ, s.v. 4.b.

πάρεδρος, -ου (mas.). *adviser, counselor*; in magical contexts, *helper divinity, familiar spirit*: LSJ and Lampe, s.v.

δεῖν ᾤετο. See note on section **(27.3)** of E1, s.v. οἴομαι δεῖν.

λοιπόν. *finally*: LSJ, s.v. λοιπός, 5.b.

κατασβέσων. fut. part. indicating purpose.

E3. CONSTANTINE'S VISION III

Eusebius *Life of Constantine* 1.37–40

At the end of the previous passage (E2), Eusebius, having described Constantine's vision and dream, suggests that at last the reader will hear of the emperor's campaign against Maxentius. But, no, instead another delay ratchets up the tension. Eusebius luridly details Maxentius's egregious behavior in Rome, burnishing the latter's credentials as a tyrant and sorcerer with an insatiable appetite for sexual depravity and violence (1.33–36). Maxentius is cast as the Egyptian Pharaoh from the biblical book of Exodus who oppresses the Israelites enslaved in his land; Constantine plays their divinely chosen liberator, Moses. Emphasizing the depths of Maxentius's depravity also justifies Constantine's invasion and staves off any sympathy for Maxentius's fate. In the beginning of the passage below, Constantine finally makes his move. In spring 312, from Gaul he crosses the Alps into Italy. He takes the town of Segusio in the Piedmont; he bests heavily armored cavalry near Turin, whose residents welcome him after the battle; and he besieges Verona, where Maxentius's forces eventually surrender. (These are the three battles alluded to in 1.37.2.) Constantine has secured the Po Valley.

Then, marching to Rome along the Via Flaminia, Constantine pitches camp north of the city, not far from where the road crosses the Tiber River on the Milvian Bridge. Maxentius waits within the city's walls. Like so many ancient battles, the details are fuzzy but the outcome is clear. Maxentius is

Giovanni Battista Piranesi, "Veduta del Ponte Molle sul Tevere," c. 1748–1778. Piranesi portrays Rome's Milvian Bridge, which lends its name to the battle fought by the emperor Constantine and his rival Maxentius in 312 C.E. Eusebius narrates the battle in *Life of Constantine* 1.37–40 (E3). *Reproduced by permission of Greenslade Special Collections and Archives, Kenyon College, Gambier, Ohio.*

defeated on the sixth anniversary, to the day, of his acclamation as emperor, on October 28, 312. After the battle, the victor Constantine enters Rome—like Jesus, who in the gospels also enters a royal city in triumph. The excerpt below is of special interest because of its possible links to two famous monuments from the emperor's reign. First, Eusebius describes a statue of Constantine erected in Rome that it is tempting to identify with the fragments of a colossal statue of the emperor now displayed in the Capitoline Museums. Second, Eusebius records an inscription (which is also known from other ancient sources, with small, revealing variations in the texts) that is similar to the inscription found on the Arch of Constantine—albeit with a significant difference at the beginning, where the latter attributes Constantine's victory over the unnamed Maxentius to the "prompting of divinity [and] greatness of mind" (*instinctu divinitatis mentis magnitudine*: H. Dessau, *Inscriptiones Latinae Selectae* [Berlin, 1892], 1:156, no. 694).

Further Reading

Exodus 14–15.19; A. Wilson, "Biographical Models: The Constantinian Period and Beyond," in *Constantine: History, Historiography and Legend*, ed. S. N. C. Lieu and D. Montserrat, 107–35 (London, 1998); E. Marlowe, "Framing the Sun: The Arch of Constantine and the Roman Cityscape," *Art Bulletin* 88 (2006): 223–42; R. Van Dam, *Remembering Constantine at the Milvian Bridge* (Cambridge, 2011), 124–46, 181–203.

(37.1) Ἀλλὰ γὰρ τούτων ἁπάντων οἶκτον ἀναλαβὼν Κωνσταντῖνος πάσαις παρασκευαῖς ὡπλίζετο κατὰ τῆς τυραννίδος. προστησάμενος δῆτα ἑαυτοῦ θεὸν τὸν ἐπὶ πάντων σωτῆρά τε καὶ βοηθὸν ἀνακαλεσάμενος τὸν Χριστόν, αὐτοῦ τε τὸ νικητικὸν τρόπαιον τὸ δὴ σωτήριον σημεῖον τῶν ἀμφ' αὐτὸν ὁπλιτῶν τε καὶ δορυφόρων προτάξας ἡγεῖτο πανστρατιᾷ, Ῥωμαίοις τὰ τῆς ἐκ προγόνων ἐλευθερίας προμνώμενος. **(2)** Μαξεντίου δῆτα μᾶλλον ταῖς κατὰ γοητείαν μηχαναῖς ἢ τῇ τῶν ὑπηκόων ἐπιθαρροῦντος εὐνοίᾳ, προελθεῖν δ' οὐδ' ὅσον πυλῶν τοῦ ἄστεος ἐπιτολμῶντος, ὁπλιτῶν δ' ἀναρίθμῳ πλήθει καὶ στρατοπέδων λόχοις μυρίοις πάντα τόπον καὶ χώραν καὶ πόλιν ὅση τις ὑπ' αὐτῷ δεδούλωτο φραξαμένου, ὁ τῆς ἐκ θεοῦ συμμαχίας ἀνημμένος βασιλεὺς ἐπιὼν πρώτῃ καὶ δευτέρᾳ καὶ τρίτῃ τοῦ τυράννου παρατάξει εὖ μάλα τε πάσας ἐξ αὐτῆς πρώτης ὁρμῆς χειρωσάμενος, πρόεισιν ἐπὶ πλεῖστον ὅσον τῆς Ἰταλῶν χώρας.

(38.1) Ἤδη δ' αὐτῆς Ῥώμης ἄγχιστα ἦν. εἶθ' ὡς μὴ τοῦ τυράννου χάριν Ῥωμαίοις πολεμεῖν ἐξαναγκάζοιτο, θεὸς αὐτὸς οἷα δεσμοῖς τισι τὸν τύραννον πορρωτάτω πυλῶν ἐξέλκει, καὶ τὰ πάλαι δὴ κατ' ἀσεβῶν ὡς ἐν μύθου λόγῳ παρὰ τοῖς πλείστοις ἀπιστούμενα, πιστά γε μὴν πιστοῖς ἱεραῖς βίβλοις ἐστηλιτευμένα, αὐταῖς ἐνεργείαις ἅπασιν ἁπλῶς εἰπεῖν πιστοῖς ἅμα καὶ ἀπίστοις ὀφθαλμοῖς τὰ παράδοξα θεωμένοις ἐπιστώσατο. **(2)** ὥσπερ γοῦν ἐπ' αὐτοῦ ποτε Μωϋσέως τοῦ τε θεοσεβοῦς Ἑβραίων γένους "ἅρματα Φαραὼ καὶ τὴν δύναμιν αὐτοῦ ἔρριψεν εἰς θάλασσαν καὶ ἐπιλέκτους ἀναβάτας τριστάτας κατεπόντισεν ἐν ἐρυθρᾷ" [Exodus 15.4] κατὰ τὰ αὐτὰ δὴ καὶ Μαξέντιος οἵ τ' ἀμφ' αὐτὸν ὁπλῖται καὶ δορυφόροι "ἔδυσαν εἰς βυθὸν ὡσεὶ λίθος" [Exodus 15.5], ὁπηνίκα νῶτα δοὺς τῇ ἐκ θεοῦ μετὰ Κωνσταντίνου δυνάμει τὸν πρὸ τῆς πορείας διῄει ποταμόν, ὃν αὐτὸς σκάφεσι ζεύξας καὶ εὖ μάλα γεφυρώσας μηχανὴν ὀλέθρου καθ' ἑαυτοῦ συνεπήξατο, ὧδέ πῃ ἑλεῖν τὸν τῷ θεῷ φίλον ἐλπίσας. **(3)** ἀλλὰ τῷδε μὲν δεξιὸς παρῆν ὁ αὐτοῦ θεός, ὁ δ' ἄρα τὰς κρυφίους μηχανὰς καθ' ἑαυτοῦ δείλαιος συνίστη. ἐφ' ᾧ καὶ ἦν εἰπεῖν, ὡς ἄρα "λάκκον ὤρυξε καὶ ἀνέσκαψεν αὐτὸν καὶ ἐμπεσεῖται εἰς βόθρον ὃν εἰργάσατο. ἐπιστρέψει ὁ πόνος αὐτοῦ εἰς κεφαλὴν αὐτοῦ, καὶ ἐπὶ κορυφὴν αὐτοῦ ἡ ἀδικία αὐτοῦ καταβήσεται" [Psalm 7.16–17]. **(4)** οὕτω δῆτα θεοῦ νεύματι τῶν ἐπὶ τοῦ ζεύγματος μηχανῶν τοῦ τ' ἐν αὐτοῖς ἐγκρύμματος οὐ κατὰ καιρὸν τὸν ἐλπισθέντα <διαρρυεισῶν> ὑφιζάνει μὲν ἡ διάβασις, χωρεῖ δ' ἀθρόως αὔτανδρα κατὰ τοῦ βυθοῦ τὰ σκάφη, καὶ αὐτός γε πρῶτος ὁ δείλαιος, εἶτα δὲ καὶ οἱ ἀμφ' αὐτὸν ὑπασπισταί τε καὶ δορυφόροι, ᾗ τὰ θεῖα προανεφώνει λόγια, "ἔδυσαν ὡσεὶ μόλιβδος ἐν ὕδατι σφοδρῷ" [Exodus 15.10]. **(5)** ὥστ' εἰκότως ἂν εἰ καὶ μὴ λόγοις, ἔργοις δ' οὖν ὁμοίως τοῖς ἀμφὶ τὸν μέγαν θεράποντα Μωϋσέα τοὺς παρὰ θεοῦ τὴν νίκην ἀραμένους αὐτὰ δὴ τὰ κατὰ τοῦ πάλαι δυσσεβοῦς τυράννου ὧδέ πως ἀνυμνεῖν καὶ λέγειν· "ᾄσωμεν τῷ κυρίῳ, ἐνδόξως γὰρ δεδόξασται. ἵππον καὶ ἀναβάτην ἔρριψεν εἰς θάλασσαν, βοηθὸς καὶ σκεπαστὴς ἐγένετό μοι εἰς σωτηρίαν·" [Exodus 15.1–2] καί "τίς ὅμοιός σοι ἐν θεοῖς, κύριε, τίς ὅμοιός σοι; δεδοξασμένος ἐν ἁγίοις, θαυμαστὸς ἐνδόξως ποιῶν τέρατα" [Exodus 15.11].

(39.1) Ταῦτά τε καὶ ὅσα τούτοις ἀδελφὰ Κωνσταντῖνος τῷ πανηγεμόνι καὶ τῆς νίκης αἰτίῳ κατὰ καιρὸν ὁμοίως τῷ μεγάλῳ θεράποντι ἔργοις αὐτοῖς ἀνυμνήσας, μετ' ἐπινικίων εἰσήλαυνεν εἰς τὴν βασιλεύουσαν πόλιν. **(2)** πάντες δ' ἀθρόως αὐτὸν οἵ τ' ἀπὸ τῆς συγκλήτου βουλῆς οἵ τ' ἄλλως ἐπιφανεῖς καὶ διάσημοι τῶν τῇδε, ὥσπερ ἐξ εἱργμῶν ἠλευθερωμένοι, σὺν παντὶ δήμῳ Ῥωμαίων φαιδροῖς ὄμμασιν αὐταῖς ψυχαῖς μετ' εὐφημιῶν καὶ ἀπλήστου χαρᾶς ὑπεδέχοντο, ὁμοῦ τ' ἄνδρες

ἅμα γυναιξὶ καὶ παισὶ καὶ οἰκετῶν μυρίοις πλήθεσι λυτρωτὴν αὐτὸν σωτῆρά τε καὶ εὐεργέτην βοαῖς ἀσχέτοις ἐπεφώνουν. **(3)** ὁ δ' ἔμφυτον τὴν εἰς τὸν θεὸν εὐσέβειαν κεκτημένος μήτ' ἐπὶ ταῖς βοαῖς χαυνούμενος μήτ' ἐπαιρόμενος τοῖς ἐπαίνοις, τῆς δ' ἐκ θεοῦ συνῃσθημένος βοηθείας, εὐχαριστήριον ἀπεδίδου παραχρῆμα εὐχὴν τῷ τῆς νίκης αἰτίῳ.
(40.1) γραφῇ τε μεγάλῃ καὶ στήλαις ἅπασιν ἀνθρώποις τὸ σωτήριον ἀνεκήρυττε σημεῖον, μέσῃ τῇ βασιλευούσῃ πόλει μέγα τρόπαιον τουτὶ κατὰ τῶν πολεμίων ἐγείρας, διαρρήδην δὲ ἀνεξαλείπτοις ἐγχαράξας τύποις σωτήριον τουτὶ σημεῖον τῆς Ῥωμαίων ἀρχῆς καὶ τῆς καθόλου βασιλείας φυλακτήριον. **(2)** αὐτίκα δ' οὖν ὑψηλὸν δόρυ σταυροῦ σχήματι ὑπὸ χεῖρα ἰδίας εἰκόνος ἐν ἀνδριάντι κατειργασμένης τῶν ἐπὶ Ῥώμης δεδημοσιευμένων ἐν τόπῳ στήσαντας αὐτὴν δὴ ταύτην τὴν γραφὴν ῥήμασιν αὐτοῖς ἐγχαράξαι τῇ Ῥωμαίων ἐγκελεύεται φωνῇ· "Τούτῳ τῷ σωτηριώδει σημείῳ, τῷ ἀληθεῖ ἐλέγχῳ τῆς ἀνδρείας, τὴν πόλιν ὑμῶν ζυγοῦ τυραννικοῦ διασωθεῖσαν ἠλευθέρωσα· ἔτι μὴν καὶ τὴν σύγκλητον καὶ τὸν δῆμον Ῥωμαίων τῇ ἀρχαίᾳ ἐπιφανείᾳ καὶ λαμπρότητι ἐλευθερώσας ἀποκατέστησα."

Notes to Eusebius Life of Constantine *1.37–40*

These notes are indebted to A. Cameron and S. G. Hall, *Eusebius: Life of Constantine* (Oxford, 1999) and F. Winkelmann, L. Pietri, and M.-J. Rondeau, *Eusèbe de Césarée, Vie de Constantin,* Sources chrétiennes 559 (Paris, 2013).

(37.1) τούτων ἁπάντων. i.e., Maxentius's maleficent acts as narrated in the preceding chapters (1.33–36). Objective gen. (Smyth 1331) triggered by οἶκτον.

ὁπλίζω. in mid., *arm oneself with* + dat: LSJ, s.v. 3.

προΐστημι. in 1st aor. mid., *choose as one's leader, put on front of one*: LSJ, s.v. A.II.1, 2. Both definitions apply here, as will soon be seen.

δῆτα. See E1, note on section **(27.2)**, s.v.

βοηθός, -οῦ (mas.). See E1, note on section **(27.1)**, s.v.

τὸ νικητικὸν τρόπαιον τὸ δὴ σωτήριον σημεῖον. Eusebius refers to the *labarum,* the Christianized military standard whose design had been supernaturally revealed to Constantine. On the *labarum,* see note on section **(30)** of E2, s.v. αὐτὴν.

προτάσσω (Attic προτάττω). *place X* (+ acc.) *in front of* (+ gen.).

ἡγέομαι. When meaning *lead,* this verb typically takes a dat.; when meaning *rule,* it typically takes a gen.: LSJ, s.v. II.1, 2.

πανστρατιᾷ. dat. sg. functioning adverbially: *with the whole army.*

(2) Μαξεντίου. On Maxentius's characterization, see also notes on section **(26)** of E1, s.v. τυραννικῇ and section **(27.1)** of E1, s.v. γοητικός. Eusebius keeps Constantine in the limelight by confining Maxentius to a gen. absolute.

οὐδ' ὅσον. *not even, not even a little bit*: LSJ, s.v. IV.2.

λόχοις μυρίοις. Two sources enumerate the opposing forces. While such figures are notoriously suspect, it should be noted that both, one pro- and the other anti-Constantine, agree that Maxentius's army was twice as big as Constantine's: Cameron and Hall, *Life of Constantine,* ad loc.

δεδούλωτο. 3rd sg. plupf. pass. ind. The plupf. is not always augmented in later Greek.

ἀνημμένος. mas. sg. nom., pf. pass. part. < ἀνάπτω. in pass., *cling to, fasten oneself to* + gen.

ἐπιὼν < ἔπειμι (εἶμι). *attack* + dat.

παρατάξει. Regarding the battles, see the introduction to this passage.

πρόεισιν. sc. "Constantine's troops" as the subject.

πλεῖστον ὅσον. *greatest part* + gen.

(38.1) ἦν. sc. "Constantine" as the subject.

εἶθ' = εἶτα. *then.*

χάριν + gen. *on account of*; here, as often, the preposition is postpositive, following the words it governs.

πορρωτάτω. *far beyond* + gen.

ἐξέλκει. Eusebius switches to historical present (Smyth 1883) to narrate the decisive battle.

τὰ πάλαι . . . κατ' ἀσεβῶν. *the ancient (words written) against the impious.* All the subsequent neu. pl. accusatives agree with this phrase; they are cumulatively the objects of ἐπιστώσατο.

ὡς ἐν μύθου λόγῳ. *as if (they were written) in a mythical account.*

τοῖς πλείστοις ἀπιστούμενα, πιστά γε μὴν πιστοῖς. Chiasmus (Smyth 3020) underscores the antithesis.

γε μὴν. *yet, however.*

ἐστηλιτευμένα. neu. pl. acc., pf. pass. part. < στηλιτεύω. *inscribe.* Translate the part. as causal.

αὐταῖς ἐνεργείαις ἅπασιν. dat. of means.

ἐνέργεια, -ας (fem.). *activity, action*, especially one set in motion by divine or supernatural forces: LSJ, s.v. 2; Lampe, s.v. B.

ἁπλῶς εἰπεῖν. *to put it simply,* a parenthetical aside.

(2) γοῦν. This particle introduces specific evidence that supports the general assertion made in the previous sentence: Smyth 2830.

ἐπί + gen. (usually with a personal name). *in the time of X*: Smyth 1689.1.b.

ἅρματα Φαραὼ. All the quotations in this chapter, save one, derive from the "Song of Moses" (Exodus 15.1–19), a hymn sung by Moses and the Israelites to celebrate the drowning of Pharaoh's army in the Red Sea. By weaving these quotations into the narrative, Eusebius creates a bricolage that serves to bridge the triumphs of Moses and Constantine. To put this a different way, Eusebius here reads the Song of Moses "typologically"; i.e., according to a hermeneutic scheme employed by Christian interpreters of the Bible in which episodes from the OT prefigure and reach their fulfillment in later events, usually those described in the NT, but here instead those manifested in the life of Constantine.

Φαραὼ. Like many non-Greek words (Smyth 284), Pharaoh is indeclinable.

τριστάτης, -ου (mas.). *captain.*

ἐρυθρᾷ. i.e., *the Red (Sea).*

κατὰ τὰ αὐτὰ. lit., *according to the same things*; i.e., *in the same way.*

πρὸ τῆς πορείας. *before his path.*

διῄει. 3rd sg. impf. act. ind. < δίειμι. Probably conative (Smyth 1895): *he tried to cross.*

σκάφεσι ζεύξας. Like Herodotus's Xerxes, who hubristically built a bridge of boats across the Hellespont (7.33–35), the tyrannical Maxentius does the same across the Tiber. Whether Maxentius actually built such a bridge is unclear, for other authors offer differing accounts of the topography of the battle and of Maxentius's defeat.

συνεπήξατο < συμπήγνυμι. in mid., *build, construct for oneself.*

ἑλεῖν. aor. act. inf. < αἱρέω.

(3) συνίστη. 3rd sg. impf. act. ind. < συνίστημι. *fashion, contrive*: LSJ, s.v. III.

ἦν. *it would be possible.*

λάκκος, -ου (mas.). *pit, cistern.*

λάκκον ὤρυξε καὶ ἀνέσκαψεν αὐτὸν. Characteristic of the poetics of the Psalms is doubling, where the same idea is presented in two different ways.

ὤρυξε < ὀρύσσω. *dig.*

(4) ἔγκρυμμα, -ατος (neu.). *hidden device.*

<διαρρυεισῶν>. mas. pl. gen., aor. pass. part. < διαρρέω. here pass. with act. meaning, *fall away, break.* The angle brackets indicate that the text's editor has added this word.

αὔτανδρος, -ον. *men and all,* here modifiying τὰ σκάφη.

ᾗ. sc. ὁδῷ.

προαναφωνέω. *prophesy.*

(5) εἰκότως. *reasonably.*

εἰ καὶ μὴ λόγοις, ἔργοις δ' οὖν ὁμοίως τοῖς . . . Μωϋσέα. *even if not in words, but in deeds, in the same way as the companions of the great servant Moses,* who joined their leader in a hymn of praise after they had crossed the Red Sea: see further note on section **(2)** above, s.v. ἅρματα Φαραὼ.

τοὺς . . . ἀραμένους. i.e., those praising Constantine's victory.

ἀραμένους. mas. pl. acc., aor. mid. part. < αἴρω. in mid., *exalt, praise*: LSJ, s.v. ἀείρω, II.

ᾄσωμεν. 1st pl. aor. act. subj. < ἀείδω. *sing.*

δοξάζω. *glorify*: Lampe, s.v. B.

σκεπαστής, -οῦ (mas.). *protector, shelterer.*

(39.1) ἀδελφός, -ή, -όν. *akin to* + dat.: LSJ, s.v. II.2.

θεράποντι. cf. "τὸν μέγαν θεράποντα Μωϋσέα" in **(38.5)** above. In the Bible and early Christian literature, the noun θεράπων is strongly associated with Moses: Lampe, s.v.

εἰσήλαυνεν. cf. Jesus's triumphal entry into the royal city of Jerusalem, as the people lauded him.

(2) σύγκλητος, -ου (fem.). *Senate.* Indeed Constantine did win the favor of the Senate by declaring an amnesty for Maxentius's supporters and even naming some of them prefects of Rome. Grateful senators are likely to have overseen the construction of the Arch of Constantine.

τῶν τῇδε. *of those in this place*; i.e., residents of Rome.

αὐταῖς ψυχαῖς. i.e., of their own accord.

ἄπληστος, -ον. *insatiable.*

λυτρωτὴν αὐτὸν σωτῆρά τε καὶ εὐεργέτην. The first title evokes Jesus and Moses (Lampe, s.v.); the second and third titles are likewise associated with Jesus but also belong to the traditional vocabulary of euergetism: see further notes on sections **(10.2)** of B3, **(6)** of D1.2, and **(27.2)** of E1.

(3) συνῃσθημένος. mas. sg. nom., pf. dep. part. < συναισθάνομαι. *perceive* + gen.

(40.1) τουτὶ = τοῦτο + the deictic suffix –ι for emphasis: Smyth 333.g.

διαρρήδην. *explicitly, expressly.*

ἀνεξάλειπτος, -ον. *indelible.*

ἐγχαράττω. *inscribe.*

φυλακτήριον, -ου (neu.). *protection, amulet*: Lampe, s.v. The apotropaic power of the cross is underscored.

(2) ὑψηλὸν δόρυ σταυροῦ σχήματι. The description is similar to that of the *labarum* found in section **(31)** of E2. ὑψηλὸν δόρυ is the object of στήσαντας . . . ἐγκελεύεται: *he ordered (them), having set up a long pole.* ἐγκελεύεται is historical pres.

ὑπὸ χεῖρα ἰδίας εἰκόνος ἐν ἀνδριάντι κατειργασμένης. *in the hand of an image of himself fashioned on a statue.* Does the (rather opaque) language suggest that Constantine had an existing statue reworked so that it bore his own image? It has been suggested that such was the case with the colossal statue of Constantine now in the Capitoline Museums.

τῶν ἐπὶ Ῥώμης δεδημοσιευμένων ἐν τόπῳ. *on a plot of public property in Rome*: Lampe, s.v. δημοσιεύω, B. The statue was erected on public land to which the residents of the city had ready access.

ῥήμασιν αὐτοῖς. i.e., what follows is a literal translation from Latin to Greek.

πόλιν . . . ἠλευθέρωσα. cf. *Res Gestae Divi Augusti* 1: "τὰ κοινὰ πράγματα ἐκ τῆς τῶν συνομοσαμένων δουλήας ἠλευθέρωσα" (C3). The language of the inscription is traditional and religiously neutral.

ἀποκαθίστημι. *restore to* + dat.

E4. CONSTANTINE REASSESSED

Julian *Caesars* 18, 30, 36–38

Julian was born in 331/32 C.E. to Julius Constantius, a half-brother of the emperor Constantine (reg. 306–37 C.E.; see E1–E3). After Constantine's death on May 22, 337, his three sons Constantine II, Constantius II, and Constans jointly came to rule the empire; to secure their positions, they had several of Julian's relatives killed, including his father and older brother. In the subsequent years, Julian, resident in the east, was steeped in Greek *paideia,* receiving a superb education from a series of gifted teachers and studying side-by-side with other future notables, both civil and ecclesiastical, including Libanius (E5–E6). He read deeply in Greek and Christian literature. At the age of twenty, he secretly abandoned Christianity in favor of a mystical Neoplatonic paganism; hence his epithet "the Apostate." In November 355, the emperor Constantius II named Julian, his cousin, Caesar (junior emperor) and deployed him to campaign against barbarian tribes threatening Gaul; Julian proved to be a disciplined and popular commander. In February 360, his troops proclaimed him emperor in Paris; en route to meet the usurper, Constantius, on his deathbed, apparently named Julian his successor in early November 361. Casting himself as a Hellenic priestly philosopher-king—and growing a beard to suit the role—Julian rapidly enacted a series of initiatives: he decentralized power, purging the imperial court, simplifying its ceremonial, and boosting the autonomy of the empire's cities; made monetary and fiscal reforms; and, most famously, promoted paganism, which was to be reorganized along the lines of the Christian church. At the head of an army deep in Persia, Julian died in battle on June 26, 363, bringing to an end a memorable reign of less than two years.

Julian's reforms met with mixed reviews. Many of his prodigious writings in Greek—Julian left more prose to posterity than any other emperor—sought to explain and justify his measures, but they tended to harm as much as help. Extant are panegyric orations; treatises; dense, theological prose hymns to pagan deities; several dozen letters; a fragmentary anti-Christian treatise, *Against the Galilaeans;* and two satires: *Misopogon (Beard-Hater),* a seriocomic, rebarbative riposte to the residents of Antioch who dared to criticize his facial hair, and *Caesars,* also known as *Symposium* and *Cronia,* dating probably to mid-December 362. Indebted to Plato, Lucian, and Plutarch, *Caesars* is set during the feast of Cronus, better known as the Saturnalia, a carnivalesque festival of social reversal. Julian relates to a friend a story he had heard from Hermes of a banquet of the gods, held in the upper air above Olympus, to which the Roman emperors and Alexander the Great were invited. For their entertainment, the gods stage a competition to determine which of their guests was the best ruler. They nominate Alexander, Julius Caesar, Augustus, Trajan, Marcus Aurelius, and then, as related in the opening of the passage below, permit one more competitor to join in.

Further Reading

Julian *Caesars* 1–17; P. Athanassiadi-Fowden, *Julian and Hellenism: An Intellectual Biography* (Oxford, 1981), 1–12, 121–60; A. Kaldellis, *Hellenism in Byzantium: The Transformations of Greek Identity and the Reception of the Classical Tradition* (Cambridge, 2007), 143–72; S. Elm, *Sons of Hellenism, Fathers of the Church: Emperor Julian, Gregory of Nazianzus, and the Vision of Rome* (Berkeley, 2012), 60–87; E. J. Watts, *The Final Pagan Generation* (Oakland, 2015), 105–26.

(18) ἐπεὶ καὶ οὗτος ἦν εἴσω τῶν ἱερῶν περιβόλων, ὁ Διόνυσος εἶπεν, "Ὦ βασιλεῦ Κρόνε καὶ Ζεῦ πάτερ, ἆρα ἄξιον ἐν θεοῖς ἀτελὲς εἶναί τι;"

τῶν δὲ “οὒ” φαμένων, “Εἰσάγωμεν οὖν τινα καὶ ἀπολαύσεως ἐραστὴν ἐνθαδί.” καὶ ὁ Ζεύς, “Ἀλλ οὐ θεμιτὸν εἴσω φοιτᾶν,” εἶπεν, “ἀνδρὶ μὴ τὰ ἡμέτερα ζηλοῦντι.” “Γιγνέσθω τοίνυν,” εἶπεν, “ἐπὶ τῶν προθύρων,” ὁ Διόνυσος, “αὐτοῖς ἡ κρίσις. ἀλλ, εἰ τοῦτο δοκεῖ ταύτῃ, καλῶμεν ἄνδρα οὐκ ἀπόλεμον μέν, ἡδονῇ δὲ καὶ ἀπολαύσει χειροηθέστερον. ἡκέτω οὖν ἄχρι τῶν προθύρων ὁ Κωνσταντῖνος.”

[In turn, the competitors deliver speeches in which each argues for the superiority of his reign, save Marcus Aurelius, who feels no need to participate since the audience is familiar with his deeds already.]

(30) Τῷ Κωνσταντίνῳ μετὰ τοῦτον λέγειν ἐπέτρεπον. ὁ δὲ πρότερον μὲν ἐθάρρει τὴν ἀγωνίαν. ὡς δὲ ἀπέβλεπεν εἰς τὰ τῶν ἄλλων ἔργα, μικρὰ παντάπασιν εἶδε τὰ ἑαυτοῦ. δύο γὰρ τυράννους, εἴ γε χρὴ τἀληθῆ φάναι, καθῃρήκει, τὸν μὲν ἀπόλεμόν τε καὶ μαλακόν, τὸν δὲ ἄθλιόν τε καὶ διὰ τὸ γῆρας ἀσθενῆ, ἀμφοτέρω δὲ θεοῖς τε καὶ ἀνθρώποις ἐχθίστω. τά γε μὴν εἰς τοὺς βαρβάρους ἦν γελοῖα αὐτῷ· φόρους γὰρ ὥσπερ ἐτετελέκει, καὶ πρὸς τὴν Τρυφὴν ἀφεώρα· πόρρω δὲ εἱστήκει τῶν θεῶν αὕτη περὶ τὰ πρόθυρα τῆς Σελήνης· ἐρωτικῶς τε οὖν εἶχεν αὐτῆς, καὶ ὅλος πρὸς ἐκείνην βλέπων οὐδὲν ἔμελεν αὐτῷ περὶ τῆς νίκης.

[Realizing that he has to say something, Constantine delivers a short speech. His exploits are mocked as trivial, their impact ephemeral; Constantine blushes. The gods then decide to ask the competitors what motivated them as rulers.]

(36) Παυσαμένου δὲ καὶ τοῦδε τοῦ λόγου, τὸν Κωνσταντῖνον ὁ Ἑρμῆς ἤρετο· “Σὺ δὲ τί καλὸν ἐνόμισας;” “Πολλά,” εἶπε, “κτησάμενον πολλὰ χαρίσασθαι, ταῖς τ᾽ ἐπιθυμίαις ταῖς ἑαυτοῦ καὶ ταῖς τῶν φίλων ὑπουργοῦντα.” ἀνακαγχάσας οὖν ὁ Σειληνὸς μέγα, “Ἀλλ ἢ τραπεζίτης εἶναι,” ἔφη, “θέλων ἐλελήθεις σεαυτὸν ὀψοποιοῦ καὶ κομμωτρίας βίον ζῶν; ᾐνίττετο δ αὐτὰ πάλαι μὲν ‘ἥ τε κόμη τό τε εἶδος,’ ἀτὰρ νῦν καὶ ἡ γνώμη σοῦ κατηγορεῖ.” τούτου μὲν οὖν ὁ Σειληνὸς πικρότερόν πως καθήψατο.

(37) Σιωπῆς δὲ γενομένης ἔφερον οἱ θεοὶ λάθρᾳ τὰς ψήφους. εἶτα ἐγένοντο πολλαὶ τῷ Μάρκῳ. κοινολογησάμενος δὲ ὁ Ζεὺς ἰδίᾳ πρὸς τὸν πατέρα προσέταξε κηρῦξαι τῷ Ἑρμῇ. ὁ δὲ ἐκήρυττεν, "Ἄνδρες οἱ παρελθόντες ἐπὶ τουτονὶ τὸν ἀγῶνα, νόμοι παρ' ἡμῖν εἰσι καὶ κρίσεις τοιαῦται γίνονται, ὥστε καὶ τὸν νικῶντα χαίρειν καὶ τὸν ἡττώμενον μὴ μέμφεσθαι. πορεύεσθε οὖν," εἶπεν, "ὅποι φίλον ἑκάστῳ, ὑπὸ θεοῖς ἡγεμόσι βιωσόμενοι τὸ ἐντεῦθεν· ἑλέσθω δ' ἕκαστος ἑαυτῷ τὸν προστάτην τε καὶ ἡγεμόνα." μετὰ τὸ κήρυγμα τοῦτο ὁ μὲν Ἀλέξανδρος ἔθει πρὸς τὸν Ἡρακλέα, Ὀκταβιανὸς δὲ πρὸς τὸν Ἀπόλλωνα, ἀμφοῖν δὲ ἀπρὶξ εἴχετο τοῦ Διὸς καὶ Κρόνου Μάρκος. πλανώμενον δὲ πολλὰ καὶ περιτρέχοντα τὸν Καίσαρα κατελεήσας ὁ μέγας Ἄρης ἥ τε Ἀφροδίτη παρ' ἑαυτοὺς ἐκαλεσάτην· Τραϊανὸς δὲ παρὰ τὸν Ἀλέξανδρον ἔθει ὡς ἐκείνῳ συγκαθεδούμενος. (38) ὁ δὲ Κωνσταντῖνος, οὐχ εὑρίσκων ἐν θεοῖς τοῦ βίου τὸ ἀρχέτυπον, ἐγγύθεν τὴν Τρυφὴν κατιδὼν ἔδραμε πρὸς αὐτήν· ἡ δὲ ὑπολαβοῦσα μαλακῶς καὶ περιβαλοῦσα τοῖς πήχεσι πέπλοις τε αὐτὸν ποικίλοις ἀσκήσασα καὶ καλλωπίσασα πρὸς τὴν Ἀσωτίαν ἀπήγαγεν, ἵνα καὶ τὸν Ἰησοῦν εὑρὼν ἀναστρεφόμενον καὶ προαγορεύοντα πᾶσιν, "Ὅστις φθορεύς, μιαιφόνος, ὅστις ἐναγὴς καὶ βδελυρός, ἴτω θαρρῶν· ἀποφανῶ γὰρ αὐτὸν τουτῳὶ τῷ ὕδατι λούσας αὐτίκα καθαρόν, κἂν πάλιν ἔνοχος τοῖς αὐτοῖς γένηται, δώσω τὸ στῆθος πλήξαντι καὶ τὴν κεφαλὴν πατάξαντι καθαρῷ γενέσθαι," σφόδρα ἄσμενος ἐνέτυχεν αὐτῷ, συνεξαγαγὼν τῆς τῶν θεῶν ἀγορᾶς τοὺς παῖδας. ἐπέτριβον δ' αὐτόν τε κἀκείνους οὐχ ἧττον τῆς ἀθεότητος οἱ παλαμναῖοι δαίμονες, αἱμάτων συγγενῶν τιννύμενοι δίκας, ἕως ὁ Ζεὺς διὰ τὸν Κλαύδιον καὶ Κωνστάντιον ἔδωκεν ἀναπνεῦσαι.

Notes to Julian Caesars *18, 30, 36–38*

These notes are indebted to R. Sardiello, *Giuliano Imperatore: Simposio, I Cesari* (Galatina, 2000).

(18) οὗτος. i.e., the philosophically enlightened Marcus Aurelius who, at the god Cronus's behest, joins the other competitors selected so far. He represents a Julianic ideal emperor, a philosopher-king with an ascetic physique, simple garb, and, of course, a thick beard.

ἄξιόν [sc. ἐστι]. *is it proper for* + inf.: LSJ, s.v. ἄξιος, II.4.

ἀτελής, -ές. *imperfect.*

φαμένων. mas. pl. gen., pres. mid. part. < φημί.

κρίσις, -εως (fem.). *trial, test.* In other words, dissolute persons may be admitted to the competition, but, being impure, they may not enter the gods' chamber.

εἰ τοῦτο δοκεῖ ταύτῃ. *if it seems good (to do) this in such a fashion.*

χειροήθης, -ες. *familiar with, amenable to* + dat.

ἡκέτω. 3rd sg. pres. act. impv. < ἥκω. *come.*

(30) μετὰ τοῦτον. i.e., after Marcus Aurelius, who declines to speak.

ἐπιτρέπω. *allow* + dat. and + inf.: LSJ, s.v. sc. οἱ θέοι.

θαρρέω. *have no fear of, feel confident about* + acc.: LSJ, s.v. 2.

τἀληθῆ = τὰ ἀληθῆ.

καθῃρήκει. 3rd sg. plupf. act. ind. < καθαιρέω.

τὸν μὲν . . . τὸν δὲ. i.e., Maxentius, whom Constantine defeated at Rome in 312, to become sole emperor of the west (E1–E3), and Licinius I, Augustus of the east, whom he bested in 324 at Chrysopolis near the Bosporus to become sole ruler of the entire empire.

διὰ τὸ γῆρας. The year of Licinius's birth is not surely fixed, but if we assume it was around 260, he would have been in his mid-sixties in 325 when he was executed by Constantine.

ἀμφοτέρω . . . ἐχθίστω. mas. dual acc.

εἰς τοὺς βαρβάρους. Julian seems to refer to Constantine's avid recruitment of barbarians for military service and the financial outlays required to support them.

Τρυφὴν. Moralizing historians of ancient Rome had for centuries tracked the corrupting effects of luxury on the Roman state. Might the word also be used here as a pun on the famed τρόπαιον of the cross that Constantine was said to have seen in the sky? See section **(28.2)** of E1 (with note, s.v. τρόπαιον) and sections **(37.1)** and **(40.1)** of E3.

ἀφεώρα. 3rd sg. impf. act. ind. < ἀφοράω.

εἱστήκει. 3rd sg. plupf. act. ind. < ἵστημι.

πρόθυρα τῆς Σελήνης. Like her votary Constantine, Τρυφή must remain on the threshold.

ἔχω + adv. *behave X*: LSJ, s.v. ἔχω (A), B.II.2.

(36) τοῦδε τοῦ λόγου. Marcus Aurelius had given a speech indicating that his goal in life was "to imitate the gods" (34).

ἤρετο. 3rd sg. aor. dep. ind. < ἔρομαι. *ask.*

χαρίζω. *give generously.* Constantine's generosity is recognized and presented more positively by other authors; Julian himself valorized philanthropy: Sardiello, *Cesari,* ad loc.

ἀνακαγχάζω. *burst out laughing.*

Σειληνὸς. In Plato's *Symposium,* Socrates is likened to a statue of the satyr Silenus (215b–d). In Julian's *Caesars,* Silenus is a Socratic stand-in for Julian.

θέλων. Translate as conditional.

ἐλελήθεις . . . ζῶν. ἐλελήθεις is 2nd sg. plupf. act. ind. < λανθάνω + supplementary part. *had it escaped you that you were living the life of a sous-chef and a beautician?* The Socratic Silenus is obliquely referring to Plato's dialogues. In the *Republic,* Plato says that an unhealthy city employs ὀψοποιοί and κομμωτρίαι (2.373b-c), among other peddlers of superfluities. The implication here seems to be that just as chefs and make-up artists seek to hide imperfections and improve on nature through artifice (cf. Plato *Gorgias* 465), so Constantine adopted Christianity to cover up his ethical blemishes and thus make him more attractive to others.

ᾐνίττετο. 3rd sg. impf. dep. ind. < αἰνίττομαι. *hint at, intimate.*

'ἥ τε κόμη τό τε εἶδος.' Quotation from Homer *Iliad* 3.55, where mighty Hector is upbraiding pretty Paris. The soldiers who declared Constantine emperor after his father's death apparently preferred him to his siblings because of his healthy appearance: Zosimus 2.9.1.

καθήψατο. 3rd sg. aor. mid. ind. < καθάπτω, a verb favored by Homer; in mid., *assail, accost* + gen.: LSJ, s.v. II.1, 2.

(37) τουτονὶ. The deictic suffix –ι is emphatic: Smyth 333.g.

ὅποι φίλον ἑκάστῳ. *wherever it pleases each of you* (to go).

βιωσόμενοι. fut. part. indicating purpose.

ἑλέσθω. 3rd sg. aor. mid. impv. < αἱρέω.

Ἡρακλέα. In the text, Hercules represents, inter alia, Greek culture.

Ὀκταβιανὸς. Octavian, later known as Augustus (reg. 27 B.C.E.–14 C.E.), associated himself with Apollo: see also notes on section **(16.4)** of C2, s.v. τό . . . προτίθεσθαι, τὸ . . . ἀρτᾶσθαι and section **(24)** of C3, s.v. ἐν τῶι ναῶι τοῦ Ἀπόλλωνος.

ἀπρίξ. *tightly.*

ἔχω. in mid., *hold on to* + gen.: LSJ, s.v. ἔχω (A), C.

τὸν Καίσαρα. i.e., Julius Caesar.

ἐκαλεσάτην. 3rd dual aor. act. ind.

(38) ἀσωτία, -ας (fem.). *prodigality.* The word also evokes the etymologically related noun σωτήρ, which is often used of God and Christ: Lampe, s.v. 1, 2.; ἀσωτία lit. means *non-salvation.*

ἵνα. *where.*

Ἰησοῦν. In a missive that is nearly contemporary with this work (*Letter* 47, 434b–d), Julian urges the residents of Alexandria to abandon their faith in Jesus and to worship the Sun; in essence, he urges the Alexandrians to imitate Constantine's conversion, but in reverse.

ἀναστρέφω. in pass., *dwell with.* Jesus lives with Ἀσωτία.

μιαιφόνος. Constantine was responsible for the deaths of his wife Fausta and his son Crispus.

ἐναγής, -ές. *cursed* or *polluted,* often because one has shed blood; *sinful,* in Christian authors: Lampe, s.v.

ἴτω θαρρῶν. *let him come boldly.*

τῷ ὕδατι λούσας. Constantine was baptized soon before his death on May 22, 337.

ἔνοχος, -ον + dat. *guilty of, subject to.*

πατάσσω. *beat, strike.*

ἅσμενος ἐνέτυχεν. The subject is Constantine.

συνεξάγω. *lead X* (+ acc.) *out of Y* (+ gen.).

τοὺς παῖδας. Constantine's sons also came to the gods' banquet (15).

τῆς ἀθεότητος. gen. of the charge after verb of punishment: Smyth 1375–76.

παλαμναῖος, -α, -ον. *blood-avenging.*

δίκας τιννύω. *exact penalty for* + gen.: LSJ, s.v. τίνυμαι. The phrase evokes the Furies in Euripides's *Orestes* (322–23).

Κλαύδιον καὶ Κωνστάντιον. i.e., Zeus gave Constantine and his sons a breather (ἔδωκεν ἀναπνεῦσαι) out of respect for Claudius II Gothicus (reg. 268–70 C.E.), whom Constantine claimed as an ancestor, and his father Constantius I (reg. 293–306 C.E.).

E5. DEFEND OUR TEMPLES I

Libanius *Oration* 30.8–13

Like the emperor Julian (reg. 361–63 C.E.; see E4), with whom he corresponded and whom he admired, Libanius was an avatar of *paideia,* the Greek system of physical, moral, and literary education that inculcated not just a profound knowledge of canonical literary texts but also a mastery of comportment and self-presentation in speech. Shared training in *paideia* defined and united the elite of the Greek east, transcending geographical boundaries and religious affiliations, as Libanius's life illustrates. A traditionalist and pagan, Libanius was born in 314 C.E. in Antioch, one of the leading cities of the eastern empire, to a wealthy, prominent family. Educated in his natal city and later in Athens, Libanius became a celebrated teacher of rhetoric in Constantinople and Nicaea and Nicomedia in Asia Minor. After declining the emperor Constantius II's (reg. 337–61 C.E.) offer of an endowed post as professor of rhetoric in Athens, Libanius returned to Antioch and taught there, also participating actively in civic politics, from 354 until his death around 393. His students included numerous luminaries from a range of religious backgrounds. Libanius has left to posterity an enormous corpus: dozens of rhetorical exercises; sixty-four orations on a variety of subjects, some of them addressed to the emperors and high imperial officials; and more than fifteen hundred letters that connected the author with a vast network of notables beyond Antioch.

Sometime between 381 and 391 (or, possibly, 392), Libanius wrote an oration "For the Temples, to the Emperor Theodosius," that is, Theodosius I, who ruled from 379 to 395 C.E. From the reign of Constantius II, and perhaps even that of Constantine (reg. 306–37 C.E.; see E1–E3), the emperors, save Julian, had issued legislation that variously restricted the practice of paganism. In his speech, Libanius decries what he perceives as illegal attacks on temples and their environs by mobs of monks and an unnamed imperial official. He urges the emperor to intervene. In interpreting this speech, it is helpful to know that religious affiliation seems less important to Libanius personally as a marker of identity than to many others of his day. Indeed, in other speeches, he demonstrates an ability to calibrate his rhetoric to appeal to the particular religious allegiances of his audience. Keeping this in mind, one may then ask: what motivates Libanius to write this oration to Theodosius? Is it a plea grounded in principle, in a commitment to freedom of religion? Or does it derive from a more pragmatic belief in the political, social, and economic benefits provided by traditional religious practices—benefits also discussed by other authors in this volume (A7)? Or is the speech less concerned with religion per se than the antisocial effects of lawless violence? Or is there another agenda at work, one more self-serving, that Libanius promotes yet keeps hidden through a sort of rhetorical misdirection?

Further Reading

Libanius *Oration* 30.1–7, 14–29; I. Sandwell, *Religious Identity in Late Antiquity: Greeks, Jews and Christians in Antioch* (Cambridge, 2007), 91–119; P. Van Nuffelen, "Not the Last Pagan: Libanius between Elite Rhetoric and Religion," in *Libanius: A Critical Introduction,* ed. L. Van Hoof, 293–314 (Cambridge, 2014); E. J. Watts, *The Final Pagan Generation* (Oakland, 2015), 191–211.

(8) σὺ μὲν οὖν οὔθ' ἱερὰ κεκλεῖσθαι <ἐκέλευσας> οὔτε μηδένα προσιέναι οὔτε πῦρ οὔτε λιβανωτὸν οὔτε τὰς ἀπὸ τῶν ἄλλων θυμιαμάτων τιμὰς ἐξήλασας τῶν νεῶν οὐδὲ τῶν βωμῶν, οἱ δὲ μελανειμονοῦντες οὗτοι καὶ πλείω μὲν τῶν ἐλεφάντων ἐσθίοντες, πόνον δὲ παρέχοντες τῷ πλήθει τῶν ἐκπωμάτων τοῖς δι' ᾀσμάτων αὐτοῖς παραπέμπουσι τὸν πότον, συγκρύπτοντες δὲ ταῦτα ὠχρότητι τῇ διὰ τέχνης αὐτοῖς πεπορισμένῃ μένοντος, ὦ βασιλεῦ, καὶ κρατοῦντος τοῦ νόμου θέουσιν ἐφ' ἱερὰ ξύλα φέροντες καὶ λίθους καὶ σίδηρον, οἱ δὲ καὶ ἄνευ τούτων χεῖρας καὶ πόδας. ἔπειτα Μυσῶν λεία καθαιρουμένων ὀροφῶν, κατασκαπτομένων τοίχων, κατασπωμένων ἀγαλμάτων, ἀνασπώμενων βωμῶν, τοὺς ἱερεῖς δὲ ἢ σιγᾶν ἢ τεθνάναι δεῖ· τῶν πρώτων δὲ κειμένων δρόμος ἐπὶ τὰ δεύτερα καὶ τρίτα, καὶ τρόπαια τροπαίοις ἐναντία τῷ νόμῳ συνείρεται. **(9)** τολμᾶται μὲν οὖν ταῦτα κἀν ταῖς πόλεσι, τὸ πολὺ δὲ ἐν τοῖς ἀγροῖς. καὶ πολλοὶ μὲν οἱ καθ' ἕκαστον πολέμιοι, ἐπὶ δὲ μυρίοις κακοῖς τὸ διεσπαρμένον τοῦτ' ἀθροίζεται καὶ λόγον ἀλλήλους ἀπαιτοῦσι τῶν εἰργασμένων καὶ αἰσχύνη τὸ μὴ μέγιστα ἠδικηκέναι. χωροῦσι τοίνυν διὰ τῶν ἀγρῶν ὥσπερ χείμαρροι κατασύροντες διὰ τῶν ἱερῶν τοὺς ἀγρούς. ὅτου γὰρ ἂν ἱερὸν ἐκκόψωσιν ἀγροῦ, οὗτος τετύφλωταί τε καὶ κεῖται καὶ τέθνηκε. ψυχὴ γάρ, ὦ βασιλεῦ, τοῖς ἀγροῖς τὰ ἱερὰ προοίμια τῆς ἐν τοῖς ἀγροῖς κτίσεως γεγενημένα καὶ διὰ πολλῶν γενεῶν εἰς τοὺς νῦν ὄντας ἀφιγμένα. **(10)** καὶ τοῖς γεωργοῦσιν ἐν αὐτοῖς αἱ ἐλπίδες ὅσαι περί τε ἀνδρῶν καὶ γυναικῶν καὶ τέκνων καὶ βοῶν καὶ τῆς σπειρομένης γῆς καὶ τῆς πεφυτευμένης. ὁ δὲ τοῦτο πεπονθὼς ἀγρὸς ἀπολώλεκε καὶ τῶν γεωργῶν μετὰ τῶν ἐλπίδων τὸ πρόθυμον· μάτην γὰρ ἡγοῦνται πονήσειν τῶν εἰς δέον τοὺς πόνους ἀγόντων ἐστερημένοι θεῶν. τῆς γῆς δὲ οὐκέθ' ὁμοίων πόνων ἀπολαυούσης οὐδ' ἂν ἴσος ὁ τόκος τῷ πρὶν ἀπαντῴη. τούτου δὲ ὄντος τοιούτου πενέστερος μὲν ὁ γεωργός, ἐν βλάβῃ δὲ ὁ φόρος. καὶ γὰρ ἂν σφόδρα ἐθέλῃ τις, τό γε μὴ δύνασθαι κωλύει.

(11) Οὕτως ἐπὶ τὰ μέγιστα τῶν πραγμάτων βαδίζει τὰ διὰ τὴν τούτων ἀσέλγειαν κατὰ τῶν ἀγρῶν τολμώμενα, οἵ φασὶ μὲν τοῖς ἱεροῖς πολεμεῖν, ἔστι δὲ οὗτος ὁ πόλεμος πόρος τῶν μὲν τοῖς ναοῖς ἐγκειμένων, τῶν δὲ τὰ ὄντα τοῖς ταλαιπώροις ἁρπαζόντων τά τε κείμενα αὐτοῖς ἀπὸ τῆς γῆς καὶ ἃ τρέφουσιν. ὥστ' ἀπέρχονται φέροντες οἱ ἐπελθόντες τὰ τῶν ἐκπεπολιορκημένων. τοῖς δὲ οὐκ ἀρκεῖ ταῦτα, ἀλλὰ καὶ γῆν σφετερίζονται τὴν τοῦ δεῖνος ἱερὰν εἶναι λέγοντες, καὶ πολλοὶ τῶν πατρῴων ἐστέρηνται δι' ὀνόματος οὐκ ἀληθοῦς. οἱ δ' ἐκ τῶν ἑτέρων τρυφῶσι κακῶν οἱ τῷ πεινῆν, ὥς φασι, τὸν αὐτῶν θεραπεύοντες θεόν. ἢν δ' οἱ πεπορθημένοι παρὰ τὸν ἐν ἄστει ποιμένα, καλοῦσι γὰρ οὕτως ἄνδρα οὐ πάνυ χρηστόν, ἢν οὖν ἐλθόντες ὀδύρωνται λέγοντες ἃ ἠδίκηνται, ὁ ποιμὴν οὗτος τοὺς μὲν ἐπῄνεσε, τοὺς δὲ ἀπήλασεν ὡς ἐν τῷ μὴ μείζω πεπονθέναι κεκερδακότας. **(12)** καίτοι τῆς μὲν σῆς ἀρχῆς, ὦ βασιλεῦ, καὶ οὗτοι, τοσούτῳ δὲ χρησιμώτεροι τῶν ἀδικούντων αὐτούς, ὅσῳ τῶν ἀργούντων οἱ ἐργαζόμενοι. οἱ μὲν γὰρ ταῖς μελίτταις, οἱ δὲ τοῖς κηφῆσιν ἐοίκασι. κἂν ἀκούσωσιν ἀγρὸν ἔχειν τι τῶν ἁρπασθῆναι δυναμένων, εὐθὺς οὗτος ἐν θυσίαις τέ ἐστι καὶ δεινὰ ποιεῖ καὶ δεῖ στρατείας ἐπ' αὐτὸν καὶ πάρεισιν οἱ σωφρονισταί, τοῦτο γὰρ ὄνομα τίθενται ταῖς λῃστείαις, εἰ μὴ καὶ μικρὸν εἶπον. οἱ μέν γε πειρῶνται λανθάνειν καὶ ἃ τολμῶσιν ἀρνοῦνται, κἂν καλέσῃς λῃστήν, ὕβρισας, οἱ δὲ φιλοτιμοῦνται καὶ σεμνύνονται καὶ τοὺς ἀγνοοῦντας διδάσκουσι καὶ γερῶν ἀξίους εἶναί φασιν αὐτούς. **(13)** καίτοι τοῦτο τί ἕτερόν ἐστιν ἢ ἐν εἰρήνῃ πολεμεῖσθαι τοὺς γεωργούς;

Notes to Libanius Oration *30.8–13*

These notes are indebted to R. Romano, *Libanio, In difesa dei templi* (Naples, 1982) and H.-G. Nesselrath's notes in *Für Religionsfreiheit, Recht und Toleranz: Libanios' Rede für den Erhalt der heidnischen Tempel* (Tübingen, 2011), 76–91.

(8) κεκλεῖσθαι. pf. pass. inf. < κλείω. *close, shut down.* It is not easy to harmonize Libanius's account with extant imperial legislation. At the time of writing, it seems that animal sacrifice had been banned, but that other ritual acts, such as the offering of libations and the burning of incense, had not yet been explicitly outlawed.

<ἐκέλευσας>. The angle brackets indicate that the text's editor has added the enclosed word.

νεῶν. mas. pl. gen. < νεώς, νεώ. *temple*; for this noun's irregular declension, see Smyth 238.

μελανειμονέω. *be dressed in black.* In the period, monks wore dun garb.

τῶν ἐλεφάντων. Plato claims that elephants were the most voracious of animals (*Critias* 114e–115a), as noted in Nesselrath, *Religionsfreiheit,* ad loc.

πόνον . . . παρέχοντες . . . τοῖς δι' ᾀσμάτων αὐτοῖς παραπέμπουσι τὸν πότον. *providing trouble to those who accompany their (the monks') drinking with hymns.* The bibulous monk is a trope of anti-Christian rhetoric in the period, and one with a long postclassical afterlife; cf. Chaucer's friar, "a wantowne and a merye": *Canterbury Tales,* prologue, line 208.

τῷ πλήθει. dat. of cause: Smyth 1517.

ὠχρότης, -ητος (fem.). *pallor.*

μένοντος . . . τοῦ νόμου. gen. absolute.

Μυσῶν λεία. proverbial: *booty of the Muses* is anything that may be looted without repercussions: LSJ, s.v. λεία (B).

καθαιρουμένων . . . βωμῶν. gen. absolutes artfully deployed with synchisis (interlocked ABAB word order), consonance (repeated consonant sounds), and repetition of the prefix κατα-, combining to convey the cacophonous tearing-down of the temples.

ὀροφή, -ῆς (fem.). *roof.*

συνείρω. *connect, string together*; here, *pile on* + dat.

(9) τολμάω. *endure,* often with reference to a difficult, unpleasant, or despicable act.

κἀν = καὶ ἐν.

καθ' ἕκαστον. *in each case*; i.e., in every attack on a temple.

πολέμιοι. The monks are portrayed as enemies of the state.

ἐπί + dat. *after*: LSJ, s.v. B.II.2.

διεσπαρμένον. neu. sg. nom., pf. pass. part. < διασπείρω. *scatter.*

ἀπαιτέω may take a double acc.: *demand X from Y.*

εἰργασμένων. neu. pl. gen., pf. dep. part. < ἐργάζομαι.

ἠδικηκέναι. pf. act. inf. < ἀδικέω. The articular inf. τὸ μὴ μέγιστα ἠδικηκέναι is predicative with αἰσχύνη.

διὰ τῶν ἱερῶν τοὺς ἀγρούς. i.e., when temples are destroyed, so too are their environs.

ὅτου = οὗτινος. *any.*

ἂν = ἐὰν, introducing a general condition.

ἐκκόπτω. The verb often refers to the loss of an eye, an image reinforced by τετύφλωταί: Nesselrath, *Religionsfreiheit,* ad loc.

προοίμια . . . κτίσεως. Earlier in the speech (4), Libanius claims that temples were the first monumental buildings erected by humankind.

(10) τοῦτο. i.e., ravagement by marauding monks.

πεπονθὼς < πάσχω.

μάτην. Take with πονήσειν, not ἡγοῦνται.

εἰς δέον. *toward what is necessary.* The rural residents think that they farm in vain, because the gods who guide their work have been abused. In a similar vein, Libanius's contemporary Symmachus (c. 340–402 C.E.), a prominent senator and pagan apologist from Italy, argues that recent famines were linked to a decline in traditional piety: *Relatio* 3.14–15.

ἐστερημένοι. mas. pl. nom., pf. pass. part. < στερέω. *deprive of, rob* + gen.

ἀπολαύω. *benefit from* + gen.

τόκος, -ου (mas.). Here the word means *(crop) yield,* but it can also refer to *childbirth*; Libanius may be hinting that attacks on the temples will ultimately affect the birthrate and therefore the agricultural manpower of the empire.

ἀπαντῴη. 3rd sg. pres. act. opt. < ἀπαντάω + dat. *amount to, meet.* Potential opt.

τούτου δὲ ὄντος τοιούτου. *and if* (or *since) this is so.*

καὶ . . . κωλύει. i.e., even if the farmer is eager to work, his inability to do so successfully impedes him.

(11) βαδίζω. *pertain.*

τούτων. *of these (men)*; i.e., the monks. τούτων is the antecedent of οἳ in the next clause.

ἀσέλγεια, -ας (fem.). *antisocial violence.* There are other examples of monastic militancy from late antiquity.

πόρος, -ου (mas.). *source of revenue*: LSJ, s.v. II.3.

τῶν . . . ἐγκειμένων, τῶν . . . ἁρπαζόντων. objective genitives (Smyth 1331) triggered by πόρος.

τοῖς ταλαιπώροις. dat. of disadvantage: Smyth 1481, 1483.

τά τε κείμενα αὐτοῖς ἀπὸ τῆς γῆς καὶ ἃ τρέφουσιν. These accusatives elaborate on τὰ ὄντα: the first item refers to crops, the second to livestock.

τὰ τῶν ἐκπεπολιορκημένων is the object of φέροντες.

τοῦ δεῖνος. *of some (god) or another.* i.e., the monks sometimes take not just the movable property of the rural residents but also their land by claiming that it belongs to a temple.

ἐστέρηνται. 3rd pl. pf. pass. ind. < στερέω.

τῷ πεινῆν. *by being hungry.* i.e., through observing a modest diet and fasting.

ἢν = ἐὰν.

ποιμένα. i.e., Flavian, the bishop of Antioch. Bishops did have some legal jurisdiction at this time, but it is not clear whether they would in this particular case. Later in the speech (19), Libanius indicates that the monks themselves had come before the bishop, apparently claiming that animal sacrifice was being practiced in the countryside.

τοὺς μὲν. i.e., the monks.

ὡς ἐν τῷ μὴ μείζω πεπονθέναι κεκερδακότας. *as if they had profited in suffering nothing worse.* κεκερδακότας = mas. pl. acc., pf. act. part. < κερδαίνω. *profit, gain.*

(12) τῆς . . . σῆς ἀρχῆς. i.e., these victims are also the emperor's subjects.

τοσούτῳ . . . ὅσῳ. To explain these correlatives schematically: A is greater than B to the same degree that C is greater than D.

χρήσιμος, -η, -ον or -ος, -ον. *beneficial, useful,* often, as here, to the state. Libanius expatiates on the economic consequences of agricultural disruption.

κηφήν, -ῆνος (mas.). *drone.* The beehive was a common metaphor for the state in antiquity: see also section **(17)** of C7.

τῶν . . . δυναμένων. partitive gen. dependent on τι.

οὗτος. sc. ὁ ἀγρός.

δεῖ. *there is need of* + gen.: LSJ, s.v. II.

σωφρονιστής, -οῦ (mas.). *disciplinarian.*

λῃστεία, -ας (fem.). *gang of bandits*: see Nesselrath, *Religionsfreiheit,* ad loc.

εἰ μὴ καὶ μικρὸν εἶπον. *if I haven't spoken out of turn.*

ὕβρισας. 2nd sg. aor. act. ind.

φιλοτιμοῦνται . . . σεμνύνονται. probably mid. rather than pass.

γέρας, -αος (contracting to -ως) (neu.). *gift,* especially one received as a token of honor; also, an *honorarium* earned by a priest for performing a ritual: LSJ, s.v.

E6. DEFEND OUR TEMPLES II

Libanius *Oration* 30.30–36

After Libanius describes the attacks on pagan temples perpetrated in the Antiochene hinterlands by marauding monks (E5) in a speech addressed to the emperor Theodosius I (reg. 379–95 C.E.), he deploys a barrage of arguments to convince the emperor to address the problem: that the monks were un-Christian vigilantes whose subversion of due process points to the rustics' innocence; that, yes, those rustics did slaughter animals in the countryside, but to provide barbecue, not to honor the gods; that forced conversions, which the monks were trying to effect, are ineffective (30.14–29). Then, in the passage below, Libanius refutes a counterargument, namely, that the elimination of temples would benefit the state. He cites examples from myth and history that demonstrate how important it is to have the gods on one's side; their support is essential to the ongoing health of the empire. It is worth noting that Libanius's position here is not novel, for he is drawing on a repertoire of traditional arguments about the interdependence of religion and the state. In fact, Libanius's learned contemporary, Quintus Aurelius Symmachus (c. 340–402 C.E.), writing in 384 when he was Urban Prefect of Rome, employs similar arguments in a petition to the emperors for the restoration of the Altar of Victory in the Senate House (*Relatio* 3). (The equally learned archbishop of Milan, Ambrose, countered Symmachus and won the day.)

Further Reading

Libanius *Oration* 30.37–55; Symmachus *Relatio* 3; M. Gaddis, *There Is No Crime for Those Who Have Christ: Religious Violence in the Christian Roman Empire* (Berkeley, 2005), 208–50; T. Sizgorich, "'Not Easily Were Stones Joined by the Strongest Bonds Pulled Asunder': Religious Violence and Imperial Order in the Later Roman World," *Journal of Early Christian Studies* 15 (2007): 75–101.

(30) Ἀλλὰ τὸ μηδ' εἶναί φασιν ἱερὰ χρήσιμον εἶναι τῇ γῇ καὶ τοῖς ἐπ' αὐτῆς ἀνθρώποις. ἐνταῦθα τοίνυν δεῖ μέν μοι πολλῆς, ὦ βασιλεῦ, τῆς παρρησίας, δέδοικα δὲ μή τινα λυπήσω τῶν ἐμαυτοῦ κρειττόνων. χωρείτω δ' οὖν ὅμως ὁ λόγος ἓν τοῦτο ἀπαιτούμενος, τὴν ἀλήθειαν.

(31) Εἰπάτω γάρ μοί τις τῶν τὰς μὲν πυράγρας καὶ σφύρας καὶ ἄκμονας ἀφέντων, περὶ δὲ οὐρανοῦ καὶ τῶν τὸν οὐρανὸν ἐχόντων ἀξιούντων διαλέγεσθαι, ποτέροις ἀκολουθοῦντες οἱ τὰ μέγιστα ἀπὸ μικρῶν καὶ φαύλων τῶν πρώτων ἀφορμῶν Ῥωμαῖοι δυνηθέντες ἐδυνήθησαν, τῷ <θεῷ> τούτων ἢ οἷς ἱερὰ καὶ βωμοὶ <καὶ> παρ' ὧν ὅ τι χρὴ ποιεῖν ἢ μὴ ποιεῖν, ἤκουον διὰ τῶν μάντεων; Ἀγαμέμνονα δὲ τὸ πανταχοῦ τεθυκέναι πλέοντα ἐπ' Ἴλιον αἰσχρῶς ἐπανήγαγεν ἢ νενικηκότα τῆς Ἀθηνᾶς αὐτῷ τὸ τέλος εὑρούσης; Ἡρακλέα δὲ τὸν πρὸ τούτου τὴν αὐτὴν καθελόντα πόλιν οὐ θυσίαις ἴσμεν τῶν θεῶν προσλαβόντα τὴν ῥοπήν; **(32)** ἔτι τοίνυν λαμπρὸς μὲν ὁ Μαραθὼν οὐ διὰ τοὺς μυρίους μᾶλλον Ἀθηναίων ἢ διὰ τὸν Ἡρακλέα καὶ Πᾶνα, θεία δὲ ἡ Σαλαμὶς οὐ διὰ τὰς <τριακοσίας> τῶν Ἑλλήνων μᾶλλον ναῦς ἢ τοὺς ἐξ Ἐλευσῖνος συμμάχους, οἳ μετ' ᾠδῆς τῆς αὐτῶν ἐπὶ τὴν ναυμαχίαν ἧκον. μυρίους <δ'> ἄν τις ἔχοι λέγειν πολέμους τῇ τῶν θεῶν εὐνοίᾳ κυβερνηθέντας καί, νὴ Δία γε, καὶ εἰρήνης καὶ ἡσυχίας χρόνους.

(33) Τὸ δὲ μέγιστον, οἱ μάλιστα τοῦτο τὸ μέρος ἀτιμάσαι δοκοῦντες καὶ ἄκοντες τετιμήκασι. τίνες οὗτοι; οἱ τὴν Ῥώμην τοῦ θύειν οὐ τολμήσαντες ἀφελέσθαι. καίτοι εἰ μὲν μάταιον ἅπαν τοῦτο τὸ περὶ τὰς θυσίας, τί μὴ τὸ μάταιον ἐκωλύθη; εἰ δὲ καὶ βλαβερόν, πῶς οὐ ταύτῃ γε μᾶλλον; εἰ δ' ἐν ταῖς ἐκεῖ θυσίαις κεῖται τὸ βέβαιον τῆς ἀρχῆς, ἁπανταχοῦ δεῖ νομίζειν λυσιτελεῖν τὸ θύειν καὶ διδόναι τοὺς μὲν ἐν Ῥώμῃ δαίμονας τὰ μείζω, τοὺς δ' ἐν τοῖς ἀγροῖς ἢ καὶ τοῖς ἄλλοις ἄστεσιν ἐλάττω, δέξαιτο δ' ἄν τις εὖ φρονῶν καὶ τὰ τηλικαῦτα. **(34)** καὶ γὰρ ἐν τοῖς στρατεύμασιν οὐκ ἴσον μὲν τὸ παρ' ἑκάστου, φέρει δέ τι τῇ μάχῃ τὸ παρ' ἑκάστου. οἷον δή τι κἀν ταῖς εἰρεσίαις· οὐκ ἴσοι μὲν ἅπαντες οἱ βραχίονες, συντελεῖ δέ τι καὶ ὁ τοῦ πρώτου λειπόμενος. ὁ μέν τις τῷ σκήπτρῳ τῷ τῆς Ῥώμης συναγωνίζεται, ὁ δέ τις ταύτῃ σώζει πόλιν ὑπήκοον, ὁ δέ <τις> ἀγρὸν ἀνέχει παρέχων εὖ πράττειν. ἔστω τοίνυν ἱερὰ πανταχοῦ ἢ ὁμολογούντων οὗτοι δυσμενῶς ὑμᾶς πρὸς τὴν Ῥώμην ἔχειν δόντας αὐτῇ ποιεῖν ἀφ' ὧν ζημιώσεται.

(35) Οὐ τοίνυν τῇ Ῥώμῃ μόνον ἐφυλάχθη τὸ θύειν, ἀλλὰ καὶ τῇ τοῦ Σαράπιδος τῇ πολλῇ τε καὶ μεγάλῃ καὶ πλῆθος κεκτημένῃ νεῶν, δι' ὧν κοινὴν ἁπάντων ἀνθρώπων ποιεῖ τὴν τῆς Αἰγύπτου φοράν. αὐτὴ δὲ ἔργον τοῦ Νείλου, τὸν Νεῖλον δὲ ἑστιάματά ἐστιν ἀναβαίνειν ἐπὶ τὰς ἀρούρας πείθοντα, ὧν οὐ ποιουμένων ὅτε τε χρὴ καὶ παρ' ὧν, οὐδ' ἂν αὐτὸς ἐθελήσειεν. ἅ μοι δοκοῦσιν εἰδότες οἱ καὶ ταῦτα ἂν ἡδέως ἀνελόντες οὐκ ἀνελεῖν, ἀλλ' ἀφεῖναι τὸν ποταμὸν εὐωχεῖσθαι τοῖς παλαιοῖς νομίμοις ἐπὶ μισθῷ τῷ εἰωθότι. **(36)** τί οὖν; ἐπεὶ μὴ ποταμός ἐστι καθ' ἕκαστον ἀγρὸν τὰ τοῦ Νείλου τῇ γῇ παρέχων, οὐδ' εἶναι τἀν τούτοις ἱερὰ δεῖ, ἀλλ' ὅ τι δόξειε τοῖς γενναίοις τουτοισὶ πάσχειν; οὓς ἡδέως ἐκεῖνο ἂν ἐροίμην, εἰ τολμήσουσι παρελθόντες γνώμην εἰπεῖν πεπαῦσθαι μὲν τὰ γιγνόμενα τῷ Νείλῳ, μὴ μετέχειν δὲ αὐτοῦ τὴν γῆν μηδὲ σπείρεσθαι μηδὲ ἀμᾶσθαι μηδὲ διδόναι πυροὺς μηδ' ὅσα δίδωσι μηδ' ἀνάγεσθαι γῆν ἐπὶ πᾶσαν ἃ νῦν. εἰ δ' οὐκ ἂν ἐπὶ τούτοις διάραιεν τὸ στόμα, οἷς οὐ λέγουσι διελέγχουσιν ἃ λέγουσιν. οἱ γὰρ οὐκ ἂν εἰπόντες δεῖν τῶν τιμῶν ἀποστερεῖσθαι τὸν Νεῖλον ὁμολογοῦσι τοῖς ἀνθρώποις συμφέρειν τὰς τῶν ἱερῶν τιμάς.

Notes to Libanius Oration *30.30–36*

These notes are indebted to R. Romano, *Libanio, In difesa dei templi* (Naples, 1982) and H.-G. Nesselrath's notes in *Für Religionsfreiheit, Recht und Toleranz: Libanios' Rede für den Erhalt der heidnischen Tempel* (Tübingen, 2011), 76–91.

(30) τὸ μηδ᾽ εἶναί . . . ἱερὰ. *the nonexistence of temples.* The articular infinitive is the acc. subject in indirect discourse; χρήσιμον is a predicate adj.

φασιν. sc. a generic "they" as the subject. At this point in the speech, Libanius segues from argumentation to refutation. He employs the rhetorical technique known as hypophora (Smyth 3029) or sermocinatio, where the speaker quashes objections raised by imaginary opponents.

δεῖ. *there is need of* + gen.: LSJ, s.v. II.

παρρησία, -ας (fem.). *freedom of speech, outspokenness.* Greek *paideia* sought to cultivate this virtue in its students, yet it also taught them to use it with discretion, especially when addressing potentates like Theodosius.

τῶν . . . κρειττόνων. partitive gen. triggered by τινα.

χωρείτω. 3rd sg. pres. act. impv.

(31) Εἰπάτω. 3rd sg. aor. act. impv.

πυράγρας καὶ σφύρας καὶ ἄκμονας. *tongs and hammers and anvils,* the instruments with which the temples were torn down. The phrase also recalls a line in Homer from a scene that describes in detail the sacrifice of a heifer (*Odyssey* 3.434): a smith uses these three tools to work the gold foil with which the beast's horns are bedizened. Libanius thus also suggests that his opponents, by misusing these implements, have rejected animal sacrifice (Nesselrath, *Religionsfreiheit*, ad loc.), which is as central to Greek culture as the authoritative author who first described it.

ἀφέντων. mas. pl. gen., aor. act. part. < ἀφίημι.

ποτέροις ἀκολουθοῦντες. *by following which (of these),* anticipating the two options Libanius presents below.

οἱ τὰ μέγιστα . . . δυνηθέντες ἐδυνήθησαν. *did the Romans, having grown from small and humble origins, grow exceedingly powerful.* δυνηθέντες ἐδυνήθησαν is an example of polyptoton, the juxtaposition of words from the same root but exhibiting different forms; the effect is difficult to capture in English.

τῷ <θεῷ>. dat. in apposition with ποτέροις. The angle brackets used here and later in the text indicate that the editor has added the enclosed word.

οἷς. dat. of possession: *(these gods) for whom (there exist)*; the antecedent of the relative is omitted: Smyth 2509.

ὅ τι χρὴ ποιεῖν ἢ μὴ ποιεῖν. indirect question after ἤκουον.

τὸ πανταχοῦ τεθυκέναι. The articular inf. is the subject.

πλέοντα agrees with Ἀγαμέμνονα.

τέλος. Since Agamemnon was murdered soon after his return home, this word may seem puzzling; one editor has in fact corrected it to κλέος: Nesselrath, *Religionsfreiheit,* ad loc.

Ἡρακλέα. Before Agamemnon, Hercules, too, had once sacked Troy.

οὐ . . . ἴσμεν. *don't we know.*

ῥοπή, ῆς (fem.). *(decisive) influence.*

(32) ἔτι τοίνυν. *moreover.* The two words indicate that another example is being adduced in support of an argument: LSJ, s.v. τοίνυν, 3.c.

λαμπρὸς. predicative: *Marathon (is) glorious.* Libanius cites two crucial battles during the Persian Wars, Marathon (490 B.C.E.) and Salamis (480), in which the gods helped the Greeks to repel the Persian invaders.

τοὺς ἐξ Ἐλευσῖνος συμμάχους. After Athens had been evacuated in anticipation of the naval battle off the island of Salamis, there was seen emerging from Eleusis, the city where the Mysteries were celebrated in honor of Demeter, a great cloud of dust, as if 30,000 men were marching out of the city; from the cloud came the cry "Iacchus," which was chanted during the secret rites. This strange sight suggested that a divine army was joining the fight to defend Greece: Herodotus 8.65.

ᾠδῆς is the Attic contracted form of ἀοιδῆς.

ἔχω. here, as often, *be able to, can.*

(33) Τὸ δὲ μέγιστον. *and (what is) most important*: LSJ, s.v. μέγας, II.4.

μέρος, -εος (neu.). *heritage* (of paganism): LSJ, s.v. 2.

ἀφαιρέω. *deprive X* (+ acc.) *of Y* (+ gen.). Although sacrifice had been banned in many parts of the empire, an exemption had been made for Rome; on February 24, 391, it was banned there as well: *Codex Theodosianus* 16.10.10.

ταύτῃ. dat. of cause (Smyth 1517): *because of this*; i.e., if sacrifice is not merely foolish but also harmful, why hasn't it been banned everywhere?

ἐκεῖ. i.e., at Rome.

τὸ θύειν. The articular inf. serves as the acc. subject of λυσιτελεῖν in indirect discourse after δεῖ νομίζειν.

δέξαιτο. potential opt.

δέξαιτο . . . τηλικαῦτα. Sacrifices in the countryside may yield lesser benefits than those made in Rome, but that doesn't mean that the former are without value.

(34) τὸ παρ' ἑκάστου. *what comes from each (individual)*; i.e., soldiers contribute to an army's success in varying degrees.

φέρει . . . τι + dat. *contributes something to.*

οἷον . . . τι. *likewise.*

κἀν = καὶ ἐν.

ὁ τοῦ πρώτου λειπόμενος. *the one who falls short of the best (rower)*: LSJ, s.v. λείπω, B.II.3.

ὁ μέν τις. sc. θεός.

σκῆπτρον, ου (neu.). *scepter,* standing here, by metonymy (Smyth 3033), for imperial power: LSJ, s.v. II.2.

ταύτῃ. i.e., for Rome.

παρέχω. *allow, enable X* (+ acc.) *to Y* (+ inf.).

ὁμολογούντων. 3rd pl. pres. act. impv.

ἔχω + adv. *behave* X.

δόντας αὐτῇ ποιεῖν ἀφ' ὧν. *having permitted Rome to do (those things) from which.*

(35) τοίνυν (*moreover*) signposts a new line of argumentation: LSJ, s.v. 3.c.

τῇ τοῦ Σαράπιδος. *the (city) of Sarapis,* the Egyptian god; i.e., Alexandria, where sacrifices were banned on June 16, 391: *Codex Theodosianus* 16.10.11.

νεῶν. mas. pl. gen. < νεώς, νεώ. *temple*; for this noun's irregular declension: Smyth 238.

φοράν. Egypt was an important exporter of grain.

αὐτὴ. i.e., Αἴγυπτος, which is 2nd declension fem.

ἑστίαμα, ατος (neu.). *feast*; i.e., religious festival.

ἀναβαίνειν. Essential to Egyptian agriculture was the annual flood of the Nile.

πείθοντα. neu. pl. nom., pres. act. part., in agreement with ἑστιάματά.

ὧν. part of a gen. absolute; the pronoun's antecendent is ἑστιάματά.

αὐτὸς = ὁ Νεῖλος.

εἰδότες. Translate as causal.

οἱ καὶ ταῦτα ἂν ἡδέως ἀνελόντες. *those who might have eliminated even these (practices) with pleasure.* On the use of ἄν, see Smyth 1848.

ἀφίημι. *permit X* (+ acc.) *to Y* (+ inf.).

ἐπὶ μισθῷ τῷ εἰωθότι. *for the accustomed reward.* Even those who object to the pagan practices by which the Nile is propitiated allow them to continue, for the ends—the financial benefits—justify the means.

(36) τἀν = τὰ ἐν.

ὅ τι δόξειε. indirect question after πάσχειν.

οὓς. i.e., τοῖς γενναίοις τουτοισὶ.

ἐκεῖνο. i.e., what follows.

παρέρχομαι. *come forward* + inf. of purpose: LSJ, s.v. VI.

τὰ γιγνόμενα. i.e., the customary religious festivals in honor of the Nile.

μετέχω. *partake in* + gen. αὐτοῦ; i.e., the feast.

ἃ νῦν. *which (the Nile is doing) now.*

διαίρω τὸ στόμα. *open one's mouth*: LSJ, s.v. διαίρω, II.2.

οὐ λέγουσι διελέγχουσιν ἃ λέγουσιν. *by not speaking, they refute what they (do) say.*

E7. BELISARIUS SAVES ROME

Procopius *Wars* 7.22.6–19

About a quarter-century after the last emperor of the western Roman Empire, the aptly named Romulus Augustulus, was deposed in 476 C.E., Procopius was born in the Greek city of Caesarea on the Levantine coast, a center of learning famed for its schools and venerable library. (Eusebius had been bishop there: E1–E3.) Caesarea was part of the Byzantine or eastern Roman Empire ruled from Constantinople, whose emperors formed a line of succession that went back to Augustus (reg. 27 B.C.E.–14 C.E.; see C2–C3). (Apropos of this, it is worth noting that "Byzantine" is a modern term; the Byzantines referred to themselves as "Romans" [Ῥωμαῖοι]). Procopius's big break came when he joined the staff of his lifelong patron, Belisarius, the gifted general whom the emperor Justinian (reg. 527–65 C.E.) tasked with bringing Africa and Italy, then controlled by barbarians, under Byzantine rule. Procopius accompanied Belisarius on his campaigns and soon became the general's confidant and right-hand man. He wrote three works: *Buildings,* a panegyric tourbook of the empire's art and architecture; the *Secret History,* a tell-all, behind-the-scenes exposé of the imperial court; and eight books of *Wars,* on the Byzantine campaigns conducted in Persia, Africa, and Italy. *Wars* is the last great work of classical historiography. It is written in Attic dialect (though about a millennium had passed since the age of classical Athens) and in method is indebted to earlier Greek historians, above all Thucydides. Procopius's narrative is typically brisk and lively, and it is often based on autopsy. For the passage below, one should know that Procopius had lived in Rome during a year-long siege by the Goths; moved by nostalgia and curiosity, he details the sights of the Eternal City in book 5 of *Wars*. He knew firsthand what would be lost were Rome to be destroyed.

By the year 540, Belisarius seemed to have brought Italy under Byzantine control, having much reduced the Ostrogoths who had dominated the peninsula from the late fifth century. But the cagey and resourceful Totila (a.k.a. Baduila) became king of the Ostrogoths in 541 and reversed many of the Byzantines' gains through a combination of force and diplomacy. In 543, he took Naples; in the winter of 545/46, he besieged Rome. In response, Belisarius mustered an army that sailed around Italy and landed in Portus at the mouth of the Tiber River. But thence he could not prevent Totila, in 546, from taking Rome, betrayed by its Byzantine garrison, its population that once numbered more than a million souls now so diminished by decades of warfare, emigration, famine, and plague that only five hundred residents remained. Rome's fate lay in Totila's hands; what would he do? In the passage below, Belisarius pleads with him to save the city, making a moving argument about what Rome represented at that moment in the history of humankind.

Further Reading

P. Llewellyn, *Rome in the Dark Ages* (New York, 1971), 52–77; R. Krautheimer, *Rome: Profile of a City, 312–1308* (Princeton, 1983), 59–87; A. Cameron, *Procopius and the Sixth Century* (Berkeley, 1985), 3–18, 188–206.

❧

(6) Γνοὺς δὲ ταῦτα ὁ Τουτίλας ἔγνω Ῥώμην μὲν καθελεῖν ἐς ἔδαφος, τοῦ δὲ στρατοῦ τὸ μὲν πλεῖστον ἐνταῦθά πη ἀπολιπεῖν, τῷ δὲ ἄλλῳ ἐπί τε Ἰωάννην καὶ Λευκανοὺς ἰέναι. **(7)** τοῦ μὲν οὖν περιβόλου ἐν χώροις πολλοῖς τοσοῦτον καθεῖλεν ὅσον ἐς τριτημόριον τοῦ παντὸς μάλιστα. ἐμπιπρᾶν δὲ καὶ τῶν οἰκοδομιῶν τὰ κάλλιστά τε καὶ ἀξιολογώτατα ἔμελλε, Ῥώμην τε μηλόβοτον καταστήσεσθαι, ἀλλὰ Βελισάριος μαθὼν πρέσβεις τε καὶ γράμματα παρ' αὐτὸν ἔπεμψεν. **(8)** οἵπερ ἐπειδὴ Τουτίλᾳ ἐς ὄψιν ἦλθον, εἶπόν τε ὧν ἕνεκα ἥκοιεν καὶ τὰ γράμματα ἐνεχείρισαν. ἐδήλου δὲ ἡ γραφὴ τάδε·

"Πόλεως μὲν κάλλη οὐκ ὄντα ἐργάζεσθαι ἀνθρώπων ἂν φρονίμων εὑρήματα εἶεν καὶ πολιτικῶς βιοτεύειν ἐπισταμένων, ὄντα δὲ ἀφανίζειν τούς γε ἀξυνέτους εἰκὸς καὶ γνώρισμα τοῦτο τῆς αὐτῶν φύσεως οὐκ αἰσχυνομένους χρόνῳ τῷ ὑστέρῳ ἀπολιπεῖν. **(9)** Ῥώμη μέντοι πόλεων ἁπασῶν, ὅσαι ὑφ' ἡλίῳ τυγχάνουσιν οὖσαι, μεγίστη τε καὶ ἀξιολογωτάτη ὡμολόγηται εἶναι. **(10)** οὐ γὰρ ἀνδρὸς ἑνὸς ἀρετῇ εἴργασται οὐδὲ χρόνου βραχέος δυνάμει ἐς τόσον μεγέθους τε καὶ κάλλους ἀφῖκται, ἀλλὰ βασιλέων μὲν πλῆθος, ἀνδρῶν δὲ ἀρίστων συμμορίαι πολλαί, χρόνου τε μῆκος καὶ πλούτου ἐξουσίας ὑπερβολὴ τά τε ἄλλα πάντα ἐκ πάσης τῆς γῆς καὶ τεχνίτας ἀνθρώπους ἐνταῦθα ξυναγαγεῖν ἴσχυσαν. **(11)** οὕτω τε τὴν πόλιν τοιαύτην, οἵανπερ ὁρᾷς, κατὰ βραχὺ τεκτηνάμενοι, μνημεῖα τῆς πάντων ἀρετῆς τοῖς ἐπιγενησομένοις ἀπέλιπον, ὥστε ἡ ἐς ταῦτα ἐπήρεια εἰκότως ἂν ἀδίκημα μέγα ἐς τοὺς ἀνθρώπους τοῦ παντὸς αἰῶνος δόξειεν εἶναι· **(12)** ἀφαιρεῖται γὰρ τοὺς μὲν προγεγενημένους τὴν τῆς ἀρετῆς μνήμην, τοὺς δὲ ὕστερον ἐπιγενησομένους τῶν ἔργων τὴν θέαν. **(13)** τούτων δὲ τοιούτων ὄντων ἐκεῖνο εὖ ἴσθι, ὡς δυοῖν ἀνάγκη τὸ ἕτερον εἶναι. ἢ γὰρ ἡσσηθήσῃ βασιλέως ἐν τῷδε τῷ πόνῳ, ἢ περιέσῃ, ἂν οὕτω τύχοι. **(14)** ἢν μὲν οὖν νικῴης, Ῥώμην τε καθελών, οὐ τὴν ἑτέρου του, ἀλλὰ τὴν σαυτοῦ ἀπολωλεκὼς ἄν, ὦ βέλτιστε, εἴης, καὶ διαφυλάξας, κτήματι, ὡς τὸ εἰκός, τῶν πάντων καλλίστῳ πλουτήσεις· ἢν δέ γε τὴν χείρω σοι τύχην πληροῦσθαι ξυμβαίη, σώσαντι μὲν Ῥώμην χάρις ἂν σώζοιτο παρὰ τῷ νενικηκότι πολλή, διαφθείραντι δὲ φιλανθρωπίας τε οὐδεὶς ἔτι λελείψεται λόγος καὶ προσέσται τὸ μηδὲν τοῦ ἔργου ἀπόνασθαι. **(15)** καταλήψεται δέ σε καὶ δόξα τῆς πράξεως ἀξία πρὸς πάντων ἀνθρώπων, ἥπερ ἐφ' ἑκάτερά σοι τῆς γνώμης ἑτοίμως ἕστηκεν, **(16)** ὁποῖα γὰρ ἂν τῶν ἀρχόντων τὰ ἔργα εἴη, τοιοῦτον ἀνάγκη καὶ ὑπὲρ αὐτῶν ὄνομα φέρεσθαι." τοσαῦτα μὲν Βελισάριος ἔγραψε.

(17) Τουτίλας δὲ πολλάκις ἀναλεξάμενος τὴν ἐπιστολὴν καὶ τῆς παραινέσεως ἐς τὸ ἀκριβὲς πεποιημένος τὴν μάθησιν, ἐπείσθη τε καὶ Ῥώμην εἰργάσατο ἄχαρι περαιτέρω οὐδέν. σημήνας τε Βελισαρίῳ τὴν αὑτοῦ γνώμην τοὺς πρέσβεις εὐθὺς ἀπεπέμψατο. **(18)** καὶ τοῦ μὲν στρατοῦ τὸ πλεῖστον μέρος Ῥώμης οὐ πολλῷ ἄποθεν, ἀλλ ὅσον ἀπὸ σταδίων εἴκοσι καὶ ἑκατὸν ἐς τὰ πρὸς δύοντα ἥλιον ἐνστρατοπεδευσαμένους ἐν χωρίῳ Ἀλγηδόνι ἐκέλευεν ἡσυχῇ μένειν, ὅπως δὴ μηδεμία ἐξουσία τοῖς ἀμφὶ Βελισάριον εἴη ἔξω πη τοῦ Πόρτου ἰέναι· αὐτὸς δὲ ξὺν τῷ ἄλλῳ στρατῷ ἐπί τε Ἰωάννην καὶ Λευκανοὺς ᾔει. **(19)** Ῥωμαίων μέντοι τοὺς μὲν ἐκ τῆς συγκλήτου βουλῆς ξὺν αὐτῷ εἶχε, τοὺς δὲ ἄλλους ἅπαντας ξύν τε γυναιξὶ καὶ παισὶν ἔστειλεν ἐς τὰ ἐπὶ Καμπανίας χωρία, ἐν Ῥώμῃ ἄνθρωπον οὐδένα ἐάσας, ἀλλ ἔρημον αὐτὴν τὸ παράπαν ἀπολιπών.

Notes to Procopius Wars *7.22.6–19*

(6) Γνοὺς . . . ἔγνω. antistasis, the repetition of a word but with different meanings.

γιγνώσκω + inf. *decide to X*: LSJ, s.v. II. Troops under Totila's aegis had just tried to traverse a heavily defended mountain pass into the region of Lucania in southern Italy, which had recently switched sides, allying itself with Byzantium. Totila's troops were soundly defeated, and many of them were killed as they fled (7.22.1–5). Such was the news that Totila received.

καθελεῖν < καθαιρέω.

ἐνταῦθά πη. *there*; i.e., in the vicinity of Rome.

ἐπί + acc. *against*: Smyth 1689.3.d.

Ἰωάννην καὶ Λευκανοὺς. The Byzantine general John was simultaneously campaigning in Lucania.

(7) τοῦ . . . περιβόλου. partitive gen. dependent on τοσοῦτον . . . ὅσον. The emperor Aurelian (reg. 270–75 C.E.) surrounded Rome with a fortified wall about twelve miles in length; in many places, it is still visible today.

ὅσον ἐς τριτημόριον. *as much as a third.* On the use of ἐς with a numeral, see Smyth 1686.1.c.

ἐμπιπρᾶν. pres. act. inf. < ἐμπίμπρημι. *burn.*

ἐμπιπρᾶν . . . ἔμελλε. Through hyperbaton (Smyth 3028), the separation of these two verbs, Procopius builds suspense. He also uses another trope that was by his time centuries old, one that was favored by Homer: one character, who "was about to do X" (μέλλω in the impf. + inf., as here), is dramatically interrupted by another: see for example *Odyssey* 6.110–14. This is a subtle yet remarkable example of continuity in Greek literature over the centuries.

μηλόβοτον. predicative with Ῥώμην.

γράμμα, -ατος (neu.). in pl., *letter*; i.e., *epistle*: LSJ, s.v. III.

(8) Τουτίλᾳ ἐς ὄψιν. *into Totila's presence*: LSJ, s.v. ὄψις, II.2.

ἕνεκα. As often, this word is postpositive; i.e., it follows the word it governs.

Πόλεως . . . ἐπισταμένων. *the designs of men who are wise and know what it is to live in a civilized way may be what fashions beauty in a city that was not beautiful before.* κάλλη and ὄντα are neu. pl. acc., the objects of ἐργάζεσθαι, which is the predicate of εὑρήματα after the linking verb εἶεν, in the potential opt. Belisarius opens his letter with politesse, circumspection, and circumlocution.

ἀξύνετος, -ον. *mindless.* Note that Procopius, like Thucydides, favors the older Attic spelling ξυν to the συν that may be more familiar: Smyth, intro. E.2.

εἰκὸς. *(it is) likely (that)* + acc. and inf.

γνώρισμα, -ατος (neu.). *marker, indicator.*

(9) ὡμολόγηται. 3rd sg. pf. pass. ind. in pass., *it has been agreed that* + nom. + inf.

(10) εἴργασται. 3rd sg. pf. dep. ind. < ἐργάζομαι.

ἐς τόσον. *to such a degree of* + gen.

τά . . . ἄλλα πάντα. direct object after ξυναγαγεῖν.

(11) κατὰ βραχὺ. *little by little, piecemeal*: LSJ, s.v. βραχύς, 2.

τεκτηνάμενοι. mas. pl. nom., aor. dep. part. < τεκταίνομαι. *build, construct.*

μνημεῖον, -ου (neu.). *memorial, reminder,* but also *tomb.*

ἐπήρεια, -ας (fem.). *insult.*

εἰκότως. *reasonably.*

(12) ἀφαιρέω. in mid., *deprive X* (+ acc.) *of Y* (+ acc.).

θέα, -ας (fem.). *sight, spectacle.* Note accent; cf. θεά, *goddess.*

(13) ἐκεῖνος, especially in the neu., anticipates what follows: Smyth 990, 1248.

ἴσθι. 2nd sg. pf. act. impv. < οἶδα.

δυοῖν . . . τὸ ἕτερον. *one of two things.* δυοῖν is neu. dual gen.

ἡσσηθήσῃ. 2nd sg. fut. dep. ind. < ἡσσάομαι + gen. *be defeated by.* Here Procopius does not use the Attic form (ἡττηθήσῃ), as might be expected.

βασιλέως. i.e., the emperor Justinian (reg. 527–65 C.E.), under whom Belisarius served.

(14) ἤν = ἐάν.

ἀπολωλεκὼς . . . εἴης. 3rd sg. pf. act. opt., periphrastic form.

τὴν χείρω σοι τύχην πληροῦσθαι ξυμβαίη. *it should happen that a worse fate be fulfilled for you.* When countenancing the possibility of Totila's defeat, Belisarius employs more delicate, indirect language.

σώσαντι, σώζοιτο. polyptoton: employing words of the same root with different endings. Saving Rome would save Totila.

λελείψεται. 3rd sg. fut. pf. mid. ind.

λόγος, -ου (mas.). *pretext, grounds for* + gen.: LSJ, s.v. III.1.

ἀπόνασθαι. aor. dep. inf. < ἀπονίναμαι. *take joy in, reap benefit from* + gen.

(15) δόξα, -ης (fem.). *reputation*: LSJ, s.v. III.

πρός + gen. *in the eyes of*: Smyth 1695.1.b.

ἐφ' ἑκάτερά σοι τῆς γνώμης. Totila's decision will be long remembered.

ἑτοίμως. *readily.*

(17) ἐς τὸ ἀκριβὲς. *accurately, correctly.*

εἰργάσατο. 3rd sg. aor. dep. ind. < ἐργάζομαι. *do X* (+ acc.) *to Y* (+ acc.): LSJ, s.v. II.2.

ἄχαρι, -ιτος (neu.). *disagreeable thing.*

σημήνας. mas. sg. nom., aor. act. part. < σημαίνω.

(18) τὸ πλεῖστον μέρος . . . ἐνστρατοπεδευσαμένους. A collective singular noun may take a plural participle as a predicate: Smyth 1044. These accusatives are the object of ἐκέλευεν.

ἄποθεν = ἄπωθεν. *far from* + gen.

ὅσον. *about*: LSJ, s.v. ὅσος, IV.3.

ἀπό. *away* (from Rome): LSJ, s.v. I.2.

Ἀλγηδόνι. This locale is not otherwise known. Assuming an Attic stade of 607 feet, Algedon would be a bit under fourteen miles west of Rome, near the coastline, just north of Portus, where Belisarius's troops were encamped.

ἡσυχῇ. adv.: *at rest.*

ᾔει. 3rd sg. impf. act. ind. < εἶμι.

(19) ἐκ τῆς συγκλήτου βουλῆς. i.e., from the Roman Senate.

SOURCES AND CREDITS

In preparing notes for the Greek passages in this volume, I consulted scholarly commentaries in a variety of languages. If a certain commentary proved especially helpful as I composed my notes on a particular passage, that work is acknowledged at the beginning of those notes. It may be cited again in the individual annotations if I am indebted to a specific observation made by the commentator.

The Greek passages are reproduced from the following sources, with occasional changes to the formatting. In some cases, section or chapter breaks have been modified or supplemented to reflect textual divisions that are now conventional.

A1. Strabo 5.3.7–8. Excerpted from *Strabonis Geographica,* ed. A. Meineke (Leipzig, 1877). Text reproduced from the Perseus Digital Library (http://data.perseus.org/texts/urn:cts:greekLit:tlg0099.tlg001). Courtesy of Creative Commons.

A2. Diodorus Siculus 5.40. Excerpted from *Diodori Bibliotheca Historica,* ed. I. Bekker, L. Dindorf, and F. Vogel (Leipzig, 1888). Text reproduced from the Perseus Digital Library (http://data.perseus.org/citations/

urn:cts:greekLit:tlg0060.tlg001.perseus-grc1:5.40). Courtesy of Creative Commons.

A3.1. Herodotus 1.94. Excerpted from Herodotus, *The Persian Wars: Books 1–2,* trans. A. D. Godley, Loeb Classical Library 117 (Cambridge, Mass., 1920). Text reproduced from the Perseus Digital Library (http://data.perseus.org/texts/urn:cts:greekLit:tlg0016.tlg001). Courtesy of Creative Commons.

A3.2. Dionysius of Halicarnassus *Roman Antiquities* 1.30.1–3. Excerpted from *Dionysii Halicarnasei Antiquitatum Romanarum Quae Supersunt,* ed. K. Jacoby (Leipzig, 1885). Text reproduced from the Perseus Digital Library (http://data.perseus.org/texts/urn:cts:greekLit:tlg0081.tlg001). Courtesy of Creative Commons.

A4. Dionysius of Halicarnassus *Roman Antiquities* 1.84.1–5. Excerpted from *Dionysii Halicarnasei Antiquitatum Romanarum Quae Supersunt,* ed. K. Jacoby (Leipzig, 1885). Text reproduced from the Perseus Digital Library (http://data.perseus.org/texts/urn:cts:greekLit:tlg0081.tlg001). Courtesy of Creative Commons.

A5. Dionysius of Halicarnassus *Roman Antiquities* 1.89–90.1. Excerpted from *Dionysii Halicarnasei Antiquitatum Romanarum Quae Supersunt,* ed. K. Jacoby (Leipzig, 1885). Text reproduced from the Perseus Digital Library (http://data.perseus.org/texts/urn:cts:greekLit:tlg0081.tlg001). Courtesy of Creative Commons.

A6. Dionysius of Halicarnassus *Roman Antiquities* 2.15.1, 2.15.3–17.1. Excerpted from *Dionysii Halicarnasei Antiquitatum Romanarum Quae Supersunt,* ed. K. Jacoby (Leipzig, 1885). Text reproduced from the Perseus Digital Library (http://data.perseus.org/texts/urn:cts:greekLit:tlg0081.tlg001). Courtesy of Creative Commons.

A7.1. Plutarch *Numa* 8.1–3. Excerpted from Plutarch, *Lives,* ed. B. Perrin, vol. 1, Loeb Classical Library 46 (Cambridge, Mass., 1914). Text reproduced from the Perseus Digital Library (http://data.perseus.org/texts/urn:cts:greekLit:tlg0007.tlg005). Courtesy of Creative Commons.

A7.2. Polybius 6.56.6–12. Excerpted from *Polybii Historiae,* ed. T. Büttner-Wobst after L. Dindorf (Leipzig, 1893–). Text reproduced from the Perseus Digital Library (http://data.perseus.org/texts/urn:cts:greekLit:tlg0543.tlg001). Courtesy of Creative Commons.

B1. Polybius 6.18, 52. Excerpted from *Polybii Historiae,* ed. T. Büttner-Wobst after L. Dindorf (Leipzig, 1893–). Text reproduced from the Perseus Digital Library (http://data.perseus.org/texts/urn:cts:greekLit:tlg0543.tlg001). Courtesy of Creative Commons.

B2. Polybius 6.53–54. Excerpted from *Polybii Historiae,* ed. T. Büttner-Wobst after L. Dindorf (Leipzig, 1893–). Text reproduced from the Perseus Digital Library (http://data.perseus.org/texts/urn:cts:greekLit:tlg0543.tlg001). Courtesy of Creative Commons.

B3. Plutarch *Flamininus* 10–11.2, 11.4. Excerpted from Plutarch, *Lives,* ed. B. Perrin, vol. 10, Loeb Classical Library 102 (Cambridge, Mass., 1921). Text reproduced from the Perseus Digital Library (http://data.perseus.org/texts/urn:cts:greekLit:tlg0007.tlg028). Courtesy of Creative Commons.

B4. Plutarch *Cato the Elder* 22–23.3. Excerpted from Plutarch, *Lives,* ed. B. Perrin, vol. 2, Loeb Classical Library 47 (Cambridge, Mass., 1914). Text reproduced from the Perseus Digital Library (http://data.perseus.org/texts/urn:cts:greekLit:tlg0007.tlg025). Courtesy of Creative Commons.

B5. Phlegon of Tralles *On Wondrous Things* 3.3–8, 3.12. Excerpted from A. Giannini, ed., *Paradoxographorum Graecorum Reliquiae* (Milan, 1965). Text reproduced from *Thesaurus Linguae Graecae: A Digital Library of Greek Literature* (stephanus.tlg.uci.edu). Used by permission.

B6. 1 Maccabees 8.1–16. Excerpted from *Septuaginta,* ed. A. Rahlfs, 9th ed. (Stuttgart, 1935). Text reproduced from *Thesaurus Linguae Graecae: A Digital Library of Greek Literature* (stephanus.tlg.uci.edu). Used by permission.

B7. Strabo 8.6.23. Excerpted from *Strabonis Geographica,* ed. A. Meineke (Leipzig, 1877). Text reproduced from the Perseus Digital Library (http://data.perseus.org/texts/urn:cts:greekLit:tlg0099.tlg001). Courtesy of Creative Commons.

C1. Appian *Mithridatic Wars* 61.250–63.261. Excerpted from *Appiani Historia Romana,* ed. L. Mendelssohn (Leipzig, 1879). Text reproduced from the Perseus Digital Library (http://data.perseus.org/texts/urn:cts:greekLit:tlg0551.tlg014). Courtesy of Creative Commons.

C2. Cassius Dio 53.16.4–17.3, 18.1–3. Excerpted from Dio Cassius, *Roman History,* ed. E. Cary, vol. 6, Loeb Classical Library 83 (Cambridge, Mass., 1917). Text reproduced from the Perseus Digital Library (http://data.perseus.org/texts/urn:cts:greekLit:tlg0385.tlg001). Courtesy of Creative Commons.

C3. *Res Gestae Divi Augusti* 1–4, 13, 24, 34–35. Excerpted from *Velleius Paterculus, Compendium of Roman History,* Res Gestae Divi Augusti, ed. F. W. Shipley, Loeb Classical Library 152 (Cambridge, Mass., 1924). Text is in public domain and is reproduced from Lacus Curtius (http://penelope.uchicago.edu/Thayer/E/Roman/Texts/Augustus/Res_Gestae/home.html), but also incorporates some editorial improvements found in J. Scheid, Res Gestae Divi Augusti: *Hauts faits du Divin Auguste* (Paris, 2007) and A. E. Cooley, Res Gestae Divi Augusti: *Text, Translation, and Commentary* (Cambridge, 2009). The square brackets indicating where the text has been reconstructed have been omitted.

C4. Philo *Embassy to Gaius* 2.8–3.21. Excerpted from *Philonis Alexandrini Opera Quae Supersunt,* ed. L. Cohn and P. Wendland, vol. 6 (Berlin, 1915). Text reproduced from Wikisource (https://el.wikisource.org/w/index.php?title=%C.E.%91%CF%81%C.E.%B5%CF%84%CF%8E%C.E.%BD_%CF%80%CF%81%CF%8E%CF%84%C.E.%BF%C.E.%BD&oldid=56690). Courtesy of Creative Commons.

C5. Cassius Dio 62.3–5. Excerpted from Dio Cassius, *Roman History,* ed. E. Cary, vol. 6, Loeb Classical Library 83 (Cambridge, Mass., 1917). Text reproduced from the Perseus Digital Library (http://data.perseus.org/texts/urn:cts:greekLit:tlg0385.tlg001). Courtesy of Creative Commons.

C6. Aelius Aristides *On Rome* 26 (14).96–101, 104. Excerpted from *Aristides,* ed. W. Dindorf (Leipzig, 1829). Text reproduced from the Perseus Digital Library (http://data.perseus.org/texts/urn:cts:greekLit:tlg0284.tlg014). Courtesy of Creative Commons.

C7. Plutarch *Political Precepts* 17, 19. Excerpted from *Plutarchi Chaeronensis Moralia,* ed. G. N. Bernardakis, vol. 5 (Leipzig, 1893). Text reproduced from the Perseus Digital Library (http://data.perseus.org/texts/urn:cts:greekLit:tlg0007.tlg118). Courtesy of Creative Commons.

D1.1–2. New Testament, Luke 2.1–7 and 20.20–26, Romans 13.1–7. Excerpted from the SBL Greek New Testament (http://sblgnt.com). Copyright 2010 by the Society of Biblical Literature and Logos Bible Software. Used by permission.

D2. New Testament, Revelation 17.1–18. Excerpted from the SBL Greek New Testament (http://sblgnt.com). Copyright 2010 by the Society of Biblical Literature and Logos Bible Software. Used by permission.

D3. Josephus *Jewish War* 2.355–357, 361, 390–402. Excerpted from *Flavii Iosephi Opera,* ed. B. Niese (Berlin, 1895). Text reproduced from the Perseus Digital Library (http://data.perseus.org/texts/urn:cts:greekLit:tlg0526.tlg004). Courtesy of Creative Commons.

D4. Josephus *Jewish War* 6.249–270. Excerpted from *Flavii Iosephi Opera,* ed. B. Niese (Berlin, 1895). Text reproduced from the Perseus Digital Library (http://data.perseus.org/texts/urn:cts:greekLit:tlg0526.tlg004). Courtesy of Creative Commons.

D5. Josephus *Jewish War* 7.123–141. Excerpted from *Flavii Iosephi Opera,* ed. B. Niese (Berlin, 1895). Text reproduced from the Perseus Digital Library (http://data.perseus.org/texts/urn:cts:greekLit:tlg0526.tlg004). Courtesy of Creative Commons.

D6. Josephus *Jewish War* 7.142–162. Excerpted from *Flavii Iosephi Opera,* ed. B. Niese (Berlin, 1895). Text reproduced from the Perseus Digital Library (http://data.perseus.org/texts/urn:cts:greekLit:tlg0526.tlg004). Courtesy of Creative Commons.

D7. *Martyrdom of Agape, Irene, and Chione* 1.2–2.1, 3–4. Excerpted from *The Acts of the Christian Martyrs,* ed. H. Musurillo (Oxford, 1972). Text reproduced from *Thesaurus Linguae Graecae: A Digital Library of Greek Literature* (stephanus.tlg.uci.edu). Used by permission.

E1. Eusebius *Life of Constantine* 1.26–28. Excerpted from *Über das Leben des Kaisers Konstantin,* ed. F. Winkelmann, Eusebius Werke 1.1 (Berlin, 1975). Text reproduced from *Thesaurus Linguae Graecae: A Digital Library of Greek Literature* (stephanus.tlg.uci.edu). Used by permission.

E2. Eusebius *Life of Constantine* 1.29–32. Excerpted from *Über das Leben des Kaisers Konstantin,* ed. F. Winkelmann, Eusebius Werke 1.1 (Berlin, 1975). Text reproduced from *Thesaurus Linguae Graecae: A Digital Library of Greek Literature* (stephanus.tlg.uci.edu). Used by permission.

E3. Eusebius *Life of Constantine* 1.37–40. Excerpted from *Über das Leben des Kaisers Konstantin,* ed. F. Winkelmann, Eusebius Werke 1.1 (Berlin, 1975). Text reproduced from *Thesaurus Linguae Graecae: A Digital Library of Greek Literature* (stephanus.tlg.uci.edu). Used by permission.

E4. Julian *Caesars* 18, 30, 36–38. Excerpted from *The Works of the Emperor Julian,* ed. W. C. Wright, Loeb Classical Library 29 (Cambridge, Mass., 1913). Text reproduced from the Perseus Digital Library (http://data.perseus.org/texts/urn:cts:greekLit:tlg2003.tlg010). Courtesy of Creative Commons.

E5. Libanius *Oration* 30.8–13. Excerpted from *Libanii Opera,* ed. R. Foerster, vol. 3 (Leipzig, 1906). Text reproduced from *Thesaurus Linguae Graecae: A Digital Library of Greek Literature* (stephanus.tlg.uci.edu). Used by permission.

E6. Libanius *Oration* 30.30–36. Excerpted from *Libanii Opera,* ed. R. Foerster, vol. 3 (Leipzig, 1906). Text reproduced from *Thesaurus Linguae Graecae: A Digital Library of Greek Literature* (stephanus.tlg.uci.edu). Used by permission.

E7. Procopius *Wars* 7.22.6–19. Excerpted from *Procopius, History of the Wars,* ed. H. B. Dewing, Loeb Classical Library 173 (Cambridge, Mass., 1924). Text reproduced from the Perseus Digital Library (http://data.perseus.org/texts/urn:cts:greekLit:tlg4029.tlg001). Courtesy of Creative Commons.